Demons, Angels, and Writing in Ancient Judaism

What did ancient Jews believe about demons and angels? This question has long been puzzling, not least because the Hebrew Bible says relatively little about such transmundane powers. In the centuries after the conquests of Alexander the Great, however, we find an explosion of explicit and systematic interest in, and detailed discussions of, demons and angels. In this book, Annette Reed considers the third century BCE as a critical moment for the beginnings of Jewish angelology and demonology. Drawing on early "pseudepigrapha" and Aramaic Dead Sea Scrolls, she reconstructs the scribal settings in which transmundane powers became a topic of concerted Jewish interest. Reed also situates this development in relation to shifting ideas about scribes and writing across the Hellenistic Near East. Her book opens a window onto a forgotten era of Jewish literary creativity that nevertheless deeply shaped the discussion of angels and demons in Judaism and Christianity.

Annette Yoshiko Reed is currently an associate professor in the Department of Religious Studies and Skirball Department of Hebrew and Judaic Studies at New York University. A scholar of Judaism and Christianity, she focuses on questions of identity and literary practice across Second Temple Judaism and Late Antiquity. Her research looks to noncanonical and other neglected sources to open new perspectives on ancient Jews and Christians. Her books include *Fallen Angels and the History of Judaism and Christianity* (Cambridge University Press, 2005) and *Jewish-Christianity and the History of Judaism* (2018), as well as a number of edited volumes.

Demons, Angels, and Writing in Ancient Judaism

ANNETTE YOSHIKO REED

New York University

CAMBRIDGE
UNIVERSITY PRESS

CAMBRIDGE
UNIVERSITY PRESS

University Printing House, Cambridge CB2 8BS, United Kingdom

One Liberty Plaza, 20th Floor, New York, NY 10006, USA

477 Williamstown Road, Port Melbourne, VIC 3207, Australia

314-321, 3rd Floor, Plot 3, Splendor Forum, Jasola District Centre, New Delhi - 110025, India

103 Penang Road, #05-06/07, Visioncrest Commercial, Singapore 238467

Cambridge University Press is part of the University of Cambridge.

It furthers the University's mission by disseminating knowledge in the pursuit of education, learning and research at the highest international levels of excellence.

www.cambridge.org
Information on this title: www.cambridge.org/9781108746090
DOI: 10.1017/9781139030847

First published 2020
First paperback edition 2022

A catalogue record for this publication is available from the British Library

Library of Congress Cataloging in Publication data
NAMES: Reed, Annette Yoshiko, 1973- author.
TITLE: Demons, angels, and writing in ancient Judaism / Annette Yoshiko Reed, New York University.
DESCRIPTION: First published 2020. | New York : Cambridge University Press, 2020. | Includes bibliographical references and index.
IDENTIFIERS: LCCN 2019038889 (print) | LCCN 2019038890 (ebook) |
ISBN 9780521119436 (hardback) | ISBN 9781139030847 (epub)
SUBJECTS: LCSH: Jewish demonology. | Angels. | Judaism–History–Post-exilic period, 586 B.C.-210 A.D. | Apocryphal books. | Dead Sea scrolls.
CLASSIFICATION: LCC BM645.D45 R43 2020 (print) | LCC BM645.D45 (ebook) |
DDC 296.3/15–dc23
LC record available at https://lccn.loc.gov/2019038889
LC ebook record available at https://lccn.loc.gov/2019038890

ISBN 978-0-521-11943-6 Hardback
ISBN 978-1-108-74609-0 Paperback

To my mother, Michiko Konishi Reed

Contents

Preface and Acknowledgments

I began this book over nine years ago, shortly before the birth of my son, and I have been working on it, on and off, in parallel with a number of other projects since then. Most of those projects trace the sort of diachronic trajectories that I characterize below as representative of the study of ancient Judaism. The idea for this book's experiment in synchronic analysis arose from a paper on demons and angels in *Jubilees* for the 2007 Enoch Seminar. What began as an inquiry into demonology, angelology, and writing, however, soon expanded to encompass an investigation into Aramaic Jewish pedagogy and the early Hellenistic age, thanks to conversations with Jonathan Ben Dov, Seth Sanders, Mladen Popović, and others at the 2011 conference on "Ancient Jewish Sciences and the History of Knowledge" organized by Ben Dov and Sanders at the Institute for the Study of the Ancient World at New York University.

This book developed in the crucible of conversations with students and colleagues at the University of Pennsylvania during a remarkable decade for Jewish Studies there. I owe much to discussions with Bob Kraft about the "tyranny of canonical assumptions," discussions with David Stern about the material histories of Jewish books and reading, discussions with David Ruderman about situating Jews within the History of Science, and discussions with Natalie Dohrmann about the need for more fine-grained approaches to the "Greco-Roman context" of ancient Judaism. And to the degree my experiments here prove successful, it is due to their honing in conversation with those whom I am honored to have had as graduate students during my decade at Penn, including Matt Chalmers, Phil Fackler, Jae Hee Han, Alex Ramos, Jillian Stinchcomb, and Philip Webster.

Earlier drafts of the Introduction and Chapter 4 were workshopped at Yale University and Brandeis University respectively, and earlier versions of Chapter 3 were presented at Columbia University, New York University, Penn's Material Texts Workshop, and Princeton University. Arguments from Chapters 1 and 2 were presented at a MoMA R&D Salon on "Angels" and at conferences at Florida State University, Princeton University, and Yale University. On demonological fronts, I am especially grateful to Tzvi Abusch, David Frankfurter, and Dale Martin, and on the history and literature of ancient Judaism, to Benjamin Breed, Simcha Gross, Todd Hanneken, Eva Mroczek, Seth Schwartz, and Jed Wyrick. Although this is quite decisively not a book about "the Bible," it has been shaped in conversation with biblicists such as Jacqueline Vayntrub, Liane Feldman, Steve Weitzman, and Esther Hamori. In addition, I would be remiss not to note that many of my best ideas came, not when at my desk or in the library, but rather on the mats training Muay Thai; if good breaks make good writing, I owe much of what is good in this book to Arjan Steve Milles, Arjan Simon Burgess, Kru Emily Bearden, and the community at Five Points Academy.

I am also grateful to and for Shaul Magid, who helped to mediate the completion of this book with love, patience, and support; I have been lucky to have the daily inspiration of a searingly smart interlocutor but – perhaps even more so – the unrelentingly honest editorial eye of a consummate writer. This book would have been written much more quickly had it not been for my son, KunKun (Alexander Reed Fleming), who has grown during its slow gestation from a delightful baby into a dazzlingly brilliant boy. But my life would have also have been far less interesting, and my world far less meaningful and magical. What I can give to him is a token of what I have been given, and I dedicate this book to my mother, Michiko Konishi Reed, who has filled my life with meaning and magic as well – not least through the reminder that the true enchantment of the world dwells in the wonder of the everyday.

Introduction

For many in contemporary societies, the imagining of unseen phenomena has been shaped by the claims of modern science. The air that surrounds us is emptied of sentient agency, animated only by the wanderings of microorganisms, the gyration of waves of sound and electricity, the movement of molecules, and the agitation of atoms and particles. That this emptiness stretches even to the skies is conveyed by our very notion of outer space – a vast and vacuous realm in which stars and planets cycle on paths guided by the laws of energy and matter, indifferent to human hopes, deeds, and suffering. Germs may be feared, and bacteria warded off, but even the harmful elements of the unseen world are conventionally conceived apart from voices that tempt and sing, eyes that watch and witness, and spirits that sizzle with ardor and anger.[1]

The contrast could not be more striking with the ancient cultures that flourished near the eastern coasts of the Mediterranean Sea and in the lands around the Tigris and Euphrates rivers. Jews, Christians, and others

---

[1] Today, of course, belief in demons and angels is hardly absent. My point here is just that it is not cosmologically constitutive within the dominant discourses that shape public life (e.g., politics, education, science, economics) and that it has been particularly marginalized from those rationalizing discourses that inform modern Western scholarship. The contrast that I am highlighting, thus, pertains to the place of transmundane powers in fundamental assumptions about how reality worked across the diverse yet interlocking cultures of the ancient Mediterranean world – differing in their details but generally sharing a sense of spiritual forces as active in the cosmos in a manner not categorically compartmentalized from political, medicinal, or scientific phenomena, nor necessarily relegated to "popular" or "esoteric" domains. See further Reed, "Knowing Our Demons"; Berger, *Rumor of Angels*, 2; Lehoux, *What Did the Romans Know*, 21–46; Lincoln, *Gods and Demons*, 31–52.

shared a view of the space around them as bustling with unseen powers.[2] When they peered into the skies, they saw sentience, and they heard the songs of stars and angels. "Demons," as Peter Brown observes, "filled the air with their subtle bodies."[3]

Ancient opinions varied as to the precise nature and purpose of these powers.[4] Rarely contested, however, was their existence. Some such creatures – it was commonly believed – shared the inhabitable earth with humankind. Some peered down from above. Others lurked below or beyond. That they could sway human lives is a conviction expressed in ancient rituals for protection, prayers of petition, tales about transmundane encounters, and narratives about the cosmic unfurling of human history.

Across the ancient Mediterranean world, the population of the otherworld often provided a symbolic language for the articulation of this-worldly concerns.[5] For those who believed in a single or dominant deity,

---

[2] For overviews on *shedim, daimones, daevas*, etc., see Lange and Lichtenberger, *Die Dämonen*; Burkert, *Greek Religion*, 179–181; Frankfurter, *Evil Incarnate*, 13–30; Timotin, *La démonologie platonicienne*; Brisson, et al., *Neoplatonic Demons and Angels*. On *mal'akim, angeloi*, etc., see Reiterer, Nicklas, and Schöpflin, *Angels*; Mach, *Entwicklungsstadien*; Schäfer, *Rivalität*; Fossum, *Name of God*; Deutsch, *Guardians of the Gate*; Tuschling, *Angels and Orthodoxy*; Cline, *Ancient Angels*. On the spirits of the dead, Johnston, *Religions of the Ancient World*, 470–495.

[3] Brown, *Rise of Western Christendom*, 482. More recently, G. A. Smith has stressed that "it is very hard, and very important, to remember that ancient demons had bodies" ("How Thin Is a Demon," 479) and that "being invisible is also not the same as being a metaphor" (482).

[4] Accessible entry-points into the topic for Egypt, Mesopotamia, and Persia include Schipper, "Angels or Demons"; Hutter, "Demons and Benevolent Spirits"; Lucarelli, "Demonology"; Lincoln, *Gods and Demons*, 31–42. For ancient Jewish examples, see Reynolds, "Understanding the Demonologies"; Stuckenbruck, "Angels and God," 45–70; Alexander, "Contextualizing the Demonology," 619–620. Among ancient Greeks, *daimôn/daimonion* could denote lesser spirits of various sorts, and these figures were attributed with tasks of intermediation between earthly and otherworldly realms that Jews associated with "angels" (*mal'akim*, etc.) as well as with "demons" (*shedim*, etc.); on the continuities and transformations in the semantic field of *daimôn* and *daimonion* in ancient Greek and late antique Christian literature, see Petersen, "Notion of Demon"; Albinus, "Greek δαίμων"; Cancik, "Römische Dämonologie"; Martin, *Inventing Superstition*; Martin, "When did Angels"; Timotin, *La démonologie platonicienne*; Brisson, et al., *Neoplatonic Demons and Angels*. For developments with respect to Greek *angeloi* and Latin *angeli*, Cline, *Ancient Angels*, 1–19. For Rabbinic, late antique, and medieval Jewish examples, Schäfer, *Rivalität*; Ahuvia, "Israel Among the Angels"; Ronis, "Do Not Go Out"; Ronis, "Intermediary Beings"; Berman, *Divine and Demonic*.

[5] Frankfurter, *Evil Incarnate*, 14–15. In what follows, I do my best to avoid the dichotomy of "natural" and "supernatural," inasmuch as it is a modern contrast predicated on distinctively post-Enlightenment epistemological assumptions (partitioning, e.g., "secular"

the appeal to malevolent powers could serve to make sense of daily life in locales dominated by devotion to multiple deities.[6] At the same time, a wide spectrum of religious and philosophical groups – monotheistic and polytheistic alike – buttressed their authority-claims through promises of freedom from the whims of capricious spirits.[7] Both between and within communities, speech and writing about demons were powerful tools in the arsenal of social exclusion and the legitimation of violence.[8]

Spirits, both wayward and benign, were also marshaled in the service of organizing and theorizing knowledge.[9] Divine messengers, angelic interpreters, and spirits of the dead embodied the conviction that truth could travel from the highest heavens down into the quotidian domains of human life.[10] Their explanatory power encompassed phenomena as diverse as disease, disaster, divination, the origins of technologies, and the efficacy of ritual action, as well as social unrest and political upheavals, past and predicted.[11] Appeals to capricious or wicked spirits proved

---

from "religious"). I retain, however, the term "otherworldly" as evoking something of the sense that human life and history are shaped not just by the world visible and accessible to humankind in the mundane cycles of everyday life but also by those invisible, above, below, beyond, etc. – or, in other words, that which ancient writings describe as requiring non-ordinary modes of travel, vision, or communication to see and know.

[6] Wey, *Die Funktionen der bösen Geister.*

[7] Denzey, *Cosmology and Fate*; Hodges, "Gnostic Liberation."

[8] Pagels, *Origins of Satan.*

[9] Not least due to the shaping of the English vocabulary of the otherworldly by Christian and Enlightenment discourses, there is no term that is quite fitting for such beings. I thus alternate between using umbrella categories like "transmundane powers" and "intermediate spirits," and the more accessible "angels" and "demons" as shorthand. Of course, strictly speaking, "demon" is anachronistic to the degree that it presumes the early Christian reinterpretation of Greek *daimon* or *daimonion* as categorically evil (e.g., Martin, "When Did Angels"; Frankfurter, "Master-Demons," 127). I do not mean to downplay the significance of this later shift. For the purposes of the present study, however, I use the English term in the looser and more inclusive sense that it is commonly found in scholarly studies of a range of global cultures from Tibet to Egypt to Iran (e.g., Dalton, *Taming of the Demons*; Lucarelli, "Demonology"; Lincoln, *Gods and Demons*, 31–52) so as to draw out some of the shared concerns noted above – and especially the contrast between the richness of premodern demonologies and the habitual neglect thereof in modern scholarship.

[10] For divine messengers, see Schipper, "Angels or Demons"; Speyer, "Divine Messenger." On the *angelus interpres* of Jewish and Christian apocalypses, as well as Persian parallels, see Collins, *Apocalyptic Imagination*, 33; Macumber, "Angelic Intermediaries." On the possibility of communication from and about the dead, see Ogden, *Greek and Roman Necromancy*; Schmidt, *Israel's Beneficent Dead.*

[11] For their association with various types of misfortune, see Frankfurter, *Evil Incarnate*, 13–30; Sorensen, *Possession*. For their association with *technê*, see Graf, "Mythical

useful for explaining human suffering on personal and global levels.[12] Likewise, appeals to heaven's lesser inhabitants served as one potent means for claiming access to secret truths about cosmic order or hidden patterns in history. Figures like angels, archons, demons, and *daimones* could thus play a part in theology, theodicy, and the theorization of the structure and the workings of the cosmos.[13] At times, as Bruce Lincoln observes, demons could function "quite literally like the black holes of a premodern cosmology, where physics, metaphysics, and ethics remain inextricably intertwined."[14]

The present study is an attempt to illumine one corner of this richly imagined otherworld. It focuses upon the representation and functions of intermediate spirits in an important but understudied corpus: the Aramaic Jewish literature of the early Hellenistic age (ca. 333–167 BCE), as preserved in so-called pseudepigrapha such as the *Astronomical Book*, *Book of the Watchers*, and related Aramaic Dead Sea Scrolls such as the *Aramaic Levi Document* and *Visions of Amram*.[15] This corpus includes the most ancient Jewish texts known outside the Hebrew Bible.[16] Among the many innovations therein is a newly expansive vision of Israel's

---

Production"; Reed, *Fallen Angels*. For the notion of spirits as agents in the efficacy of divination, see Johnston, *Religions of the Ancient World*, 371–391.

[12] The association of lower powers with personal suffering (e.g., illness, madness, unrequited love) is perhaps most poignantly expressed in "magical" materials; e.g., Luck, *Arcana Mundi*, 161–226; Bohak, *Ancient Jewish Magic*, 42–44, 88–114.

[13] One striking example of the cosmological consequences is the discourse about *daimones* in Iamblichus' *de Mysteriis*, on which see Shaw, *Theurgy and the Soul*, 130–141. With respect to Late Antiquity, Athanassiadi and Frede stress that "the angels of the one and only God belong ... to the theological *koine* of the period"; *Pagan Monotheism*, 17. For inscriptional and other evidence for non-Jewish, non-Christian reflection on *angeloi/angeli* in the Roman Empire, see Cline, *Ancient Angels*.

[14] Lincoln, "Cesmag, the Lie," 55.

[15] Throughout this book, I avoid retrojecting the late antique compendium "*I Enoch*" into Second Temple times. I refer instead to the earlier independent works collected therein by the titles conventional in current scholarship – e.g., *Astronomical Book* for *I En* 72–82 and 4Q209–211, *Book of the Watchers* for *I En* 1–36, etc. – and I consider the early Aramaic materials therein in relation to the corpus of what we now know as the Aramaic Jewish literature of the early Hellenistic age. For linguistic and other evidence for treating the earliest Enochic writings and Aramaic DSS as a "corpus," see Cook, "Qumran Aramaic"; Machiela and Perrin, "Tobit and the Genesis Apocryphon"; Perrin, *Dynamics of Dream-Vision*, 30–37, 230.

[16] "Biblical" materials that have been sometimes dated to this century include the Aramaic materials in Daniel 2–6, as well as Qohelet, 1 and 2 Chronicles, and Esther, together with various smaller additions expanding older works of biblical prophecy; see e.g. Carr, *Formation*, 184–201; Japhet, *1 and 2 Chronicles*, 23–28; Hengel, *Judaism and Hellenism*, 1.109–175.

heritage of books and knowledge, predicated on claims to special access to information *from* and *about* archangels, fallen Watchers, and wicked spirits. Heavenly and wayward angels here gain names, classes, motives, and inner lives. The origins, functions, and fates of demons are mapped and explained. These and other spirits, moreover, take on integral roles in newly intricate cosmologies, mediating the cycles of the celestial luminaries and populating the divine abode in heaven, the realms of the dead, and the ends of the earth.[17] Inasmuch as this corpus attests an unprecedented concern among learned Jews for collecting, textualizing, and systemizing a claimed totality of knowledge about transmundane powers, it marks what we might call the beginnings of Jewish angelology and demonology.[18]

THE BEGINNINGS OF JEWISH ANGELOLOGY AND DEMONOLOGY

The flourishing of traditions about angels and demons is among the most dramatic developments in Jewish literature in the centuries between the Babylonian Exile (586–538 BCE) and the compilation of the Mishnah (ca. 200 CE). In the Hebrew Bible, speculation of this sort is conspicuously absent. God is depicted as surrounded by unnamed "hosts" and "holy ones," and mysterious "messengers" (*mal'akim*) act on his behalf. Yet, as Saul Olyan notes, "no text from pre-exilic Israel presents a detailed or even basic ordering of angels into a hierarchy of divisions with specific functions and responsibilities."[19] Demons are even less of a concern. "Whether suppressed by the Hebrew Bible ... or theologically subjected to the dominion of God," as Dan Ben-Amos observes, "the biblical references to demons and demonic forces are scant."[20] What is treated mostly in passing and allusive fashion within biblical literature, however, becomes the subject of exuberantly explicit discussion in the writings from Second Temple times (538 BCE to 70 CE).[21] The explosion

---

[17] Alexander, "Enoch and the Beginnings," 231–232, 240; VanderKam, "Book of Luminaries," 367; Reed, "Enoch, Eden."
[18] I.e., demonology and angelology as thus distinct from demon-belief and angel-belief; see Chapter 1. See also below on my choice of the term "beginnings," which signals my concern to avoid the assumptions and valuations associated with the quest for a singular point of "origin"; Said, *Beginnings*, xvii; Deleuze and Guattari, *Thousand Plateaus*, 323–326.
[19] Olyan, *Thousand Thousands*, 18.   [20] Ben-Amos, "On Demons," 30.
[21] On this allusiveness and its effects see further Chapter 1.

of Jewish literary interest in angels and demons is one of the most striking intellectual shifts during these politically turbulent and culturally creative centuries, and its products proved foundational for later reflection about divinity, the cosmos, and the human condition within Judaism and Christianity alike.

In past research on Second Temple Judaism, this development was studied in retrospective terms, largely through the lens of Christian categories. Loren Stuckenbruck and Wendy North, for instance, have noted the long-standing effects of the model associated with Wilhelm Bousset (1865–1920) whereby post-exilic Judaism has been characterized as "a religious environment in which the strict monotheism of the Old Testament prophets (and Jesus himself) had been significantly weakened," due to "(a) a growing interest in angels..., (b) the rise of dualism, marked by increasingly concern with demonology, and (c) a belief in divine 'hypostates.'"[22] This model jars with much of our evidence for Second Temple Judaism but has been influential nonetheless, in part due to its resonance with Christian representations of the Judaism of Jesus' time as if a corrupted form of the piety and prophecy of ancient Israel. Among the enduring results was the scholarly tendency to treat the rise of angelology and demonology as emblematic of a purported decline in the vitality of Judaism in the period between the Exile and the life of Jesus.[23]

Already in the early twentieth century, Bousset's model was critiqued for its supersessionism. Even his critics, however, followed his assessment of angelology and demonology as essentially incompatible with monotheism and, hence, only possible within denigrated forms of Judaism, ailing from divine alienation or infected by foreign influence. When George Foot Moore (1851–1931) sought to recuperate Second Temple Judaism, for instance, he did so by rejecting "pseudepigrapha" as unrepresentative – and precisely on the grounds of their interests in angels and demons.[24] Bousset's notions of

[22] Stuckenbruck and North, *Early Christian and Jewish Monotheism*, 5–9, quote at 6. For critiques of Bousset's notion of a pre-Christian Jewish "angel cult," see also Hurtado, *One God*, 22–35; Stuckenbruck, *Angel Veneration*, 51–149.
[23] Bousset was not wholly original in this regard, but his account in *Die Religion des Judentums* (esp. 302–357) proved influential in spreading such views, especially in scholarship on the NT. On the history of research – and its echoes into the present day – see Stuckenbruck, *Angel Veneration*, 5–7; Gieschen, *Angelomorphic Christology*, 8–12.
[24] e.g., Moore, "Intermediaries." In effect, Moore counters Bousset's ideas by refracting Second Temple Judaism through yet another, later, lens and claiming Rabbinic sources as the crux of a timelessly normative Judaism from which "pseudepigrapha" (and earliest Christianity) are categorically excluded.

post-exilic decline helped to naturalize the marginalization of Second Temple Judaism as merely "intertestamental" in import, and Moore's critique further reinscribed the denigration of demonology, angelology, and "pseudepigrapha."[25] For much of the twentieth century, the literature of Second Temple Judaism was read as epilogue to the story of ancient Israel or as preface to the drama of Christian Origins, but rarely valued or studied for its own sake. The influential innovations in demonology and angelology during this period were either denigrated or downplayed.

Since the late twentieth century, explicitly supersessionist approaches to Second Temple Judaism have been increasingly eschewed even in New Testament Studies, and the study of "pseudepigrapha" has been further integrated into Jewish Studies, especially in relation to the history of biblical exegesis.[26] Nevertheless, lingering traces of older biases continue to reverberate – perhaps particularly in the treatment of angels and demons.[27] Elements of Bousset's model still echo, for instance, in the common tendency to explain the Second Temple interest in angels as compensatory for Jewish feelings of "distance" from God after the Exile.[28] Furthermore, the angelology and demonology of Second Temple Judaism are still primarily construed in terms of Christian categories – and, hence, typically with a focus on abstract concepts retrojected from later theological debates about topics like monotheism, theodicy, or Christology.[29] For the most part, research on demons and angels in Second Temple Judaism remains framed and justified primarily with

[25] Even Louis Ginzberg (1873–1953) – whose *Legends of the Jews* did so much to lay the groundwork for integrating "pseudepigrapha" into Jewish intellectual history – similarly insisted that "in the appreciation of Jewish legends, it is the Rabbinic writers who should form the point of departure, and not the pseudepigrapha" (1.xxvii). In doing so, moreover, he relegated "pseudepigrapha" to Christianity: "The pseudepigrapha originated in circles that harbored the germs from which Christianity developed later on. The Church could thus appropriate them as her own with just reason" (1.xxvii).

[26] The latter is especially due to the influence of James Kugel; see esp. his magisterial synthesis in *Traditions of the Bible*.

[27] For surveys of the relevant history of research, see Olyan, *Thousand Thousands*, 2–9; Stuckenbruck, *Angel Veneration*, 5–14; Gieschen, *Angelomorphic Christology*, 8–25; Reynolds, "Understanding the Demonologies."

[28] Recent examples include Burkes, *God, Self, and Death*, 15–17; Moss, *Other Christs*, 113–114, 255–256.

[29] Research on intermediate spirits in late antique literature, by contrast, tends to focus on the social functions of discourse about angels and demons, exploring the ramifications for religious self-fashioning and communal identities in specific historical and local settings; e.g., Brakke, *Demons and the Making of the Monk*; Kalleres, *City of Demons*; Muehlberger, *Angels*; Rosen-Zvi, *Demonic Desires*; Ahuvia, "Israel Among the Angels"; Ronis, "Do Not Go Out"; Ronis, "Intermediary Beings."

reference to so-called intertestamental trajectories, connecting the dots between Hebrew Bible and New Testament.[30] And even when these traditions are studied apart from the analytical framework of Christian biblical canons, it remains common to bring diachronic perspectives to bear on "pseudepigrapha," culling them for themes or motifs to compare with what came after.[31] Partly as a result, the proliferation of detailed literary interest in intermediate spirits has been treated as epiphenomenal to developments that prove important for later periods – whether the origins of Christianity, the development of apocalyptic literature, the spread of Jewish sectarianism, or the prehistory of Jewish mysticism.[32]

This book makes the case for a synchronic approach to understanding the beginnings of Jewish angelology and demonology, attending to the other shifts that we see within Jewish literature from the early Hellenistic age (333–167 BCE) and situating them in relation to broader cultural and intellectual changes both among Jews and across the Mediterranean world in the wake of the conquests of Alexander.[33] Accordingly, I here

[30] On "the persistence of the Bible as an anachronistic structuring principle for the study of the period," see Mroczek, *Literary Imagination*, 6.

[31] This approach has much value for highlighting the rich afterlives of Second Temple traditions (e.g., Bernstein, "Angels at the Aqedah"; Orlov, *Enoch-Metatron*; Orlov, *Dark Mirrors*; Poirier, *Tongues of Angels*; Reed, *Fallen Angels*) – not least because elements from the earliest "pseudepigrapha" survived in later traditions most persistently and pervasively in the forms of motifs. My suggestion here is that something may be lost when we study them only or primarily in this atomized fashion. For a sense of how and why such ideas crystallized in such forms in the first place, rather, it is pressing to understand how they function in their earliest known contexts as well. Throughout the present study, thus, I draw upon – and take inspiration from – more focused literary studies such as Dimant, "Sons of Heaven"; Hanneken, "Angels and Demons"; Najman, "Interpretation"; Najman, "Angels at Sinai"; Stuckenbruck, "Angels and Giants"; VanderKam, "Angel of the Presence"; VanderKam, "Putative Author"; VanderKam, "Angel Story"; VanderKam, "Demons in the Book of Jubilees."

[32] Influential examples include Boccaccini, *Beyond the Essene Hypothesis*; Elior, *Three Temples*; Alexander, "What Happened to the Jewish Priesthood." For critiques and alternates, see Himmelfarb, "Heavenly Ascent"; Himmelfarb, "Merkavah Mysticism since Scholem"; Swartz, "Dead Sea Scrolls"; Stern, "Rachel Elior on Ancient Jewish Calendars"; Boustan, "Rabbanization"; Schäfer, *Origins of Jewish Mysticism*.

[33] Among Classicists, it is conventional to refer to the "Hellenistic period" as 333–30 or 323–30 BCE – that is, spanning the time from the conquests or death of Alexander to the fall of the last surviving dynasty of his successors (i.e., the Ptolemies) to Rome. Here, I use "early Hellenistic age" to denote the first part of this period (i.e., 333–167 BCE), especially as seen from the perspective of our Jewish sources, for which the Maccabean uprising against the Seleucids (ca. 167–164 BCE) and subsequent reestablishment of native rule are major landmarks. I use this terminology in part to signal my interest in recovering neglected pre-Maccabean perspectives (see further below), and in part to resist the conventional usage of "Greco-Roman" in Biblical Studies and Jewish Studies to

experiment instead with more integrative interpretations that interweave literary analysis and cultural history through attention to the social practices and settings of writing, reading, and teaching, on the one hand, and to the cultural correlates, contexts, and consequences of the classification of knowledge, on the other. In the process, I attempt to bring new questions and intertexts to much-studied "pseudepigrapha" like the *Book of the Watchers* and *Jubilees*, in the hopes of uncovering overlooked factors in the seemingly sudden explosion of intensive interest in angels and demons in Second Temple times.

Rather than attempting to add to the splendid wealth of philological, exegetical, and theological studies of Jewish traditions about angels and demons,[34] this book tackles the challenge of situating the beginnings of Jewish angelology and demonology within its specific synchronic cultural contexts, seeking to uncover its connections to concurrent shifts in the textualization of knowledge. In this respect, I attempt a "cultural history of literature" in the sense practiced by Classicists like Tim Whitmarsh, "focus[ing] upon the role of texts ... not just as 'reflections' of history, but as active participants in the struggle to define and popularize certain perceptions of the current state of that society."[35] Accordingly, throughout this book, I am less concerned with what lies *behind* our texts

---

conflate Ptolemaic, Seleucidic, and Roman periods and cultures (see further Reed and Dohrmann, "Rethinking Romanness").

[34] The study of Second Temple traditions about angels and demons in relation to the exegesis of Genesis and other books of the Hebrew Bible has been a particularly vital area of research. For an important precedent, see Olyan, *Thousand Thousands*, and for insightful recent examples see Wright, *Origin of Evil Spirits*; von Heijne, *Messenger of the Lord*. The investigation of angels in relation to "monotheism" and mediation, and the investigation of demons in relation to "dualism" and theodicy, both continue to bear fruit as well – e.g., Deutsch, *Guardians of the Gate*; Tuschling, *Angels and Orthodoxy*; Stuckenbruck, "Angels and God"; Stuckenbruck, "Interiorization of Dualism." For ancient Jewish approaches to the problem of evil, see Brand, *Evil Within and Without*, surveying the relevant Second Temple traditions, and Rosen-Zvi, *Demonic Desires*, tracing trajectories forward into Late Antiquity.

[35] Whitmarsh, *Ancient Greek Literature*, 6, further stressing that texts "are not second-order 'evidence' for society; they are primary building-blocks of that society, as it is experienced and understood by its members." In Whitmarsh's articulation, a "cultural history of Greek texts" ideally includes the "various ways that Greeks themselves narrated their own literary history, and the role of the archive in maintaining and disseminating those narratives" – not least because the archive is shaped during centuries when "Greek identity was increasingly bound up with the study of literature" (22). Here too, I attempt a cultural history of literature precisely because of my focus on a period in which the Jewish archive was reshaped and in which textuality became more explicitly tied to Jewishness; see esp. Chapter 2.

(whether in the sense of constituent sources, exegetical logics, or hidden authorial motives) and more concerned with what is achieved *by* and *with* practices of textualizing, organizing, packaging, and transmitting knowledge.[36] I approaching the literary data, not as windows onto beliefs, but rather as evidence for practices of writing and reading as well as sites of scribal expertise.[37] Consequently, I focus on the meanings made by the form, selectivity, rhetoric, and authorizing claims of the early "pseudepigrapha" and related Dead Sea Scrolls in which we see the emergence of explicit and systematic Jewish reflection on angels and demons. To do so – I suggest – is to shed light on the making of Jewish angelology and demonology through anthological and other scribal practices with parallels across the Mediterranean world in the third and early second centuries BCE.

Accordingly, throughout this book, I resist framing my analysis of the rise of Jewish literary interest in angels and demons in terms of a quest for one moment of "origins" or "invention." Instead, I follow what Edward Said posits as a productive shift toward a concern with "beginning" as "an activity which ultimately implies return and repetition rather than simple linear accomplishment":

> ... whereas origins are divine ... a beginning not only creates but is its own method because it has intention. In short, beginning is making or producing difference; but—and here is the great fascination in the subject—difference which is the result of combining the already-familiar with the fertile novelty of human work in language.[38]

For analyzing Jewish angelology and demonology, this sense of "beginning" proves apt inasmuch as it allows for the dynamics of cultural change produced *from within* continuity, such as by collecting, recontextualizing, and reconfiguring earlier received traditions. Such coupling of change with continuity is familiar to scholars of Second Temple Judaism in relation to biblical exegesis. As Mark Smith reminds us, however, it is found already in "the Bible's presentation of history," which is best understood "not only as the record of Israel's past or as literary

---

[36] For a similar approach with respect to biblical poetry, see Vayntrub, *Beyond Orality*, there stressing the degree to which past research "focused on reconstructing the history of the text's development, and seeking it in its earliest original form, risks obscuring claims encoded in the text's very arrangement" (4).

[37] My sense of "scribe" here is akin to that recently articulated by Daniel Pioske, that is, as "artisans trained in the technologies of textuality" and who "generated, copied, and maintained texts held in common over time"; *Memory in a Time of Prose*, 4.

[38] Said, *Beginnings*, xvii.

representations of their past, but also as a response to the past, or a series of responses to it."[39] What I suggest, in what follows, is that this conversation – with and through the past – continues into the Second Temple period, in a manner marked by shifts and innovations but not by the degree of rupture presumed in the conventional characterization of this period as a "post-exilic." What we find in the early Hellenistic age is a reconceptualization of Jewish writing and knowledge, predicated on a radical expansion of the very scope of what is textualized as knowledge from and about Israel's past. Angelology and demonology are among the engines for this shift: not only does writing about transmundane powers emerge as a Jewish knowledge-practice in the early Hellenistic age, but it contributes to a newly capacious vision of the domains of Jewish scribal expertise and literary production.

DEMONOLOGY AND ANGELOLOGY AS KNOWLEDGE

Earlier prophetic and other biblical sources do offer some precedents for the ideas about intermediate spirits found within works like the *Astronomical Book* and *Book of the Watchers*. Nothing in earlier biblical literature, however, prepares us for the explicit, exuberant, and extensive treatments of angels and demons in the Aramaic Jewish literature of the early Hellenistic age. Furthermore, as we shall see, their major innovation is in the collection, organization, and textualization of diverse traditions about them – including traditions with parallels in biblical and other Near Eastern literature, but also traditions rooted in local landscapes, ritual practice, and technical expertise. In this sense, these Hellenistic-era sources fit well with David Frankfurter's characterization of "demonology" on the basis of cross-cultural examples as systemizing discourses "drawing demons out of their particular 'lived' situations and oral discussion into a speculative system," whereby new domains of elite expertise are often produced as "demons get collected from their local domains and ambiguous intentions, abstracted into lists, polarized as uniformly hostile, and speculatively combined with opposing gods or angels."[40]

Throughout this book, my interest is in analyzing and situating this systemizing discourse. For this reason, I choose to retain the terms "angelology" and "demonology," which a number of scholars of Jewish

[39] Smith, *Memoirs*, 3.   [40] Frankfurter, *Evil Incarnate*, 15, 19.

Studies have resisted.[41] In using these terms, I do not mean to imply any single, stable system of spirits in Second Temple Judaism – or even among those scribes responsible for early "pseudepigrapha" and related Aramaic writings. It would certainly be misleading to use these multiple texts to try to reconstruct a single system imagined to lie behind all of them, let alone behind earlier or other texts. My choice of this terminology, rather, reflects my particular concern for charting the emergence of a systematizing discourse about transmundane powers within Jewish literature, whereby the practice of writing about angels and demons becomes a potent site for theorizing Jewish knowledge more broadly.

In a recent study of ancient Roman sciences, Daryn Lehoux demonstrates how a focus on ancient knowledge-practices can help us to grasp "what it means to understand a world" with "different entities, different laws, different tools and motivations for studying the natural world … different ways of organizing knowledge, and sometimes different ways of understanding even the most basic levels of sensory experience."[42] In the Roman materials that Lehoux considers, "astronomy bleeds into ethics, ethics into politics, politics into theology, theology into mathematics, mathematics into harmonics, harmonics into astronomy again," and "politics cannot be cleanly distinguished from conceptions of nature, and neither of them from conceptions of the gods."[43] The period that Lehoux examines is the first century BCE to the second century CE – an era that has attracted fresh scholarly attention in recent years for the unculled richness of its evidence for the ancient theorization of knowledge. Whereas past scholars had dismissed Roman science as derivative, for instance, scholars such as Trevor Murphy have looked beyond the conservative rhetoric and anthological forms of works like Pliny the Elder's *Natural History* to highlight the cultural work done by encyclopedism, both for the prestige of Greek *paideia* and for the power of the Roman Empire.[44] Such studies, in turn, have helped to spark conversations at the intersection of Classics and History of Science concerning the ordering of knowledge in the Roman Empire and the resultant coproduction of local and imperial knowing.[45] Among the results, as Whitmarsh and Jason König note, is a new concern for how "particular

[41] e.g., Olyan, *Thousand Thousands*, 1.   [42] Lehoux, *What Did the Romans*, 8.
[43] Lehoux, *What Did the Romans*, 9.
[44] Murphy, *Pliny the Elder's Natural History*, 49–73.
[45] e.g., König and Whitmarsh, *Ordering Knowledge*; Woolf, *Tales of the Barbarians*.

conceptions of knowledge and particular ways of textualising knowledge were entwined with social and political practices and ideals."[46]

This book experiments with a similar approach to the Jewish literature of the early Hellenistic age. The angelology and demonology of this literature, as we shall see, cut across some of the most definitive partitions within post-Enlightenment Western orders of knowledge. Its demons and angels are "supernatural" insofar as they participate in unseen realms above or beyond our own, but they are "natural" insofar as they are given a causal role in the visible cycles of the cosmos or in the human mind and body. Its treatments of such spirits can be called "religious" insofar as some impinge on ethics, piety, salvation, and beliefs about the divine; "magical" in the sense that some can be manipulated by rite or speech to flee or protect an individual; and "scientific" insofar as some fit into a regular system of cosmic structures and movements. To attend to the beginnings of Jewish angelology and demonology, then, is to be challenged to look beyond the conventional modern compartmentalization of knowledge about the world, but also to look beyond the bounds of those types and topics of knowing now commonly distinguished as "religious," in general, and as "Jewish," in particular. In the process, we might be able to recover something of what has been lost in the hermeneutical exorcism of modern scholarship whereby ancient worlds have been emptied of their spirits – a task that is pressing, I would suggest, not just for an analysis of angelology and demonology, but also for an understanding of the social and cultural contexts in which angels and demons could function as foci for learned efforts to textualize, theorize, and organize other forms of knowledge as well.

RECOVERING THE ARAMAIC JEWISH PEDAGOGY OF THE EARLY HELLENISTIC AGE

Rather than trying to catalogue all the relevant references from across the Second Temple period,[47] this book focuses on the earliest extensive evidence for intensive Jewish literary interest in transmundane powers, and it ask *why* this interest arises *when* and *how* it does. This task is now

---

[46] König and Whitmarsh, "Ordering Knowledge," 3.

[47] Surveys of the relevant material include Dimant, "Sons of Heaven"; Davidson, *Angels at Qumran*; Eshel, "Demonology in Palestine"; Mach, *Entwicklungsstadien;* Reynolds, "Understanding the Demonologies"; Reynolds, "Dwelling Place of Demons; van der Toorn, et al., *DDD*; Wright, *Origins of Evil Spirits*.

newly possible, due to evidence from the Dead Sea Scrolls. Such evidence enables us to move beyond broad-based characterizations of the beginnings of Jewish angelology and demonology as "post-exilic" or "intertestamental," permitting us to pinpoint specific determinative shifts and to situate them in relation to concurrent developments. To do so, moreover, is to contribute to the broader task enabled by the discovery of the Dead Sea Scrolls – that is, to begin to understand Second Temple Judaism on its own terms.

Evidence from Qumran has made starkly clear that the Judaism of this period was not "post-biblical" or "intertestamental" in any simple senses of those terms. Not only did the discovery of multiple Aramaic copies of the *Astronomical Book* and *Book of the Watchers* reveal the antiquity of the earliest so-called pseudepigrapha (ca. third century BCE) as predating the latest book in the Hebrew Bible (i.e., Daniel; mid-second century BCE), but the ample biblical manuscripts and "paraphrases" found among the Dead Sea Scrolls have exposed the fluidity in the textual traditions surrounding a number of now-canonical books throughout much of the Second Temple period.[48] "The discovery of the Qumran manuscript collection," as Armin Lange has stressed, "provided a huge increase of literature written in a period when the late books and redactions of the Hebrew Bible were still developing."[49] The precanonical context of Second Temple Judaism is similarly underlined by multiple Hebrew copies of *Jubilees,* a possible reference to it in the *Damascus Document* (CD 16:3–4), and other evidence for the popularity and possibly authoritative status of some of what we now call "pseudepigrapha."[50] Most importantly, for our purposes, the Dead Sea Scrolls yielded an unprecedented wealth of pre-Maccabean writings, massively expanding our evidentiary basis for reconstructing Jewish intellectual history in the early Hellenistic age.

The period between the end of Persian rule over the Land of Israel (539–334 BCE) and the return of native rule to Israel under the Hasmoneans after the Maccabean Revolt (167–64 BCE) saw the conquests of Alexander and the wars of the Diadochi, after which Judaea was

[48] See further Ulrich, "Bible in the Making"; Flint, "Noncanonical Writings"; Crawford, *Rewriting Scripture*; Abegg, Flint, and Ulrich, *Dead Sea Scrolls Bible*.

[49] Lange, "Pre-Maccabean Literature," 285. For an assessment of the ramifications for the study of the Hebrew Bible, see also Carr, *Formation*, 155–203.

[50] Nickelsburg, "Books of Enoch at Qumran"; cf. Dimant, "Two 'Scientific' Fictions."

dominated first by the Ptolemies (ca. 301–200 BCE) and then by the Seleucids (ca. 200–164 BCE). Judaea was ruled by the Ptolemies for about a century – roughly around the same span of time that it was ruled by the Hasmoneans.[51] Yet the early Hellenistic age has been sorely neglected in modern research on Judaism. This neglect, as Michael E. Stone has observed, mirrors its minor place in those primary sources traditionally used to reconstruct Jewish history:

It has long been true that a major difficulty in writing the history of Judaism in the pre-Christian era is the paucity of information relating directly to the fourth and third centuries [BCE]. Certain of the biblical writings were doubtlessly redacted in this age and a few others composed in it. Nonetheless, we lack a clear picture of how Judaism developed throughout this period. Rabbinic chronology radically foreshortens this era and Josephus' brevity too reflects the poverty of the historical accounts. It is not surprising that when the sources become plentiful once more, after the start of the second century BCE, the picture of Judaism they present differs considerably from that which can be constructed for the period down to the age of Ezra and Nehemiah [in the Persian period] ... Quite new forms of religious writing had emerged ... as well as innovations in the history of ideas that were to set patterns for the succeeding millennia.[52]

It is precisely this gap that the Dead Sea Scrolls now permits us to fill. And part of what we learn when we do is its determinative place for the beginnings of Jewish angelology and demonology.

Prior to the discovery of the Dead Sea Scrolls, scholars typically associated the rise of Jewish interest in angels with the "post-exilic" shift from prophetic to apocalyptic literature and the dawn of apocalyptic eschatology in the era of the Maccabean Revolt. When one looks mainly to biblical literature, such logic makes sense. After all, as Saul Olyan notes, "the only named angels in the Hebrew Bible occur in the latter half of the Book of Daniel, a composition of the second century BCE; Gabriel is mentioned in Dan 8:16; 9:21 and Michael in Dan 10:13, 21; 12:1."[53]

After J. T. Milik's 1976 publication of the Aramaic fragments of the *Astronomical Book*, *Book of the Watchers*, and other Enochic and related materials from Qumran,[54] it became clear that the development of Jewish angelology and demonology was more complex than one might imagine from simply connecting the dots between Ezekiel and Daniel. In between are the *Astronomical Book* and *Book of the Watchers*, which the Aramaic

[51] For a summary of what we know of its economy and administration, see Bagnall, *Administrative of the Ptolemaic Possessions*, 11–24.
[52] Stone, "Book of Enoch and Judaism," 479.   [53] Olyan, *Thousand Thousands*, 15.
[54] Milik, *Books of Enoch*.

fragments revealed to be pre-Maccabean in date, likely from the century of Ptolemaic rule over the Land of Israel (ca. 301–200 BCE).[55] "Prior to this discovery," as Stone stresses, "there was no reason to suppose that . . . the cosmos and all its parts were the object of detailed learned speculation" among ancient Jews," but these writings attest "a developed 'scientific' lore about astronomy, calendar, cosmology and angelology . . . now known to have existed in the third century BCE."[56]

Only recently has it become possible to explore the ramifications. Milik's edition sparked a renaissance of research on the *Book of the Watchers* already since the 1980s, inspiring multiple scholarly efforts to rewrite the early history of apocalyptic literature.[57] The study of the *Astronomical Book*, however, was impeded both by the delay in the availability of the full range of relevant Aramaic fragments and by the lack of knowledge about ancient sciences among most specialists in Second Temple Judaism. Since the remaining fragments of the *Astronomical Book* were finally published in 2000, research on its "scientific" ideas and contexts has flourished.[58] In 2011 and 2012, two detailed commentaries on this difficult work appeared, furthering facilitating efforts to utilize it to fill the gaps in what we know of Judaism in the third century BCE.[59]

Also transformative in this regard is the recovery of a surprisingly broad array of fragments of other Aramaic sources from Qumran – the vast majority of which were otherwise unknown to us. By Devora Dimant's count, there were portions of 121 Aramaic manuscripts discovered among the Dead Sea Scrolls, constituting roughly 13 percent of the total manuscripts found in the caves near Qumran.[60] Thirty-two of these manuscripts are too fragmentary to assess at all, and a further five are too fragmentary to assess meaningfully.[61] What remains are

[55] For a recent reading of the *Book of the Watchers* in relation to Ptolemaic Palestine, see Bachmann, *Die Welt im Ausnahmezustand*, esp. 196–203, 244–245, 256.

[56] Stone, "Book of Enoch and Judaism," 488.

[57] Collins, *Apocalyptic Imagination*, 25-26, 44-59; Boccaccini, *Beyond the Essene Hypothesis*, 70-77; Himmelfarb, *Ascent*, 5-7, 9-28; Reed, "Heavenly Ascent."

[58] i.e., with the editions of 4Q208 and 4Q209 by Eibert Tigchelaar and Florentino García Martínez in DJD 36, 95–171, supplementing J. T. Milik's full publication of 4Q210 and 4Q211, and partial publication of 4Q209, in his 1978 *Books of Enoch*, 274, 287–289, 292–297. See further Ben-Dov and Sanders, *Ancient Jewish Sciences* and Chapter 3 below.

[59] i.e., Drawnel, *Aramaic Astronomical Book*, in 2011; VanderKam, "Book of Luminaries," in 2012.

[60] Dimant, "Qumran Aramaic Texts," 199; for a different count, see Berthelot and Stökl Ben Ezra, "Aramaica Qumranica," 1.

[61] Dimant, "Qumran Aramaic Texts," 199.

"eighty-four scrolls ... from twenty-nine different works, only three of which were known prior to the discovery of the scrolls."[62] Inasmuch as this material mostly seems to predate the sectarian community at Qumran, it opens a further window onto the Jewish scribal cultures of the early Hellenistic age.[63]

Much-needed editions, commentaries, and monographs on Aramaic Dead Sea Scrolls have begun to appear in the past decade, making the significance of this forgotten tradition of Jewish literary production increasingly evident.[64] These fragments provide a wealth of direct data for Jewish writing in Aramaic during Second Temple times, and they also offer important clues to the social settings within which the earliest "pseudepigrapha" first took form, also initially in Aramaic. In the process, a number of features thought to be distinctive to apocalypses – such as the lack of explicit engagement with the Torah/Pentateuch, the narrative focus on the biblical past, the relative paucity of distinctively halakhic discourse, and interest in dream-visions – have been revealed to be common to other Aramaic Jewish writings of the time.[65] Consequently, the Aramaic Dead Sea Scrolls open up the possibility of a synchronic approach to apocalypses like the *Book of the Watchers*, which have typically been studied in diachronic terms in relation to later works of the same genre.[66]

---

[62] Dimant, "Qumran Aramaic Texts," 200. By the three, she there means Tobit, *1 Enoch*, and *Aramaic Levi Document*. This is, of course, a rough count: *1 Enoch* is more properly multiple works, and *Aramaic Levi* is only indirectly related to a known work, i.e., the *Testament of Levi* in the *Testaments of the 12 Patriarchs*. Her point, however, remains.

[63] Collins, "Transformation of the Torah," 456; Collins, "The Aramaic Texts," 548–549, 552–555. On Aramaic DSS as presumably "non-sectarian" and hence often "pre-sectarian," see Dimant, "Qumran Aramaic Texts," 198–199; Puech, "Du bilinguisme"; Ben-Dov, "Scientific Writings," 360; Machiela, "Aramaic Writings"; cf. García Martínez, "Aramaica Qumranica," 439–446. Compare also Lange's count of pre-Maccabean DSS, which includes some Hebrew works as well ("Pre-Maccabean Literature," 285–286).

[64] e.g., Puech in DJD 31: 283–406; Duke, *Social Location*; Machiela, *Dead Sea Genesis Apocryphon*; Drawnel, *Aramaic Wisdom Text*; Greenfield, Stone, and Eshel, *Aramaic Levi Document* – although see already Klaus Beyer's three-volume *Die aramäischen Texte*. See further Berthelot and Stökl ben Ezra, *Aramaica Qumranica*; Dimant, "Qumran Aramaic Texts"; Dimant, "Themes and Genres"; Dimant, "Tobit and the Qumran Aramaic Texts"; Drawnel, "Priestly Education"; Machiela, "Situating the Aramaic Texts"; Machiela, "Aramaic Dead Sea Scrolls"; Machiela and Perrin, "Tobit and Genesis Apocryphon"; Perrin, "Aramaic Imagination"; Perrin, *Dynamics of Dream-Vision*; Tigchelaar, "Aramaic Texts from Qumran."

[65] Collins, "Transformation of the Torah"; Perrin, *Dynamics of Dream-Vision Revelation*.

[66] Dimant, "Themes and Genres," 16.

This book makes the case that Aramaic evidence from Qumran proves particularly transformative for our understanding of Jewish angelology and demonology, permitting us to better understand and contextualize traditions about transmundane powers in the earliest "pseudepigrapha."[67] Relevant sources in this regard include:

- proto-testamentary texts like the *Aramaic Levi Document* (1Q21, 4Q213, 4Q213a, 4Q213b, 4Q214, 4Q214a, 4Q214b), *Admonitions of Qahat* (4Q542), and *Visions of Amram* (4Q543–549; cf. 4Q540–541), and other narrative materials concerning the pre-Sinaitic past (e.g., *Genesis Apocryphon* [1Q20]; *Book of the Giants* [e.g., 1Q23–24, 2Q26, 4Q530–532]; the various patriarchal traditions in 4Q537–539);
- technical materials that span what we might call "science" (e.g., witnesses to early forms or sources of the *Astronomical Book*; esp. 4Q208) and "divination" (e.g., the astrological texts 4Q318 and 4Q561, as paralleled in part by 4Q317 and 4Q186, respectively, in Hebrew);
- the exorcistic incantations in 4Q560 (as exhibiting concerns echoed in part in Hebrew, e.g., in 4Q444, 4Q510, 4Q511, and 11Q11, with some resonances also in later Aramaic incantation bowls).[68]

As we shall see in Chapter 2, the proto-testamentary texts associated with priestly progenitor Levi, his son and Moses' grandfather Qahat, and Moses' father Amram allow us to situate the *Astronomical Book* and *Book of the Watchers* within a Jewish tradition of Aramaic scribal pedagogy that flourished in the early Hellenistic age. Together with the *Genesis Apocryphon*, the *Book of the Giants*, and various Aramaic fragments about the patriarchs, they fill in our picture of the Jewish textual creativity that surrounded the renewed focus on the pre-

[67] I here concentrate on these Aramaic materials as a result of the particular temporal focus of the present book (i.e., the pre-Maccabean portion of the Hellenistic period), for which non-sectarian texts prove most useful. Important studies situating the relevant traditions about intermediate spirits in relation to a fuller range of evidence from the DSS include Dimant, "Sons of Heaven"; Dimant, "Between Qumran Sectarian"; Eshel, "Demonology in Palestine"; Davidson, *Angels at Qumran*; Reimer, "Rescuing the Fallen Angels"; Alexander, "Contextualizing the Demonology"; Reynolds, "Understanding the Demonology."

[68] i.e., spanning Dimant's categories I–II and V in her schema in "Qumran Aramaic Texts," 200–201. The materials in her categories III, IV, and IV will supplement the above-listed materials where relevant, following her call to consider the Aramaic materials together as clues to a broader tradition otherwise almost wholly lost to us.

monarchic and pre-Sinaitic past in this period – particularly as it set the stage for *Jubilees'* magisterial synthesis in Hebrew.[69] Especially by virtue of their inclusion of narrative scenes of reading, writing, and teaching, these proto-testamentary texts provide new grounds for speculating about an Aramaic Jewish counterpart to the Greek *paideia* of the time.[70] On the one hand, as Henryk Drawnel has demonstrated, the Aramaic works associated with Levi, Qahat, and Amram reshape the memory of the biblical past in didactic terms that resonate with models of Mesopotamian scholasticism.[71] On the other hand, as Loren Stuckenbruck has shown, these works attest Jewish experimentation in Aramaic with first-person literary forms that recall Hellenistic models of *historia* and "authorship."[72]

Likewise, the technical materials among the Aramaic Dead Sea Scrolls enable the contextualization of the beginnings of Jewish angelology and demonology in relation to a broader concern with the cosmos and its workings cultivated by learned Jews in the early Hellenistic age.[73] As we shall see in Chapter 3, these include didactic lists of lunar, calendrical, physiognomic, and other information, and they thus reveal other areas of learning wholly unknown from the Hebrew Bible but richly paralleled in Mesopotamian scholasticism. As the most astonishing examples of the expansion of the scope of Jewish literary production in the era, they stand as a humbling reminder about just how much is missed when we characterize Second Temple Judaism by means of "intertestamental" trajectories. At the same time, these materials open new avenues for investigating the rise of explicit Jewish literary interest in intermediate spirits. What I shall suggest, more specifically, is that this trend may form part of the same impulse to collect, list, and organize diverse traditions about the cosmos – as well as to reframe information about them, both native and

---

[69] The pre-Sinaitic past seems to be a special preoccupation in these Aramaic materials, whereas the monarchic period is neglected; Dimant, "Qumran Aramaic Texts," 201–203.

[70] Carr, *Writing on the Tablet*, 204; Reed, "Textuality."

[71] Drawnel, *Aramaic Wisdom Text*; Drawnel, "Priestly Education"; Drawnel, "Some Notes on Scribal Craft"; Drawnel, "Form and Content."

[72] Stuckenbruck, "Pseudepigraphy."

[73] On the *Book of the Watchers*, see Coblentz Bautch, *Study of the Geography*, and on the *Astronomical Book*, Ben-Dov, "Scientific Writings"; Ben-Dov, *Head of All Years*; Popović, *Reading the Human Body*; Popović, "Physiognomic Knowledge"; Popović, "Emergence of Aramaic and Hebrew Scholarly Texts" – building on earlier studies such as Neugebaur, "Astronomical Book"; Albani, *Astronomie und Schöpfungsglaube*; Geller, "New Documents from the Dead Sea"; Alexander, "Enoch and the Beginnings"; Alexander, "Physiognomy, Initiation."

foreign, as part of a library of ancient and heavenly knowledge, claimed to be uniquely preserved among Jewish scribes since before the Flood.

Although comparably scant, the evidence for a concern with exorcism proves no less significant: it reminds us that reflection on intermediate spirits among learned Jews was not limited to the rarified realms of abstract cosmology or theology.[74] Rather, as we shall see in Chapter 4, Jewish angelology and demonology formed part of a continuum with – and drew meaning and power from – more practical concerns about the threat of demons in daily life and local spaces. Just as ancient Jewish scribes ordered their knowledge about the cosmos by writing lists of information pertaining to the cycles of the moon and sun, so they also did so by naming the demons who roamed among them and by listing the angels whom they might petition for protection.

Following Dimant, I look to these and other Aramaic materials from Qumran as the main sources for contextualizing "pseudepigrapha" like the *Astronomical Book* and *Book of the Watchers*. Following Lange and Collins, I emphasize the importance of understanding pre-Maccabean materials on their own terms. Following Stone, I do so in part to ponder this puzzle of how a period so neglected in Jewish historiography yielded "innovations in the history of ideas that were to set patterns for the succeeding millennia."

For understanding the beginnings of Jewish angelology and demon-ology, I suggest that it proves particularly pressing to attend to those elements that appear to be distinctive to the early Hellenistic age (i.e., post-Achaemenid and pre-Maccabean) – and perhaps especially to those elements that do not fit what we have come to expect from "Juda-ism" on the basis of the Hebrew Bible, New Testament, and Mishnah, or what we have come to expect from "Hellenism" and "Judaism" on the basis of the Maccabean Revolt. Diachronic perspectives on Second Temple literature have yielded a wealth of important findings concerning the afterlives of biblical traditions and the Jewish contexts in which Christianity took form. As a result of their dominance, however, there is no dearth of insightful books and articles that interpret Second Temple texts and traditions about angels and demons in relation to biblical ideas

---

[74] Eshel, "Demonology"; Alexander, "Contextualizing the Demonology"; Stuckenbruck, "Pleas for Deliverance from the Demonic"; Stuckenbruck, "Prayers of Deliverance from the Demonic"; Fröhlich, "Demons, Scribes, and Exorcists in Qumran"; Fröhlich, "Invoke at Any Time."

about God, Christian ideas about Jesus, or contemporary theological concerns like the Problem of Evil.[75] Effective studies mining "pseudepigrapha" for exegetical and mythic motifs abound.[76] So too with fascinating inquiries into their rich points of connection with the Hebrew Bible and the New Testament.[77] My interest in this book, however, is in recovering some of what is missed when the rise of Jewish interest in angels and demons in Second Temple times is investigated within teleologically diachronic frameworks that center and privilege currently canonical scriptures and the theological categories and concerns of present-day religious communities.[78]

This book focuses on the functions of angels and demons within the earliest "pseudepigrapha" and other plausibly pre-Maccabean Jewish writings in Aramaic. For contextualizing these materials, I look less to later texts and more to Jewish and other literature from the period of Ptolemaic rule over the Land of Israel. To the degree that a synchronic focus opens the way for experimentation with fresh intertexts and unculled comparanda, I suggest that it might aid us in mapping a range of possible factors spurring the emergence of intensive Jewish reflection on otherworldly spirits. What emerges, in the process, is the integral connection between the development of systematic discourses about transmundane powers and the new approaches to scribes, books, and writing that also emerge in the Jewish literature of early Hellenistic age.

---

[75] Among the superb studies approaching these materials through the lens of the problem of evil, for instance, are Delcor, "Le mythe de la chute des anges"; Stuckenbruck, "Origins of Evil"; Stuckenbruck, "Book of Jubilees and the Origin of Evil"; Brand, *Evil Within and Without*; Bachmann, "Wenn Engel gegen Gott freveln."

[76] Examples of special relevance to the present study include Dimant, "Fallen Angels"; Bernstein, "Angels at the Aqedah"; Najman, "Angels at Sinai"; Losekam, *Die Sünde der Engel*.

[77] Studies of biblical interpretation in *Jubilees* are especially plentiful; e.g., Endres, *Biblical Interpretation*; van Ruiten, *Primeval History Interpreted*; Kugel, *Walk through Jubilees*; Brooke, "Exegetical Strategies in *Jubilees* 1–2"; Crawford, "On the Exegetical Function." On biblical interpretation in early Enochic "pseudepigrapha," see Dimant, "1 Enoch 6–11"; Pomykala, "Scripture Profile"; VanderKam, "Biblical Interpretation in *1 Enoch* and *Jubilees*."

[78] i.e., as is the case whether these writings are judged *negatively* in relation to canonical materials (e.g., as a departure from biblical monotheism) or *positively* (e.g., as a prelude to the purported transcendence of "this-worldly" Judaism in "other-worldly" Christianity; as precursor to Jewish mysticism). To "describe a precanonical world on its own terms" – as Mroczek has recently shown – it is necessary to "leave teleological questions in the margins" (*Literary Imagination*, 11).

"PSEUDEPIGRAPHA" AND THE HISTORY OF JEWISH WRITING

Recent decades have seen a renaissance of research on orality, textuality, and memory across the humanities, characterized by the rejection of older dichotomies between oral and literate stages or cultures, and the exploration of the richly varied ways in which oral and textual practices can relate and interpenetrate within different historical and cultural contexts.[79] Even in highly-specialized and self-contained subfields like Biblical Studies, New Testament Studies, Patristics, and Rabbinics, investigation of such themes has created new spaces for interdisciplinary experimentation, engaging insights from settings as far-flung as ancient Athens, medieval Europe, and modern Africa.[80] Drawing on interdisciplinary discussions of the limited place of writing in premodern technologies of memory, for instance, Biblicists such as Susan Niditch, David Carr, and Joachim Schaper have remapped the uses of writing in relation to the spoken and heard word in ancient Israel.[81] Such reassessments, in turn, have prompted fresh inquiries into the formation and collection of the Torah/Pentateuch and prophetic literature, as keyed to shifts in the packaging, preservation, teaching, and transmission of knowledge in the wake of the Assyrian conquest of the Northern Kingdom of Israel (722 BCE), and during and after the Neo-Babylonian conquest of the Southern Kingdom and the exile of Judah's elites (597–539 BCE). Whereas older studies of the biblical canon focused largely on the question of *when* it was closed, newer studies have thus charted the textualization of Israel's

---

[79] e.g., Floyd, "Write the Revelation"; Carr, *Writing on the Tablet* – the latter stressing that writing could function as a "permanent reference point for an ongoing process of largely oral recitation" (4). On the persistence of old assumptions about the "Great Divide" between orality and textuality, see Vayntrub, *Beyond Orality*.

[80] For orality and textuality, scholars of ancient religions have looked especially to questions posed by Walter Ong in *Orality and Literacy*, and the evolving perspectives of Jack Goody (e.g., *Logic of Writing*; *Tradition of the Written Word*), as well as to studies such as Harris, *Ancient Literacy*. For memory, Mary Carruthers' *Book of Memory* is frequently cited as inspiration. That said, the former lines of inquiry also stand in some continuity with form-criticism within Biblical Studies, as well as extending classic works in NT Studies such as Gerhardsson, *Memory and Manuscript* and Kelber, *Oral and the Written Gospel;* the latter resonate with points made already in Yerushalmi, *Zakhor*. For useful summaries, oriented towards the utility of the discussion for the study of antiquity, see Alexander, *Transmitting Mishnah*, 1–34; Smith, *Memoirs of God*, 124–140.

[81] e.g., Niditch, *Oral World*; Carr, *Writing on the Tablet*; Schaper, "Theology of Writing"; Schaper, "Exilic and Post-Exilic Prophecy"; Schaper, "On Writing and Reciting."

remembered past and its epistemological effects with reference to specific scribal practices and pedagogies.[82]

Inspired independently by the same theoretical matrix, specialists in early Christianity and Rabbinic Judaism have eschewed older notions of orality and textuality as distinct stages of cultural development, and they have looked beyond the ideological privileging of oral transmission in the New Testament and classical Rabbinic literature to uncover the material and social contexts of textuality and orality in late antique pedagogies and literary production.[83] Among the results has been the recovery of the social lives of Scripture within post-70 Jewish and Christian communities – as variously constituted through its oral recitation and exposition, its internalization and transmission through recitation and memorization, and its repackaging in various material forms and performative settings.[84] In effect, scholars of late antique Jews and Christians have come at the problem from the other side, rethinking what the biblical past, its laws, and its stories did and meant in social worlds in which skills in reading remained rare, and even cherished writings were rarely experienced as words silently seen upon a page. Like their counterparts in Biblical Studies, they have grappled anew with questions about the hermeneutical ramifications of the gap between modern and ancient ideas of "authorship." If the advent of printing so thoroughly reshaped practices of reading, writing, and literate education in the West, for instance, what do contemporary readers miss when we try to understand ancient texts – and those who created, edited, copied, collected, and preserved them? And how can we recover a sense of the social worlds in which writings often lived, not as writing *per se*, but rather as the voice of the past rendered present in the ear and memory?[85]

I suggest that such questions prove especially pressing in the case of "pseudepigrapha" like the *Book of the Watchers* and *Jubilees* – perhaps the ancient writings that have suffered most from the imposition of modern judgments about what writing and reading *should* entail.[86]

---

[82] e.g., Schniedewind, *How the Bible*; van der Toorn, *Scribal Culture*. On the limits of this approach, however, see Newman, *Before the Bible*.

[83] Jaffee, *Torah in the Mouth*; Hezser, *Jewish Literacy*; Alexander, *Transmitting Mishnah*, esp. 9–18; Gamble, *Books and Readers*; Haines-Eitzen, *Guardians of Letters*.

[84] Stern, "First Jewish Books"; Stern, *Jewish Bible*; Stock, *Augustine the Reader*.

[85] For a focused effort to apply insights from Book History onto the study of the Hebrew Bible and Second Temple Judaism, see Mroczek, *Literary Imagination*.

[86] Najman, *Seconding Sinai*.

The category and collection of "Old Testament Pseudepigrapha" first took shape at the turn of the eighteenth century, giving voice to new anxieties about authorship, forgery, and the ramifications of new technologies of printing for reshaping the textual archive of the Christian past.[87] In this early modern context, the emphasis on the false attribution of parabiblical writings functioned to bracket the question of the antiquity and authenticity of their canonical counterparts, helping to naturalize Protestant notions of Scripture and to inoculate their Old Testaments against the critical scrutiny opened up by Reformation-era debates.[88]

The aftereffects have been deep and lasting. In comparison with those writings now comprised by "the Bible" for Jews and Protestants, those categorized as "pseudepigrapha" have suffered much scholarly neglect. These works have been analyzed largely through the lens of their retrospectively canonical counterparts, and they have been only rarely and recently studied on their own terms. Even today, their significance remains largely defined in their relational terms – labeled as "post-biblical," "inter-testamental," or "extra-canonical" literature, read as "rewritten Bible" or biblical exegesis, and treated as "New Testament background." The dominant categories and questions for research on these sources have been based upon the Hebrew Bible and the New Testament.[89] And, even though much of our evidence for Second Temple Judaism comes from "pseudepigrapha," their ancient authors have been pushed to the peripheries of sociocultural reconstructions of the history of this period, which have centered instead on currently canonical corpora.

Over sixty years after the discovery of the Dead Sea Scrolls, it is still not uncommon to find even the earliest "pseudepigrapha" read in relation to a biblical corpus imagined to be effectively set and inviolable. Even more pervasive are the subtler effects of what Robert Kraft has termed the "tyranny of canonical assumptions" whereby post-Reformation notions of Scripture have shaped the hermeneutical habits of modern scholarship[90] – whether through the imposition of abstract categories and concepts from Christian theology, or through the mining of such works for

---

[87] i.e., with Johann Albert Fabricius' *Codex pseudepigraphus Veteris Testamenti*, which was first published in 1713, followed by a second edition in 1722 and a second volume in 1723 (*Codicis pseudepigraphi Veteris Testamenti, Volumen alterum accedit Josephi veteris Christiani auctoria Hypomnesticon*); see further Reed, "Modern Invention."

[88] Reed, "Modern Invention."   [89] Stone, *Ancient Judaism*, 4–15.

[90] Kraft, "Para-mania," 17; see also McDonald, *Forgotten Scriptures*, 11–34.

clues to "intertestamental" trajectories, or through the naturalization of modern scholarly reading-practices that reinscribe the assumption of their derivative or subordinate status vis-à-vis what we now call "the Bible."[91]

As much as scholars have sought to make sense of the literary polyvalence, collective authorship, and even pseudonymity of many works in the Hebrew Bible and New Testament, for instance, they have tended to judge the same features far more harshly when they appear in "pseudepigrapha." Modern standards of logical consistency have been imposed upon their redactional layering through the application of source-critical approaches of the sort no longer utilized in the study of the Hebrew Bible or New Testament.[92] Their assertions about angels and demons have been treated as ciphers to decode, rather than constitutive of their cosmologies, and their pseudonymous and revelatory claims have been taken as signs of their derivative character, rather than products of deliberate literary choices. Martha Himmelfarb, Hindy Najman, and Eva Mroczek have shown how such authorizing strategies are often inextricable from the ethics, the epistemologies, and even the exegesis of "pseudepigrapha."[93] Nevertheless, in most research about them, the governing assumption is that their claims to preserve the words of this or that ancient luminary can only be a ruse to achieve some other aim. And, accordingly, modern scholars have generally preferred the task of speculating about the hidden motives of the authors of "pseudepigrapha" to the challenge of taking seriously their literary choices and the social worlds in which such choices made sense.

The category of "pseudepigrapha" is a distinctively modern one – a concept and corpus created in modern times from modern criteria, shaped by distinctively modern anxieties about authorial attribution.[94]

---

[91] Examples of such reading-practices include [1] the interpretation of their similarities with biblical texts automatically as "retellings" or as products of exegesis, [2] the interpretation of their differences as deliberate "departures" from an assumed norm determined by what became the most common readings of certain biblical texts in later Jewish or Christian traditions, and [3] the interpretation of their lack of explicit mention of related (or even somewhat unrelated) biblical traditions as signaling a possibly "sectarian" self-consciousness. It is not so much that these interpretations are incorrect in all cases. The problem arises, rather, when certain relationships are predetermined in the range of options that scholars even consider.

[92] See further Collins, "Apocalyptic Technique"; Reed, *Fallen Angels*.

[93] Himmelfarb, *Ascent to Heaven*, 95–114; Najman, *Seconding Sinai*; Najman, *Past Renewals*; Mroczek, *Literary Imagination*.

[94] I do not mean to imply that there are no premodern precedents for an interest in the proper attribution of texts (for examples especially germane for this study, see Wyrick, *Ascension of Authorship*). Rather, I am pointing to the distinctive configuration of such

Consequently, the study of these particular texts might especially benefit from – and contribute to – recent attempts to peer behind the Gutenberg divide. For all the richness and sophistication of recent work on orality, textuality, and education among specialists in the Hebrew Bible and post-70 Jews and Christians, attention has focused almost wholly on those ancient writings with normative force within modern-day faith-communities. Within the relevant studies of ancient Israel, the Second Temple period consistently serves as the horizon of Scripture's canonization – typically with a teleological focus on the Bibles of present-day Jews and Protestants.[95] What is epilogue for Biblicists is prologue for their counterparts in New Testament Studies, Patristics, and Rabbinics.[96] The special wealth of Second Temple evidence related to textuality and interpretation is often noted. Surprisingly little has been done, however, to investigate Jewish scribal cultures and technologies of memory from the perspective of the full range of relevant Second Temple sources, understood on their own terms.

Among the aims of this book is to contribute to this task, building on the insights of Himmelfarb, Najman, and Mroczek. The earliest "pseudepigrapha" contain an unusually high concentration of references to writing, reading, books, and teaching. Insofar as this evidence has yet fully to be brought to bear on the discussions of textuality, memory, and pedagogy in neighboring subfields, a more focused analysis may help to bridge current discussions of biblical and post-70 materials. Yet, as we shall see, such analysis also reveals the degree to which the dynamics of literary production in Second Temple times cannot be fully captured when considered only in terms of themes or motifs that come *before* or *after*. The data resist easy reduction to the conclusion of one story or the beginning of another – in part, I suggest, because of their entanglement with angelology and demonology. Much of the surviving literature from the period has been shaped in a matrix in which sharpened concerns

---

concerns in the specific modern European scholarly settings in which "Old Testament Pseudepigrapha" was created as a concept, collection, and area of study – on which see further Reed, "Modern Invention."

[95] The canonical focus is clear from the titles of major works in this area, which consistently frame their subject as the story of how "the Bible" was "made" or "became a book," the "origins of Scripture," etc., and thus treat the Second Temple period as the end of this story – e.g., Schniedewind, *How the Bible*, 165–213; van der Toorn, *Scribal Culture*, 205–264; Carr, *Writing on the Tablet*, 201–276.

[96] Esp. Jaffee, *Torah in the Mouth*, 15–38; Gamble, *Books and Readers*, 19, 23–28.

about the power of writing overlap with an intensification of interest in intermediate spirits.

To modern sensibilities, the theorization of writing, knowledge, and education might seem to be worlds apart from speculation about angels and demons. It remains, however, that the same centuries that saw the beginnings of Jewish angelology and demonology also heralded the progressive textualization of prophecy and pedagogy. What I argue in this book is that these phenomena are so tightly intertwined that one cannot pull upon one of their threads without unraveling the others. References to writing are frequently framed or supplemented with claims about angels who reveal, interpret, read, and record. Just as angels emblematize the power of knowledge from heaven to shape life on earth and to survive even the ruptures of historical catastrophe, so demons become paradigmatic of that which can be ordered and controlled by the totalizing power of heavenly knowledge recorded in writings on earth. Even in cases like *Jubilees* where the past is rewritten with an eye to older authoritative scriptures like the Torah/Pentateuch, it is not so much ossified in writing as reanimated through the infusion of spirits – angelic and demonic alike.

The intersections of angelology and writing have been profitably examined in past scholarship, particularly by Himmelfarb with reference to the *Book of the Watchers* and ascent apocalypses, and by Najman with reference to *Jubilees* and biblical interpretation.[97] This book extends and contextualizes their findings by looking to a broader array of Aramaic, Hebrew, and Greek sources from the early Hellenistic age. Whereas Himmelfarb and Najman focus on the ideology, representation, and rhetoric of writing, I here attempt to correlate their conclusions with insights from neighboring subfields, especially concerning the situated social practices of writing, reading, and teaching. Following Carr's lead, I look not only to inner-Jewish dynamics but also to broader patterns and practices across the ancient Mediterranean world.[98] I draw on the findings of recent research on Greek *paideia* (lit. education) by scholars such as Teresa Morgan and Raffaela Cribiore, as well as on attempts by Andrew Erskine, Steve Johnstone, and others to chart the politicization of books and the "invention of the library" in the Hellenistic period.[99] To situate the Jewish literature of this period,

---

[97] Himmelfarb, *Ascent to Heaven*, 95–114; Najman, "Interpretation," 381–388.
[98] Carr, *Writing on the Tablet*, 177–273.
[99] e.g., Morgan, *Literate Education*; Cribiore, *Gymnastics of the Mind*; Erskine, "Culture and Power"; Johnstone, "New History of Libraries."

I consider what Whitmarsh, Haubold, and others describe as the rise of an "archival sensibility" in Greek and Babylonian sources from the third and second centuries BCE.[100]

At the intersection of these conversations are the core questions of this book. How are we to understand the *Astronomical Book*, *Book of the Watchers*, *Jubilees*, and related Aramaic texts wherein the earliest known examples of systematic attention to demons and angels within Jewish literature are paired with some of the most intensively self-referential and explicit discussions of writing, knowledge, and education? Is there a causal connection behind this confluence of concerns? What might their relationships reveal about shifting attitudes toward knowledge and its transmission in the Jewish literary cultures of the early Hellenistic age? Does Aramaic Jewish scribalism parallel or participate in any of the broader intellectual trends of this time? And what might we learn about Second Temple Judaism by recovering a sense of the imagined worlds in which angels wrote and recited, sinned and sired demonic sons, and traveled with human scribes to the very ends of the earth? In the process of exploring these questions, I propose that a focus on writing can open a fresh perspective on long-standing debates about the determinative causes for the flourishing of Jewish angelology and demonology.

TRANSFORMATIONS OF NEAR EASTERN KNOWLEDGE IN THE HELLENISTIC PERIOD

At first sight, the beginnings of Jewish angelology and demonology might seem to resist any connection to broader developments in the Hellenistic world. Not only are the most relevant materials in Aramaic rather than Greek, but they are marked by a renewed embrace of Mesopotamian and other Near Eastern traditions. Already in 1975, however, John J. Collins and Jonathan Z. Smith published articles that arrived independently, from different directions, to much the same suggestion: the reemergence of older Near Eastern traditions in Jewish apocalypses, like Daniel and the *Book of the Watchers*, may actually have much to tell us about cultural change in the wake of the conquests of Alexander.[101]

---

[100] e.g., Whitmarsh, *Ancient Greek Literature*, 122–138; Haubold, *Greece and Mesopotamia*, 127–177.
[101] Collins, "Jewish Apocalyptic"; Smith, "Wisdom and Apocalyptic."

Scholars of Biblical Studies have habitually treated Near Eastern "influence" as an emblem of pre-exilic antiquity, while interpreting post-exilic sources in terms of resistance or assimilation to Greco-Roman culture – with divisions of periodization, selections of *comparanda*, and conventionalized reading- practices thereby naturalizing the notion of the two as mutually exclusive. Due in part to the structurally embedded persistence of old dichotomies like Greek/Near East in the study of antiquity, and "Hellenism"/"Judaism" in research on Second Temple Judaism, studies of Hellenistic-era Jewish sources have tended to neglect Near Eastern *comparanda* from the Hellenistic period, either treating their Jewish echoes as survivals from the pre-exilic past or dismissing them as akin to the return of the repressed. "One is left with the impression," as Collins notes, "that the post-exilic period was the Sheol of ancient civilization, where the myths and ideas of an earlier period led a shadowy afterlife, enjoying vitality only in so far as they were reincarnated in Jewish apocalyptic."[102]

Smith's seminal "Wisdom and Apocalyptic" starkly demonstrated the converse: in the course of showing how attention to Hellenistic-era Near Eastern scribes like Berossus could illumine the interconnection of what scholars of Judaism traditionally separated as "sapiential" and "apocalyptic," he posits parallel shifts in Near Eastern scribal cultures at the advent of Hellenistic rule.[103] Similarly countering the long-standing scholarly habit of situating Israel's engagement with Near Eastern traditions in pre-exilic periods and distinguishing them from post-exilic encounters with Hellenism, Collins' "Jewish Apocalyptic against its Hellenistic Near Eastern Environment," made the case that

if we would appreciate Jewish apocalyptic against its contemporary Near Eastern environment we must look beyond traces of literary influence between particular books to similar phenomena in the various cultures and the common or similar conditions which produced them ... [and to] parallel developments in different national traditions, each of which retained its distinctive character.[104]

When viewed from this perspective, "we can no longer consider Israelite tradition and Hellenistic syncretism as mutually exclusive alternatives."[105] What we see, rather, is how "the conquests of Alexander had a profound impact on the eastern civilizations" and how this "impact included an unprecedented circulation of ideas among the various

[102] Collins, "Jewish Apocalyptic," 27.   [103] Smith, "Wisdom and Apocalyptic," 68–74.
[104] Collins, "Jewish Apocalyptic," 27.   [105] Collins, "Jewish Apocalyptic," 34.

peoples" as well as changes in the "conditions of life" and a resultant "transformation of attitudes."[106]

Both articles have been widely cited. Puzzlingly, however, their calls for attention to Hellenistic-era Near Eastern *comparanda* have gone largely unheeded. From the 1980s to 2000s, specialist research on Jewish apocalyptic literature turned instead to investigate inner-Jewish dynamics, extending Collin's other insights into the apocalypse as literary genre and exploring the ramifications for reconceptualizing "Apocalyptic" in relation to more abstract rubrics, both old (e.g., "Wisdom") and new (e.g., "Enochic Judaism").[107] As much as specialists in Second Temple Judaism have engaged Smith's argument about the shared scribal character of "sapiential" and "apocalyptic" traditions and the development of the latter from the former (i.e., as "wisdom lacking a royal patron"),[108] moreover, surprisingly little has been done to extend the comparative endeavor on which his argument was based.

During these same decades, however, evidence has mounted for the renewed engagement with Near Eastern materials within the Aramaic Jewish literature of the Hellenistic age – including but not limited to apocalypses. The Aramaic manuscripts related to the *Astronomical Book*, for instance, attest the continued impact of Mesopotamian scholasticism on Jewish scribalism well into the Hellenistic age. Nor are these and other scientific examples unique in this regard: there are similarly cosmopolitan lineages for the knowledge collected and reframed within other Aramaic Jewish texts of the time, ranging from the Mesopotamian metrology of the *Aramaic Levi Document*, to the hybrid Greek-Babylonian geography of the *Book of the Watchers*, to the integration of Gilgamesh and Humbaba into the *Book of the Giants*.[109]

---

[106] Collins, "Jewish Apocalyptic," 27.

[107] Most influential in this regard was *Semeia* 14 from 1979, edited by Collins, as well as the reactions to it in the 1990s by Paolo Sacchi and Gabriele Boccaccini, countering the turn toward generic analysis with studies seeking to assert apocalyptic ideology and so-called Enochic Judaism as critical components of intellectual conflicts within Second Temple Judaism (e.g., Sacchi, *Jewish Apocalyptic*; Boccaccini, *Beyond*); see further Reed, "Interrogating Enochic Judaism"; Reed, "Origins of the *Book of the Watchers*."

[108] For the quote see J. Z. Smith, "Wisdom and Apocalyptic," 80, and for assessment and bibliography of the further discussion see Wright and Wills, *Conflicted Boundaries*.

[109] See further Kvanvig, *Roots of Apocalyptic*; VanderKam, *Enoch and the Growth*; Albani, *Astronomie und Schöpfungsglaube*; Stuckenbruck, "Giant Mythology and Demonology"; Drawnel, "Between Akkadian *tupšarrūtu*." On the need to update older assessments, moreover, see Sanders, "Enoch's Imaginary Ancestor."

By the standards of older dichotomous approaches to "Hellenism" and "Judaism," the choice to integrate Mesopotamian traditions might seem counterintuitive, if not paradoxical. Yet the range and character of these traditions ultimately resist reduction to the conventional trope of the recovery of ancient Near Eastern myth in isolated or esoteric "apocalyptic conventicles." New data confirm the insights made decades ago by Collins and Smith as well as their prescient calls to situate the Jewish literature of the early Hellenistic age simultaneously in relation to its Hellenistic *and* Near Eastern contexts.

Fortuitously, such contextualization is now facilitated by recent research in Classics that has articulated more nuanced characterizations of imperialism and cultural change in the Hellenistic Near East. Paul Kosmin's 2014 study of Seleucid spatial ideologies marked a watershed in this regard. Not only does Kosmin decisively destabilize older notions of a monolithic "Hellenism" marked by the top-down imperially-imposed spread of Greek culture, but he also redescribes the establishment of the Seleucid empire in terms of the multipolarity of the Near East and the precariousness of its remapping as a Macedonian domain:

Alexander's kingdom, like the Achaemenid imperial structure that he conquered and reelaborated, was a hegemonic world empire characterized by an emphasis on totality and exclusivity. The Persian Great King and Alexander monopolized legitimate sovereignty and recognized no entity as external and equivalent. The fragmentation of this all-embracing imperial formation after Alexander's death and the stabilization of independent kingdoms multiplied the royal persona and state. A diachronic succession of world-empires (Achaemenid to Alexander) was replaced with the synchronic coexistence of bounded kingdoms. The emergence of a few "Great Powers" (Antigonid Macedonia, Ptolemaic Egypt, Seleucid Asia, as well as Attalid Pergamum, Mauryan India, the Anatolian kingdoms, and Rome) gradually developed into a system of peer states with semiformalized procedures of interactions. In other words, the east Mediterranean–west Asian region settled back into the multipolarity that had characterized its Neo-Babylonian period, immediately before Cyrus' conquests and the foundation of the Persian empire, and in the famous Late Bronze Age of Amarna.[110]

Rolf Strootman's study of the interconnected and interacting court cultures of these empires, published in the same year, similarly reassesses and

---

[110] Kosmin, *Land of the Elephant Kings*, 31. Whereas Kosmin stresses boundedness with respect to the Seleucid empire, Strootman emphasizes the ideological and propagandistic promotion of Ptolemaic and Seleucid kings as "absolute rulers of empires that knew no limits" (*Courts and Elites*, 11–12). Both follow in the wake of the corrective of Kuhrt and Sherwin-White, *From Samarkhand to Sardis*, while also attenuating the assertion of continuity between Achaemenid and Hellenistic empires.

relativizes "Hellenism" as but one among many legitimating strategies used by Macedonian rulers. He stresses that the monarchies of Antigonids, Seleucids, Ptolemies, and Attalids were "hegemonic empires: supranational state systems, based on military conquest and aimed at exacting tribute rather than governing lands and populations" but also "essentially negotiated enterprises characterized by diversity"[111]:

> After the initial conquest, imperial rulers often found it difficult to consolidate their control. Since military coercion could be used only incidentally and administrative capacities and infrastructure made direct rule difficult, empires depended heavily on the cooperation and self-government of civic and provincial elites ... When necessary, the rulers of Macedonian empires interfered in local politics ... But generally speaking, subject cities and people were relatively autonomous under the umbrella of imperial overlordship ... Since cooperation with, and only rarely occupation of, autonomous cities, temples, or vassal kingdoms was vital to imperial rule, Hellenistic kingship presented itself in multiple forms, adapting to multifarious local demands. Particularly in provinces and cities, the manifestations of royal rule was brought to accord with supposed local and regional traditions ...[112]

It is in the context of the "multiform cultural roles played by the monarch" in varying local settings, in turn, that Strootman situates the imperial court culture wherein "Hellenism" came to serve as a "reference culture ... facilitating communication between the court and elite groups and creating a sense of commonwealth in states that were characterized by their political, ethnic, and cultural heterogeneity" and thus "binding the local elites to the centre."[113]

These and other recent studies of the Hellenistic period by Classicists may make it newly possible to situate our Jewish evidence from the third and early second centuries BCE within the nested cultural contexts and networks of knowledge that shaped the Hellenistic Near East.[114] Not only do Kosmin and Strootman demonstrate the value of bringing Classics into further conversation with the study of the Near East, but they

[111] Strootman, *Courts and Elites*, 7.   [112] Strootman, *Courts and Elites*, 7-8.
[113] Strootman, *Courts and Elites*, 9.
[114] Moyer, for instance, situates his own project as part of a broader trend whereby "a heterogeneous group of historians and anthropologists ... have reconfigured relations between Europe and its others as dialogical and transactional" (*Egypt and the Limits*, 35). Although ultimately skeptical of analogies imported from postcolonial criticism, Moyer takes care to stress that "Egyptian priests, as the elite within Egyptian civilization, cannot, in any case, be categorized as subaltern ... if one were to push the analogy, they would (both in the Ptolemaic era and under Persian domination) be more like the 'modernizing elites' of colonial and post-colonial states" (34).

also model the efficacy of eschewing binary models of imperial power and experimenting with more variegated approaches to the intensified interplay of local and global idioms and ideologies in the Hellenistic period. When charting Seleucid efforts at legitimation, for instance, Kosmin jettisons the older notion of Hellenization as simply the top-down imperial imposition of Greekness, and he considers the monarchic ideology of Akkadian materials like the *Antiochus Cylinder* alongside writings in Greek by Megasthenes and Berossus.[115] Likewise, in his 2013 *Greece and Babylonia*, Haubold stresses the continual production and transmission of cuneiform texts in Seleucid Babylonia as the broader context against which to understand Berossus' defense of Near-Eastern–style scribal expertise through his creative reconfiguration of king-lists, mythic materials from *Enuma Elish*, and other traditional Mesopotamian traditions in his *Babylonica*. Far from simply a "translation" of Babylonian lore into the language and idiom of Greek historiography, the *Babylonica* helps to illumine the "extraordinary period of thirty years at the beginning of the third century BCE, when Antiochus I ruled in Babylon" and "his entourage of scribes, chroniclers, and historians helped him to retrieve and replay the relevant roles from the archive of Mesopotamian literature."[116]

In emphasizing the need to abandon "the outdated notion of a one-sided Hellenization of the east," these recent studies follow the lead of Amélie Kuhrt and Susan Sherwin-White's critique of the Hellenocentrism of modern historiography on the Macedonian empires heir to Alexander.[117] The two decades since the publication of their groundbreaking *From Samarkhand to Sardis*, however, have also exposed the shortcomings of simply flipping the focus from Alexander's inventiveness to his continuities with the Achaemenids. Strootman, for instance, notes how the "postcolonial 'continuity paradigm,' i.e., the line of thought that conceptualizes the empire of Alexander and the Seleukids as essentially a continuation of the Achaemenid Empire and emphasizes the continuity of Near Eastern cultural 'traditions'" can run the risk of "capitaliz[ing] on an ahistorical synthesis of Greek ('European') and non-Greek ('Oriental') cultural systems" and

---

[115] Kosmin, *Land of the Elephant Kings*. See also now Kosmin, *Time and Its Adversaries*.
[116] Haubold, *Greece and Mesopotamia*, 127–177, quote at 127, and see 154–155 for discussion of similarities and differences with Whitmarsh's assessment of Greek materials.
[117] So Strootman, "Babylonian, Macedonian, King of the World," 76, reflecting on the impact of Kuhrt and Sherwin-White, *From Samarkhand to Sardis*.

"conceptualiz[ing] Near Eastern cultures as essentially static."[118] Instead, he calls for an approach to "social discourses and practices [as] constantly in flux and bi-directional" – an approach that he models in his own analyses of the "vital, two-way interaction of city and court."[119]

In his 2011 *Egypt and the Limits of Hellenism*, Ian Moyer brings a similar approach to bear on our evidence for the Ptolemies. Deconstructing the tendency of modern scholarship on Hellenistic Egypt to assume the "independent persistence of two ancient civilizations, one ruling, the other ruled," he investigates the array of intermediate positions navigated by indigenous elites.[120] Among the results is a fresh assessment of the Greek historiography of the Egyptian priest Manetho, not as a bridge between otherwise distinct Egyptian and Greek social worlds, but rather as a reflection of "an important, if not necessarily numerous, group of indigenous elites, who served in the Ptolemaic military or administration and were in regular communication with the new immigrant elite and even the court itself."[121] By his reading, Manetho's *Aegyptiaca* emerges as an example of "counter-discursive historiography firmly rooted in his own creative exegesis of Egyptian ways of representing the past."[122] Here too, older lists (in this case: king-lists) provide material for the creation of a new literary work that speaks to the concerns of the early Hellenistic age.[123] The result is not so much the product of the Greek introduction of "historical consciousness" into Egypt so much as an extension of earlier trends in Egyptian writing about the past in a manner shaped both by the patronage of the early Ptolemaic court (esp. under Ptolemy I Soter, r. 305–282 BCE, and Ptolemy II Philadelphus, r. 282–246 BCE) and by concerns about continuity and rupture akin to those expressed in contemporaneous Demotic sources such as the *Demotic Chronicle*.[124]

---

[118] Strootman, "Babylonian, Macedonian, King of the World," 76.

[119] Strootman, "Babylonian, Macedonian, King of the World," 77; Strootman, *Courts and Elites*.

[120] Moyer, *Egypt and the Limits*, 27.   [121] Moyer, *Egypt and the Limits*, 89.

[122] Moyer, *Egypt and the Limits*, 38, see further 96–141. He stresses that something is lost when we read this work as "the result of a Greek colonization of Egyptian historical consciousness," arguing instead for seeing it as "an indigenous attempt both to make explicit the proper historical role of the Egyptian pharaoh, and also to teach the Ptolemies and other Greeks at court to read Egyptian history in Egyptian fashion" (140–141).

[123] Moyer, *Egypt and the Limits*, 103–125.

[124] On the date of Manetho, see Moyer, *Egypt and the Limits*, 86 n. 6, and on parallels with the *Demotic Chronicle*, see 128–135 – the latter culminating with his suggestion to read the *Aegyptiaca* as "an Egyptian scholar's effort to use and to make comprehensible indigenous ways of explaining and representing the past in the process of grappling with

For reconstructing the Jewish cultural history of the third and early second centuries BCE, it may be similarly useful to set aside contrastive models of ruler and ruled, "Hellenism" and "Judaism," Macedonian oppression and Jewish apocalyptic resistance. For instance, as we shall see, the Aramaic Jewish literature of the early Hellenistic age participates in broader trends in the third and second centuries BCE toward the increased prestige of books and writing across the Hellenistic world – a shift that can be glimpsed in donative inscriptions no less than in the literature of the time, both by self-claimed Greeks and by "barbarians" like Babylonians defending the need for Near Eastern scribes even in a world remade by Greek *paideia*.[125] But at the same time, the very choice to make a Jewish literary language out of Aramaic points to a creative reconfiguration of what even counts as local knowledge – far more complex than simply the preservation or defense of some statically authentic Israelite heritage against imperial encroachment or elite assimilation.

So too with the textualization of Mesopotamian science and other Near Eastern knowledge in newly Jewish literary forms: these and other innovations within the Aramaic Jewish literature of the early Hellenistic age are inextricably local and globalizing. To the degree that Ptolemaic rule brought new questions, concerns, and challenges, some Jewish scribes answered them *from* and *with* Israel's own past, forging new models of teaching, textuality, and knowledge out of older Israelite *and* other Near Eastern materials.[126] The result was a new vision of Jewish literature and learning, articulated especially in the administrative language of the previous empire (i.e., the Imperial Aramaic of the Achaemenids) and predicated on a reimagining of Israel's past that enabled the integration of new elements of Mesopotamian science, mythology, and pedagogical practice into Jewish literature.[127]

---

the contemporary problem of historical rupture and continuity created by the end of native rule and the establishment of the Ptolemaic dynasty" (134–135).

[125] Johnstone, "New History of Libraries."

[126] As in its Egyptian counterparts, this turn to the past preceded the Ptolemies, but seems to have intensified under their rule; Moyer, *Egypt and the Limits*, 38, 84–141.

[127] For a sense of the startling range of Mesopotamian traditions in Enochic "pseudepigrapha," see Kvanvig, *Roots of Apocalyptic*; VanderKam, *Enoch and the Growth*; Albani, *Astronomie und Schöpfungsglaube*; Stuckenbruck, "Giant Mythology and Demonology"; Drawnel, "Between Akkadian *tupšarrūtu*." As we shall see, the range and character of these traditions resist reduction to the old trope of the "apocalyptic" recovery of Near Eastern "myth."

Reread from this perspective, the emergence of explicit concern for angels and demons forms part of an astonishing expansion in the scope and self-consciousness of Jewish literary production in the early Hellenistic age. It proves intriguing, thus, that its range matches the totalizing claims of Greek *paideia,* especially in the forms that this style of enculturating education was coming to define elite identity and court culture across Ptolemaic, Seleucid, and other Hellenistic empires. Just as the curriculum of *enkyklios paideia* ("common education") encompassed Greek grammar, literature, astronomy, and mathematics,[128] so Jewish scribes of the time also recast Israel's past in the image of a pedagogical ideal that included detailed knowledge about the structure, cycles, and workings of the cosmos. In the process, they innovated new literary forms at the interface of Greek ideas of "authorship" and the anonymous and collective scribal practices native to the Near East. Even as their totalizing claims echoed those of their counterparts elsewhere in the Hellenistic world, they were also distinctive – not least in presenting Jewish knowledge, teaching, and writing as the product of uniquely ancient and enduring connections with the angels who govern the cosmos and the demons thereby controlled.

CONCLUSION AND CHAPTER SUMMARY

At the heart of this book is the trajectory from the *Astronomical Book* in the third century BCE to *Jubilees* in the middle of the second century BCE. Much has been learned from the use of these and other "pseudepigrapha" to illuminate the background of Jesus, early Christianity, and Rabbinic Judaism alike; yet much remains to be discovered from and about these sources, understood on their own terms and in their own contexts. Toward this aim, this book experiments with "reversing the gaze" by placing the earliest "pseudepigrapha" at the center of the analysis and bringing in biblical and other comparanda primarily to illuminate them. Rather than forefronting biblical exegesis, for instance, I here approach both biblical and parabiblical sources through the lens of the preoccupation with writing and knowledge in works like *Astronomical Book* and *Book of the Watchers.* Following the lead of *Jubilees,* I consider traditions about Enoch and Moses in concert, and I sidestep recent specialist debates predicated on polarized dichotomies between "the Bible" and

---

[128] Morgan, *Literate Education,* 35–38.

"pseudepigrapha." Instead of assuming that any topics neglected in the Hebrew Bible must have been marked as foreign, I follow the lead of the *Astronomical Book*, *Book of the Watchers*, and *Jubilees* in treating astronomy, geography, angelology, and demonology as forms of Jewish knowledge for some scribes, and I thus attempt to recover some sense of the structures of plausibility wherein they connected such knowledge to those domains that modern readers are more accustomed to interpreting as "Jewish" and "religious" (e.g., ethics, ritual, halakha).

Chapter 1 sets the stage for this inquiry by reflecting on the lack of demonological and angelological discourses in the surviving literary remains of ancient Israel, in contrast with what is commonly found elsewhere in the ancient Mediterranean world. Rather than framing the difference in terms of the conventional contrast between "monotheism" and "polytheism," I here consider the absence of systematic discourses of demonology and angelology in early biblical literature in relation to the overwriting of divine multiplicity therein and the dominance of genealogy as an organizing principle for textualizing and organizing knowledge. Attending to the rhetoric of ambiguity surrounding creatures later categorized as "angels," I argue for the need to distinguish between the question of what Jews *believed* about intermediate spirits and the question of when Israel's scribes did and did not choose to *write* about them in explicit, systematic, and systematizing terms.

Chapter 2 makes the case for the early Hellenistic age as the determinative era for emergence of systematic written reflection on angels and demons in Jewish literature, and it explores why this development occurs when and how it did. Against the modern scholarly habit of explaining change in the Second Temple Judaism as "post-exilic," I argue for the need for more fine-grained perspectives that attend to the specificities of Achaemenid, Ptolemaic, Seleucid, Hasmonean, and Roman rule. Attention to the Aramaic Dead Sea Scrolls makes this newly possible for the Ptolemaic period, I suggest, not least by helping us to situate angelological, demonological, and other trends synchronically within the third and early second centuries BCE. Among the results is a sense of the inextricability of demonology and angelology from concurrent shifts in the practice and perception of scribes – including the repurposing of Aramaic as a Jewish literary language, the turn to the pre-Sinaitic past, and the scribalization of this past. To recover a distinctive Aramaic Jewish scribal pedagogy, moreover, is also to be able to situate the beginnings of Jewish angelology and demonology in relation to broader trends in the early Hellenistic age, within and beyond Judaism.

Chapter 3 turns to focus on the angelology of the *Astronomical Book*, considering it both in relation to Jewish redeployment of Mesopotamian astronomy and in relation to the Ptolemaic politicization of cosmological and other knowledge. On the one hand, the "scientific" interests in this and related materials from Qumran are exemplary of the cosmological concerns that inform the increased turn to angels: the intertwined interest in angelology and astronomy in the *Astronomical Book* points to the radical expansion of the very scope of knowledge deemed apt for record in writing in literary forms by Jewish scribes during the early Hellenistic age. On the other hand, its angelology is entwined with its textuality. Attention to the Aramaic fragments of the *Astronomical Book* enable us to recover some of the process whereby earlier didactic lists of astronomical and related information become compiled into a literary work in which text-based teaching becomes a model for the angelic revelation of knowledge to Enoch and his scribal heirs. Inasmuch as the angelology of the *Astronomical Book* is inextricable from its epistemology and textuality, I suggest that its concerns resonate with contemporaneous efforts by non-Jewish authors like Aratus and Berossus to rewrite received astronomical lists and related materials into newly literary, cosmological, and pedagogical forms.

Chapter 4 turns to the *Book of the Watchers* and related traditions about demons and other spirits. This apocalypse is famously the first known Jewish source to explain the origins of demons as well as to list the names of fallen and heavenly angels. To understand its innovative demonology, I first focus on the epistemological concerns and literary features that it shares with the *Astronomical Book*. Then, I turn to so-called "magical" materials from Qumran that reflect the types of local and practical demon-beliefs that are here collected and systematized into demonology. The textualization of this material in the *Book of the Watchers* parallels the archival impulse and scribal practice that we see in the *Astronomical Book*, similarly pointing to the anthological character of Enochic discourse as it shapes the beginnings of Jewish angelology and demonology. As with the angelology of the *Astronomical Book*, moreover, the demonology of the *Book of the Watchers* enables both the expansion of the expertise of Jewish scribes and the claims that the Jewish literary tradition was both more ancient than the Greeks and encompassed an even more comprehensive understanding of the cosmos.

Chapter 5 reflects on the transmission and transformation of these traditions in the wake of Seleucid rule over the Land of Israel and the Maccabean Revolt in the second century BCE. To do so, I focus on their "translation" into the Hebrew language and pentateuchal idiom in *Jubilees* – a source that similarly features an extensive concern for angels and demons. Rather than reading *Jubilees* through the lens of its parallels and departures from Genesis and Exodus, I thus consider its reception and transformation of Aramaic Jewish scribal pedagogy, its extension of the archival impulses and anthological discourse of the early Hellenistic age, and the consequences for the development and diffusion of Jewish angelology and demonology. If *Jubilees* marks the culmination and consolidation of many elements in the earlier Aramaic Jewish literary tradition, I suggest that it also marks the beginning of its end.

Throughout this book, I experiment with an approach to Second Temple Jewish literature that resists the reduction of its significance either to the history of biblical exegesis or to background for Christian Origins. Accordingly, I here look both within and beyond specialist research on Biblical Studies and Second Temple Judaism. I built on recent findings from across Jewish Studies and Religious Studies, but I also draw ideas from other subfields and disciplines such as Classics and the History of Science. In addition, I take inspiration from interdisciplinary conversations about memory, material texts, education, empire, and the sociology of knowledge. And I try to make a case for the relevance of even Aramaic Jewish literature to our understanding of the cultural history of the Hellenistic period more broadly.

Furthermore, with Lehoux, this book takes the analysis of ancient knowledge-practices as an invitation "to see how the modern categories stand up to and are challenged by a body of foreign texts and at the same time to see what new methods of reading those texts can reveal about antiquity."[129] As we shall see, the *Astronomical Book*, *Book of the Watchers*, and *Jubilees* reflect an understanding of the workings of unseen forces in the cosmos that dramatically differs from modern Western scientific views of the universe. Their treatments of angels are entangled in pseudonymous or authorizing claims of the sort commonly dismissed as "forgery" by modern criteria. Their treatments of demons form part of a theodicy far more complex and dynamic (and, by current standards: messy) than the attribution of any single, original cause for earthly evils.

Their demonology and angelology exemplify the challenges of understanding premodern demarcations of knowledge that differ radically from our own. Precisely for this reason, however, attention to them can push us

---

[129] Lehoux, *What Did Romans*, 15. See also Zerubavel, *Social Mindscapes*, 10.

to follow the lines drawn by our ancient sources as they make their own connections – from present to past, from earth to heaven, from local to global. From a modern purview, for instance, it might be tempting to dismiss ancient Jewish interest in angels and demons as a "popular" encroachment on "elite" theology and/or as a mark of "foreign influence" on Israelite monotheism. When we attend to the histories and theories of knowledge within the Aramaic Jewish literature of the early Hellenistic age, however, what might appear to us as a blurring of self-evidently separate categories is soon revealed, instead, as a window onto a world that differed in its defining demarcations. After all, as we shall see, their claims to know about angels and demons are ultimately claims about knowledge – and adduced as exemplary of what is thereby claimed to be the unique totality of what is known by Jewish scribes. In the process of grappling with their claims, moreover, we may catch glimpses of a lost world – in which demons roamed the earth, angels sang in the skies, and human acts of writing could have cosmic consequences.

I

Multiplicity, Monotheism, and Memory
in Ancient Israel

It seems likely that in ancient Israel – as elsewhere in the Near East – beliefs about transmundane powers thrived.[1] For this, however, there are only scant hints in the Hebrew Bible. Allusions to the Judaean desert as an abode of the demonic signal the likelihood that native Israelite traditions about spirits sprung from the mapping of misfortune onto local land-scapes.[2] Scattered references to goat-demons and *cherubim* recall Meso-potamian traditions about malicious spirits shaped like animals and guardian spirits with hybrid forms.[3] Names from the Mesopotamian

---

[1] Here and throughout, I follow the convention of using "ancient Israel" to refer to the culture that we now know primarily from those materials in the Hebrew Bible that reflect the period of monarchic self-rule prior to the Babylonian Exile (586 BCE) – with the caveat that many of these materials reflect some degree of post-exilic reshaping, such that "biblical," "pre-exilic," and "ancient Israelite" are not coterminous categories. My references to "early biblical literature" pertain to those materials that are in Archaic Biblical Hebrew and Standard Biblical Hebrew, excluding those in the Late Biblical Hebrew characteristic of works composed in the Persian or Hellenistic periods; on these categories and the epigraphical and literary evidence for them, see Schniedewind, *Social History*. Inasmuch as my focus here falls especially on the contrast between these "early" materials and the Jewish literature that took form during and after the third century BCE, I refrain from delving into debates about precise dates of specific texts or strata therein.

[2] E.g., Isa 34:14. I borrow the phrase "mapping of misfortune" from Frankfurter, *Evil Incarnate*, 14.

[3] On *cherubim*, Hartenstein, "Cherubim and Seraphim," 157–162; Wood, *Of Wings and Wheels*. On Sumerian and Akkadian incantations featuring demons in the forms of animals, see van der Toorn, "Theology of Demons," 65–67, and on the broader phenomenon of the use of animals "for conceptualizing demonic power," see Frankfurter, *Evil Incarnate*, 14.

demonological lexicon have echoes as well.[4] In light of the fervency with which some biblical sources condemn soothsayers, mediums, and necromancers, it seems probable that some local ritual experts claimed to control, mediate, or dispel spirits in a manner largely disconnected from the knowledge and power of Israel's monarchic and priestly elites.[5]

Nevertheless, demons are rare in the Hebrew Bible, and even references to angels are vague and allusive. In surviving literary remains of ancient Israel, terminology used to describe intermediate spirits tends to be amorphous and ambivalent. Early biblical literature attests some of the terms elsewhere or later applied to demons. But even these – as Dan Ben-Amos notes – "hover between the referential and the metaphoric, between the literal and the poetic."[6] What we find attested elsewhere as demonic names here blur into generic nouns: Resheph into flame, Deber into pestilence, Azazel into a place where a goat is sent.[7] Angels are more prevalent but no less elusive. Those who search early biblical literature for named angels with stable jobs and personalities discover, instead, anonymous *mal'akim* with slippery identities and shifting forms.

In the surviving textual remains of preexilic Israel, no effort is made to explain the origins or nature of demons or angels. Nor are there any precedents for the explicit concern in Second Temple literature to outline their relationship to humankind.[8] Biblical literature is not marked by any systematic interest in situating a plentitude of intermediate spirits within the structure and workings of the cosmos. There are no lists of demons, nor any catalogs of the personal names or ranked classes of God's heavenly retinue and otherworldly underlings. The one partial exception to this pattern – Daniel – is itself a product of the Hellenistic age.[9]

Why did intermediate spirits not attract concerted literary attention until the Second Temple period? Above, we noted the persistence of the supersessionist approach associated with Wilhelm Bousset, who deemed the rise of interest in angels and demons as a mark of Judaism's supposed

---

[4] On Lilith in this regard, as well as Resheph, Qeteb, and Deber, see van der Toorn, "Theology of Demons," 63–65; Münnich, *God Resheph* – together with the relevant *DDD* entries.

[5] E.g., Deut 18:10–11; Schäfer, "Magic and Religion," 27–28.

[6] Ben-Amos, "On Demons," 30.

[7] Smith, *Memoirs*, 151–152; Milgrom, *Leviticus 1–16*, 1021; cf. Münnich, *God Resheph*, 215–237.

[8] Wright, *Origin of Evil Spirits*, 1–3.

[9] Here and below, I thus omit Daniel from my characterization of "early biblical literature," since this work took its present form in the second century BCE.

decline after the Babylonian Exile (586–538 BCE). This chapter clears the way for exploring other explanations. By drawing on more recent specialist studies of both demonology and ancient Israel, I here reconsider the precise character of the change that we see in the treatment of transmundane powers in Second Temple times. Whereas older notions of post-exilic decline and "divine distancing" are predicated on the presumption of a pristine monotheism at the heart of Israelite exceptionalism, newer research has begun to sketch a different picture. Among my aims in this chapter, then, is to bridge the notable disjuncture between current specialist research on ancient Israel, on the one hand, and the older assumptions that ground treatments of post-exilic change in specialist research on Second Temple Judaism, on the other.

At least since Alexander Rofé, scholars of ancient Israel have recognized the relative lack of interest in angels in the Hebrew Bible and speculated about its origins in active efforts to suppress even older traditions of divine multiplicity and to promote Israel's exclusive worship of YHWH.[10] More recent studies have gone even further, hailing the seventh and sixth centuries BCE as pivotal for the articulation of what we now know as "biblical monotheism."[11] What has become clear, in the process, is that the dynamics of tradition and transformation are much more complex than any singular trajectory from biblical monotheism to post-biblical decline – not least because biblical representations of divinity are much more complex than the modern trope of Israel's invention of monotheism might lead us to expect: a number of early biblical writings appear to preserve residual parallels to traditions about demons and deities described more explicitly in other Near Eastern corpora, even as their own literary forms are shaped by a notable reticence surrounding even lesser or subordinate otherworldly powers.

The present chapter explores the purposes and poetics of this reticence. To do so, I build upon the work of Biblicists who have sought to recover ancient Israelite traditions of divine multiplicity with attention to the gaps and silences in early biblical literature.[12] For our purposes, these gaps and

[10] Rofé, *Belief in Angels*.
[11] E.g., Smith, *Early History*; Smith, *Memoirs*; Gnuse, *No Other Gods*; MacDonald, *Deuteronomy and the Meaning*.
[12] See note above as well as Smith, *God in Translation*; Sommer, *Bodies of God*; Hamori, *When Gods Were Men*; Wagner, *Gottes Körper* – and see already the essays reprinted in Halpern, *From Gods to God*. Exemplary in this regard is the common structure of *DDD* entries on biblical terms, which can only provide specific details inasmuch as they "fill the gaps" of the biblical text with parallels from the literature of other Near Eastern cultures.

silences are important data in their own right – valuable for what they might reveal about the writing practices, technologies of memory, and Hebrew scribal cultures that shaped early biblical literature. By attending to these data, this chapter thus lays the groundwork for our analysis of the writing practices, technologies of memory, and Aramaic scribal cultures that later shaped the Second Temple sources in which we first find a systematized Jewish discourse about angels and demons.

However we might speculate about what Israelites *believed* about the otherworld and its occupants before the Exile, it remains that an interest in angels and demons was not yet *textualized* in explicit or systematic terms in what was cultivated and continually transmitted of ancient Israel's literary cultures. What are the factors that shaped and patterned this textualized selectivity? Why and how did it later give way to a delight in detailing the names and functions of angels and demons in such explicitly systematic and systematizing terms? These questions form the focus of this chapter, which thus lays the foundation for our subsequent inquiry into the timing, character, and contexts of the beginnings of Jewish angelology and demonology.

The first part of this chapter looks to demonological discourses elsewhere in the ancient Mediterranean world so as to situate the relative lack of concern for intermediate spirits in the surviving products of ancient Israel's scribal cultures. Rather than culling *comparanda* for claims of "influence" or "borrowing," I here treat cross-cultural analysis as an invitation to look more closely at the concerns, contexts, and conditions that shaped the emergence of demonologies among diverse literate elites in the interlocking cultures of the ancient Mediterranean world. This analysis grounds the second part of this chapter, which experiments with explanatory strategies for discussing why discourses of this sort are lacking in the Hebrew Bible. Drawing on recent research on monotheism and memory in ancient Israel, the third part of this chapter charts the rhetoric of divine unity and the poetics of divine multiplicity in its surviving textual remains, mapping the dominant patterns in biblical references to creatures later conflated into the category of "angel," such as *mal'akim*, *bene elohim*, *seraphim*, *cherubim*, *ḥayyot*, and *ruḥot*.

Consistent with the main focus and aims of this book, and my experiment in "reversing the gaze" to place so-called pseudepigrapha at the

My point here is that the ambiguity that necessitates such scholarly efforts is significant in its own right, particularly due to the striking contrast with the later materials that form the heart of the present study.

center of my analysis, I make no claim to comprehensiveness, and I look to larger trends rather than specific texts or times. My aim is to highlight some patterns within early biblical literature that can help to bring developments in the early Hellenistic age into sharper relief. In the process, I engage some areas of specialist research on the Hebrew Bible and ancient Israel that have methodological consequences for the analysis of cultural change in Second Temple Judaism, particularly when put in conversation with comparative perspectives on demonology and divine multiplicity from across the ancient Mediterranean world.

Among the results are two distinctions that are central to this book as a whole. The first, which emerges from comparative studies of demonology, is between evidence for the pervasiveness of various local beliefs in transmundane powers within a culture, on the one hand, and evidence for the development of demonology as a practice of systematizing, organizing, and globalizing such knowledge, on the other. Many biblical writings attest the former, whether directly or indirectly. Yet they consistently lack the latter. It is by virtue of this pattern, in fact, that modern scholars read *behind* the silence of the texts and look to *comparanda* from neighboring cultures if they wish to speculate beyond what the literary record explicitly states. For our purposes here, reticence and rhetoric are important data in their own right. Not only might they tell us something about the scribal habits that shaped the surviving literature of ancient Israel, but they also push us to redescribe the beginnings of Jewish demonology and angelology with a focus on shifts in the systemization, textualization, and ordering of knowledge.

The second distinction, which emerges especially from research on Israelite monotheism, is between what Israelites in general *thought* or *believed* about seen and unseen powers, and how certain scribes *wrote* about them. "Writing in the biblical period," as Tzvi Abusch reminds us, "represented not Israelite/Judean culture, but rather 'biblical' religion, with its emphasis on prophets or cultic priests as well as its anti-magician attitude."[13] This distinction pushes us to approach our literary data, not as direct windows onto beliefs or worldviews, but rather as evidence for choices about the textualization of knowledge, the written representation of the past, and the scribal cultures that shaped them. What types of knowledge are apt for preservation, teaching, and transmission *in writing*? What is the scope of the expertise claimed by scribes, and what

---

[13] Abusch, "Exorcism," 518.

is the place of books in education and the transmission of tradition? The Hebrew Bible was shaped by quite different answers to these questions than would develop in the Aramaic Jewish literature of the early Hellenistic age – and the change is perhaps nowhere more evident than in their respective approaches to textualizing knowledge about intermediate spirits.

These two distinctions, in turn, clear the way for situating the shifts that we see in our literary evidence in relation to cultural memory.[14] In conversation with multidisciplinary research on memory, scholars such as Mark S. Smith have modeled fresh approaches to the Hebrew Bible as the product of "ongoing dialogue in ancient Israel over different versions of the past."[15] A sense of the dynamics proves particularly helpful, for our purposes, inasmuch as this dialogue hardly stops with the Babylonian Exile: there is no single moment when reflection on Israel's past ceases and when exegesis of Israel's scriptures then begins.[16] Just as the "academic study of collective memory offers important intellectual help for understanding the biblical representations of Israel's past, which includes its past recollections of its God,"[17] so too for their Second Temple counterparts, wherein the formative past – and reflection on divine, angelic, and demonic involvement therein – continued to be rewritten and reshaped in new historical and political contexts. In this chapter, we shall see how the encounter with the past was formative for the articulation of monotheism and genealogy, which appear to have largely displaced demonology as dominant systematizing strategies within those modes of literary production that shaped the Hebrew Bible. In the following chapters, we shall see how writing continued to be one powerful technology of memory-making, as Jewish scribes in the early Hellenistic age forged new approaches to angels and demons precisely by textualizing them as knowledge from and about Israel's past.

DEMONOLOGY AND MONOTHEISM IN THE ANCIENT WORLD

When seen in the broader context of the ancient Mediterranean world, the absence of sustained reflection on otherworldly spirits in ancient Israel appears as somewhat of an anomaly. Mesopotamian materials bespeak

[14] I do not mean to imply that writing and taxonomy were the *only* technologies of memory in ancient Judaism; for angelology and demonology, however, they happen to be especially important.
[15] Smith, *Memoirs*, 6.   [16] Levinson, *Legal Revision*, 95–175.   [17] Smith, *Memoirs*, 5.

efforts to outline the nature and activities of demons and lesser deities already in the second and first millennia BCE. Evidence for this trend can be found, not only in exorcistic traditions (e.g., *Udug-hul*), but also in theological reflection on the relationship of lesser powers to higher deities (e.g., *Atrahasis*; *Erra and Ishum*).[18] Something similar may be glimpsed in Persia: young Avestan sources evince the classification of transmundane powers into a hierarchy of impure *daevas* matched by a hierarchy of beneficent *ahuras*, attesting attempts to impose systematic order upon the invisible world emerging by the first half of the first millennium BCE.[19] Parallel systematizing and classifying impulses can be glimpsed even in ancient Greek literature. Whereas *daimôn* and deity (i.e., *theos*) are interchangeable in Homeric epic (e.g., *Ill.* 1.222), for example, attempts to differentiate their origins and domains become evident soon thereafter, most famously in Hesiod's *Works and Days* (e.g., *Op.* 122–126). Further reflection on the status and function of *daimones* as powers who negotiate the divide between human and divine can be found already in the writings of Plato (e.g., *Symp.* 202d–203a), which open the way for a long tradition of philosophical discourse using powers beneath the highest divinity to articulate cosmic and ontological hierarchy.[20] If comparanda of this sort draw our attention to the relative silence on such matters in the literary remains of ancient Israel, they also permit us to chart some of the social, political, and intellectual factors that elsewhere accompanied attempts at imposing order on beliefs about intermediary powers, benign and malign spirits, subordinate deities, etc., in the inter-locking cultures of the ancient Mediterranean world.

On the basis of cross-cultural data, David Frankfurter notes a recurrent pattern. It is common to find "the informal or traditional mapping of misfortune onto the environment" whereby "the local landscape becomes thus a topography of catastrophe, as place and passage become correlated to misfortune through the stories of local demons."[21] Yet, as he further notes:

...all this rudimentary systematizing of demons belongs to the oral, interactive domain of popular discussion, legend-telling, and the recommendation (or composition) of protective spells...Demon-belief in this case is context-specific to a certain affliction, to a certain group of participants in a conversation—and it is ad

---

[18] So van der Toorn, "Theology of Demons," 74–81.
[19] Hutter, "Demons and Benevolent Spirits," 27; Frankfurter, *Evil Incarnate*, 16–19.
[20] See further Albinus, "Greek δαίμων"; Timotin, *La démonologie platonicienne*.
[21] Frankfurter, *Evil Incarnate*, 14.

hoc. It is neither relevant nor conceivable to contemplate the entire range of potentially malignant spirits or to integrate them with the formal theology of the dominant religious institution.[22]

Consequently, he contrasts the "local landscapes where people really tangle with demons" with the more abstractified, second-tier practices of "collection, classification, and integration."[23] Whereas the former is *ad hoc*, the latter is shaped by totalizing aims and globalizing claims, and often associated with lists and writing.[24]

In focusing on the beginnings of Jewish angelology and demonology, this book is concerned with when, how, and why the former shifts into the latter – or, in other words, with the emergence of Jewish attempts to impose order on earlier, local, and diverse traditions about intermediary spirits. Precisely because of the likelihood that ancient Israelites had the oral and local precursors of systematic written reflection on the population of the otherworld, however, we must begin by asking *why* demonology and angelology are absent from the literary heritage of Israel as preserved in the Hebrew Bible. Frankfurter's insights thus prove especially useful inasmuch as he distinguishes the discursive practice of demonology from other modes of speech and writing about demons. After all, traditions about these and other transmundane powers can circulate widely, both orally and in writing, without sparking any systematic written reflection about their precise place in the cosmos. Our question, then, is *why* written reflection of the sort emerges in Jewish literature *when* and *where* it does. And to address this question, we must first ask *when* and *why* it does not.

The two discourses – local/practical and totalizing/conceptual – can coexist. Nonetheless, the data adduced by Frankfurter and others suggest that the former tends to be temporally prior, forming part of the environ-

---

[22] Frankfurter, *Evil Incarnate*, 15.   [23] Frankfurter, *Evil Incarnate*, 13–15.

[24] In Mesopotamian materials, Karel van der Toorn observes a similar distinction between what he terms "popular" and "scholarly" perspectives (e.g., "Theology of Demons," 62). When characterizing later Jewish and Christian traditions, Philip S. Alexander points to the doubled character of demon-belief, as encompassing both "the everyday belief in demons, and... attempts at the level of the street and market-place to deal with them," and "theological reflection... on the nature of demons, their place in the hierarchy of being and in broad scheme of things" ("Contextualizing the Demonology," 616); Alexander here stresses, however, that the ritual manipulation of demons was often a highly specialized domain, practiced by experts who transmitted their skills in lines of succession and who compiled their knowledge in written handbooks; already in the Hellenistic age, he finds evidence for the "technicalization" of this domain of knowledge and practice (616).

ments that fertilize the growth of the latter. Local traditions often provide the raw materials for priests, scribes, theologians, or philosophers to construct their systems. And these systems, in turn, take their persuasive power from their resonance with names and ideas already familiar in local cultures and rooted in local landscapes.

Accordingly, as Fritz Graf has shown, self-claimed experts, such as Greek philosophers, could use systematizing discourse about *daimones* to promote their own status as uniquely knowledgeable on cosmological and other topics transcending local concerns.[25] Yet, as Frankfurter notes, the development of demonologies frequently goes hand-in-hand with efforts to centralize ritual power in particular institutions (e.g., temples) and with attempts by classes of ritual experts (e.g., priests) to monopolize cosmological or theological knowledge. On the basis of evidence from Mesopotamia and Persia, for instance, Frankfurter points to some parallel conditions for the emergence of systematic attempts to organize otherworldly spirits into hierarchies and to subsume them into elite domains of expertise; the discursive practice of demonology, for instance, often accompanies other attempts at "appropriating and recasting local religious beliefs so as to make the temple priests and their rituals indispensable to public religious life."[26]

What, then, made ancient Israelites different in this regard? At first sight, the conventional contrast between monotheism and polytheism might seem to provide a tidy solution. This is certainly the answer that has dominated past research. In older scholarship on the history of religions, monotheism was widely celebrated as the invention of ancient Israel and its unique contribution to the progress of human civilization.[27] Partly as a result, the increased interest in angels and demons in post-exilic Jewish literature has long been framed as a phenomenon of decline or devolution, and it remains common to explain this development in terms of the trauma of the Babylonian Exile and/or blame it on the corrupting influence of the polytheism of the foreign empires that thereafter ruled the Land of Israel.[28]

---

[25] On the philosophical discourse on "magic" as an expression of authority-claims of this sort, wherein the very category took shape "originally... [in] a debate among specialists at the margin of society" at a time when "philosophers and doctors are no less marginal and less itinerant than are the purifies and begging priests," see Graf, *Magic*, 20–60.

[26] Frankfurter, *Evil Incarnate*, 15.   [27] Schäfer, *Mirror of His Beauty*, 1.

[28] For a survey of the numerous (and even recent) attempts to explain the rise of interest in angels and demons within Second Temple Judaism as a result of the "influence" of

In effect, the logic of what is still often taken as commonsensical in much scholarship on Second Temple Judaism echoes the claims in those particular biblical works that most vigorously promote Israel's exclusive worship of YHWH, by configuring all alternatives as foreign and corrupting. Perhaps not coincidentally, this is precisely the thrust of the only two biblical attestations of *shed* (pl. *shedim*), the Hebrew word that later becomes the primary term for "demon":

> They incensed him with alien things,
> vexed him with abominations.
> They sacrificed to *shedim*, no-gods,
> gods (*elohim*) they have never known,
> new ones, who came but lately,
> who stirred not your fathers' fears.
> You neglected the Rock that begot you,
> forgot the God who brought you forth.
> (Deut 32:16–18; NJPS)

> They did not destroy the nations,
> as the Lord commanded them,
> but mingled with the nations,
> and learned their ways.
> They worshiped their idols,
> which became a snare for them.
> Their own sons and daughters,
> they sacrificed to *shedim*.
> They shed innocent blood,
> the blood of their sons and daughters,
> whom they sacrificed to the idols of Canaan;
> so the land was polluted by their guilt.
> Thus they became defiled by their acts,
> debauched through their deeds.
> The Lord was angry with His people
> and He abhorred his inheritance.
> He handed them over to the nations;
> their foes ruled them
> (Ps 106:34–41; NJPS)

Below, we will consider the later extension of these ideas. For now, it suffices to note that both passages demonize divine multiplicity in the course of associating it with foreign corruption, divine distancing, and decline. In both, foreign invasion is framed as deserved punishment for

"pagan" polytheism, see Tuschling, *Angels and Orthodoxy*, 14–28. On the framing in terms of post-exilic trauma, see discussion in Chapter 2.

the failure of Israelites to limit themselves to the exclusive worship of YHWH.[29] Just as the rhetoric of these passages reveals the politicization of polemics against divine multiplicity in ancient Israel, so it also points to the prehistory of a trope long taken for granted in modern scholarship on angelology and demonology in Second Temple Judaism – namely: the explanation of Jewish interest in transmundane powers as a product of foreign "influence," alienation from God, and a decline from the ideal of pure monotheism.

Here as elsewhere, there is a danger of misreading biblical rhetoric as ancient Israelite reality, and evidence from other ancient sources can help to add perspective. That monotheism is hardly peculiar to Judaism, after all, has been emphasized in recent years both by scholars of the ancient Near East and by scholars of Greek and Roman cultures.[30] M. L. West, for instance, points to the common cross-cultural "tendency, in hymning a deity, to dwell on those aspects and accomplishments in which he or she surpassed the rest," and he posits this liturgical rhetoric as leading readily to narratives "awarding the deity in question absolute supremacy": as for Hesiod's Zeus, so too with the Mesopotamian use of "'king of the gods' [as] a standard title, applied at different times to the gods Anu, Narru, Shamash, Marduk, and Aššur."[31] Among ancient Greeks, such sovereignty also found expression in Homer's "idea of a unified divine purpose...in the phrase Διὸς νόος or Διὸς βουλή, the mind or will of Zeus," which serves to juxtapose the misunderstandings of events by men and lesser gods with the determinative plan that the reader/hearer ultimately recognizes as divine.[32]

West thus makes much the same point for Hesiod and Homer that Benjamin Sommer makes with reference to the Hebrew Bible: "Where we see a god emerging as plenipotentiary, the existence of other gods is not denied, but they are reduced in importance or status, and he is praised as the greatest among them."[33] To the degree that we can speak of ancient

[29] I.e., in the case of Ps 106, as recourse to Canaanite idols, and in the case of Deut 32, as the embrace of new *elohim*.

[30] Athanassiadi and Frede, *Pagan Monotheism*.

[31] West, "Towards Monotheism," 25–26.

[32] West, "Towards Monotheism," 23–24. Notably, West is later explicit in drawing a comparison with LXX Deut 32:8 (26–27), on which see further below.

[33] West, "Towards Monotheism," 24. Among the examples he adduces is the case of Xenophanes, whose oft-quoted slogan "One God!" continues with "the greatest among *gods* and men," such that its message is not one of a singular deity "but a god who towers above the rest" (32–33).

"monotheism," then, it is typically of a sort that "allows for the existence of many gods" in relation to "the belief that there exists one supreme being in the universe, whose will is sovereign over all other beings."[34]

Definitions of this sort defuse much of what early historians of religion like Bousset had found problematic – and thus judged as degraded or peripheral – about the interest in angels and demons in Second Temple Jewish literature.[35] Understood in this fashion, the elevation of a single deity is not necessarily incompatible with angelology or demonology. In fact, often quite the contrary. In their volume on *Pagan Monotheism*, for instance, Polymnia Athanassiadi and Michael Frede emphasize that there is more than one "way of saying that monotheism was perfectly compatible with belief in the existence of a plurality of divine beings," including but not limited to "the Platonic teaching that these beings formed a strict hierarchy subordinated to the supreme God...[as] executors or manifestations of the divine will rather than independent principles of reality."[36]

What West, Athanassiadi, and Frede posit on the basis of Greek and Roman examples has been argued on the basis of Near Eastern materials as well. Even though ancient Egyptian religiosity was characteristically marked by dynamic cosmotheism, for instance, Bernd Schipper proposes that the conceptualization of Amun-Re as supreme deity in the middle of the second millennium BCE entailed the enumeration of his protectors and by new traditions about his messengers;[37] this double development, in his view, "reflects the prevalence, professionalization, and hierarchization of a religion."[38]

That similar intellectual and social conditions might contribute to demonology is argued even more explicitly by Karel van der Toorn. On the basis of Mesopotamian examples, he posits that the more one subordinates the demonic to all-encompassing divinities, the greater is the danger that one thereby demonizes or defiles the divine, and he discusses two solutions found in the theological writings of ancient Mesopotamia:

In the first option, demons are cosmic accidents analogous to disease and other discomforts that can make life a burden. The gods offer support to the battle against these evils by granting efficacy to spells and apotropaic rites, but they

---

[34] Sommer, *Bodies of God*, 146–147.
[35] For the genealogy of "monotheism" as it has been used in Biblical Studies, see MacDonald, *Deuteronomy and the Meaning*, 5–58. As noted above, the popular notion of biblical monotheism devolving into "post-biblical" multiplicity raises more problems than it solves when set against the evidence of Second Temple Judaism.
[36] Athanassiadi and Frede, *Pagan Monotheism*, 8.
[37] Schipper, "Angels or Demons," 5–7.   [38] Schipper, "Angels or Demons," 15.

cannot eradicate them altogether. The very existence of demons defines the limits of the power of the gods. The innocence of the gods is maintained at the cost of their omnipotence. In the second option, the demons are subordinate to divine rule. The gods have either decided that there should be demons as part of the cosmological order, or they have forced the demons into their service. In either case, they become an accessory to the evils wrought by the demons, and are tainted by demonic traits themselves.[39]

Just as the theorization of intermediate spirits can contribute to the elevation of deities, so this elevation could be an engine driving the development of systematic theologies, angelologies, and demonologies as well.

Evidence from other ancient cultures, thus, exposes the limits of the explanatory power of the contrast of "monotheism" and "polytheism" – at least with respect to the question of where and when we find the development of systemizing discourses about transmundane powers.[40] Far from representing a denigration of an absolute divine singularity, angelology and demonology could sometimes accompany the elevation of one deity and the resultant reconfiguration of the structure and contours of divine multiplicity. In some cases and places, the elevation of a certain god or gods toward an all-encompassing or all-pure status could go hand-in-hand with concerted attempts by priestly and other experts to classify the levels and occupants of the otherworld, whether through the demotion of local or foreign deities to the status of his/her servants, envoys, messengers, generals, or protectors and/or through their reinterpretation as demons to whom s/he permits only a limited domain.

If Frankfurter is correct, this impulse toward classification of deities and spirits was frequently coupled with priestly professionalization, temple centralization, and the prestige of writing. Why, then, are strategies of this sort seemingly absent from the Hebrew Bible, a corpus shaped both by priestly perspectives and by ideologies of centralized sacrifice, priesthood, and kingship? Why did more biblical authors not choose to draw upon the efficacy of angelology as a strategy elsewhere used to promote certain god(s) as uniquely powerful, and/or the efficacy of demonology as a strategy for negotiating the elevation of a single deity? In what follows, we shall explore these questions, first by considering

---

[39] Van der Toorn, "Theology of Demons," 76.

[40] "The polarity 'monotheism-polytheism' has some explanatory value," as Sommer stresses, but "its explanatory value has been overestimated," not least because "it obscures connections that transcend this polarity"; *The Bodies of God and the World of Ancient Israel*, 145.

some of the dominant writing practices that shaped early biblical literature and then by surveying the treatment of intermediate spirits therein.

WRITING, GENEALOGY, AND OTHER TECHNOLOGIES
OF MEMORY IN ANCIENT ISRAEL

The texts now in the Hebrew Bible claim to speak to and for all Israel.
Those responsible for this literature no doubt saw themselves as doing so,
and their words would eventually come to shape the very notions of Israel
and Jewishness. When these works first began to take form, however,
literacy remained rare.[41] Writing was primarily the domain of scribes and
those who employed them. Even in those eras where our epigraphical data
point to the development and democratization of Hebrew alphabetic
writing, the scope was nothing akin to modern literacy.[42] The very
writtenness of biblical literature – in a richly and enduringly oral culture –
signals the unusual status of those who created it.[43]

The determinative era for this process remains a matter of debate.[44]
Most theories point to one or more of the following as significant:

- The initial period of Israelite state-formation around the tenth and
  ninth centuries BCE, as memorialized in the Hebrew Bible with

---

[41] In the ancient cultures here considered, there is nothing akin to the notion of "literacy"
that emerged in industrial societies in the modern period and shapes our contemporary
values; on the latter, see Graff, *The Legacies of Literacy*, 15–26; Graff, *The Labyrinths of
Literacy*, 175–300. For the case of ancient Israel, see Heszer, *Jewish Literacy in Roman
Palestine*, 8–9, 27–33; Niditch, *Oral World and Written Word*, 39–59; Rollston, *Writing
and Literacy in the World of Ancient Israel*, 127–135.

[42] Rollston, "Scribal Education," 49–50. On the emergence of Hebrew as a written
vernacular with a distinctive alphabetic script, see Sanders, *The Invention of Hebrew*,
there stressing the importance of developments in the ninth century BCE. On its
"democratization," see Schniedewind, *Social History*, 99–125, positing its development,
expansion, and emergence as a "Judean cultural value" concurrent with the development
of governmental bureaucracy in the eighth century BCE.

[43] Rollston, *Writing and Literacy*, 132–135, emphasizing that "the Hebrew Bible itself
attests to the literacy of elites, not the non-elite populace" (133). See further Rollston,
"Scribal Education in Ancient Israel," on the epigraphical evidence for "formal,
standardized scribal education" in ancient Israel, which similarly suggests that "scribal
elites educated scribal elites in ancient Israel" (68), inasmuch as "the lion's share of the
Old Hebrew epigraphical record does not reflect 'functional knowledge' of the script...
[but] the sophisticated knowledge of trained professionals" (60–61).

[44] Compare, e.g., Na'aman, "Sources and Composition"; Schniedewind, *How the Bible
Became a Book*, 64–117; Carr, *Writing on the Tablet of the Heart*, 163–173; van der
Toorn, *Scribal Culture and the Making of the Hebrew Bible*.

reference to the establishment of the Davidic monarchy, the unification of southern and northern tribes under David's son Solomon, and the construction of the Jerusalem Temple;

- The late monarchic period, around the eighth and seventh centuries BCE, as memorialized in the Hebrew Bible with reference to the Assyrian conquest of the northern kingdom Israel and the centralizing religious reforms of the kings Hezekiah and Josiah in the southern kingdom Judah;

- The exilic and post-exilic periods of the sixth century BCE and following, as memorialized in the Hebrew Bible with reference to the Babylonian invasion of the southern kingdom Judah and destruction of the Jerusalem Temple, the exile of elites from Judah to Babylon, their restoration in the wake of Persian conquest, and the rebuilding of the Jerusalem Temple (i.e., Second Temple) under Persian imperial patronage.

Past debates about dating biblical materials were limited largely to the internal evidence of the Bible itself, particularly as analyzed with source-critical methods geared toward recovering materials contemporaneous with the preexilic eras therein described. Resultant hypotheses tended to be circular in reasoning and contested in reception. On the one hand, comparative insights into premodern practices of composition and editing shed doubt on older source-critical principles long taken for granted among Biblicists.[45] On the other hand, attempts to backdate biblical materials met with skepticism from those suspicious of their apologetic underpinnings; in response, some so-called minimalists even posit the entire Hebrew Bible as a post-exilic product.[46]

More persuasive, in my view, are those recent studies that forefront the epigraphical record, rather than the Hebrew Bible, and trace developments in Hebrew script and language, rather than treating Scripture as the sole *telos*. "The problem," as Seth Sanders notes, "is the Bible's physical condition":

---

[45] See, most extensively, the critiques of older approaches, ample bibliography, and experimentation with different alternatives in Carr, *Formation*; cf. the newer approaches in Baden, *The Composition of the Pentateuch*.

[46] On this debate, see Davies, *In Search of "Ancient Israel"*; Lemche, *The Israelites in History and Tradition*; Nicholson, "Current 'Revisionism' and the History of the Old Testament; Dever, "Histories and Non-Histories of Ancient Israel"; Dozeman and Schmid, *A Farewell to the Yahwist?*

We only have actual biblical manuscripts from centuries after the end of the Israelite kingdoms. This means we must delve through intricate, sometimes inextricable layers of editing before we can talk about original contexts...[but] unlike biblical manuscripts, the inscriptions come from the time they speak about.[47]

Inscriptions attest the emergence of Hebrew and other written local languages in the Levant by the end of the ninth century BCE, concurrent with the spread of Assyrian imperial power and propaganda.[48] Accordingly, they reveal a productive interplay of imperial and local languages and identities that proved formative for the Hebrew Bible but is nowhere described in such terms therein.[49]

William Schniedewind makes a parallel point: one might expect Hebrew to emerge as a national language with standardized writing and scribal infrastructure at "the emergence of monarchy in ancient Israel and particularly with the reigns of David and Solomon."[50] But the epigraphical record suggests otherwise: "Scribes and writing were not nationalized but were part of transnational Canaanite culture" until the rise of the Neo-Assyrian empire that served "as a catalyst for the creation of the language of the Judean state – that is, Standard Biblical Hebrew (SBH), which would develop as the literary language of Judean scribes from the late eighth century until... the end of the sixth century BCE."[51] Accordingly, Schniedewind posits the "exile of the northern kingdom by Assyria and the subsequent urbanization of the rural south [as] catalysts for literary activity that resulted in the composition of extended portions of the Hebrew Bible."[52]

That the texts we now know as "biblical" were subject to continued reshaping long after the Babylonian Exile is evinced by the Dead Sea Scrolls, as we shall see below. Nevertheless, the postulate of preexilic settings for the initial formation of much of these materials finds support in the epigraphical record, particularly in relation to the late monarchic

[47] Sanders, *Invention*, 1–2.   [48] Sanders, *Invention*, 103–155.
[49] I.e., whereby "vernacular languages entered politics when Levantine courts borrowed the superimposed genres of an empire to communicate in a new way," after which even those outside of the circles of monarchic power could then appropriate, in turn, the power of the vernacular to shape local identity and history; Sanders, *Invention*, 6–7, and see further there 105–106, 136–152.
[50] Schniedewind, *Social History*, 51.
[51] Schniedewind, *Social History*, 74. For the history of the eighth and seventh centuries BCE, retold with a focus on the Hebrew written language, literary and other writing practices, and scribalism, see 73–125 there.
[52] Schniedewind, *Social History*, 77, there summarizing arguments made in more detail in *How the Bible*, 64–117. The importance of the era of Assyrian domination of the Levant for shaping core "biblical" materials is also stressed by Carr, *Formation*, 304–338.

period. Hypotheses of large-scale literary invention in post-exilic eras, by contrast, strain historical credulity due to their dissonance with what else we know of Jewish literary production in the Achaemenid, Ptolemaic, and Seleucid periods – not least from so-called pseudepigrapha and other materials preserved outside the Hebrew Bible.[53] In the following chapters, we shall survey some of this evidence. For now, it suffices to note that ancient Israel's scribes had a formative role in shaping the core of what became the Hebrew Bible – however narrowly or broadly one chooses to define "scribe,"[54] and however firmly or flexibly one chooses to connect them to the palace or the Temple.[55]

Above, we noted how efforts at cultic centralization, elsewhere in the ancient Mediterranean world, were often accompanied by the integration and classification of local deities, demons, etc., into totalizing conceptual systems. Why is the impulse toward centralization not paired with this particular strategy in the surviving literary remains of ancient Israel?

---

[53] I.e., most so-called minimalist approaches argue on the basis of a *lack* of evidence for preexilic datings for biblical writings, rather than on the basis of evidence *for* specific postexilic settings. Ironically, they thus tend to focus almost wholly on the Hebrew Bible, making little use of the ample evidence *outside* the biblical canon for later patterns in Jewish literary production.

[54] So already Fishbane, *Biblical Interpretation in Ancient Israel*. With respect to difference senses of "scribe," contrast the narrower sense used in van der Toorn, *Scribal Culture*, with Carr's contention that the term "scribe" was "a badge of graduation that allowed you to perform such elite roles in both Mesopotamia and Egypt. It didn't necessarily mean you spent most of your time writing and reading. In this sense the focus in some recent literature on the 'scribal' context of the formation of biblical literature is potentially misleading, at least insofar as it might lead some to think that all biblical texts were produced by full-time writing professionals" ("Torah on the Heart," 22). Note also, more recently, Pioske's definition as "artisans trained in the technologies of textuality," stressing that these "individuals...were demarcated from the vast majority of their contemporaries by being trained in the specific craft of writing and reading texts"; *Memory in a Time of Prose*, 4.

[55] E.g., Schniedewind, *How the Bible* (stressing the palace); van der Toorn, *Scribal Culture*, 82–86 (stressing the Temple); Carr, *Writing on the Tablet*, 111–116 (suggesting a shift from palace to Temple). For this, Carr points to "the Iron Age trend (also seen in Mesopotamia and Egypt) toward concentration of textuality in the temple" (169). Sanders, however, cautions against filling in the gaps in our knowledge of ancient Israel's scribes with Mesopotamian and Egyptian parallels and thereby "treating scribes across the entire ancient Near East as a kind of vast, three thousand-year-long monoculture" (*Invention*, 8–9). That said, even a focus on the Hebrew evidence allows for varying interpretations: e.g., Sanders (*Invention*, 131) posits the "relative independence" of scribes, adducing evidence for their work "outside of large institutions" in a manner more akin to artisans for hire than monarchic bureaucrats, whereas Rollston ("Scribal Education," 68) maintains that "the most reasonable position is that 'the state' was the primary aegis for scribal education in Iron II Israel."

Throughout the Hebrew Bible, one finds ample evidence for political fragmentation, on the one hand, and for the persistence of multiple cult-centers and devotion to multiple deities on the other. Much of what came to be collected therein celebrates the centralization of worship – to one God, in one Temple, ideally within one state united under the rule of one anointed king. Texts like Deuteronomy attest the importance of writing as a vehicle for the realization of this ideal, just as the Deuteronomistic History speaks to its power to shape even monarchic history.[56]

Despite its close connections with the use of writing to reconfigure local knowledge, demonology is notably absent. For this, there are many potential avenues for explanation. Among possible factors, for instance, may be the practical matter of pedagogy in a small state. Whereas Mesopotamian temples offered advanced scribal training in a variety of specializations such as astrology, exorcism, medicine, divination, and liturgical song, for instance, the scope was likely more limited in ancient Israel.[57] The epigraphical record attests "formal, standardized education" in Hebrew, as Christopher Rollston has demonstrated.[58] We lack evidence for its specific curriculum, but due to the variance in scale, the situation in this small kingdom in the Levant no doubt differed from those Egyptian and Mesopotamian milieu from which we have most of our data for Near Eastern scribal pedagogies.[59] The evidentiary gap

---

[56] See Levinson, *Deuteronomy and the Hermeneutics of Legal Innovation*, 23–52, on the textual practices that effect the cultic centralization of Deuteronomy 12, as well as Levinson, "Reconceptualization of Kingship in Deuteronomy and the Deuteronomistic History's Transformation of Torah," on Deuteronomy's subordination of royal power to cultic centralization in contrast with the Deuteronomistic History. What Levinson shows from his analysis of legal reasoning and literary practices is not dissimilar to what Sanders shows from the epigraphical record: "What we find is not an Israelite state establishing writing, but writing recruited by an Israelite state to establish itself" (*Invention*, 124).

[57] On the training of Mesopotamian scribes, see van der Toorn, *Scribal Culture*, esp. 56–59. Carr (*Writing*, 170–171) speculates that Israelite scribes likely learned "abecedaries, proverbs, instructions, hymns, and so on," after which some went on to training in law and cultic practices to serve in the Temple, while others may have had further administrative training fitting for royal service.

[58] For a survey of the relevant evidence see Rollston, "Scribal Education" – there using paleographical, orthographical, and other non-literary data to make the case for "formal, standardized education" in ancient Israel, while countering those who posit pervasive education and literacy among the populace.

[59] Sanders (*Invention*, 8) thus points to the problems with trying to fill in the gaps of our knowledge of ancient Jewish scribal culture with Egypt and Mesopotamia – "the seats of geographically large empires, richly productive economies that could support many scribes, and long continuous written traditions on the scale of three thousand years"; see his further argument to this effect in *From Adapa to Enoch*.

reminds us of crucial distinctions between ancient Israelite scribes and their better-attested Egyptian and Mesopotamian counterparts: by the time that the former were giving voice to their concerns in written form in SBH, political centralization was already becoming more of a matter of nostalgic ideal than lived reality, and even cultic centralization was shaped by the ideologies of Assyrian imperialism no less than by the recasting of Judahite traditions.

From the evidence of early biblical literature, moreover, it is clear that Hebrew scribes also made different types of choices than their counterparts across the Near East. Like elites elsewhere, Israel's monarchic, priestly, and scribal elites were faced with the challenge of the persistent and rich diversity of local traditions, identities, and practices – and thus also with the opportunity to claim knowledge and power with and over them. Even if demonology seems absent, some parallel patterns of systemizing local knowledge shaped the scribal cultures of ancient Israel, at least during the late monarchic period. The legitimacy of local shrines is assumed in some pentateuchal narratives (e.g., Gen 12:6–8, 28:21), for instance, but such sites come under critique in materials from the eighth century BCE (e.g., Hosea 4:13–15) and are constructed as foreign then and thereafter in what Baruch Halpern terms the "elite redefinition of traditional culture."[60]

Yet it was not demonology that served as the mechanism for imposing order on local dynamics of difference. If anything, it was perhaps genealogy. As Ronald Hendel notes, that the Hebrew term *toledot* ("generations," "lineage") is "the only term used in the Pentateuch to refer to its own narrative of the past."[61] Its repetition serves to connect cosmogony, primeval history, and patriarchal history (cf. 1 Chron 1–9) as well as to tie them to the reader's present. In effect, the power of the written list to order knowledge is here deployed, not to classify demons or catalog deities, but rather to sort peoples and local traditions into temporal lineages. The subgenre of the genealogical list is so pervasive in the Hebrew Bible, in fact, that it can be easy to miss what is thereby assumed and asserted – namely, the dominance of lineage as an organizing principle for structuring Israel's collective identity and cultural memory *in writing*.[62]

Hendel suggests that the literary idiom of genealogy first took form against the background of an ancient Israelite cultural landscape in which family religion remained dominant, standing in tension with state religion

---

[60] Halpern, "Sybil or Two Nations?"   [61] Hendel, *Remembering Abraham*, 105.
[62] Hendel, *Remembering*, 9–13, 33–37, 105–107.

and never wholly usurped by it.[63] Accordingly, in his view, this rubric was readily redeployed to shape the collective memory that reconfigured diverse events and groups into the single story of a single nation.[64] In Chapter 2, we shall see how this "idiom of genealogical reckoning" became newly scribalized within the Aramaic literature of the early Hellenistic age. For now, it suffices to reflect upon Hendel's characterization of the earlier shift that produced much of what we now know as "biblical" literature – that is, the shift from oral family lore to written national literature as mediated by genealogical lists. If he is correct, we might further wonder whether the relative lack of interest in angels and demons in the Hebrew Bible is partly a product of the dominance of other concerns among Israel's literary elites, whereby the impulse to centralize commerce with the divine was focused on the ongoing challenges posed by family religion and articulated through the *Listenwissenschaft* of lineage.[65]

Inscriptional and documentary data confirm the pervasiveness of genealogical, familial, and tribal idioms of collective identity throughout the Iron Age Levant.[66] Hendel points to evidence internal to the redacted Torah/Pentateuch for older and local forms of Israelite practice in which the family provided the dominant structures for the teaching and transmission of religious traditions and in which ancestral names and family metaphors provided the dominant models for expressions of collective identity (e.g., tribal, regional). It was from these threads – he suggests – that ancient Israelite scribes wove national histories, repurposing ancestral names and stories, as well as familial metaphors, in the service of collective memory on a greater scale; over the course of centuries, the oral

---

[63] I.e., the strategy was effective because it is both an "extension of the kinship structures of Israelite society" but also "a teleological form of history"; Hendel, *Remembering*, 35–36. For a detailed survey of the relevant evidence for family religion, see van der Toorn, *Family Religion in Babylonia, Syria, and Israel*, 181–286 – although there focusing instead on the use of the Exodus narrative to overwrite ancestral and tribal allegiance with national identities (287–315).

[64] Hendel, *Remembering*, 35.

[65] This is not to imply that genealogical lists are not paralleled in the ancient Near East; it is with reference to Babylonian evidence, e.g., that van der Toorn (*Family Religion*, 52–55) notes that "genealogical lists are family history in telegraphic style"; there, notably, it is clear that "the ancestor cult is the setting in which such genealogies functioned and – presumably – originated" (54).

[66] Sanders, *Invention*, 124–125. In addition, the possibility that scribal training in Israel was family-based is intriguing in connection with the use of writing to appropriate such idioms for state-centered histories, even if unverifiable from the evidence currently at hand.

ancestral tales of divided groups were thus rewritten as the tale of the single family, to which were also filiated all other known peoples, near and far. Such acts of writing and memory, in turn, enabled Israelite elites to promote monarchic rule and centralized worship by subsuming older and local stories into a teleological narrative with the people Israel and the Jerusalem Temple as its end.[67] Worship at local cult-sites was projected into the patriarchal past; local rituals granted national etiologies; and the memories of some used to construct the history of the whole.[68] For this, the genealogical list provided one major organizing principle for the written integration of diverse stories, place-name etiologies, and other older traditions linked originally to local spaces and family settings. Hendel, in effect, illumines the flip-side of the process by which other local and longstanding practices were systematically marked as "foreign" – that is, the re-conceptualization of the "local" in terms of the people as a whole by means of its writing as shared past.[69]

Significantly, for our purposes, Hendel's characterization of the *long durée* dynamics of pentateuchal memory-practices dovetails with recent attempts to redescribe the rise of Israelite monotheism. For this too, the Hebrew Bible has been reread as the product of extended processes by which the Israelite past was re-remembered through collecting, writing, reframing, and reordering local knowledge but also through selective acts of erasure. Smith, in particular, has illumined the process whereby exclusive worship of YHWH was promoted through a multi-stage overwriting of the past. In his view, what appears in retrospect as the "origins of monotheism" can be more accurately described as a "shift in divine roles [that] signals reduction of family religion in shaping the dominant cultural memory under the force of the textually more dominant traditions represented by the priestly sections of the Torah (Pentateuch) and by Deuteronomy and the Deuteronomistic History"[70]:

Traditional religion (and here for Israel read traditional religion of clans, with local "high places" and shrines) is submerged first in the face of the rising nation state, with its royal sanctuaries (here read the rise of the Judean and Israelite

---

[67] Hendel, *Remembering*, 45–56. On this feature of genealogy more broadly, see Zerubavel, *Ancestors and Relatives*.

[68] Hendel, *Remembering*, 34–36.   [69] Hendel, *Remembering*, 24–28.

[70] Smith, *Memoirs*, 157, further noting that "as a corollary of this shift, these traditions all criticize family religion and their religious practices, especially those pertaining to the dead in Leviticus 19:28, 31; 20:6, 17; Deuteronomy 14:1; 18:10–11; 26:14; 1 Samuel 28; and 2 Kings 21:6."

monarchies). This traditional religion then recedes further due to an increasing loss of traditional locus and practice of religion (here read the loss of local patrimonies and lineages and nonroyal sanctuaries especially from the eight to the sixth centuries). This loss corresponds to the appearance of new forms of elective fraternity (here read prophetic and perhaps priestly and Deuteronomic movements gathering social force in reaction to the limitations of family and monarchic religion in the eighth through the sixth centuries). At work is a rule of memory surviving in inverse proportion to historical order and power of social location: the family, with its memories generated largely through oral means, is socially weaker relative to the priestly forces behind the textual formation and transmission of texts in regional shrines, and family memory is submerged further beneath the weight of priestly lines working in sanctuaries and then filtered through royal shrines, and ultimately through the royal shrine with a single priestly hierarchy in Jerusalem.[71]

In practice, this process of overwriting involved a set of methods whereby "ancient Israel reconstituted the diversity of its deities into a single God"[72]:

- "convergence," whereby YHWH became associated with traits and traditions of the other deities denied in the course of the promotion of exclusive YHWH-worship by Israelites (e.g., Baal's cosmic enemies and titles in Pss 48:2; 68:4);
- "differentiation," whereby the "denial of 'other gods' was accompanied by the claim that older traditions formerly associated with Yahweh did not belong to Yahweh" and whereby traditional elements of Israel's religion (e.g., asherah) were reinterpreted "as features not of Israel but of foreign peoples";
- "reinterpretation of older polytheistic vestiges" (e.g., Deut 32:8–9) and related discursive shifts: "Other developments may also have worked with monotheistic language, for example, the linguistic phenomenon whereby the names of other deities become generic nouns. Thus Astarte became a term for fertility, Resheph for flame, and Deber for pestilence."[73]

---

[71] Smith, *Memoirs*, 137.   [72] Smith, *Memoirs*, 157.
[73] Smith, *Memoirs*, 151–152. With respect to Resheph, Münnich places this development later, contrasting what he sees as the appeal to a figure in Deut 32:24 and Hab 3:5 with the more metaphorical readings in Ps 78:48, Job 5:7, and Song 8:6 to propose that "the monotheising process of the Hebrew religion resulted in the demythologization of Resheph among post-exilic elites"; *God Resheph*, 237. The question of timing pivots on the interpretation of Deut 32:24, for which other senses have been suggested also by Kató, "Entdämonisierung"; Blair, *De-Demonizing*, 178–184, 194–195.

From this perspective, "biblical monotheism" is best understood, not as a theological doctrine innovated in ancient Israel, but rather as "a kind of ancient *rhetoric* reinforcing Israel's exclusive relationship with its deity."[74] Particularly in the wake of the Assyrian conquest of the northern kingdom Israel in 722 BCE, Smith shows how the emphasis on the singularity of Israel's God emerged as a "strategy designed to persuade its audience of the reality of YHWH's absolute power in a world where a foreign empire holds sway over Judah," functioning as "a kind of inner community discourse using the language of YHWH's exceptional divine status over and in all reality...in order to absolutize YHWH's claim on Israel and to express Israel's ultimate fidelity to YHWH in the face of a world where political boundaries or institutions no longer offered sufficiently intelligible lines of religious identity."[75] The monotheism that seems, in retrospect, so definitive of the Hebrew Bible is the result of an especially influential moment of recasting both Israel's past and earlier memories of it – that is, "the presentation of a single deity, read back into the biblical corpus...in priestly tradition and in Deuteronomy and the Deuteronomistic History, probably from the eighth–seventh century onward."[76]

This recasting had notable consequences, not least in naturalizing reading practices that absorbed and foreclosed other ancient Israelite understandings of divinity.[77] But it was also incomplete: "homogenization of societal narratives went only so far," Smith stresses, since "once written memory passes into a body of texts, the tradition does not seem to throw out what it forgets; instead, it tends to rewrite what it does not remember."[78] As a result, the very writing practices that forged "biblical monotheism" also permit the modern scholarly recovery of earlier perspectives on divine multiplicity. By Smith's reading, then, early biblical literature is less a monotheistic manifesto and more a partial palimpsest wherein traces of divine multiplicity persist even in the assertion of divine unity:

...the Bible's later commemorialists preserved some older vestiges about divinity in ancient Israelite religious life...Such vestiges survived displacement, conflation, and diminishment as long as they could be read, interpreted, or rewritten

---

[74] Smith, *Origins*, 9; emphasis mine. For a similar relational emphasis explored through a single text see now MacDonald, *Deuteronomy*.

[75] Smith, *Origins*, 9. See also Gnuse, *No Other Gods*, there stressing the view that all Israelites should worship YHWH predates the notion that he also ruled other nations, while the conceptualization of a single bodiless God alone in the cosmos is a far later development.

[76] Smith, *Memoirs*, 157.   [77] Smith, *Memoirs*, 158.   [78] Smith, *Memoirs*, 137–138.

according to later norms, especially a monotheistic view of God. As a result, the Bible preserves both the dominant views of later commemorialists and the vestiges of earlier memories.[79]

The task of culling these vestiges has been a rich area of research among specialists in Biblical Studies who have thereby illumined the place of polytheism, anthropomorphism, the divine court, and family religion in ancient Israel, as well as other elements effaced by the strategies of monotheistic rereading noted above, including demon-belief. In the process, scholarship on biblical literature has further demonstrated how the divine exclusivism of those passages most often cited as exemplary of ancient Israelite religion constitute only a part of the depiction of the divine within the Hebrew Bible – which, in turn, formed only part of a broader range of Israelite religiosity.[80]

For the purposes of the present study, Smith's redescription of biblical monotheism as a set of interlocking memory-practices proves useful as well. Not only does he remind us that the Hebrew Bible is not a direct window onto Israelite beliefs, but he models an approach to biblical literature as evidence *both* for the scribal practices of selection, collection, omission, reframing, arranging, and rewriting *and* for the older oral and written materials thereby reshaped. In the chapters that follow, I suggest something similar for the *Astronomical Book*, *Book of the Watchers*, *Jubilees*, and related Aramaic Dead Sea Scrolls: just as the emergence of biblical monotheism can be profitably understood as part of a broader recasting of the memory of Israel's past – expressed especially and most influentially in writing[81] – so the beginnings of Jewish angelology and demonology may mark another key moment in the reframing and rewriting of Israel's past for yet another new set of historical challenges. There too, innovation is not a matter of the sudden rupture of "origins" or "invention"; rather, it reflects the emergence of new modes of constructing continuity with the past from the past – including new approaches to negotiating divine multiplicity and unity, to ordering difference through

---

[79] Smith, *Memoirs*, 157.

[80] For an accessible summary of the literary and archaeological evidence for Israelite polytheism, see Sommer, *Bodies of God*, 148–159, and for a thoroughgoing attempt at synthesis, Day, *Yahweh and the Gods*.

[81] I.e., in the priestly portions of the Torah/Pentateuch, the book of Deuteronomy, and the Deuteronomistic History (i.e., Joshua, Judges, 1–2 Samuel, 1–2 Kings), which together form the core of what came to be conceived in later centuries as the Tanakh and Old Testament.

genealogy, and to reconfiguring the bounds of what even counts as local and foreign knowledge.

Consequently, as we shall see, it does not suffice to proclaim Jewish angels as simply Canaanite gods suppressed and later recovered in some apocalyptic resurrection of the mythic substratum of Israelite religion.[82] As with the beginnings of biblical monotheism in the eighth and seventh centuries BCE, the beginnings of Jewish angelology and demonology in the third and second centuries BCE may be best understood as part of an ongoing engagement with the past, for which writing, lists, and genealogies served as powerful technologies for both preserving and reframing memory. To understand both, moreover, it may be critical to attend to writing as social practice, anthologizing as a mode of cultural production, and the consequences of choices of script and language alike.

AMBIGUOUS ANGELS AND THE BIBLICAL MANAGEMENT OF DIVINE MULTIPLICITY

So far, we have stressed the relative lack of systematic reflection on angels and demons in the surviving products of ancient Israel's scribal cultures. But, of course, the Hebrew Bible is hardly devoid of references to such figures. Demons may be rare, but there is no dearth of references to the inhabitants of heaven and other spirits and powers aligned with Israel's God YHWH. In what follows, we shall look more closely at some of these references, attempting to draw out some of the microdynamics of the processes explored above and asking what they might mean, in practice, for the representation of transmundane powers in early biblical literature. That divine multiplicity was a component of ancient Israelite religiosity is clear, as Sommer notes, from the fact that the "Hebrew Bible at once describes and proscribes polytheistic worship among ancient Israelites throughout the preexilic period."[83] Such polemics, however, are not put into the service of what we might consider today as a "narrow, common-sense definition of monotheism as the belief that one God exists and that no deities exist other than this one God"; by this criteria – Sommer

---

[82] Or, more accurately: Second Temple Jewish apocalypses may attest the post-exilic afterlives of Canaanite gods, as Day suggests (*Yahweh and the Gods*, 232–233), even if the recovery of Canaanite myth does not suffice to explain the configuration of divine multiplicity and the intensification of interest in the otherworld attested within even the earliest apocalypses.

[83] Sommer, *Bodies of God*, 159.

reminds us – "the Hebrew Bible is not a monotheistic work, because it acknowledges the existence of many heavenly creatures in addition to YHWH."[84] There are many biblical examples of appeals to divine multiplicity to elevate YHWH, albeit marked by a persistent lack of clarity surrounding the intermediate powers that make up this multiplicity.

"According to the biblical picture," as Esther Hamori observes, "the heavenly realm is teeming with life."[85] Most prominent among them are divine messengers, holy ones (קדשים), armies/hosts (צבאות), "sons of God," *cherubim*, *seraphim*, and *ḥayyot*. Specialist research on ancient Israelite religion has tended to study these figures by reading against the grain of the reticence surrounding them, filling in the gaps of the biblical text with the more explicit statements about related figures in the literature of other cultures, and otherwise aligning them with ancient Near Eastern parallels. For our purposes, it is more pressing to attend to what is and is not said about them in early biblical literature – and the meanings made by the very silences that scholarship on these figures typically seek to fill. Later authors, translators, and exegetes would impose order on them, for reasons that we shall explore below. To understand their place in early biblical literature, however, such ambiguity may be telling. The very lack of specificity and systemization may be part of what here does the work of making meaning about Israel's God.

Significantly, for our purposes, the lack of angelological systemization in early biblical literature includes the lack of any overarching term akin to our category "angel." "The translation of *mal'āk* by 'angel' in English Bibles," as Samuel Meier has stressed, "obscures the ancient Israelite perceptions of the divine realm"; one finds no sense, as in later times, that even the "sons of God" or hosts of heaven are subsets or types of *mal'akim,* in the word's later sense as a "undifferentiated term for all of God's supernatural assistants."[86] When such assistants appear, it is most often as anonymous and countless multitudes surrounding God, as described in terms that resonate with a monarchic or military lexicon of

---

[84] Sommer, *Bodies of God*, 146, citing in this regard "angels" (see below) as well as "gods" and "sons of God" (e.g., Gen 6:2; Pss 29:1; 82:6; 86:8; 89:7; Job 1:6), and "the council of holy ones" (Ps 89:6, 8)," together with texts that "portray YHWH as surrounded by heavenly beings who attend Him or await His orders (e.g., 1 Kings 22.19–22, Isaiah 6, Ezekiel 1, Zechariah 3, Job 1.6; a similar picture is assumed in Psalm 29 and Isaiah 40.1–2)."

[85] Hamori, "The Spirit of Falsehood," 15.   [86] Meier, "Angel I," 47.

power – that is, as akin to the army, council, or court of a king.[87] When one encounters a discrete number of such figures, they tend to be described in terms that reduce them either to their functions in implementing divine will (e.g., messenger, destroyer, accuser) or to a divine attribute (e.g., presence, voice). As a result, the means of their evocation enables the use of the rhetoric of divine multiplicity to convey the enormity of the power of Israel's God, even as their anonymity serves to subordinate this multiplicity to the rhetoric of divine unity emphasizing his unique sovereignty.

Although our English word "angel" derives from the Greek counterpart (*angelos*) to Hebrew *mal'ak,* it remains that the majority of biblical occurrences of that term actually pertain to people.[88] The semantic range of *mal'ak* (pl. *mal'akim*) encompasses meanings ranging from "messenger" and "envoy," and the earliest usage of *mal'ak* is limited to those figures who fulfill these functions.[89] Although those sent by God on specific missions or with specific messages include both heavenly and human beings, there is no terminology to distinguish them.[90] One even finds cases where no effort is made to specify whether a particular messenger is human or nonhuman.[91] Whereas Second Temple and later descriptions of *mal'akim* often emphasize the glorious forms that signal their otherworldly status, even the explicitly heavenly messengers of the Hebrew Bible are described as indistinguishable in appearance from men (e.g., Gen 19:1–22; 32:25–31) and as fulfilling the same functions as their human counterparts: they are those who "perform His word" (Ps 103:20) but also representatives, escorts, and protectors. Like the human messengers of kings, they accept hospitality from those to whom they are sent, speak praise on behalf of the sender, communicate his intent, and collect debts or obligations owed to him.[92] The pattern is consistent:

---

[87] On the divine assembly in Mesopotamian context, see Smith, *Origins*, 41–53.

[88] E.g., Judg 11:13; 1 Sam 11:4; 1 Kgs 19:2; 2 Kgs 5:10.

[89] For a comprehensive survey of relevant biblical references, see Mach, *Entwicklungsstadien*, 37–51, and for comparative analysis, Meier, *The Messenger in the Ancient Semitic World*.

[90] E.g., Hag 1:13; Mal 2:7; 1 Sam 29:9; 2 Sam 14:16–20; 19:28; Meier, "Angel I," 46. Meier notes that this pattern is shared by other ancient Near Eastern cultures, which similarly lack terms specific to the supernatural messengers of deities. The Mesopotamian parallels Meir adduces, however, typically pair a high deity with a single named messenger (e.g., Nuska, Kakka), who – like the Greek Hermes – bears the distinction of crossing the otherwise unbridgeable or dangerous divide between divine and human realms.

[91] E.g., Judg 2:1–5; Mal 3:1; Eccl 5:5; Meier, "Angel I," 49.

[92] Meier, "Angel I," 47–49.

it is their function, rather than their personal identity, that is deemed worthy of mention.

The one major point of difference between human and heavenly *mal'akim*, as Meier notes, is the "reticence to provide divine messengers with personal names."[93] Unlike their human counterparts, nonhuman *mal'akim* remain consistently anonymous, at times described as an unspecified group or "camp" (Gen 32:2–3) and at times likened to forces like the wind (Ps 104:4).[94] Just as *mal'akim* are unnamed and mistaken for men, so biblical descriptions of their words and deeds sometimes elide attribution to the *mal'ak* and to the deity who sent him. Matthias Kökert, for instance, observes how the *mal'akim* of pentateuchal narrative tend not to be recognized immediately as envoys sent by God; even after they depart, "the people to whom the message was delivered generally identify him with YHWH himself (Gen 16:13; 22:14)."[95]

If modern scholars have difficulty pinning down the angels of the Hebrew Bible, it is partly as a result of what seems to be a deliberate set of literary strategies for describing the workings of divinity in the world. Exemplary, in this regard, is a biblical type-scene highlighted by James Kugel: the moment of surprise when someone realizes that a man he met or a voice he heard was, in fact, God or his messenger.[96] In the narrative world thereby evoked, the *mal'ak* is not an emissary of a distant divinity. Rather, he is "God Himself in human form, God unrecognized, God intruding into ordinary reality" even apart from human efforts to seek him out.[97]

Kugel's insight has notable ramifications for our understanding of the beginnings of Jewish angelology and demonology. By his reading, the reticence toward intermediate spirits in the literature of ancient Israel cannot be reduced to medieval or modern notions of monotheism, nor to a suppressed or less developed form of the hierarchies of later Judaism or Christianity. Such notions, in fact, may lead us to miss the meanings of these *mal'akim*. Their blurring with God may betray a studied and sophisticated ambiguity – or, perhaps more accurately, a set of literary and discursive practices of representing the otherworldly, whereby

---

[93] Meier, "Angel I," 47.
[94] On *ruḥot* here as not necessarily an impersonal force, however, see below.
[95] Köckert, "Divine Messengers and Mysterious Men in the Patriarchal Narratives of the Book of Genesis," 52.
[96] Kugel, *The God of Old*, 5–36.
[97] Kugel, *God of Old*, 34. On divine vs. human initiatives for theophanies, see 37–70.

transmundane powers are represented in terms that blur their identity with the God of Israel, on the one side, and his human servants, on the other.

What is striking, in any case, is that early biblical references to *mal'a-kim* are consistently counter-classificatory in character, and they resist any hierarchization, apart from the assertion of YHWH's primacy above them and ultimate encompassing of them. The two tendencies may be intertwined. Smith, for instance, suggests that the blurring of God and his messengers may be a reflex of the broader process whereby YHWH emerged as a single national deity, promoted as the proper subject of exclusive worship by Israelites.[98] Whatever the ultimate derivation, however, divine–angelic blurring came to serve a variety of literary, discursive, and conceptual functions in the literature of ancient Israel.[99] Such blurring, for instance, could be used to blunt the encompassing of evil within an elevated deity, by allowing for violence to be asserted as *simultaneously* separate from YHWH *and* encompassed within him. Examples include the Passover narrative in Exodus 12, in which the slaying of the first-born of the Egyptians is variously associated with an enigmatic figure called the "destroyer" (משחית; 12:23) and with God himself (12:29).[100] It is unclear whether the same fluidity of identity is assumed in the account of the first Passover in Psalm 78, where the task of slaughter is performed instead by "a company of harmful *mal'akim*" (משלחת מלאכי רעים; v. 49).[101] That the introduction of *mal'akim* could function to resolve some of the

---

[98] In Smith's view, for instance, the convergence that facilitated this process was achieved largely through the identification of YHWH with El, who "was originally the patriarch of both the divine family and many human families in ancient Israel": "With the loss of El and the melding of most of his functions with Yahweh's," he posits, "the older role of the god of the fathers as one who accompanies the family (Genesis 35:3) shifted in some texts into the role of angelic accompaniment," and as a result, vestiges of the shift remain in biblical passages that feature "the accompanying 'god of the father' and the protective angel... in grammatical apposition" (*Memoirs*, 156, citing Gen 48:15–16, 1 Kgs 19:5–9, and Ps 91:11–12 as prime examples). This speculation forms part of Smith's attempt to reconstruct the prehistory of Israelite monotheism in the movement from a four-tiered hierarchy, similar to that attested in Ugaritic *comparanda*, to the elevation of YHWH through the emptying of its middle tiers. See also Day, *Yahweh and the Gods*, 13–41.

[99] For examples of the blurring of divine identities across the ancient Near East, see Hundley, "Divine Fluidity."

[100] See Schöpflin, "YHWH's Agents of Doom," for a broad survey of biblical examples of intermediary spirits who do God's will through destruction.

[101] Blair (*De-Demonizing the Old Testament*, 194–195) proposes a similar pattern in the parallel in Deut 32:23–25, albeit with allusions to various personified evils and arrows that act on God's behalf – including *qeteb* and *resheph* – in place of the explicit reference to *mal'akim*.

tensions that came with the elevation of Israel's God, however, is suggested by the contrast between the attribution of David's census to God's anger in 2 Samuel (24:1) and its later attribution to *satan* in 1 Chronicles (21:1).[102] Here too – as perhaps also in the references to the *satan* in Job and Zechariah – some ambiguity remains. The Hebrew term *satan* is not yet a *name* for a specific figure or even a *title* for an ontologically distinct category of creatures. Like the term *mal'ak*, it is a *function* (in this case: adversary or executioner) that can be fulfilled either by a person or by an anonymous member of the heavenly court operating at God's behest.[103]

We may see something similar in early biblical references to *ruḥot* (s. *ruaḥ*) who are said to be sent by God but who are associated with causing harm or deception. Especially in the Deuteronomistic History, Hamori posits "a recurring biblical tradition of רוח as a divine agent, specifically associated with bringing destructive justice by means of falsehood."[104] Rather than a title per se, she suggests that it is a "particular *role* that is recognizable by a tight cluster of associated features" (in this case: pivoting on false prophecy): "a רוח sent by God that brings falsehood," after which "this deception or delusion leads to death, violence, or terror for those already deemed in the wrong."[105] Against the tendency of past scholarship to read biblical references to the *ruaḥ* of falsehood (1 Kings 22) and "evil spirit" (Judg 9:23–24; 1 Sam 16–19) primarily in internalized and naturalizing terms, Hamori thus argues that "there is not a systematic presentation of these spirits in biblical texts," but the "ambiguity of terminology" allows for the reading of some *ruḥot* as "an active part of the population of the heavens."[106]

[102] Schniedewind, *The Word of God in Transition*, 141, reads this passage in light of Chronicles' enhancement of elements of angelic mediation (e.g., 1 Chron 21:8), while Stokes, "Devil Made Me Do It...or Did He?," sees the function of the *satan* as more similar to that in Numbers 22.

[103] Compare, e.g., Num 22:22–35; Job 1–2; Zech 3:1–7. On this term, see further Day, *An Adversary in Heaven*; Stokes, "Satan, YHWH's Executioner." On the history of research, Stokes, "Devil Made Me Do It," 93–97; Brown, "The Devil in the Details," 203–205.

[104] Hamori, "Spirit of Falsehood," 18, there arguing that "[t]he use of רוח terminology (rather than מלאך or no reference at all to an intermediate divine being) is bound to a specific kind of work that YHWH wants to have accomplished, according to each narrative." Hamori interprets Judg 9:23–24; 1 Sam 16:14–23; 18:10–12; 19:9–10; 1 Kgs 22:19; 2 Kgs 19:7; Isa 19:13–14 as direct examples, while seeing indirect examples for variations in the tradition in Isa 29:9–10; Job 12:21; Hosea 4:12; 5:4; 9:7; 12:2.

[105] Hamori, "Spirit of Falsehood," 18, 24.   [106] Hamori, "Spirit of Falsehood," 30.

If Hamori is correct, we may find yet another example of deliberate ambiguity – albeit here blurring what *we* might distinguish as "supernatural" and "natural" as well as "external" and "internal." The semantic field of Hebrew *ruaḥ* includes wind (e.g., Gen 3:8), breath (e.g., Ps 33:6), and inclination or feeling (e.g., Num 5:14), as well as "spirit" in the sense of that which enlivens the living (e.g., Ezek 37:5–6; Qoh 12:7). Accordingly, Hamori's examples of hostile and harmful *ruḥot* also draw our attention to the blurring of different senses of the term in more positive contexts, such as in Psalms 104:4 ("He makes the *ruḥot* his *mal'akim*, fiery flames his servants") and 148:7–8 ("Praise YHWH, you who are on the earth…fire and hail, snow and smoke, *ruaḥ* of storm that executes his command…").[107] Something similar may be presumed even for the various *ruḥot* said to transport the prophet Ezekiel at God's behest.[108]

Hamori's argument is also useful, for our purposes, in highlighting the degree to which the *functions* of transmundane powers govern even the biblical representation of their *forms*. She proposes that the form of "the spirit of falsehood – intangible, able effectively to transmit a message unbeknownst to its recipient – reflects its function," with the "absence of face-to-face interaction in most texts…fitting for the purpose of deception," partly on the basis of comparison of the biblical representation of *mal'akim* as "indistinguishable from one another in heaven, but tak[ing] various forms that suit their functions when communicating with humans."[109] If she is correct, this pattern might also help us to make sense of the application of the term *mal'ak* even to envoys who do not deliver messages. Just as it is fitting that *mal'akim* appear in anthropomorphic forms to convey divine words, for instance, it also makes sense that the task of leading the Israelites would be associated variously with a *mal'ak* and with a pillar of cloud (Exod 14:19), as well as with God himself appearing in a pillar of cloud by day and a pillar of fire by night (13:21–22). Even if the blurring of the identities of *mal'akim* into God is partly a reflex of the practice of ancient messengers reading letters or degrees in the first-person voices of their senders, it has coalesced into a common pattern: just as function and identity blur, so too do function and form.

---

[107] That the latter occurs in perhaps the closest biblical counterpart to a cosmic hierarchy (i.e., Ps 148) makes the blurring of "supernatural" spirit and "natural" force especially poignant.

[108] E.g., Ezek 3:14; 11:1, 24; 37:1; 40:1. On the association of the *ruaḥ* YHWH with prophecy, see Ezek 11:5.

[109] Hamori, "Spirit of Falsehood," 30.

Much the same might be said for the association of *mal'akim* with the divine voice. Exodus, for instance, is explicit in describing how God sends a *mal'ak* to guard and lead Israel in the Wilderness (Exod 23:20–23; 32:34; 33:2), instructing them to "be attentive to him and listen to his voice...for my Name is in him" (23:21). Insofar as the simultaneity of unity and multiplicity serves in part to attenuate anthropomorphism,[110] it also underlines the danger imputed to holiness in both pentateuchal narrative and purity legislation: commerce with *mal'akim* is narratively necessitated in part due to the principle that a human being cannot "see God and live" (33:20) nor safely approach holiness apart from a purified state and site. The provisional character of the forms of God's otherworldly messengers and retinue may function, in some cases, as a mark of divine separation from the mundane spaces God nevertheless roams.

The function of marking boundaries between human and divine realms is even clearer in the case of other types of transmundane creatures in early biblical literature. Such a function can be construed negatively, as in the case of the *bene ha-elohim* (lit. "sons of God") who are said to have come to earth in the days before the Flood to take wives of the "daughters of men" (Gen 6:1–4) and who are thus implicated, even if tersely or indirectly, in the destruction of the world by flood in Genesis 6–9. Elsewhere, this boundary-marking function is expressed more positively, as with the *cherubim* who are said to guard the entrance to the Garden of Eden (Gen 3:24) and the *seraphim* who police purity in the prophet Isaiah's vision of God's presence in the Temple (Isa 6:1–7). That such guardians function in part to articulate and naturalize the priestly distinction of the Temple from the rest of Israel – and Israel's priests, people, and land from the rest of the world – is evoked by the cultic associations of *seraphim* and *cherubim*. Both convey the danger and power of the holiness that separates God from the mundane world in the course of communicating the same about the spaces and people sanctified to him. In the terse allusion to Azazel in Leviticus 16, we might glimpse a parallel patterning of an evaluative geography of pure center and polluted periphery more specifically on priestly ritual: although the term there remains ambiguous, its spatial association with the desert nonetheless evokes a sense of the demonic threat of distant and deserted spaces so as to assert

---

[110] For this suggestion, see Smith, *Early History*, 141–143, and on the rich tradition surrounding God's embodiment in biblical literature and the ancient Near East, see Hamori, *When Gods Were Men*; Sommer, *Bodies of God*; Wagner, *Gottes Körper*.

the purity of the altar, Temple, and people as effected by the rites of Yom Kippur.[111]

Whether or not we find overlapping functions for different types of heavenly creatures, the variety of biblical traditions surrounding *ser-aphim, cherubim,* and *bene elohim* cautions against the assumption that the array of figures later reread as "angels" were originally all of the same sort.[112] The term *seraph,* for instance, occurs variously to denote fiery serpents (e.g., Num 21:8; Isa 30:6; cf. *1 En* 20:7) and six-winged creatures (Isa 6:2). Inasmuch as these figures appear to mingle elements of demonic power and divine servitude,[113] they point to the capacity of the rhetoric of divine multiplicity to enable the distancing of Israel's God from direct contact with human bloodshed, while simultaneously encompassing death and violence within his domain of power.

While references to *seraphim* are scant, references to *cherubim* abound. In fact, as Alice Wood has recently noted, these are the intermediate spirits most frequently mentioned in the Hebrew Bible.[114] Contrary to modern assumptions about Israelite aniconism, moreover, the term *cherub* is most often used in historical texts to denote a cult image in the Temple or tabernacle – probably the context presumed by the texts that project these chimera into heaven as well.[115] This context is also clear from the epithet כרבים ישב (lit. ruler/dweller of the *cherubim*), which functions in a manner akin to the more common "Lord of Hosts" to

---

[111] Milgrom (*Leviticus 1–16,* 1021) posits that "[t]he most plausible explanation is that Azazel is the name of a demon...who has been eviscerated of his erstwhile demonic powers by the Priestly legislators," adding that "the banishment of evil to an inaccessible place is a form of elimination amply attested in the ancient Near East" but also that "Azazel himself is deprived of any active role...designating the place to which impurities and sins are banished." Notably, Milgrom correlates this impersonalization of the demonic with the ambiguity surrounding angels as well, noting it as akin to their blurring with natural forces in Pss 104:4 and 148:8.

[112] Mach's suggestion of a complete separation in preexilic materials between *mal'akim* and the divine court may be too polarizing, but his core insight of the precedents for the impulse to correlate various transmundane powers nevertheless seems apt; e.g., *Entwicklungsstadien,* 52.

[113] See Mettinger's entry on these creatures in *DDD,* 742–744.

[114] Wood, *Of Wings and Wheels,* 2.

[115] Wood, *Of Wings and Wheels,* 2–3, 8. By her count, the term appears ninety-one times (in addition to two cases where it is a place name), of which fifty-six refer to cult images, "mostly in historiographical accounts describing the design of sanctuaries" (8, see further 22–49), while seven occur in the divine epithet כרבים ישב, mainly in liturgical texts (9–22), and only twenty-eight "denote animate heavenly beings" (8, see further 49–138). For the last, see Gen 3:24; 2 Sam 22:1=Ps 18:11; Ezek 9:3; 10:1–9, 14–16, 18–20; 11:22; 28:14, 16 – and note that they cluster overwhelmingly in Ezekiel.

telegraph grandeur, but – Woods suggests – "always appears in cultic contexts and thus seems to reflect the temple setting."[116]

Their later metamorphosis into heavenly creatures is clearest from the Book of Ezekiel, which reflects some of the process, traced by Wood, whereby they were transformed "from apotropaic beings, guarding the divine locale, into a category of angelic beings...symbolic of divine omnipotence and universality, who carry the throne of Yahweh to the exiles."[117] As a result of their secondary identification with the otherwise mysterious ḥayyot (Ezek 8–11; cf. 3:12), together with their description in terms evocative of seraphim (1:11; 3:12; cf. Isa 6:2–6), one here sees the shift in the cherub's form from a "quadruped (1 Sam 22:11=Ps 18:11) with one face and one set of wings (Ex 25:18–22; 37:7–9; 1 Kgs 6:23–28)" to "enigmatic beasts with four faces and four wings."[118]

The term bene elohim, by contrast, stands as a poignant vestige of the limits of monotheizing impulses to overwrite what Smith calls "Israel's primordial polytheism."[119] The term elohim, the conventional plural form of the Hebrew term for "God," is itself an expression of divine elevation through multiplicity.[120] Smith further speculates that the biblical "slippage of divine identity may have been facilitated by the ambiguous character of the term (ha)elohim," which "permits the effacing of older distinctions between minor and major divinities (elohim), including messenger, the familial god, and Yahweh."[121] One might wonder if something similar is at play in the ambiguity of the term bene elohim as it is used in early biblical literature.[122] If so, it proves especially intriguing that some of the most ancient Jewish efforts to organize the otherworld

---

[116] See 1 Sam 4:4; 2 Sam 6:2; 2 Kgs; 1 Chron 13:6; Pss 80:1; 99:1; Isa 37:16; Wood, Of Wings and Wheels, 9–22, quote at 14.

[117] Wood, Of Wings and Wheels, 138. She stresses, however, that even "the passages describing the כרבים as real heavenly beings do not give us precise details concerning the rank and role of cherubim in relation to other heavenly beings" (140). Compare 1 En 20:7, in which Paradise and cherubim are under the domain of the archangel Gabriel.

[118] Wood, Of Wings and Wheels, 140; for more specifics on the diachronic development she proposes, see 95–138.

[119] Smith, Memoirs, 4.

[120] On this function of multiplicity more broadly in the ancient Near East, see Hundley, "Divine Fluidity," there stressing "multiplicity as a sign of potency" while also tracing Israelite departures from it through the lens of the priestly materials in the Torah/Pentateuch.

[121] Smith, Memoirs, 156–157. The flexibility of the term elohim is also suggested by its use in 1 Sam 28:13 in relation to the spirit of dead prophet Samuel.

[122] Compare bene elim in Pss 29:1; 89:7/89:6; and bene elyon in Ps 82:6 – the latter especially resonating with early Enochic traditions about angels.

resonate with the relatively small handful of biblical references to these particular figures – that is, as taking wives of the daughters of men (Gen 6:1–4; cf. *1 En* 6–11), as equal or associated with "morning stars" (Job 38:7; cf. *1 En* 72–82), and as among the divine court and associated with the *satan* (Job 1:6; 2:2; cf. *Jubilees*).[123]

Below, we shall explore some of the rich afterlives of these passages. For now, it suffices to note that references to *bene elohim* were a nexus for textual variation within the transmission and translation of early biblical literature. These figures, for instance, feature in the most famous example of the censorship of divine multiplicity within the Hebrew Bible. The Hebrew of the Masoretic text of Deut 32:8–9, which is paralleled by the Samaritan Pentateuch, Targum, Peshitta, and Latin Vulgate, reads as follows:

When the Most High (El Elyon) gave the nations their inheritance and divided the sons of man, he established the boundaries of the nations, according to the number of the sons of Israel. For the portion of YHWH is his people, Jacob his inheritance. (MT Deut 32:8–9)

Manuscripts of the Greek translation of Deuteronomy, by contrast, are almost unanimous in reading "angels of God" in place of "sons of Israel."[124] This variant seemed puzzling until the discovery of the Dead Sea Scrolls yielded Hebrew copies of Deuteronomy preserving yet another reading.[125] The versions of Deut 32:8b in 4QDeut[j] and 4QDeut[q] read *bene elohim* or *bene El* for *bene Israel*, raising the possibility that "sons of God" was the earliest recoverable reading,[126] which Hebrew tradents later changed to *bene Israel* and which Greek tradents rendered as *angeloi theou* ("angels of God"), whether in the course of translation or in an inner-Greek shift akin to that in LXX Gen 6:2.[127]

---

[123] The connection is most explicit in the first case; see *1 En* 6:2 and discussion in Chapter 4. Notably, however, Job 38:7 offers perhaps the clearest precedent for the association of angels and stars that is detailed in the *Astronomical Book*, while Job 1:6 and 2:2 stand in an intriguing relationship with *Jubilees'* traditions about Mastema in relation to the fallen angels and the spirits of the Giants.

[124] Brooke and McLean, *Old Testament in Greek*, 1:661.

[125] On the broader phenomenon of some Qumran biblical MSS attesting readings similar to the presumed Hebrew *Vorlage* of LXX texts, see Tov, *Textual Criticism of the Hebrew Bible*, 115–116.

[126] So Tov, *Textual Criticism*, 269, further speculating: "Within the supposed original context, Elyon and El need not be taken as epithets of the God of Israel, but as names of gods also known from the Canaanite and Ugaritic pantheon."

[127] Supporting the latter, Wevers, *Notes on the Greek Text of Deuteronomy*, 513.

What is most plausibly reconstructed as the oldest known reading of
Deut 32:8 also finds some counterpart in the version of Deut 32:43
preserved in 4QDeut[q] – also with partial parallels in LXX Deuteronomy.
Where MT Deuteronomy reads "Nations, acclaim his people, for he
vindicates the blood of his servants" for the first part of the verse
(32:43a), 4QDeut[q] has "Rejoice, O heavens, with him, and worship
him, all *elohim*, for he vindicates the blood of his sons." In the Greek,
one finds a combination of the two.[128] In the part corresponding to the
above-quoted portion of 4QDeut[q], moreover, there is internal variation
again around what is rendered there as *elohim*: Codex Alexandrinus and
several minuscules read "all sons of God" (cf. "sons of God" in Codex
Vaticanus), while a number of other manuscripts have "all *angeloi*"
instead.[129]

The evidence surrounding Deut 32:43, then, cautions us against
assuming that the "sons of God" of Deut 32:8 were already more angel
than deity. It is possible that both may have meant something more akin
to what later tradents seem to fear – or at least encompassed this possible
meaning in a deployment of deliberate ambiguity akin to the examples
noted above. In the case of Deut 32:43, the version of 4QDeut[q] elevates
Israel's God by depicting Him as the one who is worshipped by other
divine beings, while in the case of Deut 32:8, the appeal to other divine
beings functions to underline YHWH's exclusive fidelity to Israel.
Although the tradition that culminates in the MT negates both options
entirely, they were clearly still part of the textual tradition surrounding
Deuteronomy well into the Second Temple period.

The manuscript witnesses to the transmission of Deut 32:8, thus, attest
the theorization of the diversity of human cultures through their association with the multiplicity of the divine realm, but also two different later
attempts to defuse this notion: [1] a terminological shift to underline the
categorical subordination of these figures to Israel's God (i.e., from the
potentially ambiguous *bene elohim* to the unequivocally subordinate
"angels"); and [2] a more radical conceptual shift, which separates the
ordering of earthly nations totally from any transmundane associations,
drawing instead upon the coincidence of the number of the nations,
traditionally set at seventy, with the number of the progeny of the

---

[128] Among the options are that the LXX preserves the earlier form, and compressed
differently in each of the Hebrew versions, or that the Greek preserves a doublet
informed by impulse to integrate two known Hebrew versions of the verse.

[129] See Brooke and McLean, *Old Testament in Greek*, 1:666, for the precise breakdown.

patriarch Jacob/Israel. The first option finds parallels in Aramaic and Hebrew literature of the early Hellenistic age (and beyond), as we shall see below. The second, however, reminds us that at least *some* of what we are accustomed to reading as the "biblical" vision of monotheism is the product of the overwriting of divine multiplicity by later scribes and tradents.

The textual variation surrounding Deuteronomy 32 stands as a poignant reminder that not all biblical texts were fixed in the eras discussed in the present study. However common it is to treat the Second Temple period as categorically "post-biblical," this is the era of the composition of the latest texts that came to be included in the Hebrew Bible (with the latest, Daniel, postdating so-called pseudepigrapha like the *Astronomical Book* and *Book of the Watchers*). It is also the era that saw the stabilization of the forms and texts of the other books that we now call "biblical." From the evidence of the Dead Sea Scrolls, we now know that editorial variation and scribal intervention remained features of the biblical tradition well into the early Hellenistic age, and their clustering around issues like divine multiplicity and mediation, thus, attest the prevalence of some of the same concerns that we shall see later addressed more explicitly within the Aramaic Enoch tradition and related materials.

It is unclear whether overwriting of this sort clustered in Deuteronomy due to its special popularity in Second Temple times,[130] or whether we simply have more evidence for Deuteronomy due to the greater quantity of surviving manuscripts of this particular work.[131] Or perhaps a bit of both. The special place of Deuteronomy 32 in ancient Jewish piety is suggested by its prominence in special-use manuscripts like 4QDeut[j,k,l,q] that contain selected excerpts. That the readings noted above happen to be preserved in two of these special-use manuscripts is also perhaps not accidental: this pattern raises the possibility that some older readings may have survived in part due to the circulation of Deuteronomy in multiple forms and settings. In any case, its popularity may have made the matter of its precise message on divine multiplicity especially pressing to manage, with possible ambiguities increasingly perceived as problematic.

---

[130] So Crawford, "Reading Deuteronomy in the Second Temple Period."

[131] There were, for instance, twenty-nine copies of Deuteronomy found among the DSS (including one in Greek [4Q122]). The quantity is far greater than for any other part of the Torah/Pentateuch (i.e., nineteen copies of Genesis, seventeen copies of Exodus, twelve copies of Leviticus, six copies of Numbers) and is rivaled only by the thirty-six copies of Psalms in the total number of manuscripts of any work there attested.

For the purposes of the present chapter, it suffices to note that different views of divine multiplicity can be seen, not just in early biblical literature and in its later interpretation, but also within the textual history of some biblical works, the forms of which continued to remain fluid for centuries after the Exile. The message of Deuteronomy, for instance, sounds a bit different if we do not reduce its depiction of the divine to the oft-quoted monotheistic motto of 32:39 – "There is no god beside me!" We are challenged, rather, to reread the full range of references to divine unity and multiplicity in the Song of Moses through the lens of in 4QDeut^j and 4QDeut^q (i.e., as likely preserving some readings earlier than MT, but even if not, certainly reflecting a version widely circulating in Second Temple times). To do so, for instance, is to notice that the subordination of other deities to YHWH, their association with other nations, and the affiliation of YHWH exclusively with Israel are echoed by the reference to Israel's initial lack of contact with any "alien god" (אל נכר; 32:12) and the accusation of their forgetting their exclusive affiliation with YHWH to sacrifice instead to "*elohim* they had never known, new ones who came but lately" (32:17), who are condemned as *shedim* and "no-gods" (32:17, 21)[132] and who are powerless to act against YHWH (32:37–39).

Below, we shall see how this understanding of Deuteronomy makes sense as the conceptual structure upon which the authors of later texts, like the "Animal Apocalypse" and *Jubilees* (and many others after them), built up their angelologies and demonologies. For now, it suffices to note that it also makes sense in light of references elsewhere in the work to the prohibition of Israel worshipping *what* YHWH allotted instead to the nations (i.e., "the suns and the moon and the stars, the whole heavenly host"; 4:19; cf. 17:3) but also worshipping YHWH *how* the peoples of the Land serve their gods (12:31). That the worship of deities not allotted to them emblematizes the forgetting of YHWH is clear also from the identification of the sin punished by uprooting from the Land as Israel's worship of gods not allotted to them (29:25). In short, the principle of allotment that is so clearly stated in the versions of Deut 32:8b in 4QDeut^j and 4QDeut^q is implied by the logic throughout, which does not deny reality to the deities of other nations, as much as assert a principle of inversion whereby foreign-style worship is definitive of false worship for Israel, and the gods of others like demons and "no-gods" for those

---

[132] Compare LXX Deut 32:17: "they sacrificed to *daimones* not to God, to gods they did not know; new ones have come whom their fathers did not know." Note also the quotation in 1 Cor 10:20.

allotted instead to the God to whom all other gods bow down. We find no hint of concern for the question of the status of foreign worship of the deities allotted to them, or for any specific hierarchization in cosmic terms. The closest biblical precedent for demonology is epiphenomenal to the recasting of world-history to center completely on Israel and its deity.

Something similar may be at play with respect to angels as well. Although the term *mal'ak* is never used in Deuteronomy to refer to any nonhuman messenger (2:26), this work would have a powerful impact on later angelologies. Above, we noted how transmundane powers are used throughout biblical literature to telegraph divine exaltation – as exemplified by divine epithets such as "Lord of Hosts" or "rider/dweller on *cherubim*," wherein such powers have no identity apart from their use to convey the power of YHWH. In Moses' blessing of the people prior to his death in Deuteronomy, an appeal to anonymous angelic myriads serves a similar function with respect to Israel:

He (i.e., Moses) said: "The Lord came from Sinai, and dawned from Seir upon us; he shone forth from Mount Paran. With him were myriads of holy ones (קדש מרבבת);[133] at his right, a host of his own. Indeed, O favorite among peoples, all his holy ones were in your charge; they marched at your heels, accepted direction from you." (Deut 33:2–3)

Just as the later paralleling of angels and men has some precedent in references to their functions as *mal'akim* send by God, as discussed above, so the subordination of the heavenly hosts to Israel is a dynamic that continued well into the early Hellenistic age (and long beyond).[134]

What distinguishes early biblical reflections on transmundane powers from their Second Temple counterparts, then, is not a matter of belief in the existence of such spirits. The assumption of their existence – and, indeed, pervasiveness – makes possible all the various functions and allusions discussed above. The difference lies in the degree of systematic or focused literary interest in them as distinct figures with names, classes, and individualized roles to play in the cosmos and history. What is seemingly avoided, in other words, is "demonology" in the sense that Frankfurter defines as the process of "drawing demons out of their particular 'lived' situations and oral discussion into a speculative system,"

[133] On קדוש as a term used for spirits that serve God, see also Job 5:1; 15:15; Ps 89:6, 8; Zech 14:5.
[134] Schäfer, *Rivalität*, remains the most comprehensive treatment.

whereby "demons get collected from their local domains and ambiguous intentions, abstracted into lists, polarized as uniformly hostile, and speculatively combined with opposing gods or angels"[135] – that is: what we find evinced in a range of other ancient literary cultures, before and after, but only in Jewish literature from the centuries after the Exile.

Below, we shall note how this process came to reshape the remembrance of the biblical past. For now, it suffices to mention that it also left its mark on the transmission of some biblical texts, especially with their translation into Greek. The clearest examples are again in passages mentioning *bene elohim*. In the Old Greek translations of the Torah/Pentateuch, begun around the third century BCE, for instance, *bene elohim* is rendered with the literal "sons of God" (οἱ υἱοὶ τοῦ θεοῦ in LXX Gen 6:4 and some MSS of LXX Gen 6:2).[136] Some manuscripts, however, attest an alternate rendering of *angeloi theou* at LXX Gen 6:2, for which we also find external attestations beginning in the first century CE.[137] By the time of the Greek translation of Job around 150 BCE, *angeloi* for *bene elohim* has become consistent (LXX Job 1:6; 2:1; 38:7), and if the Greek Psalter can also be dated to around the second century BCE, we may find contemporaneous evidence there for the use of *angeloi* to render *elohim* as well (LXX Pss 8:5; 97/96:7; 138/137:1).[138]

Might we see here a broader pattern of defusing potentially polytheistic terminology through translation and the concurrent creation of a category akin to our own sense of "angels"? It is certainly intriguing – as Michael Mach observes – that various Greek translations of Hebrew texts attest the emergence of a technical meaning for Greek *angeloi* as denoting specifically nonhuman messengers/*mal'akim*.[139] That such lexical shifts bespeak a classificatory impulse may also be suggested by the use of *angeloi* by the beginning of the first century BCE in Greek

---

[135] Frankfurter, *Evil Incarnate*, 15, 19.

[136] Brooke and McLean, *Old Testament in Greek*, 1:13. For οἱ υἱοὶ τοῦ θεοῦ as the Old Greek, see Wevers, *Notes on the Greek Text of Genesis*, 74–78, and for further discussion, Reed, *Fallen Angels*, 116–118.

[137] e.g., Philo, *On the Giants* 6.1; Josephus, *Ant.* 1.73. It is intriguing that the reading *angeloi theou* occurs almost exclusively at Gen 6:2, the verse paraphrased in *1 En* 6:2, but almost never at LXX Gen 6:4, and that the external attestations begin to appear roughly around the same time as the Greek translation of the *Book of the Watchers*. See further Reed, *Fallen Angels*, 7, 82, 105–106, 118.

[138] For this estimate for the Greek Psalter, see Williams, "Towards a Date for the Old Greek Psalter."

[139] e.g., LXX Num 21:12. On the broader pattern as well as the exceptions see Mach, *Entwicklungsstadien*, 86–89.

translations of Aramaic texts like Daniel and the *Book of the Watchers* to render "Watchers" (עירין) as well.[140] Given the diverse character of the Greek translations of Jewish literature and their revision through multiple recensional layers over the course of many centuries, however, the evidence may be less clear-cut than might appear at first sight. This is especially the case in light of the somewhat unique situation surrounding the Greek translation of Job; the earliest Greek translation (i.e., OG Job) seems to have been only one-sixth of the length of what came down to us as the Hebrew (i.e., MT Job), and its references to *angeloi* go well beyond cases where the corresponding Masoretic text of the Hebrew reads *mal'akim, bene elohim*, or the like.[141] It is only with much caution that an isolated verse-by-verse comparison of examples plucked from different works can be used to posit any generalized "Septuagintal" tendency.

Despite the habitual presumption that "pseudepigrapha" are categorically later and dependent upon "biblical" texts, moreover there is no evidence that translations of *bene elohim* as *angeloi theou* predate the developments discussed in the rest of this study. Mach could be correct that the identification of *bene ha-elohim* with *mal'akim* and *angeloi* comes to form the heart of the classification system of Jewish angelology, ultimately enabling the rereading of diverse transmundane powers as part of a single hierarchy of what we now call "angels."[142] What is less clear, however, is whether or not this development postdates and depends upon the extensive and influential narrative traditions identifying the *bene elohim* of Genesis 6 as fallen angelic Watchers (עירין), beginning with the *Book of the Watchers* already in the third century BCE – concurrent with the start of the long process of translating the Torah/Pentateuch into Greek.[143] In fact, as we shall see below, the angelological trajectories that we see within the transmission and translation of what became "biblical" literature run parallel to what we find expressed earlier and more explicitly in so-called pseudepigrapha.

---

[140] So, e.g., Gr^Pan for *1 En* 6:2, cf. Sync. οἱ ἐγρήγοροι.

[141] For a summary of the text-history of LXX Job, see Reed, "Job as Jobab," 33–35. For more examples of its use of *angeloi*, see Gammie, "The Angelology and Demonology in the Septuagint of the Book of Job."

[142] Mach, *Entwicklungsstadien*.

[143] Furthermore, as we shall see below, classification does not center initially on the expansion of the category of *mal'akim* but often draws instead on the structuring potential of *ruhot* to encompass transmundane powers that are both beneficial and harmful to humankind.

CONCLUSION

Whatever can be said of the differences between what ancient Israelites and later Jews *believed* about intermediate spirits, I have argued in this chapter for the importance of attending to our evidence that learned Jews *wrote* about them in quite different ways in different periods. As we have seen, early biblical literature preserves only scattered hints of demon-belief; it abounds in angels but shrouds them in ambiguity. Where the data for ancient Israel differ from the data for Second Temple Judaism, then, is not so much in the lack of a sense of divine multiplicity; it is, rather, in the dearth of explicit and concerted efforts to outline, specify, name, and explain the intermediate figures therein in writing and to use them, in turn, within systematizing discourses for explaining the cosmos and the history of Israel.

In the next three chapters, we will further consider the character, causes, and timing of the shift toward explicit and systematic demon-ology and angelology in Jewish literature. Before turning to those tasks, it may be useful to reflect on methodological insights from the recent lines of research in Biblical Studies engaged above. Most significant, for this book as a whole, are insights into: [1] the problems with reducing biblical praise and description of YHWH merely to an embryonic form of what we today call "monotheism"; [2] the value of looking beyond the privileging of those biblical passages that presage medieval and modern monotheism to recover the place of such reflection within a broader spectrum of ancient Israelite religiosity; and [3] the importance of situating the rhetoric of divine unity within particular historical and social contexts, rather than assuming a timeless Jewish norm from which any notion of divine multiplicity can only be deviance or devolution. Above, we saw how such insights have helped to illumine the interplay of divine unity and multiplicity in the Hebrew Bible. What I would like to propose is that they are no less pressing for our inquiry into Second Temple Judaism.

Just as older scholarly views of Israelite monotheism resulted, in part, from the misrecognition of biblical rhetoric for ancient Israelite reality, so its idealization was also naturalized by the presentist pro-jection of modern ideas of monotheism back into the ancient past. Among the consequences is the conflation of biblical monotheism with medieval philosophical ideas about a cosmos emptied of all powers except an all-powerful God and/or with a post-Enlightenment disenchantment that denigrates any angelology or demonology as superstition.[144] Yet the path from Israelite devotion to a single deity to the modern Western notion of monotheism was a very long one – and far from a direct line.[145] Rather than supporting any notion of a unilinear development from Deuteronomy to Maimonides, later Jewish literature attests the creative tension between divine multiplicity and unity that continued to shape late antique and medieval Judaism.[146] Modern Western notions of monotheism, moreover, have their own specific history and contexts, arising – as Smith has shown – "in part from contact between modern Europeans and non-Westerners, as a way of defining the Western religious traditions in contrast to non-European cultures."[147]

Here as elsewhere, we might wish to be wary lest the temptations of teleological thinking foster a narcissistic illusion of the inherent superiority of those ancient beliefs that seem most to resemble our own. Kugel has cautioned, for instance, that evolutionary models of monotheism bring the danger of assuming that earlier ideas were simply "primitive" or underdeveloped versions of ideas familiar to us today; we miss much when we read early biblical literature through the lens of much later concepts of Israel's God as all-knowing, all-powerful, lacking a body, and inhabiting a universe in which no other deities could possibly exist.[148] Ancient Israelite views of God differ in striking ways from the Jewish and Christian theologies that were later built upon them, but they are often no less sophisticated and best understood in their own right.[149]

How, then, should we explain the relative reticence of ancient Israelite literature to name, list, catalog, and classify intermediary spirits? If this reticence should not be reduced to modern notions of monotheism as the emptying of the cosmos of all but one power, how can we account for its appeal? In my view, Smith's emphasis on the rhetorical character of ancient Israelite assertions of divine unity may point us to a productive

---

[144] Schäfer, *Mirror of His Beauty*, 1–9.

[145] Smith, *Origins*, 10–13; Schäfer, *Mirror of His Beauty*, 2–3. Contrast, e.g., Gnuse, *No Other Gods*, 321–345, who characterizes the development of "emergent monotheism" in ancient Israel as a process of "punctuated equilibrium," which culminated in the sixth century BCE. For him, this marks a major moment in the history of human thought, an "intellectual breakthrough or transformation" that he does not hesitate to describe in teleological terms (20).

[146] See Schäfer, *Mirror of His Beauty*, 1–9, and references there.

[147] Smith, *Origins*, 11. On the some of the specific political and social contingencies that contributed the valuation of monotheism in early modern Europe and contemporary North America, see 10–13 there.

[148] Kugel, *The God of Old*, 192–193. [149] Kugel, *God of Old*, xi–xii, 59–66.

way of understanding biblical treatments of divine multiplicity as well. Our extant evidence allows us only to speculate about what most Israelites may or may not have believed about transmundane powers. What we can discuss more concretely, however, is what the scribes among them deemed appropriate to set down as worthy of remembrance *in writing* and how they chose to frame it in literary forms. Approached from this perspective, angelology and demonology may not be so much suppressed as displaced: if there is anything akin to the *Listenwissenschaft* of scribal and priestly demonologies in neighboring cultures, as we have seen, it pertains not to intermediate spirits but rather to human ancestors. Genealogy structures the writing of collective memory to the degree that it perhaps obviates demonology as an organizing principle for cosmological, historiographical, and theological theorization.[150]

Together with a focus on rhetoric and writing, attention to the dynamics of cultural memory further challenges us to rethink what we are even seeking when we try to pinpoint the start of this or that phenomenon – in our case, Jewish angelology and demonology. Modern scholarship on the history of religions has been shaped by longstanding assumptions about the priority of "origins" whereby the identification of the birth of a phenomenon was thought to reveal its purest essence. Today, one rarely finds explicit assertions to this effect. Nevertheless, such assumptions remain structurally embedded in much research on ancient Judaism and Christianity – as exemplified, for instance, by philological inquiries into key terms, which commonly conflate the discovery of the derivation of a word or its first occurrence with the unmasking of its true meaning or the birth of the very concept. Newer models of cultural and intellectual change have tended to introduce more agency into this process, as is clear from the recent trend of searching for moments of "invention" rather than "origins." Yet such approaches can run the risk of unintentionally reinscribing elements of the older pattern, not least due to the Kuhnian and Foucaultian focus on rupture and on the power of elite discourse to produce revolutionary conceptual shifts.[151] Drawing insights from the

---

[150] I.e., genealogical discourse serves much the same totalizing or taxonomic functions associated elsewhere with demonological discourse – including the displacement of local sites, knowledge, and experts by scribal and other experts supported by a royal or priestly center, and the remapping of various local traditions as a periphery that gains meaning through connection to this center.

[151] That is, paradigm shifts and epistemic shifts respectively; Kuhn, *Structure of Scientific Revolutions*; Foucault, *The Archaeology of Knowledge*; cf. Deleuze and Guattari, *Thousand Plateaus*, 323–326; Fleming and O'Carroll, "Revolution, Rupture, Rhetoric."

history of science, for instance, Daryn Lehoux thus cautions that the "temptation to find points of rupture (whether positivistic or Foucaultian) can only distort the before and after pictures"; it may feel more satisfying to proclaim one's discovery of a dramatic development, but the types of changes that transform and shape cultures are often more akin to "nodes in a shifting conversation."[152]

Among the benefits of recent interdisciplinary research on memory are alternate models for conceptualizing change that encompass the concurrent continuity and discontinuity common in so many cases of religious change in particular. In the case of monotheism, we have seen how older notions of invention, revolution, and evolution do not suffice to capture the complexity and dynamism of a phenomenon that was *simultaneously* a radical rethinking and reorientation *and* a reencounter with the past. So too with the use of genealogy to rewrite Israelite local identity – in that case: quite literally a rewriting of the past with the past. And so too, I shall suggest below, with the beginnings of Jewish demonology and angelology in the early Hellenistic age.

To be sure, the task of reconstructing this dynamism comes with special challenges to modern interpreters. Not only can the ancient scribes and tradents involved thereby efface their own agency and innovation, but their acts of overwriting can make some of their most radical choices appear invisible, inevitable, or natural. To memorialize the past, after all, is also to decide what is *not* deemed worthy of remembering or recording.[153]

This chapter touched upon some of the consequences for topics like divine multiplicity in the Hebrew Bible. By means of conclusion, we might further note the effects of choices in textualizing periods and trajectories in time. Writing from the standpoint of the sociology of knowledge, for instance, Eviatar Zerubavel stresses the social contexts and consequences of conventions of periodization: "Just as society delineates the scope of our attention and concern, it also delineates our mental reach into the past by setting certain historical horizons beyond which past events are basically regarded as irrelevant and, as such, often forgotten altogether."[154]

---

[152] Lehoux, *What Did the Romans*, 15–16.   [153] See further Reed, *Forgetting*.
[154] Zerubavel, "Social Memories," 286, further stressing that "the division of the past into a memorable 'history' and a practically forgettable 'pre-history' is neither logical nor natural. It is an unmistakably social, normative convention" (288); see further Zerubavel, *Time Maps*, 82–100; Reed, *Forgetting*. His comments, notably, also have historiographical consequences, cautioning us against the temptation to overplay innovation and rupture in our own scholarly narratives about cultural change.

Within the long-duration literature of ancient Israel as we know it from the Hebrew Bible, the silent work of periodization proves especially powerful in the genealogical lists and other orchestrating logics of the redacted Torah/Pentateuch. Despite truisms among modern scholars of Religious Studies about creation as a privileged site for culture-making, for instance, cosmogony and protology there play a minor part, largely relegated to the realm of a prehistory only brought to an end with Abraham, who marks the beginning of those genealogies that mark history *qua* history thereafter.[155]

This very bracketing, however, leaves a productive space for later scribes to create innovations that are simultaneously overwritings and reencounters as well. As we shall see in the next chapter, the beginnings of Jewish demonology and angelology accompany an explosion of literary interest in the pre-Sinaitic past in the Aramaic Jewish literature of the early Hellenistic age, and systematic appeals to angels and demons first appear in works that claim to speak *from* this past. What is framed as preface in the Torah/Pentateuch becomes a space to be filled anew by demons, angels, scribes, and books. Here too, we see glimpses of an "ongoing dialogue in ancient Israel over different versions of the past."[156] And, in this sense, what we may see in the early Hellenistic age is perhaps not so much a dramatic transformation of belief or the emergence of a brand new "world-view" as a potent shift in Jewish memory and writing.

---

[155] On the modern scholarly focus on creation see Masuzawa, *In Search of Dreamtime*. This nineteenth- and twentieth-century preoccupation stands in quite some contrast to the situation in ancient Israel; indeed, even Gen 2–3 attracted surprisingly little attention prior to the first century CE.

[156] Quote from Smith, *Memoirs*, 6.

2

Rethinking Scribalism and Change in Second Temple Judaism

In the surviving literary remains of preexilic Israel one finds little system-atic concern for demons and angels, but also surprisingly little interest in primeval ages, celestial cycles, cosmic spaces, and eschatological horizons. Whether or not this reticence reflects an era in which Israel's scribes focused their literary efforts on familiar spaces, human lineages, and historical time, it challenges us to grapple with the dramatic changes in the centuries that follow. Angels and demons became the focus for inten-sive written reflection, first and tentatively in the Hebrew literature of the exilic and Achaemenid Persian periods, then later and far more exten-sively in Jewish literature written in Aramaic, Hebrew, and Greek under Ptolemaic, Seleucid, Hasmonean, and Roman rule.[1]

To the degree that past research has sought to explain the intensifica-tion of interest in angels and demons in the Jewish literature of the Second Temple period, it has been largely through speculation about Jewish feelings of distance from God in the wake of the Babylonian Exile (586–538 BCE). Still surprisingly prominent – as Larry Hurtado notes – is Wilhelm "Bousset's misleading claim, echoed by many others subse-quently, [that] the texts present the angelic hosts as intermediaries between a distant God and an elect who felt a growing sense of alienation from him and who assigned to the angels greater importance than in earlier times because God seemed so remote and inactive."[2] Despite the detailed data-driven critiques of this claim by scholars from George Foot

---

[1] See further Olyan, *Thousand Thousands*, 3–9; Collins, *Apocalyptic Imagination*; Segal, *Life after Death*, 120–124.
[2] Hurtado, *One God*, 25–27.

Moore in 1920s to E. P. Sanders in 1970s to Hurtado in 1980s, variations thereof continue to be cited as if self-evident.[3] The tidiness of the trope of divine distancing makes it tempting to repeat, and scholars often do so in passing in the course of studies dedicated to other phenomena. Even in recent studies, the intensification of interest in intermediate spirits is often explained away as answering a purported postexilic Jewish need to fill the vacuum left by an elevated deity, following the seemingly commonsensical logic that "the more exalted God becomes and the more comprehensive the deity's interests, the possibility also emerges that divine concern for any particular person or nations might be correspondingly diluted" and "weakening of divine attention to daily human events can create the sense that the distance between God and humanity is a huge and empty chasm" such that "thinkers would fill the chasm with subsidiary beings."[4]

From the perspective of modern notions of monotheism, such logic makes sense. As we have seen in Chapter 1, however, it does not fit our data for ancient discourses about divinity – either from Israel or elsewhere.[5] Furthermore, as we shall see below, the trope of divine distancing does not fit the stance or concerns of the Jewish writings in which we first find angelology and demonology explicitly textualized. Indeed, if anything, these writings are marked by an unprecedented confidence in the possibility of human access to divine knowledge, and this confidence is expressed precisely through their treatment of transmundane powers: just as their claims of knowledge about the origins and laws of demons on earth underline their claims to know "everything," so they also undergird these claims through the likening of Jewish scribes to heavenly angels.[6]

---

[3] Moore ("Christian Writings," 228–233) placed the blame on F. Weber's characterization of the God of postbiblical Judaism as remote and inaccessible in his 1880 *System der altsynagogaien palästinischen Theologie*, while Sanders (*Paul and Palestinian Judaism*, 33–40) pointed to its dissemination by Bousset and his student Rudolph Bultmann to become enshrined in NT scholarship, together with its supersessionist use to undergird readings of Paul as reacting to the purportedly empty legalism and alleged divine inaccessibility within Second Temple Judaism.

[4] Burkes, *God, Self, and Death*, 16.

[5] Peter Brown makes a similar point for Late Antiquity, pointing to the pervasive and productive "paradox that a high God, precisely because he was all-powerful, must be both immeasurably distant and, at the same time, ever-present" (*Poverty and Leadership*, 97).

[6] North and Stuckenbruck thus caution that "one is *not* to infer inaccessibility to God from stratified conceptions of the universe; *transcendence* – yes, *remoteness* – no" (*Early Jewish and Christian Monotheism*, 7). They also stress that "apocalyptic cosmologies, which involved a belief in the existence and activities of heavenly beings other than God are not – indeed were not – necessarily perceived as antithetical to 'monotheistic' convictions."

But even despite its misfit with our ancient data, the trope of postexilic "divine distancing" has been strangely tenacious.

This chapter reflects upon the reasons for the continued appeal of this old explanation, and it experiments with alternatives. To understand the beginnings of Jewish angelology and demonology, I argue that it is critical to resist generalizing the entire Second Temple period as "postexilic" but also to refrain from conflating the eras of Ptolemaic and Seleucid rule over the Land of Israel and from retrojecting post-Maccabean developments onto pre-Maccabean sources. Accordingly, I here make the case for taking seriously the clustering of our earliest evidence for angelology and demonology in the third century BCE. This chapter lays the groundwork for a synchronic approach that situates their beginnings in nested synchronic contexts: the Aramaic Jewish scribal pedagogy that we see within the earliest "pseudepigrapha" and related Aramaic Dead Sea Scrolls, concurrent shifts within other plausibly pre-Maccabean Jewish sources, contemporaneous non-Jewish texts and trends under the early Ptolemies, shared concerns in other writings by Near Eastern scribes elsewhere in the Hellenistic world, and the broader cultural shifts in the Mediterranean and Near East in the centuries following the conquests of Alexander.

The first part of the chapter interrogates the long-standing scholarly tendency to treat sources from Achaemenid, Ptolemaic, Seleucid, Hasmonean, and Roman periods as if uniformly "postexilic," noting the ramifications for naturalizing the notion that the flourishing of angelology reflects a response to the malaise of "divine distancing." I then survey our evidence for situating the beginnings of angelology and demonology more specifically in the early Hellenistic age, pointing to the clustering of such concerns especially in Aramaic.[7] The second part of the chapter considers the distinctive features of the corpus of Aramaic Jewish literature from this time, and it posits the Aramaic Jewish scribal pedagogy of the early Hellenistic age as a crucible for the development of systematic written reflection on transmundane powers. To do so, I focus on a set of proto-testamentary sources – the *Aramaic Levi Document* (1Q21, 4Q213, 4Q213a, 4Q213b, 4Q214, 4Q214a, 4Q214b), *Admonitions of Qahat* (4Q542), and *Visions of Amram* – that elevate scribes, books, and

---

[7] The value of synchronic approaches to evade the "tyranny of canonical assumptions" is also noted by Mroczek, who shows how "the call to read synchronically or synoptically, rather than hierarchically with the (proto)biblical at the top or center of the literary world, is helpful for reconsidering Second Temple literature more broadly"; *Literary Imagination*, 122.

writing, thereby voicing a new confidence in the capacity of human knowledge to resist loss to historical rupture. Lastly, I make the case for situating what we know of the Aramaic Jewish scribal pedagogy of the time in relation to the cultural changes across the Mediterranean and Near East during the era of the establishment of Ptolemaic, Seleucid, and other Macedonian empires.

It is in the early Hellenistic age that we first find explicit examples of the Jewish classification and systemization of knowledge about transmundane powers, and we can learn much about this development from a specific synchronic focus on this era. Among what we learn – I suggest – is that the beginnings of Jewish angelology and demonology may be as much about shifts in writing as about shifts in knowledge. Concurrent with the expansion of the scope of topics of Jewish literary interest, the Aramaic Jewish literature of the early Hellenistic age attests a burst of experimentation with new literary forms, including first-person narrative address, revelatory dream-visions, and other features that would later become central for new genres like the apocalypse and the testament.[8] This experimentation is accompanied by pointedly self-conscious reflections on writing, reading, scribes, and books, signaling new claims about scribal authority and expertise – for which, as we shall see, claims about angels and demons prove particularly determinative.

To understand the beginnings of Jewish demonology and angelology, I suggest that it is necessary also to look to concurrent shifts in textuality and scribal practice. This proves especially pressing, in my view, because Jewish demonology and angelology has its "beginning" in this era in the sense noted by Edward Said: we here see innovations produced *from* and *with* received traditions, through creative acts of recontextualizing or reconfiguring knowledge by "combining the already-familiar with the fertile novelty of human work in language."[9]

This phenomenon of innovation from and with received tradition has been a major focus of research on Second Temple Judaism in relation to biblical exegesis. As Mark Smith reminds us, however, it is found already in "the Bible's presentation of history," which is best understood "not only as the record of Israel's past or as literary representations of their past, but also as a response to the past, or a series of responses to it."[10] What I argue, in what follows, is that this conversation – with and

---

[8] Stuckenbruck, "Pseudepigraphy and First-Person Discourse in the Dead Sea Documents"; Perrin, *Dynamics of Dream-Vision.*
[9] Said, *Beginnings,* xvii; see discussion above in the Introduction.   [10] Smith, *Memoirs,* 3.

through Israel's past – continues into the Second Temple period in a manner marked by change and innovation, but not by the degree of rupture conventionally assumed: there is little in the Jewish literature of the early Hellenistic age to support the old caricature of the Second Temple period as a uniformly "post-biblical" age of belatedness and the consolation of exegesis. What we find, rather, are bold new claims about what is known and written by Jewish scribes – including from and about transmundane powers.

BEYOND POSTEXILIC DIVINE DISTANCING AND CANONICAL CONSTRAINTS

In past research on Second Temple Judaism, the trauma of the Babylonian destruction of the Jerusalem Temple and the Exile was adduced to explain a variety of phenomena from throughout the Second Temple period – including the new interest in angels and demons, but also the rise of Scripture, the literary practice of pseudepigraphy, the proliferation of heavenly temples and palaces, and the development of apocalyptic literature.[11] Specific articulations differ in their details. What they typically have in common, however, is the evocation of a sense of belatedness pervading the period as a whole, for which any creativity is interpreted as compensation.[12] The result has been to reinforce long-standing notions of "postexilic" Judaism as essentially "post-biblical" and/or "intertestamental"[13] – an age of alienation when Jewish longing for a lost past

---

[11] See Hanson, *Dawn of Apocalyptic*, for the classic articulation of apocalyptic eschatology and visionary literature as "due to a pessimistic view of reality growing out of the bleak post-exilic conditions within which those associated with the visionaries found themselves" (11–12). For an influential reading of the Exile as the catalyst for the rise of Scripture and its interpretation, see Kugel, *Traditions of the Bible*, 2–14. For speculation concerning the destruction(s) of the Jerusalem Temple as tied to the progressive projection of Jewish ideals into heaven, see Elior, *Three Temples*. My point here is not to deny the relevance of such theories for understanding *some* texts and trajectories, but rather to question their hermeneutical dominance and especially their conventional generalization to nearly *all* texts from over the six centuries of the Second Temple period.

[12] R. H. Charles (*Book of Enoch*, ix–x) thus stressed "the evil character of the period" in which the Enoch literature took form, opining that even "enthusiasts and mystics, exhibiting on occasions the inspiration of the O.T. prophets, were obliged to issue their works under the aegis of some ancient name," since the "Law which claimed to be the highest and final word from God could tolerate no fresh message."

[13] These categories are examples of the broader pattern, noted by Mroczek, whereby "despite our caveats about anachronism, the biblical returns as the default way by

supposedly spurred the rise of Scripture and its interpreters in a manner eventually culminating with the rise of Rabbinic Judaism, on the one hand, and when Jewish anxiety about divine alienation purportedly impelled the multiplication of mediating angels in a manner eventually culminating with the origins of Christianity, on the other hand.

Teleological narratives of this sort function to bridge the divide between the Hebrew Bible and post-70 Judaism and Christianity in a manner that speaks to present-day Jews and Christians. Yet our understanding of the texts and times in between can suffer from their imposition. Sara Japhet, for instance, observes that even biblical texts from the Persian period, like Ezra–Nehemiah, are more optimistic than their Deuteronomistic antecedents; contrary to what common scholarly generalizations about "postexilic" literature might lead one to expect, they are "not written as theodicy, aimed to justify God in the face of destruction, or as a memorial to an extinguished past."[14] Japhet points to a gap between the ancient data and modern scholarly habits of describing them:

Biblical scholarship tends to ascribe a certain finality to the "exile"... and view everything that followed in relation to it. The period of Return and Restoration or, from another perspective, the Persian period in the history of Israel, is commonly described as "postexilic," and so are its social, literary, and spiritual phenomena...In fact, however, the works that are commonly identified as "postexilic historiography" were not written under the immediate impact of destruction and exile, nor as a direct response to them.[15]

The Babylonian invasion of Judah, the demise of its monarchy, the concurrent disappearance of the office of the prophet, and the dislocation of Jewish elites had the dire socio-political effects with long-standing cultural consequences. Nevertheless – Japhet stresses – much is lost when the varied texts and transformations of the subsequent centuries are interpreted as if uniformly "postexilic."

In highlighting this habit, I do not mean to downplay the dire socio-political effects of the events surrounding the Exile or their enduring place within Jewish cultural memory. What I would like to question, however, are the sweeping narratives of postexilic change that have been pressed upon the Second Temple period as a whole. Such generalization risks diluting the particularity and the explanatory power of the Babylonian

which texts are classified, and sets the agenda for the questions we ask"; *Literary Imagination*, 7.
[14] Japhet, "Postexilic Historiography," 172–173.
[15] Japhet, "Postexilic Historiography," 145–146.

Exile, while also eliding the specificity of Jewish experiences under Persian, Ptolemaic, Seleucid, Hasmonean, and Roman empires.[16] To treat the entire Second Temple period as "postexilic," after all, is to collapse nearly 600 years of Jewish history and to foreclose the much more interesting task of situating specific changes in their specific times and settings.

Here as elsewhere, we might wish to be wary lest we misread biblical rhetoric as social reality. As Martien Halvorson-Taylor has shown, the dehistoricized generalization of "exile" has a history of its own, which includes the textualization and memorialization of the Babylonian conquest and captivity but also much besides. Long prior to 586 BCE, the association of exile with divine wrath was common across the Near East, especially in treaty curses, and this association also finds some parallels in vestiges of "preexilic thinking about the threat of exile" preserved within the Torah/Pentateuch.[17] Even after the Babylonian Exile, prophetic authors and redactors often use the language of exile, not just to describe geographical displacement or political disenfranchisement, but also to convey divine wrath and estrangement – with the latter potentially evoked even apart from a strictly historical sense of the former as delineated in space or time. In the shift from Second Isaiah (40–55) to Third Isaiah (56–66), for instance, Halvorson-Taylor posits that "exile takes on a paradigmatic, increasingly dehistoricized meaning,"[18] and in the course of the redactional formation of Zechariah, exile and restoration become refigured as terms pertaining foremost to Israel's relationship with God.[19] These prophetic traditions add new layers of meaning onto the memory of the Babylonian Exile, and they are redeployed around the time of the

---

[16] So too with post-70 rereadings of the Babylonian Exile: the effects can be felt, not just in Jewish liturgy and memory (*m. Ta'anit* 4:6; *b. Ta'anit* 29a; *b. Megillah* 5b), but also in modern scholarship. The contention of the symmetry of the catastrophes of 586 BCE and 70 CE is embodied in the very notion of "Second Temple Judaism" as suspended between them. Even historical studies have tended to privilege these two events as pivotal in a manner presumed to be more decisive, for instance, than the Assyrian conquest of the northern kingdom Israel before (722 BCE) or the Bar Kokhba Revolt thereafter (132–135 CE) or even the Maccabean Revolt in between (167–164 BCE). On the overlooked significance of the era of Assyrian dominance, see *Schniedewind, How the Bible,* 65–75, and on the overlooked significance of the Bar Kokhba revolt, see Clements, "70 CE after 135 CE."

[17] Halvorson-Taylor, *Enduring Exile,* 9, 21–38.

[18] Halvorson-Taylor, *Enduring Exile,* 109.

[19] Halvorson-Taylor, *Enduring Exile,* 151–198, there with special emphasis on the counterparts to Jeremiah's prediction of 70 years (e.g., Zech 1:12).

Maccabean Revolt as "antecedents of the second-century BCE motif of the 'enduring exile'" best known from Daniel 9, whereby "Israel can be in exile even though the people have returned to the land."[20] In the wake of the Roman destruction of the Second Temple in 70 CE, this motif took on new meanings yet again, particularly in works like 4 *Ezra*, contributing to the process whereby the memory of the Babylonian destruction of the First Temple increasingly coalesced around its conflation with the Roman destruction of the Second Temple.[21]

For Halvorson-Taylor, this trajectory proves significant inasmuch as this particular approach to "exile, in general, and the Babylonian Exile, in particular, left its mark on the formation of the biblical canon."[22] For our purposes, it is no less important for drawing our attention to how certain articulations of "postexilic" experience thus displaced others – even within the Bible, but especially beyond it. The "metaphorization of exile" that Halvorson-Taylor highlights, for instance, reinforces the Deuterono-mistic interpretation of the Babylonian conquest of Judah as divine punishment for Israel's disobedience, and it underpins the contention of decline conveyed both by the Rabbinic foreshortening of Second Temple history and by early Christian polemics against the purported corruption of Judaism at the time of Jesus.[23]

By virtue of its place in shaping both the biblical canon and its interpretation, this characterization has also informed modern narratives about the Second Temple period as an era of "postexilic" divine alienation and "post-biblica" belatedness as well as naturalizing the scholarly practice of interpreting innovation during this period foremost as consolation or compensation. For instance, even when contextualizing *Jubilees* – a work that took form over 400 years after the Exile – James Kugel characterizes its aim as communicating a "message of comfort" to those lamenting that God "had allowed the Northern Kingdom of Israel to fall to the Assyrians, never to rise again" and that "the Southern Kingdom, Judah, had similarly fallen to the Babylonians, and much of its citizenry

---

[20] Halvorson-Taylor, *Enduring Exile*, 7. This motif contravenes the assertion of the finite span of the Babylonian Exile in Jer 29:10; Isa 40:1–2; 2 Chr 36:20–23; Ezra 1:1–3; cf. 2 Kgs 25, although articulations differ as to whether exile will come to an end at a later date or only with the final eschatological renewal of cosmic order. Much of the rhetoric force of extending the exile is to evoke "change as imminent but not yet realized" (154).

[21] Halvorson-Taylor, *Enduring Exile*, 11–15; Najman, *Losing the Temple and Recovering the Future*.

[22] Halvorson-Taylor, *Enduring Exile*, 199.   [23] See further Reed, *Forgetting*.

had been exiled to Babylon."[24] In this, Kugel's approach is representative, echoing a long-standing tendency in the study of Second Temple Judaism to treat literature of this period as belated and dependent, while also limiting its creativity mainly to the nostalgic consolation of biblical exegesis. It is not just that Kugel atomizes *Jubilees* into a "treasure-house of ancient biblical interpretation" that responds to the biblical past in ways that are "designed to answer questions about the biblical narrative."[25] He characterizes the entire Second Temple period in terms of a purported "postexilic malaise" and wistful "mode of return," which in his view is exemplified by a "significant barrier" between the text of the Torah/Pentateuch and its postexilic readers, as bridged by a resultant turn to biblical exegesis, thereby and thereafter oriented toward resolving textual ambiguities, harmonizing contractions, and "filling gaps."[26]

Needless to say, Kugel's call for attention to the exegetical elements of so-called pseudepigrapha did much to inspire the renaissance in their study in the wake of the discovery of the Dead Sea Scrolls, bringing fresh attention to these materials, not just as data for Christian Origins, but also as part of a history of biblical exegesis that leads no less to Rabbinic midrash. More recent research along these same lines, however, has shed doubt on his characterization of the Second Temple period as primarily an "Age of Interpretation," questioning his base assumption of a fixed text of "the Bible" and a distinct status for "biblical" literature so soon after the Exile.[27] The more that we learn from the Dead Sea Scrolls about the writings now in the Hebrew Bible, the more difficult it becomes to imagine a Second Temple circumstance in which "the Bible" was already

[24] Kugel, *Walk through Jubilees*, 5–6 – there reading these events from the eighth to sixth centuries BCE as looming larger than the Return and periods of Persian, Ptolemaic, and Seleucid rule that followed – not even to mention the specific settings of the work's own provenance, most likely in the second century BCE. See also Kugel, *The Bible As It Was*, where he characterizes the Second Temple period as an "Age of Interpretation," describing the "dawn of a new age with regard to Scripture and its interpretation" after the Babylonian conquest (2) and crediting the "mode of return" from Exile as one of its main motives (5) – even despite drawing his evidence for this trend from sources "composed from, roughly, the third century BCE to through the first century CE" (2–3).

[25] Kugel, *Walk through Jubilees*, 1.

[26] Kugel, *Traditions of the Bible*, 4–5. In this, he is representative of a broader pattern, noted by Mroczek, whereby "texts like various parts of the Enochic corpus, Jubilees, Genesis Apocryphon, and the Qumran Psalms Scroll have been called and studied as 'rewritten Bible' or 'biblical interpretation,' even though exegesis does not seem to be *their* primary concern" (*Literary Imagination*, 8).

[27] Mroczek, *Literary Imagination*, 19–50, 118–155.

so categorically distinct. And – as Eva Mroczek has richly shown – the more that we learn from the Dead Sea Scrolls about the most ancient Jewish literary production outside "the Bible," the less possible it becomes to reduce its creativity simply to a turn to "biblical exegesis" as if compensation for some supposed "postexilic" sense of "post-biblical" belatedness.[28]

To this, we might add that even the earliest "pseudepigrapha" were penned centuries after the Exile, and, as John Collins has shown, the most ancient among them are actually the least exegetical.[29] Nor do these works cohere with what later memory-making might lead us to expect of "postexilic" Judaism as marked by belatedness, dependency, or decline. If anything, – as we shall see – they are shaped by a radical expansion of the topics and horizons of textualized Jewish knowledge as well as an audaciously innovative experimentation with new literary forms and genres.

SYNCHRONIC APPROACHES TO JEWISH ANGELOLOGY AND DEMONOLOGY

How, then, should we explain the rise of interest in angels and demons that we see in the Jewish literature of Second Temple times? Summarizing the scholarly consensus on the development of Jewish angelology, Saul Olyan points to the Babylonian Exile as the pivotal moment after which one finds the "emergence of named angels, classes of heavenly beings, angelic hierarchy, archangels, a complex of heavenly temples and cults, conflicts between good and bad angels, expanding roles of angels in the human sphere, and characterization of angels" within Judaism.[30] If we limit ourselves to materials that are now canonical among Jews and Christians in the West, this consensus makes sense: Daniel – the latest book in the Hebrew Bible – might appear to mark the efflorescence of a trajectory presaged in Ezekiel and other works of late biblical prophecy.[31] Inasmuch as Daniel is also characterized by a notable lack of any direct engagement with the divine, moreover, it is perhaps not surprising that past scholarship tended to correlate the angelological impulse within

---

[28] Mroczek, *Literary Imagination*, 138–139.
[29] Collins, "The Transformation of the Torah in Second Temple Judaism"; Dimant, "The Qumran Aramaic Texts and the Qumran Community," 202.
[30] Olyan, *Thousand Thousands*, 3.   [31] Olyan, *Thousand Thousands*, 15.

Second Temple Judaism to a perceived need for mediation in an era of purported postexilic estrangement.

It is certainly the case that angels gain new prominence already in late biblical prophecy written during and after the Exile: *cherubim* become part of the vivified architecture of God's chariot-throne (e.g., Ezek 1; 10), for instance, and *mal'akim* are commissioned with the tasks of revealing knowledge, showing sights, and explaining visions to chosen men (e.g., Ezek 40–48; Zech 1–6).[32] Nevertheless, nothing quite prepares us for the explosion of interest in intermediary spirits in the Jewish literature of the early Hellenistic age. In the wake of the conquests of Alexander, explicit written reflection on angels massively intensifies, and it is coupled with a new concern for cataloguing the origins, names, nature, and purpose of demons.[33] Until recently, little could be said of this shift, in part because so little was known of the broader context or concerns of Jewish literary production in the period between the end of Achaemenid rule in the Land of Israel in the fourth century BCE and the beginnings of the tensions that lead to the Maccabean Revolt in the mid-second century BCE.[34]

Prior to the discovery of the Dead Sea Scrolls, the Maccabean-era Daniel was widely considered to be the first and paradigmatic apocalypse.[35] This chronology, however, was overturned with Milik's publication of the Aramaic Enoch fragments in 1976, which revealed the greater antiquity of both the *Astronomical Book* and *Book of the Watchers* (ca. third century BCE).[36] The ramifications for the history of

[32] Tigchelaar, *Prophets of Old*, 250–252; Himmelfarb, *Ascent to Heaven in Christian and Jewish Apocalypses*, 11–12, 73–74; Davidson, *Angels at Qumran*, 35; Schöpflin, "God's Interpreter," 188–198; Hartenstein, "Cherubim and Seraphim," 173–178; Macumber, "Angelic Intermediaries"; Melvin, *Interpreting Angel Motif*. Also notable is the prediction of God's "holy ones" accompanying him in the age of eschatological judgment in Zech 14:5.

[33] On the possibility that רוח הטמאה in Zech 13:2 already denotes a demonic power, see Lange, "Spirit of Impurity," 264–265. This relatively allusive association, however, still stands in stark contrast to the explicitly demonological lists, narratives, and aetiologies of a work like the *Book of the Watchers* (on which see Chapter 4).

[34] Even as recently as 2005, e.g., one could bemoan that "we lack the evidence to reconstruct Judaism in the third century BCE with any degree of certainty" – as I myself did in Reed, *Fallen Angels*, 58!

[35] The dominance of Daniel is an example of the broader pattern, noted by Mroczek (*Literary Imagination*, 15), whereby "the Bible and individual books set the agenda for the study of early Jewish literature...distort[ing] our reading of the ancient evidence."

[36] The Aramaic Enoch fragments from Qumran consist of seven manuscripts preserving the *Book of the Watchers* and other parts of *1 Enoch* (i.e., 4QEn[a-g]) – including copies containing this book by itself (esp. 4QEn[a]) and also compiled together with the *Book of Dreams* and *Epistle of Enoch* (esp. 4QEn[c]) – and also four other manuscripts that Milik

apocalypses have been explored for four decades, transforming our understanding of revelation and eschatology in Second Temple Judaism and early Christianity.[37] But no less significant – I suggest – are the ramifications for the beginnings of Jewish angelology and demonology. With the aid of these and other data from Dead Sea Scrolls, it is now newly possible to avoid the conflation of exilic and Persian-period trends with Hellenistic-era developments and to reassess the causes and contexts of this shift within Second Temple Judaism. New evidence, moreover, permits us to peer beyond the bounds of received canonical corpora – not least to situate Daniel itself in relation to its precedents in early Enochic and other Aramaic Jewish literature of the early Hellenistic age.

When we look beyond the Hebrew Bible to consider sources from the earliest "pseudepigrapha" and related Aramaic Dead Sea Scrolls, we find that most of the features conventionally deemed characteristic of "post-exilic" trends in the treatment of transmundane powers can be found in the Aramaic Jewish literature of the third and early second centuries BCE – long after the Exile but prior to Daniel. Daniel may feature the only hierarchy and naming of angels in the Hebrew Bible.[38] But decades before, as Bennie Reynolds has stressed, the *Book of the Watchers* lists seventeen distinct angelic personages in just a single chapter.[39] This work goes on to list seven additional figures by name as archangels, outline their functions, describe the heavenly abode of God and His angels in Temple-like terms, recount the transgressions of their fallen brethren and its effects on human history, and map the specific spaces at and beyond the ends of the earth where wayward angels and the spirits of the dead await final judgment. In its angelology, moreover, it is preceded by the even older *Astronomical Book*, which appeals to the angelic leader of the

---

identified as containing only the *Astronomical Book*, always copied by itself (i.e., 4Q208–4Q211). For the fragments see Milik, *Books of Enoch*, 273–297 and plates XXV–XXX; Stuckenbruck in DJD 36, 3–7; Tigchelaar and García Martínez in DJD 36, 95–171; Drawnel, *The Aramaic Astronomical Book from Qumran*. For Milik's discussion of dating, see *Books of Enoch*, 7–22, and for a recent reassessment, Drawnel, *Aramaic Astronomical Book*, 73.

[37] For syntheses thereof see Collins, *Apocalyptic Imagination*; Himmelfarb, *Apocalypse*.

[38] Olyan, *Thousand Thousands*, 17–18. There are intermediate spirits elsewhere in biblical literature that bear what could be read as titles (e.g., angel of the Lord in Exod 23:20–21; destroying angel in 2 Sam 24:16/1 Chron 21:15; angel of the covenant in Mal 3:1; angel of His presence in Isa 63:9; *satan* in Job 1–2; Zech 3; 1 Chron 21:1), but Daniel is the only biblical text in which "a sense of hierarchy has emerged, since archangels are distinguished."

[39] I.e., *1 En* 6; Reynolds, "Understanding the Demonologies," 103.

celestial luminaries, Uriel, to articulate astronomical and calendrical concerns that are also unprecedented in biblical literature.

Already by the third century BCE, the *Astronomical Book* and the *Book of the Watchers* distinguish between different classes of some what we now call "angels" (e.g., Watchers [עירין], holy ones [קדישין]),[40] and they attach personal names to a number of specific angels, both heavenly and fallen.[41] Just as the *Book of the Watchers* includes lists of the names of fallen angels and archangels, so the *Book of the Giants* soon extends this naming, agency, and personalization to the Watchers' hybrid sons.[42] The *Astronomical Book* and *Book of the Watchers* both dwell upon the place of angels within the cosmos and human history, and especially in the case of the *Book of the Watchers*, this concern extends also to fallen angels and evil spirits, occasioning the theorization of the acts and domains proper to creatures of spirit and creatures of flesh. In both, moreover, angels are charged with the governance of celestial and natural phenomena, and stars and winds are associated with angels and spirits with differing degrees of directness – ranging from the apparent equation of the two to the use of the former as a metaphor for the latter.[43] In addition,

---

[40] The relevant Aramaic fragments attest references to "sons of heaven," "holy ones" (קדישין), and "Watchers of heaven" (עירין די שמיא) or simply "Watchers." In the Greek and Ethiopic versions of these texts, we often find the terms commonly used to translate Hebrew *mal'ak* (Gr. ἄγγελος; Eth. *mal'ak*), but the equivalent Aramaic term does not appear among the surviving fragments. It is unclear whether this is an accident of preservation or whether this reflects a later shift in terminology. There are some cases where an Aramaic fragment reads עירין and the Greek and Ethiopic translations read ἄγγελοι and *malā'ekt* respectively, likely reflecting the later association of the term עירין with the fallen Watchers in particular; see further Nickelsburg, *1 Enoch 1*, 43–44, 140–141. On the term "watcher" (Aram. עיר; Gr. ἐγρήγοροι; Eth. *teguh*) as the name for angels and/or members of a specific class of angel, see Dimant, "Fallen Angels," 32–33; Davidson, *Angels at Qumran*, 38–39, and compare Daniel 4.

[41] Black, "Twenty Angelic Dekadarchs."

[42] Some of these names draw on Mesopotamian mythology (esp. Gilgamesh epic); Stuckenbruck, "Giant Mythology," 320–337.

[43] Although we do find an appeal to the cycles of stars and seasons as a model for human righteousness in the Nature Poem at the beginning of the *Book of the Watchers* (*1 En* 2–5), these cycles are not explicitly linked to angels, as they are in the *Astronomical Book* (75:3; 75:1; 80:1; 82:13). Indeed, the association between Nature and angels is far more fraught in the *Book of the Watchers*. Some of the names of the fallen angels are derived from astronomical bodies and meteorological phenomena (6:7), and they are credited with corrupting humankind by teaching of divination from lightning, stars, shooting stars, earth, sun, and moon (8:3). An association of angels and stars may be implicit in 18:15–16, but that passage occurs in the context of the stars' transgression of their appointed tasks and their resultant imprisonment. Only the passing reference to the "paths of the angels" in 18:5, in the context of the movement of the winds, may

the *Book of the Watchers* describes angels as serving a priest-like function in heaven.[44] Archangels hear prayers said on earth, look down from heaven, and intercede with God on behalf of humankind (8:4–9.11; cf. Zech 1–2); one of their kind, Sariel, is even entrusted with the task of informing Noah of the impending Flood, thus acting on God's behalf to save him and his family from destruction (10:1–3). Likewise, the Enochic *Book of Dreams* and *Epistle of Enoch* (second century BCE) include allusions to the fallen angels as well as angelic scribes, shepherds, teachers, and Watchers of humankind.

Nor are such interests limited to Enochic writings. The Book of Tobit, also written in Aramaic (ca. 225–175 BCE?), specifies the names of both archangelic intercessor (i.e., Raphael) and demonic foe (i.e., Asmodeus).[45] Its narrative includes an explicit account of exorcism – a practice that is possibly also associated with Abraham in the roughly contemporaneous *Genesis Apocryphon*.[46] In the *Aramaic Levi Document* (third century BCE) and *Visions of Amram* (early second century BCE?), we find early expressions of the idea of "two spirits" – good and evil – struggling in cosmic opposition, and *Aramaic Levi* may also provide us with our earliest explicit example of the interpretation of *satan* as an unequivocally demonic power, from whom one might pray for protection.[47] The highly fragmentary but intriguing Aramaic *Words of Michael* (4Q529; 6Q23) even seems to be framed as "the words of the book which Michael addressed the angels," presumably referring to the archangel of that name; it makes mention of Gabriel as well.[48]

Here as elsewhere, new evidence thus yields new opportunities. As more and more materials from the Dead Sea Scrolls have been published, our knowledge of the Jewish literature of the early Hellenistic age has been radically expanded. "Before the Dead Sea Scrolls were found," as Armin Lange observes, "33 of the 38 non-biblical pre-Maccabean texts from Qumran were known only in part or not at all."[49] Not only do these

---

preserve a trace of a more positive association between angels and natural cycles. See further Chapter 3.

[44] Esp. *1 En* 14:8–25; Himmelfarb, *Ascent to Heaven*, 20–23.

[45] Nowell, "The 'Work' of the Angel Raphael"; Reiterer, "Archangel's Theology"; Owens, "Asmodeus"; Ego, "Den er liebt sie"; Barker, "Archangel Raphael." Notably, the demonic name Asmodeus is Persian in origin.

[46] On their relationship see Perrin, "Tobit's Context and Contacts in the Qumran Aramaic Anthology"; Machiela and Perrin, "Tobit and the *Genesis Apocryphon*."

[47] Greenfield, Stone, and Eshel, *Aramaic Levi Document*, 21, 30–31.

[48] See further Puech in DJD 31:1–8.   [49] Lange, "Pre-Maccabean Literature," 285.

materials help to fill a long-standing gap in our knowledge of Second Temple Judaism, but they provide significant evidence for the prominence of Aramaic in Jewish literary production under Ptolemaic and Seleucid rule.[50] Even if the evidence does not permit any certain conclusions about presectarian provenance for most or all of the many Aramaic manuscripts attested at Qumran – most of which are simply too fragmentary to date – the prominence of Aramaic in these materials remains striking. These materials, as Daniel Machiela notes, attest "a cluster of Jewish writings later than the principally Hebrew literature that would eventually coalesce into the canonical Hebrew Scriptures (and the Christian Old Testament"), yet largely earlier than the principally Hebrew compositions of the Hasmonean and Herodian periods (i.e., *Jubilees*, 1 Maccabees, and the sectarian Dead Sea Scrolls)."[51] As Machiela, Devora Dimant, Andrew Perrin, and others have richly shown, this literature thus allows us to recover a formative yet forgotten renaissance of Jewish literary production, particularly in Aramaic, in the early Hellenistic age.[52]

BEYOND "HELLENISM" AND "JUDAISM"

If the history of the Jews in the century of Ptolemaic rule over the Land of Israel (ca. 301–200 BCE) remains a mystery, it is in part because there were few sources prior to the discoveries at Qumran but also in part because shifts within pre-Maccabean materials have been commonly conflated with later texts, ideas, and developments.[53] The Maccabean

---

[50] See Klaus Beyerm's three-volume *Die aramäischen Texte* and Émile Puech's two *Textes Araméens* volumes (i.e., DJD 31 and 37) as well as discussion in Dimant, "Qumran Aramaic Texts"; Dimant, "Themes and Genres"; Tigchelaar, "Aramaic Texts from Qumran"; García Martínez, "Scribal Practices in Aramaic Texts"; Berthelot and Stökl ben Ezra, *Aramaica Qumranica*.

[51] Machiela, "Aramaic Writings of the Second Temple Period and the Growth of Apocalyptic Thought," 114–115.

[52] See above and also Machiela, "Situating the Aramaic Texts from Qumran"; Machiela, "The Aramaic Dead Sea Scrolls"; Perrin, "The Aramaic Imagination"; Perrin, *Dynamics of Dream-Vision Revelation*. Notably, much of this discussion has centered on what this new material might tell us about the origins of a Jewish and Christian apocalyptic "outlook" or "worldview" – an issue that I here sidestep, as noted above, by virtue of my experimentation with a more synchronic approach (cf. Grabbe, "Seleucidic and Hasmonean Periods").

[53] Elsewhere, I have pointed to the tendency to interpret the *Book of the Watchers* in terms of the more separatist sentiments found in Enochic writings from the Maccabean era, such as the "Animal Apocalypse" (Reed, *Fallen Angels*, 58–83; Reed, "The Textual Identity, Literary History, and Social Setting of *1 Enoch*," 290–291; see also Himmelfarb,

Revolt (ca. 167–164 BCE) looms large in the study of Second Temple
Judaism – not least because of its aftermath, which included the return of
native rule to the Land of Israel under the Hasmoneans, the emergence of
sectarian groups like the Qumran *yaḥad*, and the spread of competing
visions of Israel such as those of Pharisees, Sadducees, John the Baptist,
and Jesus. The century prior to the Revolt, by contrast, tends to be
characterized somewhat telegraphically – often with recourse to the trope
of the conflict of "Hellenism" and "Judaism" famous from the descriptions of events in the mid-170s BCE within even later sources (e.g. 2 Macc
4:7–17).[54]

The tendency to read the third century BCE as preface to the Revolt has
been revived most recently in a line of research interpreting ancient Jewish
apocalypses as "resistance literature." The applicability of this approach to
Maccabean-era historical apocalypses like Daniel, "Apocalypse of Weeks,"
and "Animal Apocalypse" is amply demonstrated in the recent monographs
on the topic by Richard Horsley and Anathea Portier-Young.[55] Both critique
the blinkered isolationism of much past research on apocalypses, and they
model the value of situating these texts within their socio-historical contexts.
But to the degree that they reinscribe the traditional privileging of Daniel –
the only apocalypse in the Hebrew Bible – as a paradigmatic apocalypse,
they also run the risk of conflating pre-Maccabean and Maccabean-era
sources and circumstances. In both Horsley's *Revolt of the Scribes* and
Portier-Young's *Apocalypse against Empire*, for instance, the *Astronomical
Book* is treated in passing, and even the *Book of the Watchers* is adduced
mainly as precursor to developments that culminate with Daniel.[56]

To reconstruct the imperialism that the Jewish authors of these early
apocalypses purportedly resist, moreover, Portier-Young draws heavily

---

A Kingdom of Priests, 40–45; Collins, "Transformation of Torah," 456). Much the same
might be said for the "scientific" concerns with lunar, solar, and other cycles attested in the
Astronomical Book, which have suffered from their conflation with the calendrical
controversies of later times.

[54] On this tendency and for a broader critique, see Schwartz, *Imperialism and Jewish
Society*, 23–24. Notably, the contrast is not even as clear as it might seem in 2
Maccabees – a text which, as Himmelfarb has shown, is itself "at once Jewish in its
piety and Greek in its mode of expression"; "Judaism and Hellenism in 2
Maccabees," 20.

[55] Horsley, *Revolt of the Scribes*, 19–104; Portier-Young, *Apocalypse against Empire*.
Especially valuable in this regard is Portier-Young's detailed engagement with
interdisciplinary theories about imperial resistance (3–48).

[56] Horsley, *Revolt of the Scribes*, 47–62; Portier-Young, *Apocalypse against Empire*, 15–23,
286–312.

upon the retrospective accounts of the Maccabean Revolt in 1 and 2 Maccabees – even to the degree of treating the latter's construction of "Judaism" and "Hellenism" as reflecting "real tensions" throughout the entire period of Hellenistic rule.[57] Yet there is little evidentiary support for retrojecting 1–2 Maccabees' accounts of the crisis in the mid-170s BCE onto the prior century of Ptolemaic rule (ca. 301–200 BCE). Writing of this period, for instance, Seth Schwartz observes that "although the history of Yehud/Judaea ... in much of the period is obscure, the apparent institutional stability of Judaea suggests that the impression of calm created by the silence of the sources, preceding the well-attested dynamism and disorder of the two-and-a-half centuries beginning in 170 BCE, is no mirage."[58] Partly as a result, he questions the scholarly tendency to frame "Hellenism as a defining issue in Jewish society after 332 BCE" and the assumption that "differing attitudes to Hellenism ... generated social fissures and even conflict" even in the Ptolemaic period.[59] Culling pre-Maccabean literature for clues to reactions to Hellenization yields scant results: "it demonstrates that the search in Jewish sources for Greek influence and native resistance in the form of opposition to Hellenism is largely misguided."[60] Schwartz thus calls, instead, for "a more subtle search for cultural reorientation."[61]

---

[57] This is most extensive in Portier-Young, *Apocalypse against Empire*, 49–77, where the early Hellenistic period is analyzed for the sake of "Setting the Stage for Resistance." Her superb study suffers, in my view, from taking the accounts of 1–2 Maccabees too much at face value. Her focus on Antiochus' "motives" as centered on a deliberate "program of terror" to "unmake the Judean world" (216), for instance, fits well with the rhetorical representation of empire within the retrospective accounts of 1–2 Maccabees but is less plausible from the historical perspective of what we know of the logistics of administering the vast Seleucid empire. It may be worth recalling the caution offered already by Susan Sherwin-White and Amélie Kuhrt against the scholarship tendency to read non-Greek sources of the early Hellenistic age through automatic assumptions of a stance of resistance to Hellenistic rule; "it is hard to believe that foreign rule, as such, was a *new* reason for resistance since the Achaemenid empire had already established a long-lived suzerainty over the people and places comprising the Seleucid empire," they note, stressing also that "the nexus 'oppression-rebellion'... is, after all, an unsatisfactory simplification" (*From Samarkhand to Sardis*, 137). For a more nuanced approach to the Maccabean Revolt in relation to what we now of the Seleucid empire and native responses to its spread even beyond Judaea, see Kosmin, *Time and Its Adversaries in the Seleucid Empire*, 219–228.

[58] Schwartz, *Imperialism*, 22.   [59] Schwartz, *Imperialism*, 22–36, quote at 23.

[60] Schwartz, *Imperialism*, 31. Notably, in his more recent work (*The Ancient Jews from Alexander to Muhammad*, 35–36), Schwartz dismisses the effects of Hellenization on "the handful of Jerusalemite literate elites who were responsible for all the surviving writing in Hebrew and Aramaic" and looks instead to "others, at or beyond the fringes of the clerisy, who had a more direct experience of what a Greek empire meant" such as the Tobiads.

[61] Schwartz, *Imperialism*, 31.

In what follows, I suggest that we might see something of this subtler cultural reorientation in the Aramaic Jewish scribal pedagogy of the period, which the Aramaic Dead Sea Scrolls now enable us to reconstruct. The texts of this corpus, as John J. Collins notes, "are often thought to be presectarian, and most of them surely are," and "they are part of the literary heritage of the third and early second centuries BCE."[62] Furthermore, as Collins has shown, they exhibit enough differences from Maccabean-era and later writings that this corpus can serve as a source of evidence for charting changes within Judaism before and after the Revolt – and, I shall further suggest below, perhaps under Ptolemaic and Seleucid rule as well.[63]

Frustratingly fragmentary but surprisingly extensive, the Aramaic Dead Sea Scrolls help to reveal the broader contexts of previously known works like the *Book of the Watchers*, Tobit, and Daniel, while also dramatically expanding our evidentiary base for understanding Judaism in the early Hellenistic age – prior to the Maccabean Revolt, on the one hand, and the establishment of the Qumran *yaḥad* on the other. In the process, attention to this newly recovered corpus may aid us in situating shifts within Jewish scribal cultures within the broader cultural milieu of the Hellenistic Near East in a manner that moves beyond old reified contrasts of "Hellenism" and "Judaism." Indeed, the repurposing of the Achaemenid administrative language of Aramaic as a Jewish literary language may be a telling datum in its own right for signaling the complexity of cultural reorientations among ancient Jews – not least because it seems to intensify, not in the Persian period as one might expect, but rather with the advent of Hellenistic rule across the Near East, and particularly under the Ptolemies. So too, as we shall see, with the textualization of a variety of topics and materials unrepresented in the Hebrew Bible but richly paralleled in Mesopotamia and elsewhere in the Near East.

[62] Collins, "Transformation of Torah," 456; on his logic here, see further Collins, "Aramaic Texts," 548–549, 552–555. On Aramaic DSS as presumably "non-sectarian" and hence often "pre-sectarian," see Dimant, "Qumran Aramaic Texts," 198–199; Puech, "Du bilinguisme"; Ben-Dov, "Scientific Writings in Aramaic and Hebrew," 360. Although the correlation cannot serve as a blanket assumption, it does seem to be a general pattern – or, at least, enough so that our understanding of post-Persian, pre-Maccabean Palestine hinges on attention to Aramaic materials understood on their own right, rather than read through the lens of later Hebrew materials.
[63] Collins, "Transformation of Torah," 458.

"Concentrating on Qumran Aramaic literature," as Devora Dimant has shown, "has the merit of remaining within a relatively homogenous corpus, well defined from the literary and historical points of view."[64] To focus on this corpus, moreover, is to reveal some of what has been missed in the tendency to read "pseudepigrapha" diachronically through the rubric of genre. The *Book of the Watchers*, for instance, has been studied largely from the perspective of apocalypses and apocalypticism – and hence in a trajectory with Daniel and Revelation as well as the later works compiled in *1 Enoch*.[65] Here and after, I build upon the ample research on apocalypses that revolutionized our understanding of Second Temple Judaism since the late 1970s,[66] but I do not take apocalypses, apocalyptic worldviews, or apocalypticism as my main analytical lens. I attempt, rather, is to situate the beginnings of Jewish angelology and demonology in the third and early second centuries BCE, and I thus experiment instead with a synchronic approach that cuts across the retrospective divides of literary genres like the apocalypse and testament.[67]

SCRIBES, TEXTUALITY, AND TEACHING IN ARAMAIC DEAD SEA SCROLLS

The Aramaic Jewish literature of the early Hellenistic age includes many of the earliest known Jewish writings outside of the Hebrew Bible, but they do not bear marks of a self-consciously "post-biblical" belatedness. In many of them, in fact, we find quite the opposite – namely, the assertion of continuity with and from the biblical past, stretching back even beyond moments of rupture like the Flood. Perhaps most telling, in this regard, is a cluster of precedents to the literary genre of the testament, now known from the Aramaic Dead Sea Scrolls.

---

[64] Dimant, "Themes and Genres," 16.

[65] On how much is lost when works like the *Book of the Watchers* are studied only through the lens of "generic definitions based on heterogenous specimens, coming from different regions and different historical periods," see esp. Dimant, "Themes and Genres," 16.

[66] I.e., especially in the wake of the appearance of *Semeia* 14 in 1979; see esp. Collins, "The Jewish Apocalypses"; Collins, "Apocalyptic Technique"; Collins, *Apocalyptic Imagination* – as well as the recent reassessment in *DSD* 17.3 (2010).

[67] It remains been debated, for instance, whether the *Astronomical Book* formally counts as an "apocalypse" (VanderKam, "Book of Luminaries," 359, 367–368; Collins, *Apocalyptic Imagination*, 59–62), and this work – as we shall see in Chapter 3 – also challenges us to think beyond our modern categories of "religion" and "science." On *Jubilees* in relation to apocalypses, see now Hanneken, *The Subversion of Apocalypses in the Book of Jubilees*.

The genre of the testament is characterized by the textualized dramatization of the moment at which a biblical patriarch or prophet, sensing his impending death, calls his progeny around him so as to pass along his final teachings. Even before the discovery of the Dead Sea Scrolls, this genre was known from much later "pseudepigrapha" like the *Testaments of the 12 Patriarchs*.[68] Consistent with the dominance of source-critical studies thereof, the discovery of related fragments among the Dead Sea Scrolls was initially met with excitement about the possibility of recovering the sources behind them (esp. *Aramaic Levi Document* for *Testament of Levi*). When analyzed on their own terms, however, these fragments prove just as illuminating for Jewish memory, scribalism, and literary production in the early Hellenistic age.[69]

Works like the *Testaments of the 12 Patriarchs* took form in Greek under Roman rule, during the first two centuries CE, and their depiction of deathbed teaching reflects ideas about death and teaching that intersect with Roman trends of the time.[70] What we now know as their earlier precedents, by contrast, took form in Aramaic in the third or second centuries BCE, and are marked by quite different ideas of textuality and pedagogy. When the only testaments known were the later examples in Greek from the first and second centuries CE, the appeal to deathbed speeches could be assumed to be an interest with exemplary figures of righteousness, such as Abraham and Job, and/or on figures that can serve as positive and negative *exempla*, such as the sons of Jacob. What we see now that we have their Aramaic precedents from the third and second centuries BCE, however, is that this genre of writing about teaching at death was initially just as much about writing as about teaching – and perhaps especially about death as metonym for rupture and the power of writing to resist it.[71]

To textualize deathbed teaching in a testament is to invoke an ideal of intergenerational familial transmission (e.g., father–son) as a didactic

---

[68] The full-fledged genre is not attested in full form until the first century CE. Yet one finds an intensification of testamentary tropes within Second Temple Judaism that begins in the literature of the early Hellenistic age (esp. third and second centuries BCE; e.g., Tobit 14; *1 En* 79:1; 81:1–82:4; 83:1; 85.1; 91:1–3; *Jub* 21; 36). Other examples include 1 Maccabees 2:49–70, *LAB* 19, 23–24, and 33; *2 Enoch* 14–18; *2 Baruch* 43–47. See further Collins, "Testaments," 329; Reed, "Textuality."

[69] See further Reed, "Textuality between Death and Memory."

[70] I.e., including an emphasis on teaching from *exempla* as well as the popularization of wills and testaments and a broader Roman surge in the "epigraphical habit" of monumentalizing the dead; Reed, "Textuality."

[71] I here summarize an argument that I make in more detail in Reed, *"Textuality."*

ideal, narrative frame, and literary occasion. Yet the very act of textualizing this ideal belies some anxiety about the adequacy of the characteristic orality of familial teaching to ensure the trustworthy preservation of knowledge across generations. This points to a major difference, then, with what is usually cited as its main biblical precedent – namely, Genesis 49. Jacob's blessings of his sons are there reported without any self-reference to the writtenness of the form in which the reader encounters them; there is no explanation of how they came to be written down, nor explicit explanation of who present might have done so. In fact, there is no reference anywhere in Genesis to writing of the sort that could explain who among the gathered would have even been able to transcribe such words into writing or transmit such writings such that they survive intact into the time of the reader. In the Torah/Pentateuch, writing may be mentioned in relation to the life and death of Moses, but not so at the death of Abraham, nor the death of Isaac, nor the death of Jacob, nor even the death of the Egyptianized Joseph. As in most of biblical literature, rather, the text's own textuality is as if invisible, and the agency of its own scribal agents is effaced.

How did Moses learn to write, and from whom? This is a question that even Deuteronomy leaves unanswered and unexplained. But this is also precisely the question answered by proto-testamentary texts among the Aramaic Dead Sea Scrolls. The *Visions of Amram* (4Q543–547),[72] for instance, introduces itself in its first line as a "Copy [פרשגן] of the writing of the words of the Visions of Amram, son of Qahat, some of Levi, that he revealed to his sons and what he advised them on the day of his death" (4Q543 1; 4Q545 1a i; 4Q546 1).[73] Thus it also rewrites Amram, father of Moses (Exod 6:18; Num 3:17–19), as a scribe and author. Amram does not only describe his dream-visions, for instance, but stresses that he himself "wrote" it down right after having dreamt it, as "I awoke from the sleep of my eyes."[74]

Related testamentary writings are attributed to the rest of the figures cited in its first line, again with explicit references to writing that reframe

---

[72] For the text, Puech, *Qumrân Grotte 4XXII*, 283–406. On its structure, Drawnel, "Initial Narrative," 525–526.

[73] The Aramaic term פרשגן occurs also in Ezra (4:11, 23; 5:6; 7:11) to refer to a copy of a letter, and in Esther (3:14; 4:8; 8:13), to a written transcript of a decree. In LXX Esther, it is rendered by Greek ἀντίγραφον – the same term used in the formulaic openings each to the twelve sections of the *Testaments of 12 Patriarchs*.

[74] On the vision, see Duke, *The Social Location of the Visions of Amram*, 19–25.

each of them as scribes. In *Admonitions of Qahat* (4Q542),[75] it is Amram's father who is the first-person voice, and he commands his sons to take care of "the inheritance which your fathers gave you," which includes "truth, justice, uprightness, perfection, purity, holiness, and the priesthood," but also "all my writings as witness that you should take care of them" (4Q542 1 ii 10–12).

And so too for Levi in the *Aramaic Levi Document*. The deathbed teachings of Levi are of concern also in the *Testament of Levi* and in a manner marked by notable source-critical connections. But the death of Levi meant something quite different in the third century BCE than in the second century CE. Of Levi it is here stressed, as for Qahat, that he learned "reading and writing and the teaching of wisdom," and that his sons "will inherit them" (ALD 13.15), and he commands "my sons," in turn, to transmit "reading and writing [ספר]"[76] and "the teaching of wisdom [מוסר חכמה] to your children" (ALD 13.4–5). When Levi writes of what he himself learned from his forefathers, moreover, it includes teachings from Jacob and Isaac (e.g., law of the priesthood; ALD 6.1–10.14) but also teachings that "Abraham commanded me" from what "he discovered in the book of Noah" (ALD 10.10). The moment of teaching in preparation for death is here an occasion for assurances about continuance in the face of rupture. Reading, writing, and books here loom large as emblems that ensure that continuance.

In these Aramaic texts from the early Hellenistic age, scribal literacy is asserted to be central to the inheritance passed from Abraham, Isaac, and Jacob to Levi, as from Levi to his son Qahat, and from Qahat to his son Amram, and – it is thus implied – to Amram's son Moses as well. Moses' writing, during life and prior to his own death, is retrospectively provided with a chain of precedents from his father Amram to his grandfather Qahat to his great-grandfather Levi before them. The implication is that the memory of these men, and their own forefathers, was preserved in trustworthy forms *in writing*, even across the rupture of the family's entry and enslavement in Egypt. It is precisely by highlighting the linkage of genealogy, succession, and knowledge that connects Moses to Levi, via Amram and Qahat, that these works interweave scribal literacy,

---

[75] This work survives in a single fragment from around the end of the second century BCE. For the text, see Puech, "Le testament de Qahat"; for discussion, Drawnel, "The Literary Form and Didactic Content of the 'Admonitions (Testament) of Qahat'." I here follow the English translation in García Martínez and Tigchelaar, *DSS Study Edition*, 2:1083.

[76] Drawnel renders the term as "scribal craft."

priesthood, emulation, and wisdom as threads of continuity both backward from Moses to Abraham and forward from Moses to the reader/hearer in the early Hellenistic age.

SCRIBALIZING MOSES AND JEWISH KNOWLEDGE

To be sure, the scribalization of Moses does have some precedent already in the Torah/Pentateuch, especially in relation to teaching and succession. The contrast is thus instructive. When textuality is first mentioned in the narrative of the Torah/Pentateuch, it is in relation to the transmission of memory from Moses to Joshua (Exod 17:14; cf. Deut 25:17). Especially after Exodus 24, the linkage of writing with the maintenance of transgenerational memory becomes a recurrent theme: Moses is portrayed as one who writes down words spoken by God (24:4; 34:28), seemingly at his own initiative but in a manner increasingly paralleled by divine acts of covenantal writing (Exod 24:12; 32:15–16; 34:1; Deut 4:13; 5:22; 9:10; 10:2, 4). Likewise, throughout Deuteronomy, references to reading and writing serve to explain how Moses' *torah* (lit. "teaching") came to be passed on to those after him.[77]

Such passages proved enormously influential in shaping later ideas about Scripture, especially when reread in terms of a modern sense of the bookishness of the Bible.[78] Throughout both the Torah/Pentateuch as well as the historical books of the Hebrew Bible, however, textuality is not the only or dominant technology of either teaching or memory. If anything, reading bears an ambivalent status: reliance on texts for preserving teaching comes with the threat of their physical loss – a danger embodied by the divinely inscribed tablets destroyed at Sinai in Exodus 32 as well as by the long-forgotten scroll of Moses' *torah* said to be rediscovered in 2 Kings 22.[79] Just as the fate of the tablets signals a sense of the fragility of writing as a physical instantiation of divine speech, so the fate of Moses' *torah* also points to a perception of textuality that differs strikingly from the equation of writing and permanence common in the modern West: the scroll that is archived is there not treated as

---

[77] On writing in Deuteronomy, see Schaper, "A Theology of Writing," 99, there stressing how "the importance of writing is stressed all the way through Deuteronomy, right across the boundaries demarcated by classic literarkritische investigations."

[78] On what is lost in the process see Mroczek, *Literary Imagination*.

[79] Indeed, one of the most striking features of the books explicitly mentioned in the Hebrew Bible is how often they are lost and destroyed; see now Rainbow, "Textual Loss."

knowledge that is possessed or accessible to all, but rather as akin to knowledge lost – with the attendant dangers of straying from the covenantal obligations therein inscribed for remembrance.

This is consistent with the treatment of reading and writing throughout the Torah/Pentateuch, wherein the physical text is presented as a record of speech that gains power through speech and memory. That text is hand-maiden to speech is communicated both from the semantic field of קרא, the Biblical Hebrew verb "to read," and from the narrative representation of reading throughout the Hebrew Bible. The verb קרא can mean reading, calling, proclaiming, or inviting; "the whole semantic field," as Daniel Boyarin stresses, "is that of speech acts."[80]

Far from modern notions of literature as privately read for leisure and pleasure, this public and oral reading is the ideal of textuality that is elevated in and by the Torah/Pentateuch.[81] Even when writing is first mentioned in Exodus 17:14, for instance, it is in the context of a divine instruction to "write as a reminder in a book" (כתב זאת זכרון בספר) to "recite it in the hearing [lit. put in the ears] of Joshua. Likewise, when Exodus later describes how Moses heard, repeated, and wrote commandments from God (24:3–4), it stresses how he then "took the record [lit. book] of the covenant and read it aloud to [lit. in the ears of] the people," who then respond as if they had heard God's own speech: "All that the Lord has spoken we will do and heed" (24:7). It is also with a sense of the purpose of writing as record and reminder that Deuteronomy self-referentially warns of what will occur "if you do not diligently observe all the words of this *torah* [lit. teaching] that are written in this book" (28:58) while promising prosperity "when you heed the voice of the Lord your God (כי תשמע בקול יהוה אלהיך) by observing his commandments and decrees that are written in the book of this *torah* (בספר התורה הזה)" (30:10).[82]

---

[80] Boyarin, "Placing Reading," 12. I here follow his approach of culling "scenes of reading" from texts toward an "ethnography of reading"; the effectiveness of this approach, notably, is not predicated on the historical accuracy of the events described, inasmuch as it culls the verisimilitude of the narratives themselves, also with an eye to semantic fields of the specific terms therein used. To Boyarin's examples we might add Isa 29:18, which describes the Day of the Lord as a time when "the deaf shall hear the words of a scroll" – presuming, it seems, that sight alone does not suffice to "read."

[81] Boyarin, "Placing Reading," 10–11.

[82] This notion of writing as aid to memory and script for speech is similarly clear in the passing of succession to Joshua; God's call to him in the beginning of the work "to act in accordance with all the law that my servant Moses commanded you" (1:7) there includes the instruction that "the book of this *torah* shall not depart from your mouth (לא־ימוש ספר התורה הזה מפיך)" (1:8). Later, Joshua is depicted as having built an

Yet this ideal of the succession of teaching – as passing smoothly from man to man by divine command, ratified by public reading and monumental writing – is also the ideal from which the Deuteronomistic History depicts decline in the age of the divided monarchy. It may be tempting to treat 2 Kings 22 as a narrative about the importance of the textualized *torah*, inasmuch as it recounts how the high priest Hilkiah "found the book of the *torah* in the house of the Lord" during the reign of Josiah (22:8), leading to the realization that the disasters that had befallen Israel had resulted from the forgetting of the covenantal obligations inscribed therein. But the narrative is predicated on the limits of writing to ensure memory: it was when the contents of this book fell from mouth and memory that people cease from acting "as prescribed in this book of the covenant," and it was not until the king "established the words of the *torah* that were written in the book that the priest Hilkiah had found in the house of the Lord" that the covenant was renewed (23:24). The archived book here emblematizes lost knowledge, and the account of its recovery is a story about the reactivation of writing through oral recitation: Hilkiah gives the scroll to the scribe Shaphan to read, after which the scribe also "read it before the king" (22:10), who "heard the scroll of the *torah*" and asked the priests to "inquire of the Lord on my behalf" (22:13). That writing and reading does not suffice to vouchsafe this knowledge, moreover, is underlined by the need for confirmation by a prophetess and divine oracle (22:14–20). In early biblical literature, it is this ideal of reading as a "public, oral and illocutionary speech-act" that is represented as enabling written words to live in hearing, memory, and action.

Especially in light of what we know of the limited literacy in ancient cultures, it seems plausible that this literary representation of reading reflects something of the social reality of how most Israelites likely interacted with books – through the ear and not the eyes.[83] This makes it all the more striking, however, that it effaces precisely the power and agency of those who made this interaction possible. Skills of writing and reading

---

unhewn stone altar on Mount Ebal "as is written in the book of Moses' *torah*" (ככתוב בספר תורת משה; 8:30–31) and as inscribing a copy on the stones themselves, writing (כתב) it before the people and then reading (קרא) it to them (8:32–34). Such acts, however, are not presented as part of Joshua's regular activities as much as evoked as emblems of smooth succession (8:35). Accordingly, thereafter, writing need not be evoked again until the narrative nears Joshua's own death (24:25 –27).

[83] See Carr, *Writing on the Tablet*, also for comparative data concerning ancient texts as aids to the internalization of information through memory.

need to be taught, and even if most people did not have them, someone must write that which is read to them, copy the words to ensure their survival, and recite it aloud to be heard. Yet in most early biblical literature – including the narrativized scenes of reading and writing therein – scribes are either omitted or reduced to secondary actors.[84]

The very writtenness of biblical literature belies the role of scribes in mediating the succession of knowledge attributed to the written teachings of Moses and Joshua as heard, remembered, and heeded by the people Israel and its kings. On the basis of the dynamics of legal revision within Deuteronomy, for instance, Bernard Levinson shows how the "ineluctable connection between religious renewal and textual reworking brings into clear focus the role of the technically trained scribe as the agent of cultural change."[85] But this makes it all the more striking that the scribes responsible for early biblical literature did not mark their own authorial or editorial agency. Rather, as Levinson stresses:

> In the Hebrew Bible, not a single text, legal or otherwise, is definitively attributed to the actual scribe responsible for its composition ... Except for the prophets, biblical authors never speak explicitly in their own voice. Instead they employ pseudonyms or write anonymously.[86]

---

[84] Passing references to scribes place them as fixtures in the Temple and palace, just as passing references to the practice of writing suggest that it was used for a wide range of purposes in ancient Israel, as elsewhere in the ancient Mediterranean world. The use of writing to record military exploits, for instance, is suggested by the quotation from the "Book of the Wars of the Lord" in Num 21:13–15; its use in relation to land-surveying is mentioned in Joshua 18:9 and its use in genealogical records in Neh 7:5. Letter-writing is mentioned in 2 Sam 11:14 and elsewhere, and mention is made of the practice of transcribing songs for the purpose of teaching them to the people in 2 Sam 1:18. Most extensive, and perhaps most telling, are the repeated references to written chronicles of monarchic events in 1 and 2 Kings, which repeatedly point the reader to what is inscribed as record in the "Book of the Acts of Solomon" (ספר דברי שלמה), the "Book of the Annals of the Kings of Israel" (ספר דברי הימים למלכי ישראל), and "Book of the Annals of the Kings of Judah" (ספר דברי הימים למלכי יהודה). Such references attest the use of writing to add to progressively expanded monarchic records and the practice of archiving of such materials – in contrast to the ideal of writing and reading as social speech-act noted above. Consequently, they also betray the character of 1–2 Kings as themselves the products of acts of literary shaping and selectivity from a broader body of written materials. Such references thus hint at the range of activities pursued by the otherwise self-hidden scribes who shaped what we now know as the biblical tradition – perhaps including the maintenance of such monarchic records and other types of documents as well as using access to such archives to create new works meant for hearing and remembering.

[85] Levinson, *Legal Revision and Religious Renewal in Ancient Israel*, 89.

[86] Levinson, *Legal Revision*, 28.

Levinson posits this pattern as closely connected to a distinctive feature of ancient Israelite legal discourse: "The concept of divine revelation of law [which] distinguishes Israelite religion from all of the other religions of the ancient Near East."[87] Yet, as he notes, the "erasure of the identity of the human author extends far beyond legal texts in the Bible."[88] The implied guarantor of the stability and permanence of what is written is not the royal or civic archive, temple library, or even scribal school, but rather the divine source claimed for the teachings, as activated on earth within the speech, memory, and deeds of the people who hear and heed them.[89]

It is here where Hellenistic-era Aramaic works like the *Aramaic Levi Document*, *Admonitions of Qahat*, and *Visions of Amram* mark a radical shift. It is not just that scribes become visible. Scribes are here explicitly asserted as the true custodians of Israel's divinely revealed heritage of knowledge ever since the pre-Sinaitic past. There is a sense, of course, in which even such claims are predicated on the precariousness of writing. It is the reality of textual loss that grounds the plausibility of the very claim that a hitherto unknown book written by Levi, Qahat, or Amram, could surface suddenly in the third or second century BCE. Yet there is a major difference from what is assumed of books and scribes in 2 Kings 22 and what we find in these Aramaic Dead Sea Scrolls. In the latter, the implication is that books can be unknown to the populace without being really lost or forgotten: the textualized knowledge therein can run secret along a line of scribes, and that line is asserted to be none other the line from Levi to Moses. The continuance of this knowledge, moreover, is marked by the transmission of texts as among the inheritance passed from father to son, in anticipation of death and thus resisting its rupture.[90] Far from the idealization of spoken and public of acts of reading that we see in the Torah/Pentateuch, one finds the explicit textualization of a pointedly scribal perspective in these Aramaic Dead Sea Scrolls. Here, writing and books become an emblem of authority, and the memory of the knowledge therein is proclaimed as safe in scribal stewardship.[91]

---

[87] Levinson, *Legal Revision*, 22.   [88] Levinson, *Legal Revision*, 28.

[89] One may find some sense of writing as effective in itself, especially to bind a covenant with curses in Deut 29:20–21, 27 – although 28:61 notes that punishments may even go beyond what is written.

[90] *Jubilees* later traces the line back to Enoch, stressing as well how what Levi inherited at the death of Jacob was no less than a library – and with the aim, moreover, for Levi to "preserve them and renew them for his sons until this day" (45:16). See Chapter 5 below.

[91] Samuel Thomas reads the non-death of scribes like Enoch in similar terms: "Being a scribe makes one immortal at least insofar as death may be overcome in the transmission, elaboration, and new life of sacred tradition"; "Eternal Writing," 588.

To what degree should we interpret this claim as a matter of Hellenistic-era Jewish scribes newly asserting their own authority by textualizing their own lived experience and projecting it back into the distant past? It is intriguing in this regard that their images of scribal practice appear to mirror some of what we otherwise know about Israel's scribes, especially in the evocation of a familial educational setting. On the basis of epigraphical evidence, for instance, Christopher Rollston argues for some degree of "formal, standardized scribal education in ancient Israel," and he posits that its setting was less likely any monumental building akin to what we would now consider a "school."[92] Rather, in his view, "Israelite scribal education would have been located, for the most part, in a domestic context, such as the home of a scribe."[93] If so, the distinction between scribal families and others would have been stark: "written documents would have been a rarity in the homes of non-elites," whereas access to textuality in "the lives of the sons and daughters of scribes, however, would have been much different."[94]

Rollston supports this contention with comparative evidence from Mesopotamia and Egypt, but he also – significantly for our purposes – points to two pieces of evidence from the early Second Temple period: the mention of scribal families in 1 Chronicles 2:55 and the prosopographical data from Elephantine attesting the same pattern among Jews in Egypt.[95] Whatever we might reconstruct for preexilic Israel, then, it does seem plausible that the scribalism that is narratively dramatized with respect to the pre-Sinaitic past in these Aramaic Dead Scrolls may be sketched with some verisimilitude for postexilic Jewish scribal pedagogy.

In light of the work of Henryk Drawnel, we may be able further to situate this scribalization of the Jewish past as produced – at least in part – by scribes for scribes. Drawnel makes a case for reading *Aramaic Levi, Admonitions of Qahat,* and *Visions of Amram,* together with the Enochic *Astronomical Book,* as didactic literature, and he thus posits a tradition of Aramaic pedagogy among Jewish scribes, as marked by an embrace of Mesopotamian models and a preoccupation with issues of Jewish priestly knowledge, practice, and pedagogy.[96] If Drawnel is correct, we might

---

[92] Rollston, *Writing and Literacy,* 91, 115–116, 122–126.

[93] Rollston, *Writing and Literacy,* 116.   [94] Rollston, *Writing and Literacy,* 125.

[95] Rollston, *Writing and Literacy,* 123.

[96] Even if Drawnel's speculations are sometimes more specific than can be supported by the evidence (e.g., *An Aramaic Wisdom Text from Qumran,* 61–63), his main argument remains compelling. See also Drawnel, "Form and Content," 64–65; Drawnel, "Priestly Education in the Aramaic Levi Document."

speculate as to one of the main settings that shaped the Aramaic Jewish literature of the early Hellenistic age – namely: circles of scribes who claimed for themselves the status of the true custodians of Israel's remembered past and ancestral knowledge, in part through appeal to their own skills of reading and writing.[97] In the Hebrew literary cultures that shaped early biblical literature, scribes seem to have written into the history of Israel only in somewhat peripheral terms, with a near-invisibility at the sidelines of the scenes of reading focused instead on covenant, king, and people. In the Aramaic literary cultures of the early Hellenistic age, the scribe is moved to the center of a past that is thereby reframed in terms of the transmission, teaching, and preservation of knowledge *in writing*.

Significantly, for our purposes, this new centering of scribalism similarly marks those Aramaic Jewish writings in which we first find such an explosion of explicit interest in angels and demons. In works like the *Astronomical Book* and *Book of the Watchers*, the antediluvian sage Enoch emerges as a paradigmatic scribal exemplar and serves to anchor an anthological discourse in which a capacious array of topics become newly integrated into the Jewish literary tradition – including but not limited to angelology and demonology. As we shall see in Chapters 3 and 4, the confluence may not be coincidental: the elevation of the scribe proves pivotal for understanding the angelology and demonology of the *Astronomical Book* and *Book of the Watchers* in their own literary and historical contexts, not least because this elevation was achieved in large part through an extended parallel between scribes and angels as well as the projection of scribal pedagogy and practice back into the Sinaitic past, onto the angels, and up into the heavens.

---

[97] I refrain here from a detailed treatment of priesthood in relation to this scribalism, for which see already Himmelfarb, *Kingdom of Priests*, 11–84. Priests and scribes were distinctive groups of elites at the time – not least since belonging to the former is predicated on ancestry, while the latter "profession was open to any Jewish man of requisite intelligence and sufficient means to undertake the education" (11). Yet it is clear that "by the beginning of the second century BCE, some learned scribes had come to understand their profession in priestly terms" (45). In some cases, this might reflect the overlap of scribal training with priestly lineage, as in the case of those men whom we know to have been both (e.g., Ezra and perhaps ben Sira). In other cases, it might reflect the scribal appropriation of the more traditional domains of priestly prestige.

PROSE, PEDAGOGY, AND THE PAST IN THE ARAMAIC
DEAD SEA SCROLLS

So far, we have focused on shifts in the literary representation of Jewish
knowledge and teaching in relation to scribes, books, and writing, and it
is on this basis that we have speculated about an Aramaic Jewish scribal
pedagogy that might be heuristically distinguished from the Hebrew
scribal cultures that shaped earlier biblical literature. Notably, there are
also further reasons to distinguish it from what came both before and
after. Analyzing the linguistic features of Qumran Aramaic, for instance,
leads Edward Cook to conclude that it represents "a generally uniform
synchronic corpus, consisting of ... didactic-religious texts written in a
formal or literary register."[98] Furthermore, as Daniel Machiela and
Andrew Perrin have shown, the Aramaic texts found among the Dead
Sea Scrolls exhibit significant clusters of content and concern consistent
with a corpus cultivated in a common setting.[99] Just as Drawnel points to
Jewish scribes and/or priests with an interest in Mesopotamian scholasticism, so Perrin also posits their derivation from "close-knit scribal circles
in the fourth to second centuries BCE" – that is, largely from the period of
Ptolemaic rule over the Land of Israel.[100]

Below, we will ponder the puzzle of why an Aramaic Jewish scribal
pedagogy with close ties with Mesopotamian scholasticism might find its
first flourishing under Ptolemaic rule. First, however, it proves useful to
sketch out some of the salient features that we see in its literary products,
wherein we can glimpse shifts in scribal practice alongside the shifts in the
representation of scribes. Most notable, for our purposes, are three features that distinguish the Aramaic Jewish literature of the early Hellenistic
age from their earlier Hebrew counterparts: (1) the prominence of first-
person prose; (2) an exuberant expansion of topics of Jewish literary
concern to include topics not treated in early biblical literature but
common in Mesopotamian scholasticism and/or Greek *paideia*; and
(3) an intensive interest in the pre-Sinaitic past.

---

[98] Cook, "Qumran Aramaic," 363.
[99] Machiela and Perrin, "Tobit and the Genesis Apocryphon."
[100] Drawnel, "Priestly Education"; Perrin, *Dynamics of Dream-Vision Revelation*, 230.
   Perrin rightly cautions against imagining such circles in terms of older tropes about
   "apocalyptic conventicles" or "fringe groups," due both to the broader orientation of
   this literature and our evidence for the reception of some of them as authoritative and
   otherwise influential, even beyond Judaea (231).

Prior to the discovery of the Dead Sea Scrolls, the use of first-person prose in "pseudepigrapha" like the *Book of the Watchers* was commonly interpreted in terms akin to modern notions of forgery and/or as a pious fiction in resistance of the purported postexilic cessation of Jewish prophecy. The evidence from the Aramaic Dead Sea Scrolls, however, led scholars to notice a broader pattern. These and other Aramaic sources of the time, as Loren Stuckenbruck observes, attest a sudden rise in the use of the first-person within Jewish literary practice.[101] In fact, with the partial exception of Tobit (cf. 1:1–3:6), "most of the remaining works preserved in Aramaic reflect the use of the first person."[102]

Stuckenbruck suggests that the growth of first-person speech forms part of a flowering of Jewish literary experimentation in Aramaic in the wake of the conquests of Alexander, as forged in reaction to, and interaction with, Hellenistic ideals of historiography and "authorship."[103] In the following chapters, we will see how this first-person voice contributes to the development of sophisticated literary structures wherein narrative framing is used to textualize diverse received traditions, supplementing older scribal technologies like *Listenwissenschaft* for the articulation of angelology and demonology in particular. For now, it suffices to note that the use of the first-person prose marks a striking departure from the characteristic anonymity of earlier Hebrew works. It is a departure, moreover, that functions even further to assert scribal agency – serving to remind the reader/hearer that writing is predicated on a writer and thereby relocating the authority of a text in the expertise of those trained to read and write.[104]

The elevation of scribalism and experimentation with new literary forms is also accompanied by a radical expansion of what is claimed as the epistemological domain of scribal expertise, encompassing a number of topics never or rarely textualized in earlier biblical literature. Even prior to the discovery of the Dead Sea Scrolls, scholars had noticed the rise of concern for topics like angels, demons, and eschatology in early

---

[101] Stuckenbruck, "Pseudepigraphy," 307–315.
[102] Stuckenbruck, "Pseudepigraphy," 302.
[103] Stuckenbruck, "Pseudepigraphy," 307–315.
[104] Note the complex of anxieties about succession and the elevation of writing already in Deuteronomy 32 and paralleled by the *Words of Ahiqar*, as explored in Weitzman, "Lessons from the Dying." Our findings here, however, suggest that the activation and redeployment of these precedents took place as part of the articulation of Aramaic Jewish scribal pedagogy in counterpoint to Greek *paideia* – a phenomenon persuasively charted in Carr, *Writing on the Tablet*, 201–272.

"pseudepigrapha"; this phenomenon, however, was largely studied in relation to apocalypses and apocalypticism, often through the retrospective lens of the New Testament Book of Revelation. With the further Aramaic evidence from Dead Sea Scrolls, we are now able to situate apocalypses like the *Book of the Watchers* and Daniel as part a broader tradition of Jewish literary production in Aramaic, which was significant for the history of apocalypses and apocalypticism literature but hardly limited to it. Likewise, we see now that the Hellenistic-era expansion of topics of Jewish literary concern is not limited to apocalyptic concerns. What we find in our Aramaic sources, rather, includes the rise of systematic written reflection on angels, demons, eschatology, and the afterlife, but also the expansion of Jewish literary production to encompass technical or "scientific" knowledge about the cosmos and its workings.

The early Hellenistic age, as Jonathan Ben-Dov and Seth Sanders have shown, marks a watershed in the history of Jewish knowledge:

For the first time in Jewish literature, we find astronomy and cosmic geography—secrets lying beyond the traditionally understood and immediately visible world—in the Astronomical Book of Enoch and the Book of the Watchers. Texts like the Aramaic Levi document and the Qumran physiognomies extend these interests from the stars to the measurement of materials and the human body. In these sources we find precise new ways to divide up and understand the world. The knowledge they present is of a sort unprecedented in Jewish sources because it contains detailed, systematic rules and observations about the physical world—what scholars of Greece and Babylon have long studied as ancient science.[105]

Was this knowledge new to Jews in the early Hellenistic age or just newly written down? Perhaps a bit of both. In some cases, we may be seeing ideas that have been integrated therein by virtue of new patterns in the circulation of knowledge across the Hellenistic Near East in the wake of the conquests of Alexander and the rise of the empires of his successors. In other cases, what seems new in these literary texts may be much older didactic lists or other received traditions that were long familiar to Jewish scribes but became textualized and/or integrated into newly literary forms during this period. When scribes were beginning to write themselves more explicitly into their narrative literature, they also seem to have textualized

---

[105] Ben-Dov and Sanders, "Introduction," 11, further stressing how "Taken together, moreover, these texts exhibit overlaps with the topics and traditions of ancient Babylonian and Hellenistic sciences, including "astronomical calculations of the movements of the heavenly bodies and length of the days, sexagesimal (base-60) metrology, simple forms of zodiacal astrology, and physiognomic interpretation of the body" (16).

and narrativized more elements from their own pedagogy, training, and expertise, as well as more of what they knew of Mesopotamian and other Near Eastern traditions.

For this, as we shall see in Chapter 3, angelology proves central. Knowledge about the cosmos is often framed as what is known to Jewish scribes by virtue of their special connections to the very angels who help govern cosmic cycles. Far from the skepticism about the human capacity for knowledge of the cosmos that we find in biblical books like Job, works like the *Book of the Watchers* celebrate the knowledge known to Jewish scribes with a new emphasis on totality and certainty: Enoch, for instance, there claims that "from the words of the Watchers and holy ones, I heard *everything* (Aram. [שמעת אנה] כלה וקדישין [עירין] מלי ומן),[106] and as I heard *everything* from them, so I also understand what I saw (Gr^Pan: καὶ ὡς ἤκουσα παρ' αὐτῶν πάντα καὶ ἔγνων ἐγὼ θεωρῶν; *1 En* 1:2). We will explore this angelological claim to knowledge further below; for now, it suffices to note that it is paired with a claim to preserve knowledge from the distant past – as emblematized by the antediluvian sage Enoch but not limited to him.

In the textualized deposits of Israelite memory in the Torah/ Pentateuch, the periods prior to Moses are notably terse – foreshortened, fragmented, and framed as mere preface to a history that only truly begins with Moses himself. But it is precisely this pre-Sinaitic past to which the earliest "pseudepigrapha" and Aramaic Dead Sea Scrolls turn anew. The antediluvian age is the focus of concern in the Enochic *Astronomical Book* (4Q208–211) and *Book of the Watchers* (4Q201–206), both of which are well represented in Aramaic fragments from Qumran, as well as in the Enochic *Book of the Giants* (e.g., 1Q23–24, 2Q26, 4Q530–532). The patriarchal past is similarly treated in detail within *Genesis Apocryphon* (1Q20) as well as in the various Aramaic fragments about Jacob and others in 4Q537–539. And, as we have seen, there are efforts to link them together, and forward to Moses in the *Aramaic Levi Document* (1Q21, 4Q213, 4Q213a, 4Q213b, 4Q214, 4Q214a, 4Q214b), *Admonitions of Qahat* (4Q542), and *Visions of Amram* (4Q543–549; cf. 4Q540–541).

---

[106] Here following the fragmentary Aramaic of 4Q201 col. i line 3, as reconstructed in Milik, *The Books of Enoch*, 142; Nickelsburg, *Apocalyptic and Myth in 1 Enoch 1*, 137. The corresponding clause in Gr^Pan reads καὶ ἁγιολόγων ἁγίων ἤκουσα ἐγώ.

The overall pattern, as Dimant notes, is quite striking:

Twenty-one Aramaic manuscripts deal with events connected with the Flood; eighteen scrolls are devoted to the lives of the Patriarchs. The Genesis Apocryphon covers both subjects ... Thus scrolls concerned with the Flood and the Patriarch's history account for *nearly half* of the eighty-three readable Aramaic texts.[107]

Their interest in the pre-Sinaitic past, moreover, is mirrored by a lack of interest in other periods:

... *nothing* in the Aramaic corpus parallels the intensive interest of the Hebrew texts [of the Dead Sea Scrolls] in later Israelite history. *No* Aramaic work deals systematically and in detail with Moses and Joshua, the period of the Judges, or the kingdoms of Judah and Israel. For that matter, *nothing* in Aramaic is related to the biblical Prophets.[108]

This Aramaic corpus thus stands in contrast with earlier Hebrew materials but also with later ones. For example, those texts from the Dead Sea Scrolls that bear the marks of the particular views of the Qumran *yaḥad*, which are post-Maccabean and in Hebrew, make mention of the pre-Sinaitic past only rarely and passingly.[109]

If part of what is distinctive about Aramaic Jewish scribal pedagogy is in this remaking of the memory of the pre-Sinaitic past, moreover, it is only rarely in a manner that can be reduced to biblical exegesis. However tempting it might be to read these writings in terms of our expectations of the literature of Second Temple times as "postexilic" and thus "post-biblical" or essentially exegetical, this corpus includes works that predate the latest book now in the Hebrew Bible (i.e., Daniel) and which took form during a time that the texts of some now-biblical writings were still in flux.[110] If anything, they speak from and to a prolonged process whereby particularly periods and purviews of Israel's past eventually came to be elevated – and, as such, they might help us to recover something of the broader process of preserving and pruning memory, of which the elevation of what is now-biblical literature, as textualized touchstone and increasingly centralized interpretative nexus for that past, was but one part.

---

[107] Dimant, "Qumran Aramaic Texts," 201–202.
[108] Dimant, "Qumran Aramaic Texts," 203.
[109] I.e., "systematic reworking of narratives dealing with pre-Sinaitic times is shared *only* by the Qumran Aramaic corpus and the parabiblical non-sectarian texts"; Dimant, "Qumran Aramaic Texts," 202.
[110] I.e., it exemplifies the degree to which, as Armin Lange notes, "the discovery of the Qumran manuscript collection provided a huge increase of literature written in a period when the late books and redactions of the Hebrew Bible were still developing"; "Pre-Maccabean Literature," 285.

LOCALISM, HEUREMATOGRAPHY, AND COMPETITIVE HISTORIOGRAPHY

Previously, we noted Stuckenbruck's speculation of some connection between the adoption of first-person prose in Aramaic Jewish literature and the common use of this form in Hellenistic historiography, and below, we shall consider how the claims to totalizing knowledge in these same sources may resonate with the politicization of knowledge by early Ptolemies. Is it possible also to explain the timing of this turn to the pre-Sinaitic past? On the one hand, as noted in Chapter 1, this creativity is partly made possible by the spaces left by the earlier memory-making of the Hebrew scribal culture that shaped the Torah/Pentateuch. Yet, on the other hand, the choice also makes meaning in its own time.

Noting Greek examples of the culling of older lore and literature toward a newly intensified concern for local origins and identity, for instance, Susan Alcock has pointed to "the power of heroic past in a Hellenistic present":

These were times that saw collective history become a matter for study, collation, and recording. Stress was laid upon recovering and celebrating origin myths and legends, on establishing pedigrees running back into the mists of time. In part, this self-consciousness appears a product of the threat to the independent life of small cities ... The right to privilege, the very right to existence, increasingly had to be demanded upon historic grounds. Yet this search transcended matters of mercenary self-protection ... Ancestries and origins, invoked through myth and ritual, could be used to claim kinship with other cities, to establish status, and to secure identity. Heroes were especially instrumental in the process, for they above all possessed a comprehensible genealogy, capable of yielding plausible chronologies and webs of inter-relationships. Hellenistic scholars charted the generations, measuring with what Veyne termed "the thread of time" the distance between heroes and the present day. Genealogy provided that longed-for sense of local history and identity, and the heroic age anchored that thread of time. Elite legitimation, civic prestige, symbolic protection, a sense of communal identity: all of these may go some way to explaining the appeal of a Hellenistic heroic past.[111]

With respect to Ptolemaic Egypt, Ian Moyer has similarly explored "the roles of Egyptian subjects in the so-called fringes of copenetration where Greek discourses on Egyptian history and culture were created," as new expressions of localism that cannot be reduced either to the assimilation

---

[111] Alcock, "The Heroic Past in a Hellenistic Present," 30, 33–34, there stressing that "these cults are not necessarily new ... but some intensification of cult practice in this epoch seems to take place."

of Greek traditions or to the static preservation of Egyptian traditions in isolation from them.[112]

For understanding the turn to the pre-Sinaitic past in the Aramaic Jewish literature of the early Hellenistic age, the comparison with Berossus' *Babyloniaca* is also illuminating. Writing in the third century BCE, this Babylonian scribe similarly pairs a local concern for lineages of knowledge with a globalizing claim to possess a totality of knowledge from the distant past:

In the first year there appeared from the Red Sea in a place adjacent to Babylonia a beast named Oannes. It had the whole body of a fish, but under the head, a human head grew beside underneath the head of the fish and feet of a human likewise grew beside from the tail of the fish. It had a human voice. Its image is still preserved even now. He says that this beast spent the day with men, touching no food. It gave men the knowledge of letters and sciences and crafts of all types [παραδιδόναι τε τοῖς ἀνθρώποις γραμμάτων καὶ μαθημάτων καὶ τεχνῶν παντοδαπῶν ἐμπειρίαν]. It also taught the founding of cities, the establishment of temples, and the introduction of laws and land-measurement, and showed them seeds and the gathering of fruits [καὶ πόλεων συνοικισμοὺς καὶ ἱερῶν ἱδρύσεις, καὶ νόμων εἰσηγήσεις καὶ γεωμετρίαν διδάσκειν, καὶ σπέρματα καὶ καρπῶν συναγωγὰς ὑποδεικνύναι]. In general, it taught men everything that is connected with a civilised life [καὶ συνόλως πάντα τὰ πρὸς ἡμέρωσιν ἀνήκοντα βίου παραδιδόναι τοῖς ἀνθρώποις]. From that time nothing further has been discovered. (BNJ 680 F 1b; trans. G. De Breucker)

Through Oannes, Berossus stakes his claim for Babylonian scribalism as the ultimate seat and source of "everything that is connected with civilized life," and he asserts that this totality of knowledge is accessible to him and his fellow scribes by virtue of an unbroken line in its transmission from the distant past.

Mark Geller has recently raised the possibility that Berossus originally wrote his *Babyloniaca* in Aramaic.[113] If so, the parallels would be all the more striking. But even if Berossus wrote in Greek, as is usually surmised, it remains a useful intertext inasmuch as it reflects a parallel response to some of the same conditions.[114] The *Babyloniaca* counts among many examples of the previously noted turn to local lineages and histories of knowledge across the Hellenistic world, but it is also a specific expression of the defense of the continued significance of Near Eastern scribalism in a new imperial context.

---

[112] Moyer, *Egypt and the Limits of Hellenism*, 34, 84–141.
[113] Geller, "Berossus on Kos."
[114] On differences between Ptolemaic and Seleucid rule, however, see Chapter 5.

Although written under Seleucid rather than Ptolemaic rule, it is notable that claims of this sort were also known to some Jews. In fact, a concern to counter such claims is found in the earliest known Jewish source in Greek that reflects awareness of the claims about knowledge that we find within the Aramaic Jewish literature of the early Hellenistic age – that is, so-called Pseudo-Eupolemus. Writing in the second century BCE, he asserts that the Babylonians only learned of astronomy through the Jews, who owe this knowledge to Enoch and the angels:

Abraham ... also discovered astronomy and the Chaldaean art [ὃν δὴ καὶ τὴν ἀστρολογίαν καὶ Χαλδαικὴν εὑρεῖν] ... And this one, because of a command of God, having gone to Phoenicia settled there. And teaching the Phoenicians the turnings of the sun and the moon, and all other such things, he pleased their king [καὶ τροπὰς ἡλίου καὶ σελήνης καὶ τὰ ἄλλα πάντα διδάξαντα τοὺς Φοίνικας εὐαρεστῆσαι τῶι βασιλεῖ αὐτῶν] ... When a famine occurred, Abraham escaped to Egypt with his whole household and settled there ... And Abraham, living in Heliopolis with the priests of the Egyptians, taught them many new things, and he was the one who introduced astronomy and the other arts to them [συζήσαντα δὲ τὸν Ἀβραὰμ ἐν Ἡλιουπόλει τοῖς Αἰγυπτίων ἱερεῦσι πολλὰ μεταδιδάξαι αὐτούς, καὶ τὴν ἀστρολογίαν καὶ τὰ λοιπὰ τοῦτον αὐτοῖς εἰσηγήσασθαι], saying that the Babylonians and he himself had found out these things, tracing their discovery to Enoch, and this one [i.e., Enoch] was the first to discover astronomy, not the Egyptians [φάμενον Βαβυλωνίους ταῦτα καὶ αὐτὸν εὑρηκέναι, τὴν δὲ εὕρεσιν αὐτῶν εἰς Ἐνὼχ ἀναπέμπειν, καὶ τοῦτον εὑρηκέναι πρῶτον τὴν ἀστρολογίαν, οὐκ Αἰγυπτίους]. Because the Babylonians say that Belus was the first, who is Kronos; that from him Belis and Cham were born; and this one [i.e., Cham] begot Chanaan, the father of the Phoenicians; and that from him a son Choum was born, who is called by the Greeks Asbolos, the father of the Ethiopians and the brother of Mestraeim, the father of the Egyptians. The Greeks say that Atlas discovered astronomy; and that Atlas and Enoch are the same. And that Enoch had a son Mathousalas, who came to know everything through the angels of God, and that we thus came to learn [sc. everything]' (τοῦ δὲ Ἐνὼχ γενέσθαι υἱὸν Μαθουσάλαν, ὃν πάντα δι' ἀγγέλων θεοῦ γνῶναι, καὶ ἡμᾶς οὕτως ἐπιγνῶναι)." (Eusebius, *Praep.ev.* 9.17.3–9 = BNJ 724 F 1)[115]

In the next chapter, we will return to this passage to discuss the early reception of the *Astronomical Book*. For our present purposes, it is useful as evidence for Jewish awareness of the intensified concern for local lineages and cross-cultural claims to antiquity, attesting the participation of some Jews alongside Babylonians in Hellenistic heurematography.

Heurematography – the practice of tracing the discoverers of specific skills, sciences, and arts – emerged as an arena for cross-cultural competition and reflection on intercultural exchange among those cultures now

[115] Here following the translation of T. Kaizer with minor revisions.

newly connected by Macedonian empires.[116] Surviving fragments from
Eudemus of Rhodes (ca. 330–285 BCE), for instance, attest an interest in
the inventors of mathematics and astronomy already by the late fourth
century BCE. In this, Eudemus extends the curiosity about the origins of
specific *technai* that had been among the hallmarks of ancient Greek
ethnography, as first attested in the sixth century BCE and consolidated
as part of the reflection on Greekness and cultural difference during and
after the Persian Wars.[117] But just as the conquests of Alexander facilitated
the diffusion and development of technical and other knowledge across an
increasingly interconnected Eurasia, so the empires of his successors also
fostered fresh interest in lineages of knowledge among non-Greeks as well.

The previously quoted passage from Berossus speaks to its resonance
among some scribes in Seleucid Babylonia, and what we know of the
writings of Manetho attests parallel concerns among some Egyptian elites
writing in Greek under Ptolemaic rule.[118] That some Jews addressed the
same issues is suggested by the excerpts from Pseudo-Eupolemus and other
Greek Jewish authors preserved via Alexander Polyhistor.[119] Taken
together, these sources point to the early Hellenistic age as an era in which
Babylonians, Egyptians, and Jews were making competing claims to
antiquity and priority in knowledge, each emphasizing – mostly in Greek –
how the wisdom of the Near East ultimately undergirded all that was valued
and claimed by the Greeks. What distinguishes Pseudo-Eupolemus, however, is precisely where his assertions overlap with contemporaneous Aramaic Jewish literature. He does not just claim Jewish cultural priority for the
invention and cross-cultural transmission of astronomy; rather, he relativizes any competing claims by tracing Jewish knowledge to angels.[120]

As with Pseudo-Eupolemus, the Aramaic Jewish sources surveyed
above reflect an intensified interest in tracing local lineages and a
redeployment of older genealogical traditions to speak more specifically
to the history of knowledge. They make local claims that resonate in a
newly global perspective. In this sense, some of their departures from
earlier biblical literature resonate with intellectual trends and concerns in

[116] Zhmud, *The Origin of the History of Science in Classical*, 117–165
[117] Kleingünter, "*Protos Heuretes*"; Lovejoy and Boas, *Primitivism and Related Ideas in Antiquity*, 382–388.
[118] Momigliano, *Alien Wisdom*.
[119] Sterling, *Historiography and Self-Definition*, 20–225.
[120] See, however, Chapter 3 below for discussion of the somewhat similar appeal to *Dike* by Aratus.

the Hellenistic Near East. When we situate them in this broader context, however, we can also see what is distinctive therein.

Perhaps foremost are their claims about transmundane powers. On the one hand, when we situate the Aramaic Jewish literature of the early Hellenistic age within broader intellectual trends across the Near East, we see that its angelology is not just a claim about angels: it is also (and perhaps foremost) a claim about knowledge. But, on the other hand, it is no less a claim for what is unique about Jewish knowledge, wherein cosmology encompasses angelology no less than astronomy and wherein knowledge from angels vouchsafes the truth and totality of technical and other knowledge about the cosmos and its workings. Like Berossus, the Jewish scribes responsible for this literature defend Near Eastern wisdom with an appeal to its extreme antiquity and the unbroken scribal transmission of books and writing. Like Pseudo-Eupolemus, however, they simultaneously situate their own expertise as ultimately beyond any earthly history or human lineage, uniquely linked to angelic teaching and the timelessness of direct knowledge of the heavens.

JEWISH WRITING IN ARAMAIC IN THE EARLY HELLENISTIC AGE

Like many intellectuals in the early Hellenistic age, across the Mediterranean and Near East, the Jewish scribes responsible for the Aramaic Dead Sea Scrolls reflect anew about the distant past, remake its lineages to fit their present, and reshape local knowledge in response to new imperial realities. They appeal to figures of extreme antiquity to lay claim to the newly prestigious cross-cultural domain of astronomy. But unlike some of their fellow Jews – like Pseudo-Eupolemus – they resist adopting the new prestige language of Greek, and they also resist the alignment of the biblical past with Greek mythology and the importation of Greek ethnographical or philosophical tropes.

But why, then, do they choose to write in Aramaic? For some time, Aramaic may well have been among the languages of everyday speech in the region, but prior to the early Hellenistic age, Jewish use of Aramaic seems largely documentary and epistolary rather than literary.[121]

---

[121] I.e., "literary" in the sense of having some narrative features but also in the sense of written works meant for continued copying and study in their own right, rather than short-duration or single-context use for record, etc. As Cook has recently shown, the linguistic and generic range for Qumran Aramaic suggests that it is not simply a record

Hebrew, thus, would seem to be the more obvious choice for those learned Jews who chose not to write in the new prestige language of Greek. Seth Schwartz, for instance, notes the continuing use of Hebrew among some Jews of the time as akin to the continued use of other local languages by indigenous elites: "In the third century, literate Jews connected with the central Judaean institutions continued to write in traditional ways, in archaizing Hebrew for the most part, and in traditional genres, just as priests in Egypt and Mesopotamia continued to writes texts in hieroglyphic Egyptian and cuneiform Akkadian well into the Hellenistic period."[122] If these comparanda caution us against characterizing the Hellenistic age only on the basis of materials in Greek, they also sharpen the puzzle of why we find a renaissance of Jewish literary production in Aramaic in the third century BCE.[123]

This choice, in my view, may be related to what we have seen of the self-conscious scribalism of this literature as well as its newly expansive approach to knowledge. Sanders, for instance, notes how "Aramaic became a cosmopolitan language of scholarship during the Persian period," when it "lost its quality as the vernacular of local kingdoms and become the common script of empires."[124] Under the Achaemenids, Sanders surmises that the use of Aramaic may well have seemed invisible: "pervasive in the training of writers all over the ancient Near East by the fifth century BCE, Aramaic was a scribal culture whose power resided precisely in the fact that it did not seem like a culture at all."[125] In Mesopotamia, thus, one thus finds "cuneiform scholars adopting the

or reflection of the full range of oral and other usages of Aramaic by Jews during the Second Temple period; whether or not the surviving corpus has been shaped by some self-conscious selectivity about the topics or genres apt for writing in this particular language, it remains the product of a seemingly synchronic tradition of literary production with a notably limited range: "Aramaic may have been consciously used in certain genres and not in others. Recently scholars have emphasized certain common genres or thematic elements in the Qumran Aramaic compositions, which, they say, suggest that Aramaic was a consciously chosen medium for those genres and/or themes (and, by implication, not for other genres and/or themes) ... In such a case, Aramaic is unrepresentative in genre by cultural choice, not by historical accident. Nevertheless, this does not affect our major point, in that in terms of the ideal totality of Palestinian Aramaic, QA is *unrepresentative*"; "Qumran Aramaic," 361.

[122] Schwartz, *Ancient Jews*, 34, listing some psalms, 1–2 Chronicles, and Qohelet as Hebrew writings plausibly situated in the Hellenistic period; he includes the *Book of the Watchers* as an example of the literature of this period as well, although not signaling the significances of its use of Aramaic.

[123] For a full survey of past explanations for why Jews in the early Hellenistic age wrote in Aramaic, see Machiela, "Situating the Aramaic Texts," 98–106.

[124] Sanders, *From Adapa*, 195.   [125] Sanders, *From Adapa*, 196.

alphabetic parchment medium whose dominance the Persian empire had established," and "by the Hellenistic period it had replaced cuneiform as the default writing system in many parts of the Near East."[126] The transmission of these traditions in Aramaic likely facilitated the exportation of elements of Mesopotamian scholasticism into Judaea and elsewhere. Yet it also enabled its globalization into a newly cross-cultural ideal of scribal expertise:

Saturated in originally Mesopotamian scholarly discourse but removed from the clay media to which it had long been attached, Aramaic scribal culture circulated free from the material markers of Babylonian identity. For the Judean scribes who copied Darius' Behistun inscription or the Samaritans who drew up their contracts with Neo-Babylonian legal formulae, Babylonian scribal culture was no longer marked as foreign knowledge. It was now simply scholarship, their own unmarked universal heritage as experts and scholars.[127]

If Sanders is correct, Aramaic might have actually been an obvious choice for Jewish scribes to articulate the newly expansive visions of knowledge that we find in the earliest "pseudepigrapha" and related Dead Sea Scrolls. On the one hand, if what we have characterized as Aramaic Jewish scribal pedagogy took form among Jews trained as what Sanders calls "Aramaic parchment-scribes," it would certainly help to explain their access to astronomical, cosmological, didactic, and other elements of Mesopotamian scholasticism – that is, not just by virtue of training in Aramaic for Achaemenid imperial administration but also because of its status as a Near Eastern *koine* for a translocal cosmopolitan scholasticism.[128] On the other hand, its prior "invisibility" would have made its repurposing richly possible, rendering it a potent resource for innovating new forms of Jewish scribal pedagogy and literary production.

But why would this Jewish literary repurposing of Aramaic flourish especially in the early Hellenistic age? At first sight, the timing might appear puzzling if not paradoxical. Yet – in my view – this is precisely why it is so telling, as a pointed and poignant choice in an era marked by the politicization of lineages of knowledge and the intensification of cross-cultural claims to knowledge. The choice to write in Aramaic embodies

---

[126] Sanders, *From Adapa*, 196.

[127] Sanders, *From Adapa*, 196. Compare Machiela's suggestion, following Elias Bickerman and Ben Zion Walchoder, that Aramaic was chosen for its internationalism and broad reach; "Situating the Aramaic Texts," 100–102.

[128] On "the role of Aramaic as a cultural vehicle in the transmission of Babylonian science" in particular, see Ben-Dov, *Head of All Years*, 287 and discussion below in Chapter 3.

the defense of the continued significance of Near Eastern scribalism against the globalizing and totalizing claims of Greek *paideia*. At the same time, it enables the appropriation of astronomical and other elements of Mesopotamian scholasticism *as originally Jewish* in an era in which new empires were increasingly cultivating Greek as the language of both imperial administration and the enculturation of elites. Consequently, the choice is in some ways akin to the choice to link their cosmological knowledge to angels: even as they rewrite the history of Jewish knowledge with a newly capacious scope that draws upon a cosmopolitan scholasticism, they do so by radically centering Israel, and its scribes, as the sole nexus of revealed knowledge about the cosmos.

CONCLUSION

The beginnings of Jewish angelology and demonology resist tidy explanation as either external or internal in cause.[129] It cannot be reduced simply to foreign "influence" or explained merely through the cataloguing of parallels. The isolation of inner-Jewish dynamics also proves insufficient. Doubts about divine justice during and after the Babylonian Exile may well help account for some of the resonance of certain ideas about wayward, impure, or evil spirits, and certain ideas about angels may have been popular due in part to their power to assuage an alienation nursed in nostalgia for native kingship. Broad-based appeals to postexilic theological crisis or malaise, however, do not suffice to explain *why* such ideas emerged so intensively precisely *when* they did – that is: in Jewish writings in Aramaic from the third and second centuries BCE. To answer such questions, we must look to what else we know of these centuries, within and beyond Judaism.

This chapter has looked to broader changes that we see in the Aramaic Dead Sea Scrolls, noting their intensive interest in pre-Sinaitic figures, the scribalization of the Jewish past with appeal to such figures, and the resultant assertion of an ancient and unbroken lineage of knowledge,

---

[129] One could go further, in fact, and suggest that this phenomenon exposes the limited explanatory power of approaches that treat "Judaism," "Hellenism," and "the ancient Near East" as if self-contained entities with stable centers and clear-cut boundaries; for, as we shall see, Israel's Near Eastern cultural contexts remain generative for Jews long after Babylon's fall to Persian and Macedonian empires – albeit in new ways – and the circulation of knowledge in the Near East contributes to forging Hellenistic elite culture as well as Second Temple Judaism.

vouchsafed by Jewish books, scribes, reading, and writing. If these features mark a departure from what we know of earlier Hebrew scribal cultures from the Bible, they resonate with the concerns of "apocrypha" and "pseudepigrapha" also known in Aramaic. If this new evidence thus enables a characterization of what is distinctive about the Aramaic Jewish literature of the early Hellenistic age – across genres – it also opens a synchronic perspective on the explosion of explicit and systematic concern for angels and demons therein.

What I have suggested then, in this chapter, is that the beginnings of Jewish angelology and demonology might be best understood as part of the Hellenistic-era articulation of a newly expansive vision of Jewish knowledge and scribal expertise. The next two chapters explore the microdynamics of this development – first in relation to the angelology of *Astronomical Book* and its relationship to astronomy, and then in relation to the demonology of the *Book of the Watchers* and its relationship to "magic." Consistent with my experimentation with a more synchronic approach, I look to the function of transmundane powers within each work, analyzed with attention to the earliest manuscript evidence and contextualized with primary appeal to other Aramaic and pre-Maccabean sources. Extending my efforts above to map their nested cultural contexts, I also juxtapose these Aramaic Jewish sources with a variety of Greek and non-Jewish intertexts from the third and early second centuries BCE, exploring the possibility of correlating and contextualizing their concerns with broader cultural trends of the time, especially under Ptolemaic rule and across the Hellenistic Near East.

Reflecting on the cultural effects of ancient empires, Greg Woolf posits two types of localism – one generated by isolation but the other "more purposive, in the sense that it is formed consciously."[130] Scholars have tended to treat nearly all Jewish distinctiveness as the former sort of localism. What I would like to suggest, in what follows, is that the Aramaic Jewish literature of the early Hellenistic age – and its innovative angelology and demonology – make more sense as the latter. To the degree that this literature reflects its imperial context, it is not in relation to the type of resistance that we later see within Maccabean-era apocalypses like Daniel. If the many unprecedented features within the Jewish literature of the early Hellenistic age signal innovations within Jewish

---

[130] Woolf, "Afterword: The Local and the Global," 190. Writing of the Seleucid empire, Kosmin similarly stresses that "indigeneity is a relational strategy, not an inherent property" (*Time and Its Adversaries*, 11).

scribal cultures with the shift from Achaemenid to Ptolemaic rule, they speak less to any dichotomous conflict of "Judaism" and "Hellenism" than to a subtler "cultural orientation" of the sort sought by Schwartz.

Writing of the Roman Empire, Woolf reflects on those types of imperial cultures that "connected people, generated diasporas, facilitated travel [and thus] created conditions in which even local history marked itself as global,"[131] and Whitmarsh reminds us that "local identities are not static, 'authentic,' immured against change, but in constant dialogue with the translocal," especially in the wake of "a phase of rapid globalization [that] sees an intensification of consciousness of localism."[132] That these features arguably find precedent already in the new Macedonian empires has been recently shown by Paul Kosmin in relation to the range of indigenous responses to Seleucid rule, which include antiquarianism and historicism no less than resistance.[133]

The change that we see in the Aramaic Jewish literature of the early Hellenistic age is similarly local and global. On the one hand, it is marked by the intensive cultivation and theorization of knowledge, which draws on the threads of earlier Israelite and other Near Eastern traditions to reimagine the pre-Sinaitic past and rewrite the history of Jewish knowledge with and about angels and demons. On the other hand, it thus remakes local Jewish knowledge in a manner that resonates with the broader trends of its time, retheorizing local knowledge in a manner that made meaning within newly globalizing contexts – including the Ptolemaic politicization of books and knowledge as well as the "archival sensibility" and self-archaizing turn to heroic pasts that we see across Ptolemaic, Seleucid, and other empires.[134]

Although relatively isolated in comparison to their Babylonian and Alexandrian counterparts, Jewish scribes may have had their own reasons to engage in efforts to reorder local knowledge in a newly globalizing and totalizing manner. Their claims, after all, serve to defend to the necessity of traditional scribes within a Jewish society in which Aramaic literacy and priestly lineage no longer sufficed to ensure a place within the administrative apparatus. If the fortunes of the non-priestly Tobiads are any indication, the status of Jewish priests and scribes under Ptolemaic rule may have been more precarious than under the Achaemenids. It may

---

[131] Woolf, *Tales of the Barbarians*, 73.   [132] Whitmarsh, "Thinking Local," 2–3.
[133] Kosmin, *Time and Its Adversaries*.
[134] Whitmarsh, *Ancient Greek Literature*, 122–138; Haubold, *Greece and Mesopotamia*, 127–177.

not be coincidental, then, that so many Aramaic Jewish texts from the pre-Maccabean period emphasize the pedagogical power of scribalism and reshape the memory of Israel's past and prehistory in their own image. They recast Israel's ancestral heritage of knowledge as explicitly bookish, elevate scribes as its true custodians, and extend the domains of their own claimed expertise.

This Jewish repackaging of received knowledge into new literary forms finds parallels across the Hellenistic world. Much like scholars working under Ptolemaic patronage, like Callimachus, and Greeks elsewhere, like Aratus, they give voice to an "archival sensitivity" marked by the reordering of local and imperial knowledge in newly totalizing terms, and they reflect the rising prestige of books and writing in Ptolemaic and other empires in the third and second centuries BCE. Both their embrace of angelology and their choice to write in Aramaic, however, signal their distinctiveness as well. Jewish scribes of the time invoked the cosmopolitanism of an age prior to the conquests of Alexander, which strikingly excludes Greeks (and Macedonian rulers with investments in Greekness) from the history and knowledge thereby celebrated. And in the process, as we shall see in Chapters 3 and 4, they scribalized and textualized the Jewish past to assert that scribes from Enoch to Levi to Moses have always known more and written more – not just about the inhabited world but also about the cosmos and what lies above and beyond, where demons lurk and angels sing.

3

Writing Angels, Astronomy, and Aramaic
in the Early Hellenistic Age

Although largely neglected in the study of Judaism, the third century BCE has been heralded as pivotal for the cultural history of the West – not least because of seismic shifts pertaining to knowledge, books, education, and the cultural politics of the past.[1] By the dawn of this century, the wars for primacy among Alexander's successors had resulted in the splintering of his conquered domains and the rise of the new Hellenistic dynasties of the Ptolemies, Seleucids, and Antigonids. New forms of elite enculturation soon emerged, evolving to match the administrative needs of Macedonian monarchs consolidating control over precarious new empires in far-flung domains.[2] "Within a few decades," as Teresa Morgan notes, Greek *paideia* "developed from an assortment of practices by which the young of certain Greek states were raised in their own culture, into something like an integrated and autonomous system which could be used by ethnic Greeks or non-Greeks, anywhere, at any time, with (relatively) predictable results and implications."[3]

---

[1] Here and below, my concern is for what we might call the "long third century BCE" – that is, the period after Alexander but before the Maccabees, with particular focus on the period of Ptolemaic rule over the Land of Israel. The *Astronomical Book* likely hails from earlier in this period, and the *Book of the Watchers* a bit later.

[2] On what such administration entailed in the case of the Ptolemies, see Monson, *From the Ptolemies to the Romans* – there outlined with a focus on Egypt and in relation to continuities and discontinuities with later Roman rule – and in the case of the Seleucids, Kosmin, *Land of the Elephant Kings*; Kosmin, *Time and Its Adversaries*.

[3] Morgan, *Literate Education in the Hellenistic and Roman Worlds*, 22, stressing that this development occurred with surprising speed, even despite the lack of centralized institutions for its standardization or promulgation: "By the third century BCE, on the evidence of the papyri, most of its elements were established in the order in which they

Classicists have done much to illumine the enculturating effects of Greek *paideia* and its power to make Greeks and elites of others – including but only Macedonians.[4] On the one hand, as Morgan observes, this "Attic-language, literary education which the Macedonians put into operation ... helped to develop and maintain a concept of shared greek-ness in areas where Greeks of all cities ... now found themselves defined as a group ... scattered and few among peoples who had thriving languages, cultures, and social structures of their own."[5] On the other hand, as Raffaella Cribiore reminds us, "most of the Greeks in the Eastern world could not claim to be born in Greece or to be of recent Greek descent, but they could speak a common language, read and write in an artificial Greek of the past, and follow the same aesthetic and ethical ideals endorsed by education."[6] In a newly multipolar Mediterranean world, new forms of Greek *paideia* thus modeled the power of education to overcome exile: "Cultivated individuals and students considered themselves exiles of an ideal country—Greece—and yearned to belong to that distant world, of which they were citizens by virtue of the texts that they read and the values they encountered through reading."[7]

The ideal of a globalizing horizon to Greekness was hardly new. Already in the fourth century BCE, Isocrates declared *Hellenismos* extric-able from lineage and mediated by pedagogy.[8] What was new, however, was the implementation of this ideal on a transregional scope, under the aegis of imperial power, and with a new emphasis on literacy and

---

would be maintained for nearly a thousand years ... This testifies not only to the urgent need for such a system in the early Hellenistic period ... it also reminds us how efficient communications could be throughout the Hellenistic (and Roman) world" (24).

[4] Here, too, political and cultural dynamics were mutually reinforcing: it was in part due to its utility as a means "to mediate and enable the co-operation of non-Greeks ... [and] to keep control of the army, economy, and administration," as Morgan notes (*Literate Education*, 23), that it also emerged as "a symbol of status and identity with the ruling minority."

[5] Morgan, *Literate Education*, 22.

[6] Cribiore, *Gymnastics of the Mind*, 9. Morgan (*Literate Education*, 22) similarly emphasizes how this "Attic-language, literary education which the Macedonians put into operation ... helped to develop and maintain a concept of shared greekness in areas where Greeks of all cities ... now found themselves defined as a group ... scattered and few among peoples who had thriving languages, cultures, and social structures of their own."

[7] Cribiore, *Gymnastics of the Mind*, 9.

[8] Isocrates, *Panegyricus* 50. Notably, Isocrates also wrote of the limits of *paideia*, especially in relation to natural talent and practice, and he was particularly suspicious of specialized training; see, e.g., *Antidosis* 187–192; *Panathenaicus* 28–29; *Sophists* 14; Poulakos, *Speaking for the Polis*, 91–104.

textuality.[9] Consequently, much more than a difference in time and locale separates Isocrates' assertion that "all who speak skillfully are pupils (μαθητάς) of the city" of Athens, from Andron's claim, centuries later, that "Alexandrians are the educators (οἱ παιδεύσαντες) of all the Greeks and the barbarians."[10] Whether or not Isocrates intended his words as an expression of local pride, his claims took on translocal connotations when correlated with imperial ideologies, cultivated in courts, and concretized in archives and libraries.[11] In the crucible of an emergent court culture linking the new Hellenistic empires, Greekness itself was reinvented – as Rolf Strootman has shown – with pretensions of "a distinct, non-ethnic, supranational form of culture, tending to smooth the regional differences among Greeks and redefine Greek culture in the light of a more cosmopolitan world view."[12] The Alexandrian Mouseion and its library are but the most famous expression of the cultural politics whereby rulers like the Ptolemies performed highly visible acts of patronizing scholars, scrolls, and knowledge.[13] The results included what Tim Whitmarsh describes as the archival culture of Hellenistic Alexandria.[14] Yet they also went far beyond, encompassing other acts of imperial and aristocratic book collection, newly intensified efforts at textualizing and anthologizing older traditions, and the reworking of technical and other lists into newly literary forms.

Much has been written about the ramifications of Greek *paideia* and Ptolemaic culture politics for setting dynamics into motion that would

[9] On the place of books in Greek *paideia*, see Cribiore, *Gymnastics of the Mind*, 137–201. On "Ptolemaic culture politics," see Erskine, "Culture and Power in Ptolemaic Egypt" – there speculating, albeit in passing, about whether this new emphasis on writtenness might reflect something of their Egyptian milieu.

[10] Isocrates, *Antidosis* 296; Athenaeus, *Deipnosophists* 4.83.184b; FrGrH 246 Fr1. The latter writer is otherwise unknown; see further Hashiba in BNJ 246; Whitmarsh, *Ancient Greek Literature*, 7–9.

[11] Cf. Thucydides 2.41.1; Poulakos, *Speaking for the Polis*, 78–92.

[12] Strootman, *Courts and Elites in the Hellenistic Empires*, 10 – i.e., thus new in its imperial repurposing and contexts even as it drew upon "pan-Hellenic concepts of Greekness that had already been developing before the Hellenistic age" (11).

[13] Erskine ("Culture and Power," 38) points to these two institutions as "products of the Hellenistic age and of the competition which arose between the successors of Alexander" and as "encapsulat[ing] the ideology and policy of the early Ptolemies," and Harder ("From Text to Text," 96) further points to the "fact that the position of the librarian was coupled with that of the tutor of the Ptolemaic princes." Whatever the accuracy of specific details here, this image does seem to preserve something of broader cultural shifts in Hellenistic period – on which see now Johnstone, "A New History of Libraries and Books in the Hellenistic Period."

[14] Whitmarsh, *Ancient Greek Literature*, 122–138.

come to shape the Roman Empire and, eventually, the making of the modern West.[15] The question that concerns us here, in this chapter and the next, is whether we glimpse any immediate effects within Judaism – not just in Alexandria but in Judaea and its environs as well.

Prior to the discovery of the Dead Sea Scrolls, Jewish literary evidence for the early Hellenistic age was scant, and scholars could only speculate about the shifts in Judaea during this momentous century of cultural and political change across the Mediterranean world. Some sense of such shifts could be inferred from sources in Greek from Alexandria, such as the *Epistle of Aristeas*, and the fragments of Greek Jewish authors preserved via Alexander Polyhistor. Some sense of the momentousness of this century could also be inferred from the differences in Jewish literary production before and after – not least on topics like angels and demons. As noted above, however, it is only recently that we are able to map these shifts in more specific terms, thanks to new evidence from the Dead Sea Scrolls.

With the discovery and publication of the Aramaic Enoch fragments from Qumran, it became clear that the oldest known "pseudepigrapha" were taking form when Judaea was under Hellenistic imperial rule, having come under Ptolemaic control after the Battle of Ipsus (301 BCE). With the completion of the publication of the Dead Sea Scrolls, we are now able to situate these "pseudepigrapha" within a broader Aramaic literary tradition – not only limited to apocalypses. As we have seen in Chapter 2, the pre-Maccabean writings known to us from the earliest "pseudepigrapha" and the Aramaic Dead Sea Scrolls make up the largest corpus of surviving Jewish literature from the period of Ptolemaic rule over the Land of Israel, and they point to a circle of Judaean scribes who did not embrace the new prestige language of Greek, nor retain the Hebrew of those older Jewish scribal cultures that wrought early biblical literature, choosing rather to repurpose the Achaemenid administrative language and Near Eastern *koine* of Aramaic. It is within the products of their distinctive scribal pedagogy, moreover, that we find the first surviving examples of explicit and systematic Jewish reflection on angels and demons.

The present chapter explores the microdynamics of this development with a focus on angelology. To do so, I bring recent insights into Hellenistic knowledge-practices into conversation with the one of the most

---

[15] See König and Whitmarsh, "Ordering Knowledge in the Roman Empire," 8–9.

puzzling texts from this time – namely, the *Astronomical Book*. Even prior to the discovery of the Dead Sea Scrolls, a version of the work was known from chapters 72–82 of the Ethiopian compendium *1 Enoch*. In the form preserved there, it offers a first-person account from the antedi-luvian sage Enoch, who recounts what the angel Uriel showed him of the cycles of the moon, sun, stars, winds, and weather, and what Enoch, in turn, wrote and taught of this knowledge to his son Methuselah. With the discovery of related Aramaic fragments at Qumran, this work was revealed to be more ancient than scholars had suspected, hailing from the late fourth or third century BCE.

Due to this early date, the *Astronomical Book* is one of the sources that can most plausibly be used to fill the silence of what was previously known of Judaism in the early Hellenistic age. To the degree that it fills this silence, however, it does so in a manner that challenges our very notion of what "Judaism" even entails – and how and why it should react to "Hellenism." The Aramaic fragments point to a probable date for the work early in the period of Ptolemaic rule over the Land of Israel. These fragments, however, are also marked by a greater degree of astronomical concern than the later Ethiopian versions, and they reveal the depth of the debts of the *Astronomical Book* to much older Mesopotamian traditions.

At first sight, the dependence on Babylonian calendrical astronomy might seem to signal a tradition either sealed off from the effects of Hellenization or reacting sharply against them. This was what Michael E. Stone suggested in the 1980s, for instance, in the wake of the partial publication of the Aramaic Enoch fragments from Qumran and Otto Neugebauer's preliminary assessment of the calendrical science therein.[16] More recent analyses of its connections to Babylonian lunar theory have revealed the situation to be far more complex. Matthias Albani established the connection to the astronomical and calendrical ideas current in Babylonian scholarly circles around the time of the redaction of MUL.APIN (ca. 700 BCE), and after the full publication of the relevant fragments (esp. 4Q208), Jonathan Ben-Dov and Henryk Drawnel demonstrated its continued debts to Mesopotamian science and scholasticism.[17] By situating the *Astronomical Book* in the context

[16] Stone, "Enoch, Aramaic Levi, and Sectarian Origins," 251–252; Neugebauer, "The 'Astronomical Chapters' of the Ethiopic Book of Enoch"

[17] Albani, *Astronomie und Schöpfungsglaube*; Ben-Dov, *Head of All Years*; Drawnel, *Aramaic Astronomical Book*. Ben-Dov stresses the broad scope of possibilities for the time of the initial Jewish contact with such traditions, ranging from Neo-Babylonian to Hellenistic periods (245–247).

of other calendrical materials now known from Qumran, moreover, Ben-Dov established ancient Jewish engagement with Babylonian astronomy to be more sustained than previously assumed – that is, with adoption of MUL.APIN-type models as well as concepts arising subsequent to them.[18] Nor was calendrical astronomy the only avenue of Jewish engagement with the "scientific" and technical discourses of the ancient Mediterranean world. Mladen Popović has demonstrated from the evidence of another Aramaic fragment, 4Q561, how Jewish scribes were familiar with some elements of Greek physiognomy.[19] Together with the Hebrew fragment 4Q186, this evidence reveals the degree to which "Second Temple period Judaism participated in forms of learning that were current in surrounding cultures."[20] Inasmuch as these materials point to intellectual interchange with Mesopotamian as well as with Hellenistic traditions, they dispel the mirage of a monolithic "Judaism" in encounter with a monolithic "Hellenism" in the Second Temple period.

How, then, should we understand the timing of the formation of the *Astronomical Book*? Seth Sanders summarizes the problem as follows:

> ... it is not possible to explain the new Jewish interest in mathematics and astronomy [in the *Astronomical Book*] through Greek influence. This is because it mainly draws on elements that had existed in the ancient Near East for centuries before its emergence in texts of the third century BCE. The new material first appears in Aramaic, not Greek; it is in a dialect—Standard Literary Aramaic—formed already in the Persian period; and it derives directly from a Babylonian scientific tradition that was itself one of the main influences on early Greek mathematics and astronomy.[21]

Albani, Ben-Dov, Drawnel, Sanders, and others have demonstrated that the *Astronomical Book* preserves knowledge from scribal traditions centuries prior to the formation of the text itself, and they have speculated about a range of possible dates for the intellectual interchanges that mediated their knowledge to Jewish scribes and enabled its inner-Jewish

---

[18] Ben-Dov, *Head of All Years*.

[19] Popović, *Reading the Human Body*, 68–118. Popović also points to the Hebrew fragment 4Q186 as offering "exceptional textual evidence for physiognomic and astrological learning in antiquity in general" inasmuch as physiognomics is there used "to determine a person's zodiacal sign" ("Physiognomic Knowledge in Qumran and Babylonia," 151, 165; also Popović, *Reading the Human Body*, 18–54, 119–208; Alexander, "Physiognomy, Initiation, and Rank in the Qumran Community").

[20] Popović, "Physiognomic Knowledge," 150–151.

[21] Sanders, "I Was Shown Another Calculation," 75.

cultivation.[22] In this chapter, thus, I would like to build upon their insights to ask a different set of questions, oriented instead to its literary forms and formation. Whatever and wherever the ultimate origins of the content collected within the *Astronomical Book*, why do we find it first textualized, in these particular forms, specifically when and how we do? Why would learned Jews living under Hellenistic rule, in the third century BCE, write about Babylonian astronomy in Aramaic?[23]

The timing of the formation of the *Astronomical Book* is certainly puzzling when we read it through the lens of later ideas about "Judaism" and "Hellenism." I shall suggest that it makes sense, however, when we follow the theorization of writing within the work itself and attend to the choices made by the scribes who collected, selected, rewrote, and reframed the knowledge therein. When we do so with reference to the relevant Aramaic fragments, in particular, we may be able to draw out some of the scribal practices and settings that mediated its very emergence as literature, as well as some of the ways in which this process dovetailed with broader archival, pedagogical, and other intellectual trends of the early Hellenistic age. And to do so – I shall here argue – is also to recover the neglected significance of the *Astronomical Book* for the emergence of Jewish angelology.

THE ENOCHIC *ASTRONOMICAL BOOK* AND ANCIENT SCIENCES

Earlier Israelites no doubt reflected upon the cosmos and likely even studied its cycles. What they do not seem to have done, however, is to write about these topics in explicit terms – or as Ben-Dov puts it: to compose "complete treatises dedicated to systematic scientific genres, as opposed to sporadic statements."[24] Yet this is precisely what we find evinced so densely and decisively in the Aramaic Jewish literature of the early Hellenistic age, beginning already with its earliest known exemplar.

The *Astronomical Book* is the oldest known example of the expansion of the scope of Jewish literary production during the early Hellenistic age,

[22] Albani, *Astronomie und Schöpfungsglaube*; Ben-Dov, *Head of All Years*; Drawnel, "Some Notes on Scribal Craft and the Origins of the Enochic Literature"; Drawnel, "Between Akkadian tupšarrūtu and Aramaic SPR"; Sanders, *From Adapa*; Ben-Dov and Sanders, *Ancient Jewish Sciences and the History of Knowledge in Second Temple Literature*.

[23] I address this particular question in more detail – with some overlapping arguments – in Reed, "Writing Jewish Astronomy in the Early Hellenistic Age."

[24] Ben-Dov, "Ideals of Science," 109.

and it is also the most astonishing. Even prior to the discovery of the Dead Sea Scrolls, this work was known to modern scholars from chapters 72–82 of the Ethiopian compendium *1 Enoch*. In the form preserved there, it offers a first-person account from the antediluvian sage Enoch concerning what the angel Uriel showed him of the cycles of the moon, sun, stars, seasons, and weather, and what Enoch, in turn, wrote and taught of this knowledge to and through his son Methuselah. As with other materials in *1 Enoch*, the *Astronomical Book* attracted fresh scholarly attention after the discovery of related Aramaic fragments among the Dead Sea Scrolls. The first publication of these fragments in 1976 focused largely on the seven manuscripts preserving other parts of *1 Enoch* (4QEn^{a-g}), including, but not limited to, the *Book of the Watchers*, which is represented both by itself (4QEn^{a,b}) and copied together with the *Book of Dreams* and/or *Epistle of Enoch* (4QEn^{c-e}). J. T. Milik identified four other manuscripts as containing only the *Astronomical Book*, always copied by itself (4Q208 – 4Q211 = 4QEnastr^{a-d}).[25] Milik dated the earliest among them, 4Q208, paleographically to the third or early second century BCE, and on that basis, posited the *Astronomical Book* as the most ancient work within *1 Enoch*.[26]

Despite its antiquity, the *Astronomical Book* has attracted much less attention than the *Book of the Watchers*. There are a number of reasons for this relative neglect – mostly quite practical. Modern readers of the *Book of the Watchers*, for instance, can readily recognize any number of features that became common or conventional within later apocalypses and related writings, as well as glimpsing the first known attestations of some ideas with very long afterlives within Judaism, Christianity, and Islam, including traditions concerning Enoch, heavenly ascent, fallen angels, demons, and the fate of the dead.[27] The form and content of the *Astronomical Book*, by contrast, is frustratingly opaque to those without specialist background in ancient sciences, in general, and Babylonian astronomy, in particular.

---

[25] For the fragments, see Milik, *Books of Enoch*, 273–297 and plates XXV–XXX; Tigchelaar and García Martínez in DJD 36.95–171; Drawnel, *Aramaic Astronomical Book*.

[26] Milik, *Books of Enoch*, 7–22. On the *Astronomical Book* as the oldest part of *1 Enoch*, see also VanderKam, *Enoch and the Growth of an Apocalyptic Tradition*; Kvanvig, *Roots of Apocalyptic*. For a recent reassessment and defense of Milik's dating of 4Q208, see Drawnel, *Aramaic Astronomical Book*, 73. Drawnel also affirms the third century BCE as a "reasonable assumption" for dating the work more broadly (51).

[27] See, e.g., Reed, *Fallen Angels*; Reeves and Reed, *Enoch*.

The challenge of studying the *Astronomical Book* is compounded by the character of the surviving textual witnesses. Those studying the *Book of the Watchers* encounter relatively few issues when trying to align fragments of the Aramaic with the text of the later Ethiopic translation, and they are able to consult multiple overlapping witnesses to the intermediary Greek. By contrast, the *Astronomical Book* survives in only a few lines of Greek,[28] and the divergences in the Aramaic and Ethiopic witnesses frustrate even basic efforts to align fragment with text.[29] In addition, the arduous work of correlating these textual witnesses was delayed by Milik's selectivity in the first edition of the Aramaic Enoch fragments. Despite identifying four manuscripts as copies of the *Astronomical Book*, his 1976 edition reproduced only two of them in full.[30] Those studying the other sections of *1 Enoch* attested at Qumran have had the full array of Aramaic evidence at their fingertips for almost forty years. But during most of that time, even basic work on the *Astronomical Book* could progress only tentatively.[31]

It was not until 2000 that complete editions of the fragments of the remaining two manuscripts (4Q208, 4Q209) were fully published and accessible, thanks to Eibert Tigchelaar and Florentino García Martínez.[32] Since then, research on the *Astronomical Book* has seen a renaissance, particularly in relation to reconstructing the scientific principles and intellectual background of its calendrical astronomy.[33] In this, scholars have been aided by other materials from among the Dead Sea Scrolls, which have revealed a broader context for its focused interest in the movements of the moon and sun, not just as a precursor to later controversies over the proper calendar for the Jerusalem Temple (cf. *1 En* 75:2), but also as part of a broader tradition of technical knowledge within the Judaism of the time.[34]

---

[28] At most! See P. Oxy. 2069 frg. 3 ≈ *1 En* 77:7–78:1 + 78:8; Milik, "Fragments grecs du livre d'Hénoch," 333–341; Chesnutt, "Oxyrhynchus Papyrus 2069 and the Compositional History of Enoch."

[29] VanderKam, "Book of Luminaries," 351.

[30] Milik, *Books of Enoch*, 273–297, includes 4Q210 and 4Q211 but only part of 4Q209, and omits 4Q208.

[31] Groundbreaking work in this period included Albani, *Astronomie und Schöpfungsglaube*.

[32] The two had published an initial transcription and translation in their 1997 *DSS Study Edition* – which marked the first time that any portion of 4Q208 had been published.

[33] See now Ben-Dov and Sanders, *Ancient Jewish Sciences*.

[34] Esp. Ben-Dov, *Head of All Years*; Ben-Dov, "Scientific Writings"; Popović, "The Emergence of Aramaic and Hebrew Scholarly Texts." Ben-Dov, in particular, shows how recent work has been aided by the availability of further relevant cuneiform materials as well.

In fact, as Ben-Dov has demonstrated, the *Astronomical Book* is the fountainhead of a dynamic Jewish intellectual tradition surrounding the 364–day calendar, which was shaped by continued engagement with Babylonian ideas.[35]

The *Astronomical Book* and other technical materials from Qumran showcase an aspect of ancient Jewish intellectual culture that is almost wholly lacking from the Hebrew Bible and classical Rabbinic literature.[36] Yet Ben-Dov makes a persuasive case for understanding Jewish cultivation of Babylonian and Greek scientific knowledge as more than mere "borrowing." By his reading, the evidence from Qumran demonstrates that "the Jewish scientific tradition ... constituted an integral part of the astronomical knowledge current in the Ancient Near East during the Persian and early Hellenistic periods," but it also suggests that "the emulation of this knowledge in Jewish circles lead to a new synthesis, perceptibly different from the main streams of astronomical teaching existent in Babylonia, Greece, Egypt, and India ... a self-contained intellectual construct."[37] Ben-Dov characterizes this tradition as simultaneously a crossing-point between cultures and its own distinctive synthesis, spanning astronomy, astrology, geography, metrology, physiognomy, and exorcism.[38] What I shall suggest, in what follows, is that we might add angelology and demonology to the list – and that angelology, in particular, is part of what facilitated the Jewish textualization of cosmological information into newly literary and narrativized forms.

Like Ben-Dov, I am more interested in analyzing ancient theories and categories of knowledge than in judging them against modern criteria of scienticity. Accordingly, this chapter does not address the questions of whether or not the content of the *Astronomical Book* counts as "*real science*" or whether it is "outdated" by external criteria of "progress."[39]

---

[35] Ben-Dov, *Head of All Years*, 9–10, 21–68, 158–244.
[36] On the latter, see Alexander, "Pre-emptive Exegesis"; Schäfer, "From Cosmology to Theology"; Reed, "Was There Science in Ancient Judaism"; cf. Séd, *La Mystique Cosmologique Juive*.
[37] Ben-Dov, *Head of All Years*, 1; see further 276–278, 286–287
[38] Ben-Dov, *Head of All Years*, 6–7; Ben-Dov, "Scientific Writings," 380–381.
[39] Accordingly, I here use the category "astronomy" in its broadest sense as pertaining to the systematic study of celestial phenomena, particularly as perceived in antiquity, rather than trying to judge what counts as "*really* astronomy" vs. "astrology," "calendar science," or the like. Needless to say, there are notable differences between Babylonian mathematical astronomy and Greek astronomy after Hipparchus, on the one hand, and the discussion of celestial cycles in the *Astronomical Book*, Aratus' *Phaenomena*,

In bracketing such concerns, I follow the lead of recent research in the History of Science that has eschewed teleological presentism in favor of a renewed engagement with cultural history.[40] Studies on topics ranging from Roman encyclopedism to the early modern colonial sciences of Asia and Africa have pointed to the value of situating specific knowledge-endeavors within their own socio-political contexts, particularly in cases where imperial power may be at play in sustaining hierarchies of knowledge or structuring the connectivity of local traditions of education and expertise.[41] Partly as a result, recent research at the intersection of Classics and the History of Science has pointed to the cultural work done by anthologizing technical knowledge – and thus the value, as Jason König and Tim Whitmarsh note, of asking how "particular conceptions of knowledge and particular ways of textualising knowledge were entwined with social and political practices and ideals."[42] Along these lines, Emma Gee and Katharina Volk have helped to recover the import of writers like Aratus and Manilius, who were influential in antiquity but neglected in modern scholarship due to judgments about the derivative character of their astronomy and their lack of any discoveries of their own.[43] Just as fresh attention to such figures reveals much about the place of astronomy in the power-knowledge complex of the ancient Mediterranean world, so too – I propose – with the *Astronomical Book.*

In focusing on the process of the textualization of such knowledge therein, I also extend recent shifts in the scholarly conversation about ancient Jewish sciences. Earlier discussion focused largely on the form of the *Astronomical Book* known from *1 Enoch* 72–82 and centered on the question of whether or not the authors deliberately adopted outdated

---

Berossus' "astronomical fragments," etc., on the other. My interest here is in understanding the cultural continuum that connected them *in antiquity*, rather than in distinguishing those particular knowledge-enterprises that contributed to lines of scientific development that made "progress" toward our own understanding of the universe today.

[40] So already Kuhn, *The Structure of Scientific Revolutions*, 1–3, 137–141. See more recently Dear, "What Is the History of Science the History Of?," 406; Roberts, "Situating Science in Global History," 10; Cuomo, *Technology and Culture in Greek and Roman Antiquity*, 3–4; Principe, "Alchemy Restored"; Lehoux, *What Did the Romans.*

[41] e.g., Chambers & Gillespie, "Locality in the History of Science"; Elshakry, "When Science Became Western"; Roberts, "Situating Science in Global History"; König and Whitmarsh, *Ordering Knowledge.*

[42] König and Whitmarsh, "Ordering Knowledge," 3.

[43] Gee, *Aratus and the Astronomical Tradition*; Volk, *Manilius.*

Babylonian models in resistance to newer Hellenistic ideas.[44] Discussion in the past decade, however, has been less concerned with questions of progress (e.g., who discovered what first) and more concerned with questions of pedagogy (e.g., how, where, why, and by whom accumulated scientific knowledge was systematized, preserved, taught, and transmitted). Popović, in particular, has pressed for attention to the literary framing of the scientific materials found at Qumran.[45] Much can be learned from culling such materials for content to compare with the products of similar knowledge-enterprises in other cultures. Nevertheless – as Popović stresses – if we wish to understand the "context of transmission of scholarly knowledge," we must ask: "what textual formats or genres of scientific writings are attested? And what sort of authorial strategies did ancient Jewish scholars pursue?"[46]

Inasmuch as the scientific concerns of the *Astronomical Book* are unparalleled in the Hebrew Bible, it may be tempting to look to this work for evidence for the origins of Jewish "scientific thought."[47] Yet it is unclear whether literary evidence could suffice to answer a cognitive question of this sort.[48] What such evidence can help us to investigate, however, is when, where, how, and why some Jewish scribes chose to record selected technical knowledge about the natural world *in writing*.[49] Even if the surviving data do not span the sum total of ancient Jewish interest in the cosmos, they remain quite telling. In the case of the *Astronomical Book*, it is clear that its literary formation cannot be conflated with the first moment of Jewish contact or concern with calendrical

---

[44] Most influentially: Stone, "Enoch, Aramaic Levi," 251–252, building upon the assessment of Neugebauer, "Astronomical Chapters." Stone's assessment was answered by Alexander, "Enoch and the Beginnings," who pushed the date of the *Astronomical Book* back so as to locate Jewish interest in science as contemporaneous to the so-called Greek miracle. Note, however, that Neugebauer's judgment was based mainly on the Ethiopic version; on the resultant distortions, see Drawnel, *Aramaic Astronomical Book*, 244–245.

[45] Popović, "Emergence"; Popović, "Networks of Scholars."

[46] Popović, "Emergence," 83.

[47] Most influentially: Alexander, "Enoch and the Beginnings."

[48] On the limitations of cognitive approaches to the history of science, and their special dangers when paired with potentially reified cultural identities (e.g., "Jewish," "Greek," "Chinese," "Western"), see Rochberg, "A Consideration of Babylonian Astronomy Within the Historiography of Science"; Brennan, "The Birth of Modern Science."

[49] I take inspiration here also from the distinction that Tzvi Langermann makes for later materials: "I am *not* asking when Jews first began to evince an *interest* in science. The question I want to answer is when Jews first *wrote* Hebrew texts whose primary purpose was the exposition of scientific knowledge" ("On the Beginnings of Hebrew Scientific Literature," 169–170; emphasis mine).

astronomy: the lunar theory therein bears the marks of older debts to Babylonian science.[50] What we see in the early Hellenistic age are intensive and creative efforts to textualize this and related information in newly anthologized and narrativized forms.[51]

When we look to the broader context of the ancient Mediterranean world, the timing of these efforts proves poignant. Indeed, as Volk has noted:

> The Hellenistic period witnessed an unprecedented flourishing of Greek mathematical astronomy, fuelled by contact (following the conquests of Alexander the Great) with Mesopotamian observational records and methods of calculation, by the development of trigonometry, and by the patronage offered to scientists by powerful rulers. The compilation of detailed star catalogues, Eratosthenes' calculation of the circumference of the earth, Hipparchus' discovery of the procession of the equinoxes, and the endeavor to model planetary movements with the help of epicycles and deferents – to name just a few achievements – all fall within this same golden age of ancient science, the third and second centuries BC.[52]

If we focus on the scientific content of the *Astronomical Book* and try to fit it within straight lines of progress traced toward modern Western science, the choice to preserve older Babylonian models might seem like "a deliberate act of archaism ... aris[ing] either from the conscious rejection of Greek science, or else from the creation of a social context into which such science did not penetrate."[53] What I shall suggest, however, is the choice makes sense when we follow Classicists like Volk in viewing the third century BCE through the double lens of science and literature. Even discoveries such as those of Eratosthenes and Hipparchus were not isolated from their contexts: they were shaped by the newly intensified imperial patronage of knowledge in the Hellenistic period, and they form part of the same cultural continuum as the concurrent "widespread non-specialist interest in things having to do with the stars."[54]

---

[50] Drawnel, *Aramaic Astronomical Book*, 47–49.

[51] It is because of this distinction that I am wary of following those who suggest that the Babylonian origins of the science therein necessitates a Babylonian provenance for the work itself (e.g., Albani, *Astronomie und Schöpfungsglaube*, 270; Drawnel, *Aramaic Astronomical Book*, 53, 301). For a recent argument against Babylonian provenance on the grounds of the broad diffusion of the model underlying 4Q208 by the third and second centuries BCE, see now Duke and Goff, "The Astronomy of the Qumran Fragments 4Q208 and 4Q209" – there building on Popović, "Networks of Scholars," 171.

[52] Volk, *Manilius and His Intellectual Background*, 25–26

[53] Stone, "Enoch, Aramaic Levi," 252.   [54] Volk, *Manilius*, 27.

Rather than asking why the *Astronomical Book* does not integrate new discoveries by thinkers like Hipparchus, we may learn more from comparing it to a work like Aratus' *Phaenomena*. Written around 276 BCE in the Antigonid court, this Greek didactic poem contributed nothing new to the science of its time. Nevertheless, as Volk reminds us, "this did not prevent his poem from being used for centuries as an astronomy textbook – even though the work, far from being comprehensive, amounts to little more than a catalogue of constellations plus a list of paranatellonta (stars that rise simultaneously with signs of the zodiac) and discussion of (largely unastronomical) weather signs."[55] Below, we will explore some of the concerns and strategies shared by Aratus and the *Astronomical Book*. For now, it suffices to call upon the *Phaenomena* as an example of the cultural work done by textualizing and anthologizing older technical knowledge in new didactically-oriented literary forms – particularly in the third century BCE.

In my view, the distinction between scientific thought and scientific writing proves especially critical for understanding the *Astronomical Book*, due to the complexity of the textual witnesses to this work. Especially after the publication of 4Q208 and 4Q209, one can no longer treat the version of the *Astronomical Book* in *1 Enoch* as if basically equivalent to the text's original form. When one compares the Aramaic fragments to the Ethiopic text of *1 Enoch* 72–82, "it is obvious that something drastic happened in the journey from one to the other," as James VanderKam has noted.[56] Even as the evidence from Qumran thus complicates our efforts to analyze the work's content, it thereby opens up opportunities to investigate its form and formation. Rarely are we so lucky to have so many early manuscripts of a work and so many clues to the patterns of fluidity that preceded its textual stabilization. Not only do these data provide a check on source-critical hypotheses about *1 Enoch*, but they also permit a rare peek into the process by which new types of knowledge – nowhere represented in the Hebrew Bible – came to be integrated into Jewish literary cultures in Second Temple times.

What I shall suggest, more specifically, is that the manuscript evidence for the *Astronomical Book* preserves something of the process of its development into what David Carr calls "long-duration" literature – that

---

[55] Volk, *Manilius*, 27. Its rich reception-history (on which see now Gee, *Aratus*) also points to the striking differences between ancient and modern ideas of Science. As much as Hipparchus is celebrated now for his contribution to scientific progress, for instance, it is perhaps telling that the only work of his to survive is his commentary on Aratus!

[56] VanderKam, "Book of the Luminaries," 351.

is, writing meant for continued copying and studying, in contrast to writing meant for short-duration or single-context use or for archiving or display as record.[57] To consider the full range of the Aramaic fragments relevant to the *Astronomical Book*, alongside the Greek and Ethiopic witnesses, is perhaps to catch glimpses of a dynamic process of textualization whereby didactic lists came to be compiled and reshaped, in part through the addition of first-person notices evoking the cross-cultural sapiential ideal of a father teaching his son. This move from list to literature eventually culminated with the integration of astronomical data into the biography of the antediluvian sage Enoch – as part of the cosmological knowledge that he learned from the angel Uriel during his otherworldly journeys and later taught to his son Methuselah.[58] Attention to the Aramaic manuscripts from Qumran, however, reveals the association with Enoch to be far less prominent than one might expect; Enoch, in fact, may be absent from the first stages of the work's history. What mediates the inclusion of astronomy within the domain of Jewish knowledge, instead, is angelology.

In light of its textual history, the authorizing strategies of the *Astronomical Book* cannot be reduced simply to the appeal to Enoch to provide a "religious" pedigree for Jewish interest in "science" or to "domesticate" Mesopotamian "alien wisdom." Rather, as we shall see, the manuscript evidence tells a more complex story, and it resists the retrojection of modern dichotomies like "religion" vs. "science" or "Judaism" vs. "Hellenism."[59] As a result, attention to its literary forms and formation may open the way for situating the *Astronomical Book* in the third century BCE, alongside parallel efforts by Greeks and Babylonians to lay claim to astronomy and cosmology through creative acts of literary reframing and mythic retelling. It also helps to highlight the character of its inner-Jewish innovation – that is, as less a matter of heurematography than angelology.[60] In the course of rewriting older didactic lists into

---

[57] Carr, *Writing on the Tablet*, 10.

[58] The idea of Enoch's otherworldly journey with Uriel as guide is attested also in the *Book of the Watchers* (esp. 1 En 33; cf. Gen 5:24). As Stuckenbruck notes (*1 Enoch 91–108*, 157–161), Methuselah is mentioned already in the *Astronomical Book* (76:14; 82:1) but becomes more prominent later in the Aramaic Enoch tradition; e.g., *1 En* 83:1; 85:1–3; 91:1–2; 92:1; cf. Gen 5:21.

[59] See further Reed, "Ancient Jewish Sciences and the Historiography of Judaism."

[60] On heurematography see Chapter 2 as well as Kleingünter, *Protos Heuretes*; Thrade, "Erfinder II"; Reed, "Ancient Jewish Sciences"; McCants, *Founding Gods, Inventing Nations*.

Jewish literature – as we shall see – the Jewish scribes responsible for the *Astronomical Book* project angels both into the cycles of the celestial bodies and into the very practice of Jewish scribal pedagogy, as those who mediate the sight of knowledge written on and about the heavens. In the process, they offer a precise and systematic treatment of angels that is unprecedented in earlier Jewish literature.

FROM DIDACTIC LISTS TO LONG-DURATION LITERATURE

In the past, scholars had tended to treat the Ethiopic version of the *Astronomical Book* as basically equivalent to its original form. The full publication of 4Q208 and 4Q209 in 2000, however, unsettled any such assumptions. Despite the intersections of the Aramaic and Ethiopic manuscripts, there is simply no way to read the fragments of 4Q208–4Q211 as scraps of the original Aramaic *Vorlage* behind the Ethiopic of *1 Enoch* 72–82. Nor is this fluidity merely the product of translation; there are notable differences already among the Aramaic fragments. The variance among the textual witnesses to the *Astronomical Book,* and the problems of textual identity that they pose, thus frustrate the recovery of any one single original, core, or *Ur*-text. Precisely because of this variance, however, the manuscript evidence helps us to reconstruct some of the micro-dynamics of the process by which elements of Babylonian astronomy came to be textualized as a topic of Jewish literary concern and reframed as remembrance of Israel's pre-Sinaitic past.

Following Milik's paleographical dating of the four relevant Aramaic manuscripts, we can chart a relative chronology with 4Q208 at the end of the third or beginning of the second century BCE, 4Q210 and 4Q211 in the middle of the first century BCE, and 4Q209 at the turn of the eras.[61] In all of the Aramaic manuscripts, astronomical material is more prominent and detailed than in the version of the *Astronomical Book* known in Ethiopic translation from *1 Enoch* 72–82. Narrative material, by contrast, is far less extensive in the Aramaic, and the surviving fragments preserve no traces of the names of Enoch, Uriel, or Methuselah.

The oldest manuscript, 4Q208, contrasts most starkly with *1 Enoch*: it has no direct textual parallel at all with the version of the *Astronomical Book* known in Ethiopic. One of its editors, Eibert Tigchelaar, went so far as to ask whether 4Q208 can be characterized as a "copy" of the

---

Astronomical Book, since it "need not have been an Enochic writing *per se*."[62] Its preserved text consists of a list of excruciatingly exhaustive information about lunar visibility, which finds only indirect echoes in the version of the *Astronomical Book* embedded in *1 Enoch* (cf. 73:4–8). One of the two manuscripts from the first century BCE, 4Q211, exhibits a similar pattern: its treatment of the seasons and weather finds no exact counterpart in *1 Enoch*, even though there is some overlap in concern (cf. *1 En* 82:20).[63] The other manuscript from the first century BCE, 4Q210, preserves portions of three consecutive chapters of *1 Enoch*.[64] Evinced in the latest Aramaic manuscript, however, is the emergent unity of a textual tradition that might otherwise seem like diffuse reflections on common themes. This manuscript, 4Q209, survives in twenty-six fragments, and contains text that overlaps with 4Q208, 4Q210, and portions of *1 Enoch* 76–79 and 82 – including counterparts to the use of first-person speech to frame astronomical data.[65]

The manuscript evidence confirms that the processes of compilation and redaction that resulted in the *Astronomical Book* were already well under way within the Aramaic stage of the tradition, prior to Greek and Ethiopic translation.[66] The four Aramaic witnesses offer snapshots of a textual tradition in motion:

Fragment number and date (Milik)	Parallels with other Aramaic MSS	Points of connection with *1 Enoch* 72–82
4Q208/4QEnastr[a] 3rd to early 2nd c. BCE = "synchronic calendar" (Milik, VanderKam) or "calculation of lunar visibility according to the monthly pattern" (Ben-Dov, Drawnel)	Shared material with 4Q209 frg. 1–22, 29–34, 36–41	No direct textual parallels, but some shared subject matter with *1 En* 73:4–8 (i.e., brief description of the first two days of the monthly lunar calculation).

[62] Tigchelaar, "Some Remarks on the *Book of Watchers*," 145.

[63] VanderKam ("Book of Luminaries," 566–568) summarizes the theories concerning the original location of this material after *1 En* 82:20 but advises caution in this regard.

[64] I.e., *1 En* 76:3–10 and 76:13–77:4 in 4Q210 frg. 1 ii; 78:6–8 in frg. 1 iii.

[65] I.e., *1 En* 76:13–77:4 in 4Q209 frg. 23; 77:1–2 in frg. 24; 78:16[?]–17 and 79:1–4 in frg. 26; 82:9–13 in frg. 28.

[66] The evidence of 4Q209 definitively counters Matthew Black's notion (*The Book of Enoch*, 10) that the *Astronomical Book* was an invention of the Greek translators of other Enochic writings.

4Q211/4QEnastr[d] 1st c. BCE		*Possibly preserving* *material that once came* *after 1 En 82:20?*
4Q210/4QEnastr[c] 1st c. BCE	Textual parallels with 4Q209 frg. 23	Textual parallels with portions of *1 En* 76–78
4Q209/4QEnastr[b] 1st c. BCE/CE	Textual parallels with 4Q210 1 ii 1–10, 14–20; some shared subject matter with 4Q208 (i.e., list of monthly patterns of lunar visibility)	Textual parallels with portions of *1 En* 76–79 and 82

Given their early dates, the fragments provide an invaluable check on source-critical theories based primarily on the Ethiopic, while also counter-balancing the tendency to interpret the *Astronomical Book* through the lens of the other Enochic writings collected alongside it in *1 Enoch*. When we abandon the quest for an "original" and reverse the arrow of analysis, moreover, we glimpse clues to the social settings and scribal practices that shaped the Aramaic Jewish literature of the early Hellenistic age.[67]

Useful, in this regard, are two new commentaries on the *Astronomical Book*, which approach the evidence from the opposite directions. Drawnel's 2011 commentary takes 4Q208–4Q211 as its lemma, bringing in *1 Enoch* only where it proves useful to illumine the fragments.[68] Accordingly, his commentary embodies the possibility of reading the Aramaic manuscripts (esp. 4Q209) on their own terms. By contrast, VanderKam's 2012 commentary is structured around the version preserved as chapters 72–82 of *1 Enoch*, and he uses the Aramaic fragments to help elucidate the parallel or related Ethiopic passages to which they relate.[69] The

---

[67] On problems of "textual identity" as opportunities to understand premodern literary practices and on the value of rereading evidence traditionally used for source-criticism and text-history in terms of redaction-history and reception-history, see further Reed, *Fallen Angels*, 16–57; Reed, "Textual Identity"; Schäfer, "Aufbau und redaktionelle Identität"; Schäfer, "Tradition and Redaction in Hekhalot Literature"; Swartz, "Three-Dimensional Philology."

[68] Drawnel, *Aramaic Astronomical Book*, 2–3. Drawnel chooses titles for the texts that communicate his contention of their essential continuity, calling them the "*Aramaic Astronomical Book*" and the "*Ethiopic Astronomical Book*," respectively.

[69] VanderKam, "Book of Luminaries," 335, 351–368. VanderKam chooses titles for the two that emphasize their unique textual identities, calling them the "Aramaic *Astronomical Book*" and the "Ethiopic *Book of the Luminaries*" respectively.

aggregate insights of his commentary convey the value of the Aramaic for illumining the prehistory of *1 Enoch* 72–82.

Coming from opposite directions, the two commentaries thus model the value of moderate approaches to reconstructing the work's textual history – cautious against conflating the Aramaic and the Ethiopic but also wary to separate 4Q208 completely from the array of known witnesses to the *Astronomical Book*. Like Ben-Dov before them, Drawnel and VanderKam answer more minimalist approaches by highlighting the cohesion of the tradition reflected in 4Q208–4Q211.[70] They look to 4Q209 as most definitive of the *Astronomical Book* in its Aramaic form and the only unequivocal Aramaic evidence for its "compound text," while treating the other manuscripts with caution and leaving open the possibility that some may be more accurately labeled as "sources" rather than "copies."

Taken together, the insights of Drawnel and VanderKam push us to set aside the search for a single original and approach the Aramaic fragments as evidence for the literary activity that lead to the form of the *Astronomical Book* that we know best from 4Q209 – which, moreover, can be deemed the end of one process only insofar as it also approximates the beginning-point of another process, from which the version in *1 Enoch* 72–82 eventually emerged. Nor are such processes limited to these two products. The Aramaic fragments certainly provide a firmer evidentiary basis for reconstructing the prehistory of *1 Enoch* 72–82, but they also demonstrate the limits of treating *1 Enoch* as the tradition's sole *telos*. After all, as Ben-Dov has shown, 4Q208–4Q210 are not only witnesses to the prehistory of *1 Enoch*: the textual fluidity that they attest is no less a product of the intensive scribal activity surrounding the 364-day calendar in Second Temple Judaism.[71] "Members of this tradition," he stresses, "studied the original texts and copied them, as well as reworking them into more systematic astronomical treatises."[72] Especially if we wish to recover the pre-Maccabean forms and settings of the *Astronomical Book*, it thus does not suffice simply to trace a line from 4Q208 to *1 Enoch*

[70] Drawnel, *Aramaic Astronomical Book*, 39–53; VanderKam, "Book of Luminaries," 341–345; cf. Ben-Dov, *Head of All Years*, 69–77 – addressing concerns raised by García Martínez, *Qumran and Apocalyptic*, 47–60; Tigchelaar, "Some Remarks," 145.
[71] Ben-Dov, *Head of All Years*, 21–68, 116–118.
[72] Ben-Dov, *Head of All Years*, 281, stressing that this process often involved "revisions of the raw data of the EMLV." Although he himself sometimes uses the language of "the original AB," his insights into its "flexibility of textual transmission" open the way for a different approach (75–76).

72–82; we must also attend to the survival of material remains from so many formative moments in between – the products of which continued to be copied in the late Second Temple period for the different purposes they continued to serve.

Instead of imposing a teleological model of literary formation on the *Astronomical Book*, it may be more useful to draw models from research on other premodern Jewish examples of collective and fluid literary production.[73] Research on Hekhalot literature, for instance, has demonstrated the value of attention to the variance among the manuscripts for helping to "lay bare the scribal processes of composition, redaction, anthologizing, and designation," especially when paired with a "modular approach, by which the careful analysis of how units have been arranged, combined and juxtaposed within areas of manuscript traditions can yield both synchronic and diachronic results" – as Michael Swartz suggests.[74] Rather than attempting to array all the textual witnesses to the *Astronomical Book* around a single "author" or "original," we might similarly approach them as evidence for the orchestrating logics of a tradition in motion – with some synchronic and simultaneous dynamics, but also some diachronically accruing results. A list of moments and movements that are recoverable from the surviving evidence might include:

1 The textualization of lunar theory in Aramaic, as exemplified by the lunar visibility list in 4Q208 and 4Q209 (i.e., what Milik called the "synchronic calendar" and Ben-Dov designates as "EMLV").

2 The compilation of Aramaic didactic lists of other astronomical and cosmological information, as attested by 4Q211.

3 The reworking of lists into treatises, as attested in part by 4Q210 and possibly also laying behind the parallels between *1 Enoch* 72–75 and 77–79 + 82:4ff.

4 The creation of the "compound text" known from 4Q209 through the combination of astronomical lists and cosmological materials, as achieved through the structuring rubric of "calculations" but also through the evocation of cosmic order under the leadership of angels and the addition of first-person framing notices that evoke the didactic trope of knowledge passed from father to son (i.e., what

---

[73] Especially as explored by Peter Schäfer in articles such as "Aufbau und redaktionelle Identität," "Tradition and Redaction," and "Research into Rabbinic Literature." For the full bibliography, see now Swartz, "Three-Dimensional Philology" – there bringing insights from late antique Jewish literature into conversation with New Philology.

[74] Swartz, "Three-Dimensional Philology," 539.

Drawnel and VanderKam call the "*Aramaic Astronomical Book*" [AAB]).

5 The continued editorial activity that shaped the earliest core of the version now known to us in Ethiopic, as approximated by *1 Enoch* 72–79+82 and marked by the abbreviation of the older lunar lists (cf. *1 En* 73:4–8)[75] and by further narrativization (i.e., what Drawnel calls the "*Ethiopic Astronomical Book*" [EAB] and VanderKam calls the "*Book of the Luminaries*"). It is possibly at this stage that the first-person didactic discourse becomes explicitly associated with Uriel and/or Enoch – an association presumed in *Jubilees* 4:17–20 (mid-second century BCE; cf. Pseudo-Eupolemus *apud* Eusebius, *Praep.ev.* 9.17.9).[76]

6 The editorial insertion of chapters 80–81, likely with the aim of enhancing the *Astronomical Book*'s connections with other Enochic works, as first attested in the Ethiopian manuscripts of *1 Enoch* (i.e., fifteenth century CE and following) where the text is preserved in a full form in a secondary translation from the Greek. These chapters may have been known to Tertullian (*De cultu fem.* 1.3; third century CE) but are attested late as part of the *Astronomical Book* and may have arisen in another context, perhaps somehow related to the *Book of the Watchers*.[77]

7 The translation of the work into Greek, probably by the first century CE, and later from Greek into Ethiopic, around the fifth and sixth centuries CE. The former is attested in P.Oxy. 2069 (late fourth century) but may be presumed already in *2 Enoch*, while the latter is known from many but much later manuscripts (i.e., fifteenth century and following). The paucity of Greek evidence does not permit any firm conclusions about the timing of this translation in relation to #6 and #8, nor about the timing of the Ethiopic translation in relation to #9.

8 The anthological impulse to combine the *Astronomical Book* – always copied in separate scrolls from other Enochic writings at

---

[75] That the longer lunar list preceded the abbreviated form is demonstrated by Ben-Dov, *Head of All Years*, 60–77.

[76] If so, there is warrant for placing this development before the mid-second century BCE; see below.

[77] Parallels with the *Book of the Watchers* are explored in Nickelsburg, *1 Enoch 1*, 333–344. The connection with Tertullian's allusion to Enoch's teaching of Methuselah in *De cultu fem.* 1.3 is intriguing but not decisive in establishing the precise forms of the Enochic writings known to him.

Qumran – with other materials related to Enoch, as attested in the fourth-century Greek fragment of the work, P.Oxy. 2069, which preserves some verses from the *Astronomical Book* (frg. 3; *1 En* 77:7–78:1 + 78:8) and some verses from the *Book of Dreams* (frg. 1–2; *1 En* 85:10–86:2 + 87:1–3).[78] Interestingly, this fragment departs from most of our Greek evidence for Enochic writings, which attests their independent circulation (e.g., *Book of the Watchers* in Syncellus) and/or their copying alongside Christian writings (e.g., *Epistle of Enoch* in Chester-Beatty/Michigan Biblical Papyrus XII; *Book of the Watchers* in Codex Panopolitanus).[79]

9 The compilation of the work as part of *Maṣḥafa Henok Nabiy* ("Book of Enoch the Prophet") – what Western scholars now call *1 Enoch* – where it forms part of an extensive compendium structured around Enoch's biography.[80] Although the specific configuration of works in *1 Enoch* is attested only in Ethiopic, it is possible that it goes back to a Greek compendium of the same or similar shape.[81]

In compiling such a list, I do not mean to imply that the textual history of the *Astronomical Book* can be reduced to the chronological arrangement of the surviving witnesses. There are reasons, as we shall see, to follow Ben-Dov's sense that some form of it "existed as a coherent whole rather than a selection of excerpts ... at an early stage" and to follow Vander-Kam's suggestion of pre-Maccabean settings for the intensive spurts of literary activity surrounding the work (i.e., not just #1–#3 above, but also

---

[78] It is unclear whether this anthological impulse should be associated with the translation or transmission of these materials in Greek. In any case, it is important to stress that P.Oxy. 2069 does not evince a full Greek form of *1 Enoch*; see below.

[79] Chester-Beatty Michigan Biblical Papyrus XII (ca. 4th c.) preserves part of the *Epistle of Enoch* (97:6–107:3) alongside Melito's *Homily of the Passion* and parts of an Ezekielian writing, while Codex Panopolitanus (5th/6th c.) preserves most of the *Book of the Watchers* (*1 En.* 1:1–32:6 + 19:3–21:9) copied with parts of the *Gospel of Peter* and *Apocalypse of Peter*. See further Nickelsburg, "Two Enochic Manuscripts."

[80] This collection compiles the *Book of the Watchers* (*1 En* 1–36), *Similitudes* (*1 En* 37–71), *Astronomical Book* (*1 En* 72–82), *Book of Dreams* (*1 En* 83–90), and *Epistle of Enoch* (*1 En* 91–105), as well as smaller units (e.g., *1 En* 106–7 + 108).

[81] Scholars differ in the degree to which they attempt to create a straight line connecting 4QEn^c (1st c. BCE) with *1 Enoch* – and hence also in the degree that they take seriously or dismiss the Greek witnesses; e.g., Dimant, "The Biography of Enoch and the Books of Enoch"; Greenfield and Stone, "Books of Enoch and Traditions of Enoch"; Nickelsburg, *I Enoch 1*; Reed, "Textual Identity"; Stuckenbruck, *1 Enoch 91–108*, 5–16; Knibb, "Book of Enoch or Books of Enoch."

#4–#5).[82] For our purposes, moreover, the dominant patterns prove more pressing than the specific details. We can limit ourselves to those elements that speak to the questions of the present chapter: how and why did astronomy come to be framed as part of Jewish knowledge and literature in the early Hellenistic age, and what was the place of angelology in this process?

The earliest stages (#1–#3) remain shrouded in the most mystery, not least because the only witnesses to them are quite fragmentary. Two of the oldest manuscripts, 4Q208 and 4Q211, exhibit only indirect connections with *1 Enoch* (cf. 73:4–8; 82:15–20), and even the direct parallels in 4Q210 (cf. 76:3–77:4; 78:6–8) are far from verbatim. All three, moreover, preserve lists with no evidence of narrative framing. It is here where the analyses of Ben-Dov and Drawnel prove most useful, inasmuch that they mobilize the work's science to reconstruct a sense of the matrix of these lists in a Jewish intellectual tradition that drew upon Mesopotamian models but also developed them.[83] This context, for instance, helps to explain the earliest manuscript, 4Q208, which may have contained only the calculation of lunar visibility according to the monthly pattern (#1 above).[84] Whatever its precise scope, Ben-Dov notes that it is "the closest one comes to a translation of an Akkadian astronomical text to a Western vernacular during this early period," raising the possibility of "the role of Aramaic as a cultural vehicle in the transmission of Babylonian science."[85] The lunar theory preserved in 4Q208 and in the parallel portions of 4Q209, moreover, differs enough from the corresponding portions of *1*

[82] Ben-Dov, *Head of All Years*, 73, 281; cf. Black, *Book of Enoch*, 10. As shall become clear below, I am convinced both from what we know of the rest of the Aramaic Enoch tradition (Stuckenbruck, *1 Enoch 91–108*, 5–16) and from Ben-Dov's characterization of the 364DCT (*Head of All Years*, 21–67) that it makes sense in terms of relative chronology to situate the *Astronomical Book* in the early Hellenistic age – i.e., pre-Maccabean. The relevant evidence is carefully gathered, sorted, and assessed by VanderKam, "Book of Luminaries," 339–350.

[83] Ben-Dov, *Head of All Years*, 69–118; Drawnel, *Aramaic Astronomical Book*, 260–310.

[84] Drawnel, *Aramaic Astronomical Book*, 72–73. Contrast the approach of VanderKam ("Book of Luminaries," 342), who argues – especially against Tigchelaar – for the possibility that 4Q208 "was an Enochic astronomical work that contained more than the synchronistic calendar." By his reading, the lunar material therein already presupposes the system of celestial gates described in *1 Enoch* 72 (357).

[85] Ben-Dov, *Head of All Years*, 287. By this time, as Sanders notes (*From Adapa*, 194), "Aramaic had been used in court chanceries as a language of Mesopotamian scholasticism for over 400 years," such that "the most complex documents of Mesopotamian science were widely circulated among Aramaic-parchment scribes by the Seleucid period." See further Chapter 2.

Enoch to warrant crediting it with a unique identity, even if it is "not an independent comprehensive astronomical treatise but simply represented one list in a broader astronomical corpus."[86]

Whether simultaneous to the textualization of this model of lunar visibility (#1) or soon thereafter, other lists pertaining to the stars, winds, earth, and seasons were also copied, systematized, and textualized (#2–#3). For understanding their aims and settings, Drawnel's findings again prove useful. Interpreting the fragments apart from the *telos* of *1 Enoch* and eschewing the retrojection of later literary genres, such as apocalypses and testaments, he highlights points of connection with Mesopotamian cuneiform sources and Aramaic Dead Sea Scrolls. When he points to the pattern of "formulaic sentences with fragment notations" in 4Q211 (frg. 1 ii–iii), for instance, he does so largely on the basis of what he reads as parallels in the section of *Aramaic Levi Document* "dedicated to the metrological order of weights and measures presented in the context of liturgical instruction."[87] In his view, both reflect knowledge of "simple arithmetic exercises in Babylonian scribal education," raising the possibility that "exercises based on cuneiform models ... found their way into liturgical and astronomical texts" among Jews in Second Temple times.[88] The precise origin of the content of these lists is less pressing for our present purposes. What is significant is that the earliest stages in the textual formation of the *Astronomical Book* (#1–#3) both attest and reflect the use of written aids for teaching.

For a sense of the topics covered by this Jewish pedagogy, the overlaps with *1 Enoch* 76–78 in 4Q210 are also telling. Parallels include portions of the lists pertaining to the twelve gates of the winds (4Q210 frg. 1 ii 1; cf. *1 En* 76:3–10), the division of the earth and location of Paradise (frg. 1 ii 2a+b+c; cf. *1 En* 76:13–77:4), and the waxing and waning of the moon (frg. 1 iii; cf. *1 En* 78:6–8). Due to the fragmentary character of 4Q210, it is unclear whether or not this manuscript originally included a first-person notice akin to that which concludes the list of the wind's gates in

---

[86] See the discussion of EMLV in Ben-Dov, *Head of All Years*, 72–73, 116, 280–281, quote at 281. Drawnel (*Aramaic Astronomical Book*, 31) posits "conscious literary activity" as evident even in the list of 4Q208.

[87] I.e., ALD 31–47 by his numbering; Drawnel, *Aramaic Astronomical Book*, 33.

[88] Drawnel, *Aramaic Astronomical Book*, 33. By his reading, the *Astronomical Book* and *Aramaic Levi* have the "same literary style: short sentences with tabular numerical notations that find their origin in Babylonian scribal literature" (58). This insight buttresses his broader argument for "a didactic context for the transmission of the whole compendium" of the *Astronomical Book* as well – at least in its early Aramaic forms (35).

1 Enoch 76.[89] What is clear, however, is that the sole portion of the *Astronomical Book* that deals with the earth formed part of the tradition already at a relatively early stage (#3):[90]

Aramaic, 4Q209 frg. 23 lines 3–10 + 4Q210 frg. 1 col. ii lines [14]–20	Ethiopic *1 Enoch* 77:1–3
[The east is called east because it is] the first.	The first quarter is called "eastern" because it is the first,
The south is called "south" because there the Great One lives and in (?) [ ] forever *blank*	and the second is called "south" because there the Most High will descend and especially there the one who is blessed forever will descend.
The great quarter (is called) the western quarter because there [ ] the heavenly [st]ars [come], and hundreds/vessels set and hundreds/vessels enter, and all of them are stars. For this reason, it is called "the west"	The name of the quarter on the west is "diminished" because there all the heavenly luminaries diminish and go down.
[The north (is called) "north] because in it all the entities that set hide, gather, and go around; they go to the east side of the sky [ea]st because from there the vessels of the sky rise; and also "orient" because from there/hundreds rise [ ] the earth.	The fourth quarter whose name is "north" is divided into three parts.
One of them for the dwelling of the sons of men in it; and one of them [...]	One of them is the dwelling-place of men (*māxdar la-sab'*).
[and one of them] for the deserts and for ...	And another: seas of water, and the deeps, and forests, and rivers, and darkness, and mist.
[... and for the *parde*]s of righteousness.	And another part: the garden of righteousness (*gannata ṣedq*).

[89] I.e., *1 En* 76:14: "The twelve gates of the four quarters of the sky are completed; all their laws and all their punishment and their prosperity – I have shown you everything, my son Methuselah." See below on Aramaic evidence for first-person notices.

[90] Translations here follow Tigchelaar, "Eden and Paradise," 62; Coblentz Bautch, *A Study of the Geography of Enoch I 17-19*, 200–201; VanderKam, "Book of Luminaries," 482; cf. Milik, *Books of Enoch*, 290. Note that in the Ethiopic, this split is depicted as a three-fold division of the northern quadrant of the earth, while the Aramaic fragments describe a three-fold division of the entire world (VanderKam, "1 Enoch 77, 3," 274–275).

The dominant pattern in the rest of the *Astronomical Book* is to contextualize material about the moon, primarily in relation to the sun and the
stars; this pattern informs the doublets in *1 Enoch* 72–82, for instance,
leading Ben-Dov to speculate about two earlier parallel efforts to create
calendrical treatises.[91] For our purposes, it suffices to note that 4Q210
already attests a broader cosmological impulse whereby the scope of scribal
Listenwissenschaft is further expanded to encompass both the division of
the earth and the gates for the wind (Aram. רוח; Eth. *nafās*).[92] It is intriguing
that the material about the wind overlaps with the only positive treatment
of the study of the stars in the *Book of the Watchers* (*1 En* 34:1–36:2; cf.
8:1–3), while the material about the earth represents the *Astronomical
Book*'s sole foray into mythic geography. 4Q210 does not just attest a core
of materials known in fuller forms from the "composite text" of 4Q209
and the version of the *Astronomical Book* preserved in *1 Enoch*: it
embodies the purview that made them possible. Evoked here is a newly
totalizing Jewish cosmology that looks especially to the intersections
between heaven and earth, charting the winds/spirits that flow between
them and mapping the "*pardes* of righteousness" at their bounds.[93]

It is only at the next stage (#4), however, that we might speak of the
emergence of the *Astronomical Book* as a long-duration text – that is, as a
work that begins to take on a stable literary form and which is framed in
terms that enable its reading and copying even apart from the specific
contexts of the initial usage and utility of the information compiled
therein. As noted above, 4Q209 contains overlaps of text and content
with 4Q208 but also with 4Q210 and *1 Enoch* 76–79 and 82. Parallels
with the version in *1 Enoch* include passages pertaining to the division of
the earth (as attested in the overlapping portions of 4Q209 frg. 23.3–10
and 4Q210 1 ii 14–20, corresponding to *1 En* 77:1–4; see above) and
material about the celestial bodies and their rulers (as attested in 4Q209
frg. 28, corresponding to *1 En* 82:9–13; see below). Most importantly, for
our present purposes, 4Q209 also preserves two structuring devices:
material is framed by the designation *ḥeshbon* ("calculation")[94] and by

---

[91] Ben-Dov, *Head of All Years*, 116–118.

[92] VanderKam ("Book of Luminaries," 471) stresses that weather and winds formed part of
the scope of astronomy in MUL.APIN as well.

[93] 4Q209 frg. 23.9: ‏קושטא ס[ולפרד...].

[94] I.e., חשבון in 4Q209 frgs. 25.3; 26.7; 27.3. Compare the use of the term "law" [Eth.
te'zāz] to designate sections of *1 En* 72–82: 72:2 ("first law of the luminaries"), 73:1
("second law"), 74:1 ("another course and law"), 78:10 ("another law"); VanderKam,
"Book of Luminaries," 410.

first-person notices that present the content of the work as what "I was shown"[95] and what "I am telling you, my son."[96] Even as the inner-Aramaic parallels evince the continuation of the same types of scribal activity that shaped the earlier tradition, the presentation of units as "another calculation," "the final calculation," etc., signals an anthological self-consciousness, while the first-person notices herald the narrativization that later becomes so central for the Aramaic Enoch tradition.

We shall return below to discuss these framing and first-person notices in more detail. For now, it suffices to note that the innovation evident in 4Q209 is predicated on continuity. Consistent with the probable didactic settings of 4Q208, 4Q210, and 4Q211, the first-person notices in 4Q209 conjure a scene of a father teaching his son. What is evoked is a trope familiar from sapiential traditions from across the Near East.[97] Yet it is also a recurrent feature of Aramaic writings with didactic themes ranging from the *Words of Ahiqar* to the proto-testamentary Jewish texts that we examined Chapter 2.

Inasmuch as Enoch is not explicitly mentioned even in most chapters of the version of the *Astronomical Book* known in Ethiopic, it is perhaps not surprising that none of the Aramaic fragments preserve his name. More telling, however, is the lack of reference even in 4Q209 to Uriel – the angel so central to the authorizing claims of the version of the *Astronomical Book* in *1 Enoch* 72–82. There, the promise to provide accurate information about celestial cycles is predicated on the claim to knowledge directly from this "holy angel [*mal'ak*] who was with me who is their leader [*marāḥihomu*]" (72:1; cf. 33:3). No such claims are found in 4Q209, and it is unclear whether the omission is an accident of preservation. It is possible that an early form of the *Astronomical Book* invoked a didactic setting for the transmission of knowledge apart from any explicit claim about either Enoch or angels.

If so, it is especially notable that 4Q209 does attest an important precedent for the angelification of celestial cycles on which the appeal to Uriel is eventually predicated. Part of *1 Enoch* 82 – the key chapter of the *Astronomical Book* for establishing a hierarchal celestial order

[95] I.e., אחזית in 4Q209 frg. 25.3; cf. *1 En* 74:1–2; 78:9–12.
[96] 4Q209 frg. 26.6: וכען מחוה אנה לך ברי; on the relationship with *1 En* 79:1, see VanderKam, "Book of Luminaries," 352, and below.
[97] See further Wright, "From Generation to Generation"; Reed, "Textuality."

governed by angelic leaders [Eth. *marāḥəyān*] – is preserved in 4Q209 frg. 28 (cf. *1 En* 82:9–13)[98]; Drawnel reconstructs the text as follows:

0 [And this is the order]
1 [of the stars that set according to their places, to] their appointed times, to their months, to their signs. And [these are the names of their leaders who watch so that they enter according to their times,]
2 [according to their orders, to their times, to their months, to] their [ru]le, according to all their stations. The fo[ur leaders who divide the four parts of the year]
3 [enter first; and after them—the three hundred and sixt]y heads (ראשי) o[f] [thousands who separate the days; and after them enter the four leaders]
4 [who are added to the heads of thousands who se]parate the d[ays, and to the leaders who divide the four parts of the year. And these heads of thousands are between]
5 [the leader and their leader, and one is added behind their position. And th]ese are the names [of the leaders who separate the four parts of the year][99]

Are some or all of these "leaders" meant to be understood as angels? In the version preserved in Ethiopic, the term "angel" is used only of Uriel, while the term "leader" [*marāḥi*, pl. *marāḥəyān*] is variously associated with Uriel (*1 En* 72:1; 74:2; 75:3; 79:6) and with "luminaries" [*bərhānāt*], both anonymous and named (e.g., Milkiel, Helemelek, Mele'eyel, Narel; 82:13).[100] On the one hand, the absence of the term "angel" is less conclusive than it might seem at first sight; as noted in Chapter 1, Hebrew *mal'ak* and its cognates may not yet denote an umbrella category encompassing creatures like *bene elohim*, *seraphim*, *cherubim*, *ḥayyot*, and *ruḥot* by the third century BCE.[101] On the other hand, there is no known form of the *Astronomical Book* that makes any effort to specify which of these "leaders" and "luminaries" are and are not sentient, and the ambiguity appears deliberate. Across the various versions of *1 Enoch* 82, the function of these lists is not to argue either for or against an equation of stars with angels (cf. Job 38:7) but rather to

---

[98] On *1 En* 82:9–20 as expressive of the "Hierarchy of Time" of the *Astronomical Book*, as distinctive from the earlier EMLV, see Ben-Dov, *Head of All Years*, 22–24.

[99] Drawnel, *Aramaic Astronomical Book*, 200–201.

[100] For a comparison with the leader-stars in MUL.APIN and other Mesopotamian writings see Ben-Dov, *Head of All Years*, 25–27.

[101] This ambivalence allows for 2 *Enoch*'s later reworking of these traditions to enhance the angels (e.g., 14:2–3) but also helps to explain why some scholars, like VanderKam ("Book of Luminaries," 404), can limit the *Astronomical Book*'s angels to Uriel, whereas others, such as Koch ("The Astral Laws," 124–125), can describe it as an "angelization" of MUL.APIN's astronomy.

extend the hierarchy of divine dominion to include every entity involved in the cycles of the skies and the seasons.

This piling up of levels upon levels, and leaders upon leaders, evokes divine grandeur in a manner akin to the evocation of myriads in Deuteronomy 33:2–3, and the conjuring of a heavenly continuum between God's "this-worldly" and "otherworldly" servants has precedent in the image of the sun, moon, stars, and angels praising him in Psalm 148:1–6.[102] What is new in the *Astronomical Book*, however, is the claim to know, teach, and write exact knowledge about their names, their movements, and their organization. In the orchestration of astral and angelic agents of divine order, we may thus glimpse something of the reasons why the scribal *Listenwissenschaft* used to teach and textualize the movements of the moon and sun later came to be reframed as the teaching of an angelic leader of the luminaries.

Missing from the Aramaic, by contrast, are clues to why and when this knowledge came to be projected back into the antediluvian past and associated with Enoch. For this, we must turn to *1 Enoch* 72–82 and use internal literary criteria to reconstruct the earliest forms of the version now preserved there in secondary Ethiopic translation. Due to the striking differences in theme and language in chapters 80–81, there is warrant for following the longstanding scholarly consensus and treating these two chapters as a later addition to an earlier version consisting largely of *1 Enoch* 72–79 and 82 (i.e., #5 above).[103] This version of the *Astronomical Book* is plausibly understood as the product of editorial activity on a "compound text" akin to what is attested by 4Q209 (#4).[104] Paralleled material, as we have seen, includes the twelve gates of the winds, the division of the earth, the leaders of the celestial cycles, and the use of first-person framing as speech from a father/teacher to his son/student. In terms of content, the most striking point of difference is absence of the detailed lunar visibility list found in 4Q208 with overlaps in 4Q209. In *1 Enoch* 73:4–8, 74:3–10, and 78:6–8, there is some reflex of the earlier interest in lunar theory, but the list itself is conspicuously absent.[105] This leads VanderKam to wonder if it might have been extracted for separate

[102] There is also some precedent in the treatment of *ruḥot* in Hebrew hymnology and prophecy, e.g., Pss 104:2–4; 148:7–8; Ezek 3:14; 11:1, 24; 37:1; 40:1; see Chapter 1.
[103] Charles, *Enoch*, 148; García Martínez, *Qumran and Apocalyptic*, 57–60; Nickelsburg, *1 Enoch 1*, 334–344; Olson, *Enoch*, 275–276.
[104] VanderKam, "Book of Luminaries," 352–357.
[105] VanderKam, "Book of Luminaries," 352–357. Whatever the original location of the material in 4Q211, it is also absent here.

circulation as a reference work, concurrent with its omission from the "compound text" to enable the creation of the further narrativized version that we find preserved in chapters 72–79+82 of *1 Enoch*.[106] If so, its extraction may attest an emergent distinction between didactic lists used as textual tools for teaching, such as we find preserved in 4Q208 and 4Q211, and the *Astronomical Book* as a literary work, associated with Uriel and increasingly aligned with the biography of Enoch in *1 Enoch* 72–79+82.

Whether the association with Uriel and Enoch occurred concurrently with, before, or after the omission of the lunar visibility list, it marks the transition from a fluid textual tradition preserving information to be studied by scribes to the consolidation of a long-duration text to be studied and copied for its own sake. Below, we will look more closely at the authorizing strategies that accompanied and enabled this transition. For now, it suffices to note that there is some support for placing this transition in the pre-Maccabean stages of the work's formation. Not only does the *Book of the Watchers* appear to depend on a version of the *Astronomical Book* already aligned with Enoch, but Pseudo-Eupolemus and *Jubilees* express varying degrees of familiarity with astronomical knowledge associated with angels and Enoch.[107] The detailed discussion of Enoch's writings in *Jubilees* 4:17–21, in particular, supports the contention of the circulation of some form of the *Astronomical Book* associated with Enoch by the mid-second century BCE.[108]

Later developments in the history of the *Astronomical Book* (i.e., #6–#9 above) are less pressing for our purposes. They do, however, help to highlight what is not yet present in its plausibly pre-Maccabean forms. It is only with the addition of chapters 80–81 (#6), for instance, that astronomical and cosmological teachings become set in relation to

---

[106] VanderKam, "Book of Luminaries," 357, noting that "if one subtracts the full synchronic character from the Aramaic text, the Aramaic looks much more like the Ethiopic booklet." Cf. Drawnel, *Aramaic Astronomical Book*, 29–30.

[107] See further Drawnel, *Aramaic Astronomical Book*, 49–51; VanderKam, "Book of Luminaries," 343–345.

[108] For varying assessments of the specific Enochic works presumed there, see Collins, *Seers, Sybils, and Sages in Hellenistic-Roman Judaism*, 290–291; Nickelsburg, *1 Enoch 1*, 71–76; VanderKam, *Enoch and the Growth*, 114–117; VanderKam, *From Revelation to Canon*, 312–325; Reed, *Fallen Angels*, 87–89; Bergsma, "The Relationship between Jubilees and the Early Enochic Books"; Knibb, "Which Parts of 1 Enoch Were Known to Jubilees," 254–262. Stuckenbruck (*1 Enoch 91–108*, 5) posits that those who composed *1 Enoch* 91–108 in the second century BCE "were probably aware of the core of the *Astronomical Book* (i.e., 72:1–80:8; 82:4b–20)."

Enoch's heavenly journey and his access to heavenly books. These chapters also introduce eschatological themes more akin to those found in later Enochic writings. George Nickelsburg has thus suggested that these chapters may have originally been related to the *Book of the Watchers*,[109] and VanderKam posits that their placement in their present setting might even belong "to an editorial layer or layers in which a redactor or redactors joined the astronomical sections with the other parts of the Enochic corpus."[110]

Whatever the precise origins of these chapters or the exact timing of their addition to the *Astronomical Book*, it is telling that efforts of this sort were even necessary. Although some manuscripts from Qumran (esp. 4QEn^c) attest anthological activity combining other Enochic materials to the *Book of the Watchers*, all known Aramaic manuscripts related to the *Astronomical Book* are copied separately. Its compilation with other Enochic materials may have even awaited its translation (#7). Our earliest evidence for this impulse is not until the sole Greek fragment, P.Oxy. 2069, which dates from the late fourth century CE and attests the copying of the *Astronomical Book* alongside the *Book of Dreams*. This Greek papyrus fragment is even more poorly preserved than the Aramaic manuscripts surveyed above, but – as Randall Chesnutt observes – it remains "our only evidence in any language prior to the Ethiopic compilation that the *Astronomical Book* was combined with another of the works that comprise what is now called *1 Enoch*."[111]

Whether the current placement of chapters 80–81 (#6) occurred before or after the translation of the work (#7) and/or its combination with other Enochic writings (#8), these literary practices shape the series of later shifts in the textual tradition that culminated with its inclusion in *1 Enoch* (#9). This anthological act added new levels of meaning: not only are the lists resituated in relation to Enoch's heavenly journey, but they are also absorbed into a continuum of ethical, cosmological, historical, and

---

[109] Nickelsburg, *1 Enoch 1*, 333–344; the strength of his insights into their connection remains, even if one does not accept the entire theory of an early Enochic Testament outlined there.

[110] VanderKam, "Book of Luminaries," 366.

[111] Chesnutt, "Oxyrhynchus Papyrus 2069," 504. In light of the evidence of other Greek MSS, we should be wary of assuming that the pairing of the *Astronomical Book* with the *Book of Dreams* necessarily attests a broader compilation akin in scope to *1 Enoch*. Syncellus' excerpts also seem to presume the separate circulation of the *Book of the Watchers* as one among multiple known books associated with Enoch. See further Reed, "Textual Identity."

eschatological teachings that Enoch is said to have learned from angels and passed on to his son Methuselah. It is due to this anthologizing act that the lists embedded therein would have an even longer afterlife, especially in Ethiopia. Attention to its late antique settings and effects, however, underline the importance of investigating the pre-Maccabean literary activity surrounding the *Astronomical Book* apart from the lens of its current context within the compendium that we now know as *1 Enoch*.[112]

SEEING, READING, AND REVELATION IN 4Q209 AND *1 ENOCH* 72–79+82

Whereas the anthological logic of *1 Enoch* fosters a reading of the works therein with Enoch as the central unifying theme, the Aramaic fragments from Qumran (4Q208–4Q211) challenge us to look to other authorizing strategies that may have been more prominent in the earliest stages of the *Astronomical Book*. As noted above, the Aramaic fragments contain no confirmation of the names Enoch, Methuselah, or Uriel. Although it is possible that this is an accident of preservation, their absence draws our attention to an interesting pattern: even in the Ethiopic, Enoch is far less central to authorizing these materials than one might expect. As Drawnel notes, "the name of Enoch does not appear even once in chapters 72–79 and 82:4–20, that is, in the main core of the texts that deal with astronomical and calendrical matters."[113]

But if not to associate astronomy with Enoch, why else would Jewish scribes rework lunar and other lists into new literary forms? To answer this question, it proves useful to look more closely at place of first-person notices within its textual history and to try to determine their function, first in the "composite text" attested by 4Q209 (#4) and then in the more narrativized version preserved in *1 Enoch* 72–79+82 (#5). There are only

---

[112] Knibb stresses that "the Ethiopic Book of Enoch represents *at the oldest* a fifth-sixth century translation of a Greek text that can into existence in the first century CE; they represent (a) new edition(s) of the original Aramaic" and "belong in different literary and historical contexts" ("Book of Enoch or Books of Enoch," 40; emphasis mine).

[113] Drawnel, *Aramaic Astronomical Book,* 36. He adds that "Methuselah, Enoch's son, appears only once in a similar didactic context" (i.e., 76:14) and that the name Uriel is also unattested in the Aramaic, further raising the possibility that the "position of teacher" that he takes "may have been originally anonymous, similar to the role of the 'son' who receives instruction in 4Q209 frag. 26.6."

two examples decisively attested in the former,[114] but both are telling, especially when we compare them to the corresponding verses of the latter:

First-person statements in the Aramaic *Astronomical Book*	Corresponding verses in the Ethiopic *Astronomical Book* (*1 En* 72–82)
4Q209 frg. 25.3: 3 [ ]another calculation I was shown for it that it went [	*1 En* 74.1–2: Another course and law [*meḥwār we-te'zāz*] I saw [*re'iku*] for it; by that law it carries out the monthly courses. All this, Uriel the holy angel... showed me. I wrote down their positions as he showed me and wrote down their months as they are...
4Q209 frg. 26.6–7: 6 its [light] alone. Now I am telling you, my son. *blank* [7 [ ] a calculation. He showed m[e	*1 En* 79.1–2: Now, my son, I {i.e., Enoch} have shown you everything, and the law [*šer'āt*] of all of the stars of the sky is completed. And he showed me all their law for each day...

In both cases, the first-person voice is used to evoke moments of teaching and to signal the transmission of exact knowledge about the cosmos. In fact, these two passages (frg. 25.3 and frg. 26.7) represent two of the three occurrences of the term *ḥeshbon* ("calculation") in 4Q209. As noted above, this term signals the self-conscious categorization of the information thereafter conveyed and may reflect early efforts at coaxing received lists into a literary structure. Even though the fragmentary form of 4Q209 preserves only three examples, the likelihood that this structuring was more extensive is signaled by the corresponding Ethiopic: the two words therein attested as counterparts to *ḥeshbon* – namely, *tə'zāz* ("law," "command") and *šer'āt* ("order," "ordinance") – serve a similar structuring function throughout *1 Enoch* 72–79+82.[115]

The difference between the two versions is perhaps clearest when we compare the "paternal report" of 4Q209 frg. 26.6 to *1 Enoch* 79:1. When

---

[114] The first-person is less decisively attested in 4Q209 frg. 23.1–2 + 4Q210 frg. 1 ii 14, which corresponds to *1 En* 76.14 ("The twelve gates of the four quarters of the sky are completed. All their laws and all their punishment and prosperity – I have shown you everything, my son Methuselah"). In addition, parallels to *1 En* 77:1–4 in 4Q209 frg. 23.3–10 + 4Q210 frg. 1 ii 14–20 may possibly support the reconstruction of the first-person "I saw" in the Aramaic corresponding to 77:4 ("I saw [*re'iku*] seven lofty mountains...").

[115] Whereas uses of *tə'zāz* cluster in the first half of the work (e.g., *1 En* 72:2, 35; 73:1; 74:1; 76:14), *šer'āt* is used to introduce information about the moon and stars in the second half (*1 En* 78:10; 79:1, 2, 5; 82:4, 9, 10, 11, 14, 20).

read in the broader context of *1 Enoch*, the latter resonates with the testamentary features of the Aramaic Enoch tradition.[116] On the evidence of 4Q209 frg. 26.6, however, we must grapple with the possibility that the connection with Enoch and Methuselah may not have been present or significant in the "compound text" attested in 4Q209. "The Aramaic fragment here does not give the name of the teacher or that of the student," Drawnel notes, "and it does not seem to be a casual omission"; there is a space at the end of the relevant line, and the name is omitted even in the corresponding Ethiopic.[117] At least at an early stage in the work's formation, it is possible that "the didactic context of knowledge transmission did not originally require a particular name to be inserted," and the evocation of "the action of the knowledge transmission from an anonymous teacher to an anonymous student" may have sufficed to "suggest a didactic context for the transmission of the astronomical knowledge in a rather unequivocal manner."[118] If Drawnel is correct, this first-person notice serves to invoke a general situation of teaching – consistent with the sapiential trope of father-to-son address and its proto-testamentary extension in Aramaic in the *Aramaic Levi Document*, *Admonitions of Qahat*, and *Visions of Amram*. It may have been only at a later stage when this unnamed "I" became linked to Enoch.

The other decisive example of a first-person notice in the Aramaic fragments, 4Q209 frg. 25.3, refers to the reception of knowledge rather than its transmission: "another calculation [*ḥeshbon*] I was shown" (cf. *1 En* 74:1–2). This statement has received much attention, most recently by Sanders, in relation to the possibility that scientific thought was associated with apocalyptic visions already in the early stages of the *Astronomical Book*.[119] A closer look, however, suggests that the process of association may have been a bit slower and less direct. Drawnel's interpretation is again helpful inasmuch as he attempts to make sense of this passage apart from the tropes developed in the *Book of the Watchers* and later

---

[116] This line may be the earliest precedent for the testamentary element of the Aramaic Enoch tradition; compare *1 En* 81:1–82:4; 83:1; 85:1; 91:1–3, and see further Stuckenbruck, *1 Enoch 91–108*, 15–16, 158–159; Stuckenbruck, "Pseudepigraphy," 303–305, 310. It is too early to speak of a literary genre of "testament" *per se* in this period; as Collins notes ("Testaments," 325) "the independent genre of the testament only emerges in the Hellenistic Age, and is poorly attested even then apart from the *Testaments of the Twelve Patriarchs*." I discuss this problem further in Chapter 2 and Reed, "Textuality."

[117] Drawnel, *Aramaic Astronomical Book*, 36 – although, to be sure, some Ethiopic manuscripts of *1 En* 79:1 here add the name of Enoch's son Methuselah.

[118] Drawnel, *Aramaic Astronomical Book*, 36.   [119] Sanders, "I Was Shown."

apocalypses. He reasons that the sense of showing here "certainly does not refer to the actual 'seeing' of an abstract process ('calculation' [*ḥeshbon*]), but to its mental understanding either by an oral explanation, or in the process of reading, or perhaps both," and he draws attention to a parallel in the *Aramaic Levi Document* attesting "the same metaphorical use of *ḥ-z-y* in the didactic context."[120] For Drawnel, thus, this line reveals a didactic practice specific to the earliest Aramaic stages of the text's formation – "the knowledge that is being transmitted as a written text that lies in front of the student."[121] Consequently, it is best understood against the background of pedagogical practices involving consultation of texts, charts, and schematic maps, as known from cuneiform literature, and with reference to the visual register of Akkadian verbs for reading (e.g., *amārum* [G] and *kullumu* [D]); following his interpretation, the first-person notices in 4Q209 are less akin to the biblical pseudepigraphy of later times than to colophons of cuneiform scientific tablets specifying that only "the one who knows may show [the tablet] to the one who knows."[122]

For our purposes, the question of the precise relationship to cuneiform materials proves less pressing. What is significant is that 4Q209 (i.e., #4 above) appears to attest the literary conjuring of the very settings of scribal teaching in which lists like 4Q208 and 4Q211 were used for text-based knowledge transmission (#1–#2). The ramifications are even more striking than Drawnel recognizes. The *Astronomical Book* is virtually unique among ancient Jewish texts in figuring the process of teaching as reading but also in figuring the process of reading as a primary visual activity. Within the Hebrew Bible and classical Rabbinic literature alike, emphasis falls instead on what is heard and what is remembered. As noted in Chapter 2, the Torah/Pentateuch consistently privileges the oral and aural dimensions of both pedagogy and textuality, representing the ideal act of reading – as Daniel Boyarin has stressed – as a "public, oral and illocutionary speech-act."[123] Even in Rabbinic midrash, the life of a studied book resides primarily in mouth and memory, and only secondarily (and rarely) as visible words seen on a page: exegesis might seem to elevate the Torah's textuality, but – as David Stern has shown – "rabbis knew the Bible primarily as a heard, memorized text."[124]

---

[120] Drawnel, *Aramaic Astronomical Book*, 36–37. Here the verb is חזי in pa'el, whereas it occurs in haph'el in *ALD* 84.
[121] Drawnel, *Aramaic Astronomical Book*, 37.
[122] Drawnel, *Aramaic Astronomical Book*, 38–39.   [123] Boyarin, "Placing Reading," 15.
[124] Stern, "The First Jewish Books and the Early History of Jewish Writing," 181.

Significantly, for our purposes, this sense of reading as speech-act is presumed even in those biblical passages commonly cited as evidence for the postexilic textualization of revelation. Ezekiel may see much, for instance, but he ingests his scroll through his mouth, and he is commanded to prophesy by speaking in the hopes that his words will be heard (Ezek 2:8–3:4); or, as Joachim Schaper puts it: "the prophet is first given the written word, which then has to be transformed into the spoken word."[125] So too even in other exemplars of the Aramaic Enoch tradition: the *Book of the Watchers* appeals to Enoch's skills of writing and status as scribe, but it nevertheless depicts his own acts of transmitting knowledge through older prophetic models of hearing, speaking, and proclaiming.[126] At times, Enoch there speaks about the need to "see," such as in his opening call to observe natural cycles, and at times he speaks of what he himself has seen and been shown by angels, whether in heaven or at the ends of the earth.[127] Missing, however, is the closed circuit of sight that is elevated within the *Astronomical Book*, wherein what is seen is then shown, again to be shown and seen again, at least partly in written form – in a manner more akin to the lineage of scribal skills and scrolls evoked by the *Aramaic Levi Document, Admonitions of Qahat,* and *Visions of Amram.*

---

[125] Schaper, "Exilic and Post-Exilic," 324–342.

[126] As I have noted elsewhere (Reed, "Pseudepigraphy and/as Prophecy"), the *Book of the Watchers* stays closer to older prophetic patterns of the earthly transmission of divine revelation, as consisting of oral proclamations; in *1 En* 2–5, for instance, speech-formulae are used that echo the account of the prophecy of Balaam in Numbers 23–24. Unlike the *Astronomical Book*, it gives no account of its own origins-as-writing. It is framed, rather, as the contents of what was spoken when "Enoch ... took up his parable [מתלוהי] and said ..." (*1 En* 1:2; 4QEn^a 1 i 2; cf. Num 24:15). An interesting example of the resultant tension within Enochic literary tradition can be found in *1 En* 93:1, for which the attested Aramaic parallels *1 En* 1:2 (4QEn^g iii 23: "Enoch took up his parable and said"), whereas the Ethiopic reads "Enoch was speaking from his books"; see further Stuckenbruck, *1 Enoch 91–108*, 65–69.

[127] Comparison with the *Book of the Watchers* is especially intriguing inasmuch as parts of *1 En* 76–77 from the *Astronomical Book* are paralleled there, reworked to fit the structure of Enoch's journey in *1 En* 34:1–36:2. There, the language of sight is also expressed in first-person formulae of seeing and been shown, but it has been redeployed to fit the narrativized account of Enoch's travels, guided by angels. If such formulae have their prehistory in the visual consultation of written materials within didactic settings, they here rise to the model for reimaging the mechanics of the revelation of heavenly knowledge to earth. The parallels thus speak to the literary creativity by which these different senses of the semantics and mechanics of vision came to be intertwined to take on new meanings overlaid upon the old.

One would certainly not want to go as far as Drawnel in positing that the whole "literary genre of a heavenly journey probably developed from the kind of didactic literature attested in the *Aramaic Astronomical Book*."[128] On the evidence of this work, however, we might posit the distinctively visual reading-practices and pedagogy of Aramaic Jewish scribalism – and their ideological elevation and literary abstractification in the *Astronomical Book* – as among the crucibles for the new emphasis on the transcendent power of sight in the apocalyptic and related literature of late Second Temple times.

In the context of the textual formation of the *Astronomical Book*, this visual rhetoric bears other resonances too. Surveying references to seeing and showing in both Aramaic and Ethiopic versions of the work, for instance, VanderKam notes how this rhetoric is consistently used in relation to patterns and phenomena visible in nature, and he thus argues for a connection to practices of observing celestial cycles.[129] In my view, we need not choose between Drawnel's emphasis on the visuality of scribal textuality and VanderKam's emphasis on seeing as metonym for scientific observation. Determinative, rather, is the overlap between the specialized scribal use of sight, on the one hand, and the power of the eyes to enable earthly access to knowledge about divine cosmic order, on the other. It is not until the addition of chapters 80–81 (i.e., #6 above) that Enoch's seeing and showing are physically relocated to the heavens.[130] But even prior to the introduction of the heavenly journey as a narrative setting for Uriel's teachings in the *Astronomical Book*, the rhetoric of visuality functions to assert scribal expertise as coterminous with claims of access to the divine cosmic order inscribed on the cycles of the skies.

Eventually, this sense of scribal expertise would become embodied in the exemplar Enoch.[131] Yet, in *1 Enoch* 72–79+82, the angel Uriel still remains more prominent. Enoch's identity as first-person speaker is there implied by references to "my son Methuselah" (76:14; 82:1), whereas

---

[128]   Drawnel, *Aramaic Astronomical Book*, 37, there explaining this contention as "because Enoch's travels in *1 En.* 17–19 and 20–36 have uncontestable points of contact with the *AAB*." For biblical precedents for the *Book of the Watchers*, however, see Himmelfarb, *Ascent*, and for Mesopotamian precedents, Sanders, *From Adapa to Enoch*.

[129]   VanderKam, "Enoch's Science," 60–61.

[130]   Drawnel, *Aramaic Astronomical Book*, 37.

[131]   Even if the connection is made somewhat later than we might expect within the Aramaic Enoch tradition, the linkage of heavenly journey and scribal exemplar has ancient precedents in Mesopotamian traditions surrounding Adapa; see further Sanders, *From Adapa to Enoch*.

Uriel's role as authorizer is emphasized through multiple mentions of his name and repeated enumeration of his roles (e.g., 72:1; 74:2; 75:3–4; 78:10; 79:2, 6; 82:7). At the very beginning of the work, for instance, the rhetoric of visuality is deployed to claim Uriel as the ultimate source for all the knowledge that follows:

The book [*maṣḥaf*][132] about the motion of the heavenly luminaries, all as they are in their kinds, their jurisdiction, their time, their name, their origins, and their months which Uriel, the holy angel [*mal'ak*] who was with me who is their leader [*marāḥihomu*], showed me ['*ar'ayani*]. The entire book about them, as it is, he showed me and how every year of the world will be forever, until a new creation lasting forever is made. (*1 En* 72:1)

Right at the beginning of this version of the *Astronomical Book*, the older didactic sense of showing is thereby repurposed for the aim of authorizing the work as the record of revelations from the angelic leader of the luminaries. Nor is this theme limited to the opening lines. Throughout *1 Enoch* 72–79+82, statements about acts of showing become claims of angelic revelation that are simultaneously assertions of angelic governance over the cycles of the natural world:

For Uriel the angel whom the Lord of eternal glory set over the heavenly luminaries, in the sky and in the world, showed me ['*ar'ayani*] the sign, the seasons, the years, and the days (cf. Gen 1:14) so that they may rule the firmament, appear above the earth, and be leaders of days and nights—the sun, the moon, the stars, and all the serving entities that go around in all the heavenly chariots. In the same way, Uriel showed me twelve gates open in the disc of the sun's chariot ... (*1 En* 75:3–4)
    Uriel showed me ['*ar'ayani*] another ordinance [*šer'āta*]... (*1 En* 78:10)
    This is the appearance and the likeness of each luminary that Uriel, the great angel who is their leader, showed me ['*ar'ayani*]. (*1 En* 79:6)

To us, astronomy might seem quite far from angelology. It is telling, however, that this does not seem to have been the case for those who shaped and read the *Astronomical Book*. We have seen already how 4Q209 (frg. 28; quoted above) includes a list of celestial luminaries that conveys the divine order of the cycles of the year and the cosmos. The connection of astronomy and angelology is even clearer in the version preserved in Ethiopic by virtue of the doubled designation of Uriel as celestial "leader" [*marāḥi*] and "angel" [*mal'ak*]. Consequently, the claim to preserve knowledge learned from "the angel whom the Lord of eternal

---

[132] The self-designation as "book" departs from the dominant pattern in *1 Enoch* (1:1; 37:1; 83:1; 91:1; 92:1; 93:1; cf. 108:1) so is not likely just a later relic of its anthological combination with other Enochic writings there.

glory set over the heavenly luminaries, in the sky and in the world" (75:3–4) functions both as an authorizing strategy for the work and as an affirmation of angelic oversight over the movement of the sun, moon, and stars. Whether or not any other entities described as "leaders" are meant to be understood as "angels" *per se*, Uriel embodies the conviction of a smooth continuum between what we might seem to us like self-evidently separate "natural" and "supernatural" phenomena. By contrast, God's heavenly abode is here connected to the earthly domains of humankind as if by a plentitude of evenly-spaced steps.[133] Among the ramifications is the inclusion of both angels and celestial cycles among the components of the workings of the cosmos that are said to be seen, taught, and written by Jewish scribes.

If angelology here forms part of the same field of scribal *Listenwissenschaft* as astronomy, meteorology, cosmology, and the calendar, it is in part because of the angelification of Jewish scribal pedagogy. Not only does the version of the *Astronomical Book* in *1 Enoch* 72–79+82 begin with a self-conscious statement of its own status as "book" [*maṣḥaf*] (72:1; quoted above), but it explains its own origins-as-text by pairing Uriel's showing with Enoch's writing:

Another course and law [*meḥwār we-te'zāz*] I saw [*re'iku*] for it {i.e., the moon}; by that law it carries out the monthly courses. All this, Uriel the holy angel ... showed me. I wrote down their positions as he showed me and wrote down their months as they are ... (*1 En* 74:1–2)

---

[133] The presentation of a tiered hierarchy of angelic and celestial "leaders" and "luminaries" thus runs directly counter to the division of realms above and below moon that was common in Greek (and later Roman) scientific and philosophical thought. On Aristotle's influential iteration of the difference – and its epistemological ramifications for the limits of human inquiry – see Falcon, *Aristotle and the Science of Nature*. On this "distinction between the 'sublunary' world of corruptible bodies, and the celestial world of the permanent and divine" as it underlies even Ptolemy's defense of the discipline of astronomy as "midway between theology (immortal and imperceptible objects) and physics (mortal and perceptible objects) as a discipline concerned with the very special class of objects which though immortal are nevertheless perceptible and hence scientifically comprehensible," see Beck, *Brief History of Ancient Astrology*, 4. That it also influenced some Jewish views of the cosmos is suggested by Philo's triadic division in *QG* 4.8 (*apud* Genesis 18) with [1] the incorporeal and intelligible world, whose cause is God Himself; [2] the perceptible world established in the fifth element (i.e., *aether*), which is ruled by God's "Creative Power" and which is a "more wonderful and divine essence, [as] unaltered and unchanged in relation with these things below," and [3] the world of "sublunary things ... made out of the four powers, earth, water, air, and fire, admitting generation and corruption," overseen by God's "Regal Power" (cf. *Fug* 97ff; Dillon, *The Middle Platonists*, 169–170).

The knowledge that Enoch – and, hence, the reader – is here "shown" is linked to Uriel's exalted status as the "leader" of the luminaries (also 79:6), and its written form is presented as proof and product of the uniquely scribal access to him. Just angelic pedagogy is posited as the ultimate origin for the lunar and other didactic lists now transmitted amongst Jewish scribes on earth, so their practices of scribal teaching, reading, and writing are elevated through association with angels – with the embodiment of this elevation presented as the *Astronomical Book* itself.

Within *1 Enoch* 72–79+82, there are also some telling differences between the first-person framing notices about what Uriel showed Enoch, those about Enoch says "I saw," and those about what Enoch taught Methuselah. We have noted how the language of showing is infused with angelology. First-person notices about Enoch's own acts of seeing, by contrast, stand in the greater continuity with the patterns in the "compound text" of 4Q209 as surveyed above. In some cases, consistent with the connection of sight with scientific observation, the didactic "I" claims to have seen the "laws" of regularity in celestial cycles or the positions of the heavenly bodies moving on those cycles:

After this law [*te'zāz*] {i.e., of the sun} I saw [*re'iku*] a second law [*te'zāz*] of the smaller luminary whose name is the moon. (*1 En* 73:1)
    ... I saw [*re'iku*] their positions, as the moon rises and the sun sets during those days." (*1 En* 74:9)
    ... I saw [*re'iku*] chariots in the sky traveling in the world above those gates in which the stars that do not set revolve. (*1 En* 75:8)

In other cases, consistent with the connection of sight with scribal reading-practices and pedagogy, Enoch is presented as seeing the structures of the heaven and earth, described in a manner more in line with a written map or diagram:

I saw [*re'iku*] six gates through which the sun emerges, and six gates through which the sun sets ... (*1 En* 72:1)
    ... At the boundaries of the earth, I saw [*re'iku*] twelve gates open for all the winds ... (*1 En* 76:1)
    ... I saw [*re'iku*] seven lofty mountains ... I saw [*re'iku*] seven rivers ... I saw [*re'iku*] seven large islands in the sea and on the land ... (*1 En* 77:4–5, 8)[134]

---

[134] As noted above, the evidence of 4Q209 frg. 23.3–10 and 4Q210 frg. 1 ii 14–20 is not decisive but does at least signal the possibility that a first-person statement of seeing similar to *1 En* 77:4 might have been present in the tradition either in or before the "compound text."

What is preserved here, in effect, is something of the doubly didactic sense of sight evoked already in the first-person notices in 4Q209.

Within *1 Enoch* 72–79+82, references to Enoch's acts of showing and telling serve to extend this didactic sense to speak to the mechanisms by which knowledge is preserved on earth. In this version of the *Astronomical Book*, there is only one reference to the act of showing in which no one is mentioned by name, and it occurs in the parallel to the "paternal report" of 4Q209 frg. 26.6–7 (see above). This passage, *1 Enoch* 79:1–2, is an exception to the overall pattern whereby the teachings of the didactic "I" are marked as Enochic through the explicit mention of the name of his son Methuselah. The anonymity of *1 Enoch* 79:1–2 may preserve a relic of an earlier stage of the tradition. Nevertheless, comparison of the two versions highlights an interesting shift in emphasis. Whereas the Aramaic emphasizes the act of teaching ("Now I am telling you, my son"), the Ethiopic stresses the completeness of what is transmitted ("Now, my son, I have shown you everything").

The other two references to Enoch's acts of showing and telling in *1 Enoch* 72–79+82 feature this version's only two references to Methuselah. These passages are marked by the same totalizing rhetoric:

The twelve gates of the four quarters of the sky are completed. All their laws and all their punishment and prosperity – I have shown you everything, my son Methuselah. (*1 En* 76:14)
... Now, my son Methuselah, I am telling you these things and am writing down. I have revealed all of them and have given you the books about these things. My son, keep the book written by the hand of your father so that you may give it to the generations of the world. (*1 En* 82:1)

In these two passages, it is made explicit that he who was the student now becomes the teacher, and it is implied that the practice of teaching makes the scribe who knows astronomy akin to the very angel who leads the heavenly retinue. Enoch here takes the place of Uriel as the one who shows and teaches knowledge about the structure and workings of the cosmos. Inasmuch as Enoch passes along "everything," Methuselah is in a position to do the same – and so on, and so on, and so on, up to the reader today. What enables the equation of angel and scribe is also what enables the confident assertion of the completeness of the transmission of knowledge both from heaven to earth and from past to present – that is, an unprecedented confidence in the power and permanence of writing. Enoch is here said to show Methuselah "everything" he was shown by Uriel in the sense of telling his knowledge but also in the sense of writing it down and giving him the books.

The blurring of teaching and textuality in *1 Enoch* 72–79+82 signals the tenacity of the didactic dynamics of sight in 4Q209: it is because one teaches with books, which are seen and read in the process, that the transmission of those books can ensure the completeness of the knowledge shown by teacher to student, from generation to generation. As the self-claimed product of Enoch's own scribal hand, these texts enable the continued survival of knowledge and enliven the continued practice of teaching. What is assumed, moreover, is that the teachers in question are scribes – those accustomed to reading with the eye, rather than with the ear, and to writing books with their hands, rather than composing with their voices. Scribes and scrolls are here elevated as that which enables knowledge to travel across vast expanses of time by virtue of bridging heaven and earth as well.

In this sense, the *Astronomical Book* both embodies and expresses the power of textuality to transcend place and time. Its form and formation resonate especially with the power of what Carr categorizes as long-duration texts, wherein the written word "makes language permanent, depersonalizes language, decontextualizes expression, and adds normativity" and "formalizes, generalizes, and perpetuates features and intentions of language – cutting it loose from momentary and context-bound utterance."[135]

For Carr, this distinction is significant in relation to those works that later came to constitute the Hebrew Bible. My suggestion, here, is that it pertains also to some of the so-called pseudepigrapha that were taking shape around the same time as the latest biblical texts. Works like the *Astronomical Book* similarly provide "reference points for a broader process of education by which nascent scribes were taught both cultural values and literacy at the same time."[136] The witnesses to its literary formation surveyed above, in fact, permit a rare glimpse into "the project of education ... so central to the creation and transmission of long-duration texts (and vice versa)."[137] Whereas biblical examples often reflect upon the limitations of human knowledge, moreover, the

---

[135] Carr, *Writing on the Tablet*, 10. As noted above, Carr uses this category as a means of acknowledging the many different uses of writing in ancient cultures, while also distinguishing those elements most prominent in literary works meant for continued copying and study.

[136] Carr, *Writing on the Tablet*, 19.

[137] Carr, *Writing on the Tablet*, 19, there arguing that such writings also "played a key role in an overall project of ensuring cultural continuity from age to age and from place to place."

emergence of the *Astronomical Book* is accompanied by an unprecedented confidence in the completeness of what can be known and taught. Its transition from list to literature may be transformative, but the product thus retains something of the power of scribal *Listenwissenschaft* – both to order knowledge and to teach it.

ASTRONOMICAL KNOWLEDGE IN ARATUS, BEROSSUS, AND PSEUDO-EUPOLEMUS

The previous chapter noted the pointed concern for pedagogy in much of the Aramaic Jewish literature of the early Hellenistic age.[138] So far in this chapter, we have seen how the textual tradition surrounding the *Astronomical Book* proves particularly resonant in this regard: it preserves early examples of written lists likely used as tools for teaching technical knowledge to Jewish scribes, alongside evidence for their compilation, framing, and narrativization into newly literary forms – largely through didactic tropes. A concern with teaching, moreover, is what unites the multiple authorizing strategies nested therein. When we initially hear the first-person voice in 4Q209, it is couched in terms of the didactic trope of a father speaking to his son, and the associated language of sight and showing is primarily pedagogical prior to its reworking as angelic revelation. Even the association of angelology and astronomy in *1 Enoch* 72–82 is achieved by projecting the practices of scribal pedagogy first onto Uriel and then up into the heavens.

Is it just a coincidence that this concern coincides with the consolidation and spread of new forms of Greek *paideia* that we noted at the beginning of this chapter? To explore this question, it proves useful to engage an intertext that exemplifies the "widespread non-specialist interest in things having to do with the stars" in the third and second centuries BCE - namely, Aratus' *Phaenomena*.[139] As noted above, the *Phaenomena* is the most prominent example of this broader trend, and it also provides an especially intriguing parallel to the literary practices that shaped the *Astronomical Book*, including the reframing of lists of astronomical and related information about time, seasons, and weather into new literary forms with distinctively didactic features.[140]

---

[138] See also Reed, "Textuality"; Reed, "Writing Jewish Astronomy."

[139] Volk, *Manilius*, 27.

[140] Didactic features include mnemonics like acrostics; Jacques, "Sur un acrostiche d'Aratos." The use of Aratus in pedagogical settings is confirmed by the survival of a

As Douglas Kidd notes, Aratus "gives a display of his artistry and ingenuity in making technical material from prose sources compatible with the demands of Hellenistic poetry."[141] The result was not just to redeem poetry from the philosophical denigration of its capacity to convey rational truths (e.g., Plato, *Rep* 607b–608a; Aristotle, *Poetics* 1447b) but also to reframe technical material about the cosmos as revealed knowledge apt for use in education.[142] To do so, Aratus models his poem on Hesiod's *Works and Days* (esp. *Phain.* 1–18; 98–136; cf. *Op.* 1–4; 109–201; 213–85).[143] Its beginning rewrites the famous opening of that work so as to present the cycles of the skies as "signs" revealed by Zeus:[144]

Let us begin with Zeus, whom we men never leave unspoken. Filled with Zeus are all highways and all meeting-places of people, filled are the sea and the harbours; in all circumstances, we are dependent on Zeus. For we are also his children, and he benignly gives helpful signs to men, and rouses people to work, reminding them of their livelihood, tells when the soil is best for oxen and mattocks, and tells when the seasons are right both for planting trees and for sowing every kind of seed. For it was Zeus himself who fixed the signs in the sky, making them into distinct constellations, and organized stars for the year to give the most clearly defined signs of the seasonal round to men, so that everything may grow without fail. That is why men always pay homage to him first and last. Hail Father, great wonder, great boon to me, yourself and the earlier race! And hail Muses, all most gracious! In answer to my prayer to tell of the stars in so far as I may, guide all my singing.
(Aratus, *Phaen.* 1–19; trans. Kidd)

third- or fourth-century school commentary on it (P.Berol. inv. 5865); see Maehler, "Der 'Wertlose' Aratkodex"; Cribiore, *Gymnastics of the Mind*, 142–143; Miguélez-Cavero, *Poems in Context*, 243–245.

[141] Kidd, *Aratus*, 12.

[142] As Gee stresses, "poetry carries with it the status of revealed knowledge, from Homer onward," and Aratus' work shared in this status even as it was also "seen by at least one of its earliest commentators as designed to impart technical knowledge, therefore open to corrections of a technical kind" (*Aratus*, 22). It is worth recalling too that poetry has a special place within Greek *paideia*, in contrast to the more limited and specialized engagement with philosophical and other prose works; see, e.g., Cribiore, *Gymnastics of the Mind*, 201–203. The poetic form meant that Aratus' astronomical work could be used in didactic settings alongside Homer and Hesiod.

[143] Kidd, *Aratus*, 8–10; Hunter, "Written in the Stars"; Gee, *Aratus*, 24–29, 185–88.

[144] Hunter ("Written in the Stars") notes the contrast: "The *Works and Days* presents us with an all-powerful and all-seeing Zeus who is concerned with justice, but whose mind (*nóos*) is changeable and hard-to-know (483–484), and who has hidden from men the means of a life free from toil," while Aratus' Zeus "while also being all-seeing and concerned with justice, openly assists mankind through the omnipresence of 'signs' (*Phain.* 10–13) ... Zeus himself set signs in heaven, marking out the constellations, and for the whole year he thought out which stars should most of all give men signs of the seasons, so that all things should grow without fail."

In place of the Hesiodic assertion that "the gods keep the means of life hidden from humans,"[145] Aratus proclaims Zeus as the one who "benignly gives helpful signs to humans."[146] He too calls upon Muses for inspiration. Here, however, it is not only the Muses who "tell of Zeus" (*Op.* 1); the "signs" [σήματα] that Zeus himself set in the skies are also revelatory.

That celestial "signs" in the skies mediate divine knowledge comes further clear in Aratus' innovative depiction of personified Justice (Gr. *Dike*) as simultaneously Muse and constellation (*Phaen.* 96–136). Here too, new points are made through Hesiodic rewriting – in this case, interweaving the myth of *Dike* (*Op.* 213–285) with the myth of the Four Ages (*Op.* 109–201). "By turning *Dike* into a star," as Gee demonstrates, "Aratus makes Hesiod's narrative of decline into a closed loop in which the notion of cyclicality replaces the Hesiodic timeline."[147] This move, in turn, contributes to the work's broader aim "to assimilate the Hesiodic mode of didactic poetry to philosophical notions of the cyclicality of the universe."[148] Nor is the appeal to divine revelation limited to the proem and later mythological asides. When Aratus later exhorts his readers to "take pains to learn" about the stars, for instance, he presents them as useful for navigation but also exemplary of what Zeus communicates to humankind:

For we men do not yet have knowledge of everything from Zeus, but much still is hidden, whereof Zeus if he wishes will give us signs anon; he certainly does benefit the human race openly, showing himself on every side, and everywhere displaying his signs. Some things the moon will tell you, for example, when halved on either side of full, or again when she is full, and other things the sun will tell you when rising and again in warnings at the beginning of night. (Aratus, *Phaen.* 769–775)

His subsequent exhortations to the reader to "observe [σκέπτεο] the moon," "pay attention [τοι μελέτω] to the sun," etc., are thus presented in terms of receptivity to revealed knowledge. The technical materials thereby framed might seem outdated or unscientific when we judge them by the standards of the new discoveries of the time (not least because of the errors that Hipparchus himself notes in his commentary to it). Nevertheless, Aratus makes no claim that the science here is new. Indeed, far from it: his claim is that the science is quite old, if not timeless, and through that claim, the universality of cosmic cycles is drawn into the

---

[145] Hesiod, *Op.* 42: κρύψαντες γὰρ ἔχουσι θεοὶ βίον ἀνθρώποισιν.
[146] Aratus, *Phaen.* 5: ὁ δ' ἤπιος ἀνθρώποισι δεξιὰ σημαίνει.   [147] Gee, *Aratus*, 24.
[148] Gee, *Aratus*, 18.

privileged cultural domain of the *mythoi* of the Greeks and into the practical domain of Hellenistic pedagogy.

Gee argues that Aratus' *Phaenomena* is "the first accessible coalescence of astronomical data with a cosmology which embraces the world in all its levels, including human morality," and she makes a persuasive case in the context of the Greek literary tradition.[149] But, as we have seen, much the same description could be applied to the *Astronomical Book* in relation to the Jewish literary tradition.[150] For understanding the century in which both took form, the comparison may be instructive.

I have no intention to argue for any direct lines of "influence" linking the two works. The wide diffusion of Aratus' *Phaenomena* eventually included Jewish readers – as is clear from the direct quotation of its opening lines by Aristobulos in the second century BCE and by the Book of Acts in the first century CE.[151] The early date of the *Astronomical Book* makes a connection of this sort more tenuous. For our purposes, arguments about direct dependence are also unnecessary. For understanding something of the broader context of the formation of the *Astronomical Book* as charted above, this intertext proves useful as a particularly prominent example of the intensification of interest in astronomy and cosmology in the third century BCE. By virtue of its extreme popularity, the *Phaenomena* also serves as a barometer of sorts for the shifting practices of pedagogy that prompted the synthesis of older astronomical data into new literary forms, similarly shaped by new cosmological, ethical, and didactic concerns. Parallels of anthological aim and practice, moreover, prove poignant enough that one cannot help but wonder if the *Astronomical Book* can be read as a separate and parallel product of some of the same conditions.

Most importantly, for our purposes, juxtaposition with Aratus' *Phaenomena* also helps to highlight the theorization of knowledge achieved by the angelology of the *Astronomical Book*. The figure of *Dike* in the *Phaenomena*, after all, fulfills much the same function as Uriel in *1 Enoch*

---

[149] Gee, *Aratus*, 18.

[150] What Aratus here does for Hesiod, moreover, the Aramaic Enoch tradition eventually does for Genesis, expanding its framework to include the newly prestigious domain of astronomy while also mediating access even to those untrained in the relevant *technai*.

[151] Acts 17:28; Clement, *Strom.* 5.14.101.4; Eusebius, *Praep.ev.* 13.12.6–7; van de Bunt-van den Hoek, "Aristobulos, Acts, Theophilus"; Gruen, "Jews and Greeks as Philosophers," 414–415; Edwards, "Quoting Aratus." The possibility that ben Sira was aware of this work is explored in Calduch-Benages, "The Hymn to the Creation (Sir 42:15–43:33): A Polemic Text?"

72–79+82. Aratus first describes the constellation *Parthenos* (Virgo) as "daughter of Astraeus ... the original father of the stars" (98–99; cf. *Theogony* 378–382). He then opines about "another tale current among men":

> ... once she actually lived on earth, and came face to face with men, and did not ever spurn the tribes of ancient men and women, but sat in their midst although she was immortal. And they called her Justice: gathering together the elders, either in the marketplace or the broad highway, she urged them in prophetic tones to judgments for the good of the people. At that time they still had no knowledge of painful strife or quarrelsome conflict or noise of battle, but lived just as they were; the dangerous sea was far from their thoughts, and as yet no ships brought them livelihood from afar, but oxen and ploughs and Justice herself, queen of the people and giver of civilized life, provided all their countless needs. That was as long as the earth still nurtured the golden age. (Aratus, *Phaen.* 100–14; trans. Kidd)

Dike is said to have engaged selectively with the Silver Age, albeit "rebuking them for their wickedness," never speaking to them face-to-face, and fleeing for the mountains (120–130). It was not until the Bronze Age – "the first to forge the criminal sword for murder on the highways, and the first to taste the flesh of ploughing oxen" (131–132) – that *Dike*, "conceiving a hatred for the generation of men, flew up to the sky and took up her abode in that place, where she is still visible to men by night as the Maiden by conspicuous Bootes" (133–136).

A later Enochic work, the *Parables of Enoch* (ca. first century BCE/ CE), contains a similar tale about how personified Wisdom found no adequate home among humankind and thus made her dwelling in heaven among the angels instead (*1 En* 42:1–2; cf. 94:5; cf. Sir 24:7–11). Whereas the *Parables of Enoch* dramatizes the distancing of divine knowledge from humankind, however, both Aratus and the *Astronomical Book* invoke celestially associated mediating figures to assert its continued accessibility. Even though Aratus appeals to the famous Hesiodic schema of the successive denigration from the Golden Age, for instance, he does not describe the departure of Justice from humankind in terms of decline. Rather, by equating *Dike* with the constellation *Parthenos*, he is able to stress her status as "still visible" – a component of Zeus' helpful communication to humankind through the "signs" in the skies.[152] The point is

---

[152] Gee (*Aratus*, 29) stresses that this connection seems original to Aratus and, as a result, "*Dike* as *Parthenos* is now cyclical, a part of the zodiac... [and] as Aratus himself tells us elsewhere (*Ph* 497–499), part of the zodiac is always visible above the horizon, part revolves below. She is always there, periodically as well as predictably visible."

doubly made when Aratus claims *Dike* as Muse: not only does she emblematize the accessibility of knowledge from Zeus through our sight of the skies, but she is figured as among the inspiring powers that enable its accessibility through didactic poetry like the *Phaenomena* itself.

Something similar may be at play in the identification of the angel Uriel *both* with the leader of the celestial luminaries at the head of the hierarchy of seasonal time *and* with the teacher who "shows" the "calculations" of their cycles to the *Astronomical Book*'s first-person scribal "I." Even as the multiplication of myriads of leaders upon leaders conveys the grandeur of God and the vastness of the heavens, Uriel vouchsafes the predictability of the orderly governance of the cosmos and the availability of knowledge about this orderliness to humankind. Here too, the accessibility mediated through the sight of the skies is paired with the accessibility mediated by writing. In the process – as for Aratus – an emphasis on the visible cycles of the moon, sun, stars, and seasons serves as symbolic of all that the highest deity chooses to reveal to humankind.[153]

The comparison may also help to highlight some of what is at stake in the pairing of Uriel with Enoch. In both cases, the primeval past is evoked as a time of intimacy between heaven and earth: just as Justice herself advised the elders of Aratus' Golden Age, so Uriel's connection to Enoch also evokes an antediluvian era when scribes learned about celestial cycles from the angels themselves. This makes it all the more striking, however, that neither tells a narrative of decline. Instead, the evocation of loss serves to occasion the assurance of a continued connection. In both cases, this connection is described through images of knowledge transmission that conjure the power of pedagogy to preserve truths across even vast expanses of space and time. He who learns the constellations listed by Aratus knows when *Dike* is predictably visible. Jewish scribal readers of the *Astronomical Book* are similarly assured that they can look up to the skies to see the celestial luminaries lead by Uriel – the very angel who is also connected to them through a lineage of teaching embodied by the book itself. In effect, both Aratus and the *Astronomical Book* appeal to transmundane mediators of astronomical knowledge to assure their readers of the potent simultaneity of mythic past and didactic

---

[153] For both Aratus and the *Astronomical Book*, this is partly achieved by interweaving technical knowledge about the skies with information about its contact points with lived human experience (e.g., weather, seasons, calendar). Or, in other words, what scholars of the History of Science might dismiss as their inclusion of "unastronomical" information proves significant for the meaning of both works, particularly in relation to their cosmological claims and ethical ramifications.

present – and, as a result, the capacity of knowledge, rightly taught, to travel smoothly even across moments of radical historical disjuncture.

Interestingly, in both cases, the epistemological functions of these mediating figures are mirrored by their literary functions. By Gee's reading, for instance, Aratus' *Dike* "is both real and mythical, a star and a symbol," and this is central to her function to help "unite, perhaps for the first time, astronomy and cosmology":

As a goddess, she is part of an ethical system, a cosmology, in which the world is engineered in such a way as to favour particular conduct, illustrated through a linear model human development; as a constellation, she is part of a cyclical astronomical system. Because of her status as both mythic figure and constellation, a dual status given to her by Aratus himself as the originator of the identification of between Dike and the constellation *Parthenos*, she stands as a metaphor for the association between the technical and the mythical central to Aratus' undertaking.[154]

Dike's role as "an active participant in the cycles of the cosmos" makes her "a Muse appropriate to the coexistence of poetry and philosophy" for Aratus.[155] Similarly, the evocation of Uriel as angel functions to fuse ethical and technical discourses into a newly integrative pedagogical ideal. To ask which "leaders" of the luminaries in the *Astronomical Book* are and are not "angels," then, may be as misplaced as to wonder whether Aratus' *Dike* is a constellation, a personified principle, or a goddess.[156] Here too, it may be the very overlap that makes meaning – both on the level of the work's theorization of knowledge and on the level of its literary structure. Just as Aratus rewrites Hesiodic myth to mediate the transfer of astronomical information into the literary genre of didactic poetry, so the Jewish scribes responsible for transforming didactic lists into the long-duration text of the *Astronomical Book* use angelology to mediate the inclusion of astronomical information into the literary heritage of Israel.

In the shared concerns of Aratus and the *Astronomical Book*, we may glimpse part of the reason for the cultural potency of technical

---

[154] I.e., it is because she is depicted as mediating the "link between astronomical data (the positions of the constellations) and the human understanding of the world as a whole (cosmology)" that she helps to justify the importation of astronomy into the domains of philosophy and the genre of poetry; Gee, *Aratus*, 34–35.

[155] Gee, *Aratus*, 23.

[156] Or, in other words, Aratus offers a contemporaneous example of a blurring of the divine realm and the celestial realm that cannot be reduced simply to an "either/or" choice of whether or not stars are gods.

information about celestial cycles, in particular, for diverse elites in the early Hellenistic age. At a time when the ancient Mediterranean world was newly splintered into a multipolarity of competing imperial centers, the claim made by Aratus and the *Astronomical Book* is that one can be taught to look to the skies to see a predictable and cyclical order under one just and benevolent divine ruler, who reveals knowledge to human-kind through the visible world, as if writing cosmic truths on and with the skies. Inasmuch as human sight is what enables the connection, it is perhaps not surprising that Aratus uses idioms of visibility to express the earthly availability of divine knowledge, just as both the *Phaenomena* and the *Astronomical Book* also figure understanding as the act of being shown, seeing, and being taught how and what to see. Thus construed, technical materials about astronomy could provide powerful tools for new written reflections on knowledge in the early Hellenistic age in part because they enable grand claims about cosmic and divine truths along-side quite practical assurances about their continued accessibility here on earth – through the eyes and through education.

The rewriting of *Enuma Elish* and translation of Near Eastern monar-chic ideology into Greek language and idiom in Berossus' *Babylonica* offers yet another example of the reworking of older knowledge into new literary forms in the third century BCE. There is a possibility, as noted above, that this work also integrated some astronomical material. The relevant excerpts have suffered much scholarly neglect due to Neu-gebauer's judgments of their scientific content as "primitive" by the criteria of the Babylonian mathematical astronomy known from cuneiform sources.[157] Yet, as John Steele has recently shown, they may be an important source for recovering Hellenistic-era efforts by Babylon-ian priests to rework older materials into the idiom of "philosophical cosmological tradition."[158] Although the questionable authenticity of this material makes any comparison precarious, it thus presents an interesting point for triangulation with Aratus and the *Astronomical Book* – raising the possibility that even some Babylonian priests of the time were discuss-ing celestial cycles for aims that were more cosmological or epistemo-logical than "scientific" *per se*.

---

[157] This was the judgment of Neugebauer, "Survival of Babylonian Methods," 529.
[158] Steele, "The 'Astronomical Fragments' of Berossos in Context," 99–111, quote at 109. Berossus predates Aratus, and the two also have in common the specification of the days of the moon's phases (108).

To the degree that Berossus is engaged in a similar enterprise to the *Astronomical Book*, however, his *Babylonica* is ultimately oriented towards kingship rather than education. He thus draws upon different elements from their shared Near Eastern cultural heritage, even as he engages in a parallel literary activity of culling this heritage to rewrite the antediluvian past for a changing Hellenistic present. His project fits with the concerns of court cultures of the time in a manner akin to Aratus but distinct from the *Astronomical Book*. The triangulation thus helps to bring the literary choices within the *Astronomical Book* into sharper relief. Here, as we have seen, the language of leadership is reserved for Israel's God and His orderly heavenly hierarchy of luminaries and angels. Yet the divine abode is far from distant. What Berossus culls for political theory, the *Astronomical Book* reworks into the beginnings of a newly detailed angelology, predicated – as for Aratus – on the assurance of the accessibility of heavenly knowledge here on earth.

Furthermore, as noted in Chapter 2, Berossus claims Babylonian cultural primacy due to the revelation of all knowledge already with Oannes before the Flood, going so far as to claim that "From that time nothing further has been discovered" (ἀπὸ δὲ τοῦ χρόνου ἐκείνου οὐδὲν ἄλλο περισσὸν εὑρεθῆναι; BNJ 680 F 1b). In the *Astronomical Book*, we find a similar emphasis on totality alongside an appeal to antediluvian age, but there is no explicit assertion of Jewish cultural primacy. That the *Astronomical Book* could be used to make a similar argument is suggested by the surviving excerpts associated with Pseudo-Eupolemus.[159] As we have seen, these excerpts explicitly engage competing claims to cultural priority in astronomical and divinatory lore, arguing that Babylonians, Egyptians, and Phoenicians all owe their knowledge of these *technai* to Abraham and Enoch. What is myth for the Greeks, moreover, is here claimed as part of Israel's recorded history: "The Greeks say that Atlas discovered astrology," Pseudo-Eupolemus asserts, only to reveal that "Atlas and Enoch are the same" (*Praep.ev.* 9.17.9).[160]

[159] *Apud* Eusebius, *Praep.ev.* 9.17, 9.18.2 = BNJ 724 F1–2. On Pseudo-Eupolemus' possible familiarity with Berossus' history, see Sterling, *Historiography*, 201–202. Following Freudenthal (*Alexander Polyhistor*, 82–103), many scholars have speculated about the Samaritan origins of this author, citing the reference to Mt. Gerizim in *Praep.ev.* 9.17.5 (e.g., Sterling, *Historiography*, 187–190). The evidence, however, remains inconclusive; for a reassessment, see Gruen, *Heritage and Hellenism*, 146–150.
[160] Notably, Atlas appears under the entry on astrology in Pliny's long list of "culture-heroes": "Atlas son of Libya [invented] astrology – but some say the Egyptians and still others, the Assyrians" (*Nat.hist.* 7.61.57).

Did Pseudo-Eupolemus, writing in the second century BCE, know some form of the *Astronomical Book*? The possibility is signaled by his even more specific assertion that this knowledge circulates among the Jews due to Enoch and his son Methuselah "who learned everything through the help of the angels of God, and thus we gained our knowledge."[161] If so, Pseudo-Eupolemus draws upon an element of the *Astronomical Book* that is as timely as it is potent – namely, its assertion of the study of celestial cycles as a pivotal component of Jewish pedagogy even in the antediluvian past. Attuned to the power of astronomy as an emblem of "barbarian wisdom" that long predates the Greeks, Pseudo-Eupolemus activates the utility of Enoch for competitive historiography. Just as the Manetho and Berossus mobilized indigenous sources to celebrate the antiquity of the Egyptians and Babylonians to and for Ptolemies and Seleucids, so Pseudo-Eupolemus appears to draw upon the *Astronomical Book* together with pentateuchal texts and/or traditions to try to create a similar place for Israel in the antediluvian past and the Hellenistic present. To do so, moreover, he appeals to the special connection with angels, articulated with the same themes of unique Jewish scribal access and completeness that are so prominent in the *Astronomical Book*: it was not just through sages of great antiquity – he argues – but also and ultimately "through the angels of God" (δι' ἀγγέλων θεοῦ) that "we gained our knowledge," and the knowledge taught from angels to Jewish sages encompassed "everything" (πάντα).

Was something similar already at play in the process of the formation of the *Astronomical Book*? It is certainly intriguing to wonder whether its integration of Mesopotamian science and scholasticism functioned, in part, as an appropriation of knowledge with prestigious connotations of extreme antiquity, paralleling or answering the claims about Egypt cultivated in the Ptolemaic court and the claims about Babylon cultivated in the Seleucid court.

To be sure, it is unclear whether the Jewish scribes responsible for the *Astronomical Book* would have encountered the lunar theory of 4Q208 and 4Q209 as "foreign" or Babylonian rather than Jewish or simply scribal. Inasmuch as such knowledge is not textualized in literary forms in what we know of earlier Jewish literature from the Hebrew Bible, however, the timing of its reframing as ancient Jewish scribal lore remains

---

[161] Eusebius, *Praep.ev.* 9.17.9: τοῦ δὲ Ἐνὼχ γενέσθαι υἱὸν Μαθουσάλαν, ὃν πάντα δι' ἀγγέλων θεοῦ γνῶναι, καὶ ἡμᾶς οὕτως ἐπιγνῶναι. See further Reed, "Abraham as Chaldean Scientist and Father of the Jews."

striking. In Greek literature, the study of the stars is so closely connected with Mesopotamia that the term "Chaldean" could mean either a Babylonian priest or an astrologer from any locale, and even Greek innovations were sometimes remembered as Babylonian in origin.[162] Writing in Greek, Pseudo-Eupolemus deftly exploits this connection when he calls upon Abraham's Chaldean origins to posit Israel's "scientific" contribution to world civilization.[163] Whereas his appeal to Abraham treats Israel's knowledge as comparable to those of other peoples, however, he also doubles his claim of priority in the "Chaldean *techne*" through a second and separate aetiology that uses angels to stress its uniqueness in a manner strikingly akin to what we have seen in Aramaic in the *Astronomical Book*: here too, the ultimate origins of human knowledge about the stars are angelic teachings to Enoch as taught, in turn, to Methuselah. Consequently, attention to Pseudo-Eupolemus – as with Aratus and Berossus – shows us some of what was at stake in claiming and reframing astronomical knowledge in the early Hellenistic age, but it also points poignantly to the power of the claim that the scribes of Israel are uniquely the students of angels.

CONCLUSION

In this chapter, I have proposed that the *Astronomical Book* is not merely a reservoir of lunar and other information, attesting the integration of Babylonian astronomy into Jewish scribal pedagogy: it is also the product of intensified Jewish literary activity in Aramaic in the early Hellenistic age. As far as we know, the scribes responsible for this work had no precedents in Hebrew for their literary reworking of technical data about astronomical and cosmological cycles. To the degree that the surviving witnesses permit us to glimpse something of the process of its emergence as a long-duration text, we can infer that this process was enabled – not initially through the association with Enoch – but rather through anthologizing didactic lists with a cosmological impulse, inserting first-person notices evoking a scene of scribal teaching, and connecting both celestial cycles and scribal pedagogy with angels, by means of the association with

---

[162] The Aramaic counterpart appears to be more mantic in connotation – or at least this is the sense in Dan 1:4, where Daniel and his friends are described as "young men ... versed in every branch of wisdom, endowed with knowledge and insight, and competent to serve in the king's palace; they were to be taught the literature and language of the Chaldeans."

[163] Reed, "Abraham as Chaldean."

Uriel. What the *Aramaic Levi Document, Admonitions of Qahat*, and *Visions of Amram* project into the pre-Sinaitic past, the *Astronomical Book* associates with angels.

This process has notable angelological consequences. Far from ambiguous spirits with fleeting forms, the transmundane powers of the *Astronomical Book* are given specific names and set roles in the governance of the cosmos, in the transmission of knowledge from heaven to earth, and especially in the practices of teaching, reading, and writing here asserted to connect them. The trope of angelic teaching, moreover, is precisely what enables its elevation of Jewish scribalism and its new claims about the completeness of the knowledge therein preserved and transmitted.

In what follows, we will turn to explore the further cultivation of this angelology and its extension into demonology, beginning with the *Book of the Watchers*. Before turning to these tasks, it may be useful to return to reflect on two of the broader questions raised above: can we glimpse any effects of Hellenization, in general, and the spread of Greek *paideia*, more specifically, in the Aramaic Jewish literature of the early Hellenistic age? Why did learned Jews living under Hellenistic rule, in the third century BCE, write about Babylonian astronomy in Aramaic? In this chapter, I have suggested that the answers to these questions may be interconnected. To the degree that we find parallel concerns in the *Astronomical Book* and the writings of Aratus and Berossus, however, the catalyst was not contact with Greek ideas *per se*, but rather the culture politics of the third century BCE wherein claims about knowledge loomed large and whereby older practices of *paideia* became more tightly tied to writing, reading, and books.

If the *Astronomical Book* resists reduction to the binary opposition of "Judaism" and "Hellenism" still common in the study of Second Temple Judaism, it fits well with the more sophisticated assessments of identity and imperialism in recent research in Classics. As noted above, Whitmarsh and others have looked to the Greek literature of the Hellenistic age when discussing Ptolemaic claims to be the guardians of all the wisdom of the Greeks, the new emphasis across Hellenistic empires on the patronage of textualized knowledge and the possession of physical books, and the self-consciously archival efforts in this period to collect, compile, and rewrite older traditions, often with totalizing claims about the completeness of the knowledge thereby possessed.[164] Yet it was not

---

[164] Whitmarsh, *Ancient Greek Literature*, 122–138.

86   *Demons, Angels, and Writing in Ancient Judaism*

just that Alexandria's library was later matched in Pergamum under the Attalids, or that Greek poets from across different empires collected, reworked, and displayed a dazzling scope of antiquarian, technical, and other knowledge, expressing a new confidence in the possibility of textualizing all human knowledge. The emergence of Greek as a new cosmopolitan *koine* is clear from the example of Aratus' *Phaenomena*, created in the Antigonid court yet widely diffused thereafter, and it is also clear from the self-conscious "translation" of native traditions into Greek historiographical idioms by authors like Berossus and Manetho. That some Jews were attuned to the emergence of Greek as a prestige language is attested by the beginnings of the translation of the Torah/Pentateuch and other Hebrew literature into Greek as well as the Greek writings of Jews like Pseudo-Eupolemus and others preserved via Alexander Polyhistor, and it even finds poignantly explicit expression in the *Epistle of Aristeas*, which represents the translation of the Torah/Pentateuch into Greek as the product of an imperially-sponsored act of including Jewish knowledge in a library embodying the totalizing claims to knowledge among the Ptolemies.

The Jewish scribes responsible for the *Astronomical Book* did not form part of the competing yet interconnected court cultures – recently examined by Strootman – in which such knowledge was cultivated in Greek in the Hellenistic Near East.[165] Yet their efforts may attest some of the wider rippling effects. Together with the other evidence for ancient Jewish sciences noted above, the *Astronomical Book* reminds us of the continued vitality and prestige of Mesopotamian sciences and scholasticism even so many centuries after the fall of Babylon to Cyrus (539 BCE), and it signals the importance of developments in the early Hellenistic age for inspiring new literary reworkings of Near Eastern knowledge – with some Egyptians, Babylonians, and Jews doing so in Greek (e.g., Manetho, Berossus, Pseudo-Eupolemus), while Egyptian scribes like the creators of the *Demotic Chronicle* did so in Demotic, and Babylonian scribes like the creators of the *Antiochus Cylinder* and the "Uruk List of Kings and Sages" did so in Akkadian.[166]

What the *Astronomical Book* evinces, perhaps more decisively than any Jewish document of its time, is how a renewed cultivation of local identity, knowledge, and literature could entail the reconfiguration of

[165] Esp. Strootman, *Courts and Elites*.
[166] Moyer, *Egypt and the Limits*, 128–135; Haubold, *Greece and Mesopotamia*, 127–177.

what even counts as "native" and "foreign" knowledge. The knowledge that its scribal creators present as ancient Jewish lore includes Babylonian astronomy, and they chose to textualize this knowledge in Aramaic, the imperial language of the previous rulers and the cosmopolitan *koine* of the intercultural intellectualism of the Near East prior to Alexander. The ramifications are no less globalizing, in their own ways, than the competing epistemological claims of the Hellenistic empires of the time. Nor should the boldness of such a move perhaps surprise us; this case of the interweaving of local and globalizing claims to Jewish and non-Jewish lineages of language and knowledge, after all, contributes to an even bolder claim – namely, that Jewish scribes are akin to the very angels who lead the celestial cycles and, as such, uniquely tradents and guardians of true heavenly knowledge here on earth.[167]

If the *Astronomical Book* is any indication, angelology played a part in the repurposing of Aramaic from a Near Eastern administrative scribal skill into a language of Jewish literary creativity and cultural memory, as well in the assertion of the archaic Jewishness of Mesopotamian scholasticism and the expansion of the scope of knowledge thereby claimed for the literary heritage of Israel. To the degree that the *Astronomical Book* matched or countered Greek *paideia*, it was by means of an angelology that enabled the creative reworking of older Israelite and Mesopotamian traditions into a new vision of Jewish scribal pedagogy expressed primarily in Aramaic – far more prominent, textualized, and cosmologically and epistemologically totalizing than its Hebrew antecedents.

To be sure, the integration of Near Eastern traditions has ample precedent in earlier biblical literature. Within the Aramaic Jewish literature of the early Hellenistic age, however, claims about angels help to mediate the textualization of these and other topics either ignored or suppressed therein – including astronomy, cosmology, ouranology, protology, eschatology, and the afterlife. This integration, in turn, contributes to a newly totalizing vision of Jewish scribal expertise, harking back to the Achaemenid-era cosmopolitanism of the Near East while also making a claim to its knowledge as a specifically *Jewish* scribal patrimony since even before the Flood. To the degree that Mesopotamian scholasticism and the Aramaic language are here claimed as an ancient intellectual

---

[167] See also Sanders, *From Adapa*, 197, for the linkage of "the death of native kingship and the rise of Aramaic media" with a shift "from genres of power to genres of knowledge" in both Judaean and Babylonian scribal cultures.

and literary heritage preserved first and most fully by Israel, it is by virtue of the Jewish scribal contention of unique totalizing access to heavenly knowledge from and about the angels. This contention, in turn, set the stage for the further expansion of the scope of the knowledge textualized as the ancient literary heritage of Israel's pre-Sinaitic past– as we shall see in the next chapter – even into the domain of the demonic.

4

Textualizing Demonology as Jewish Knowledge and Scribal Expertise

Across the Mediterranean world, the early Hellenistic age (333–167 BCE) was marked by intensified efforts to collect, catalogue, and textualize knowledge. Not only did Greek literature and literacy occupy a central place in the pedagogical enculturation of elites within the new empires of Alexander's successors, but their patronage of polymaths and papyrus rolls by the Ptolemies, in particular, embodied an aspiration to possess all the wisdom of the world. The totalizing horizon of such claims recalls the universalizing rhetoric of Achaemenid Persian imperial discourse.[1] The emphasis on textuality, however, signals a reorientation with significant cultural consequences. Within a newly multipolar imperial landscape, Macedonian monarchs faced the challenges of legitimizing rule over areas to which they bore no connection of landedness or lineage.[2] Claims about books and knowledge achieved what could not be claimed for territory: even if no one empire could allege – like the Achaemenids or Alexander – to rule all the known world, it was possible to purport to possess all of its books and wisdom.[3]

---

[1] Strootman, "Hellenistic Imperialism and the Ideal of World Unity."

[2] In noting a shift, I do not mean to imply the total lack of globalizing territorial claims; after all, Callimachus proclaims that Ptolemy II "shall rule over the Two Countries and over the lands that lie beside the sea, as far as the edge of the earth, where the swift horses always bring the sun" (*Hymn to Delos* 4.169–170), and Theocritus' encomium for the same king proclaims that "the whole sea and all the land and the roaring rivers are fueled by Ptolemy" (*Id.* 17.92); see further Strootman, "Hellenistic Imperialism," 47–50.

[3] For a recent account of the period emphasizing multipolarity, see Kosmin, *Land of the Elephant Kings.*

Most celebrated, in this regard, are the products of Ptolemaic support of sciences and scholasticism in the newly transnational prestige-language of Greek. The success of such efforts still resounds in the cultural memory of the West through the image of the Egyptian city of Alexandria, founded by Alexander in 331 BCE. Not only did the early Ptolemies attract and support a number of immigrant intellectuals to the *polis*, but its state-sponsored shrine to the Muses boasted a substantial archive of papyrus rolls. "The scale of collecting that the Ptolemies engaged in surpassed all previous endeavors," Benjamin Acosta-Hughes and Susan Stephens surmise, "and that was undoubtedly the point: for the upstart city without traditions or history to possess the greatest literary accomplishments of the Greek past, just as it sought to collect and so to control a vast array of objects, among them rare stones and animals."[4] In the process, Ptolemaic and other acts of amassing books and patronizing scholarship made archival and epistemological claims central to cross-cultural competition.[5] Among the cultural effects posited by Classicists like Jason König and Tim Whitmarsh was to inspire a "totalizing gesture" among poets, scholars, and scientists in and beyond Egypt:

The Alexandrian Library (later imitated in Pergamum and elsewhere) brought the whole world into a single city, broadcasting the glory of the Ptolemaic rule that had provided the conditions for its possibility. And a whole range of scholars imitated and influenced that totalising gesture in their individual works. Zenodotus, for example, Homeric editor and lexicographer and first head of the Library; Callimachus, whose poetry flaunts its own dazzling generic flexibility, in combination with designedly abstruse bibliographical and historical knowledge; and most prodigiously of all, Eratosthenes, whose work covers mathematical, chronographical, geographical, philosophical and literary scholarship. Others outside Alexandria followed similar paths: Theophrastus, the successor of Aristotle in the Athenian Lyceum; Aratus, the poet-scholar based in Pergamum; and Posidonius, the extraordinary polymath of the second to first centuries BCE, who prospered in Rome.[6]

---

[4] Acosta-Hughes and Stephens, *Callimachus in Context*, 12. For the echoes in later memory, see, e.g., Dio Chrysostom 32.36, and on the enduring power of this image into the Middle Ages and beyond, Delia, "From Romance to Rhetoric."
[5] The Ptolemies were uniquely situated to do so, as Erskine notes: "Their secret weapon in this culture war was their control over the supply of papyrus"; "Culture and Power," 46.
[6] König and Whitmarsh, "Ordering Knowledge," 8–9. They point to precedents in "Aristotle's project of systematising knowledge across an enormous range of different subjects," but emphasize the concretization of such aims particularly in the Hellenistic era due to the "uniquely concrete links between the projects of political organisation and cultural systematization" under the Ptolemies and others.

The degree to which the intellectual shifts of the early Hellenistic age can be causally correlated to specifically Ptolemaic projects remains a matter of debate.[7] But whether as a direct consequence of the Library of Alexandria, or as an extension of the same translocal trends of textualization that made it possible, it remains that a number of Greek authors of the time turned to compile and catalogue received knowledge, repackaging older teachings, texts, and traditions in new literary forms.[8] The early Hellenistic age saw what Steven Johnstone calls the "invention of the library" and the "political objectification of the book" but also an intensification in the textual cultivation of *polis*-based and pan-Greek pasts as well as the anthologizing of non-Greek knowledge under the auspices of a newly global and/or "Greek" gaze.[9]

There is no doubt that some Jews of the time were aware of these developments. It is, in fact, through Jewish eyes that we first glimpse them. The most ancient among all extant witnesses to the Library of Alexandria is a Greek Jewish text that engages in self-conscious reflection about this totalizing epistemological project and the prospect of the inclusion of Israel's literary heritage therein.[10] Writing in the second century BCE, the unknown author of the *Epistle of Aristeas* points to the Ptolemaic desire to collect "all the books in the known world" (ἅπαντα τὰ κατὰ τὴν οἰκουμένην βιβλία; *Ep.Ar.* 9), and he frames the tale of the Greek translation of the Torah from Hebrew in terms of the imperially sponsored integration of Jewish wisdom into an imperial library with globalizing pretensions. Whatever this text might tell about the Septuagint, it is our oldest evidence of any sort for this celebrated Library, and it preserves a poignant glimpse into Ptolemaic culture politics as seen from the periphery of the city's elite Greek and Macedon

---

[7] See Johnstone, "New History of Libraries," 349, on approaching "the history of the Library of Alexandria ... as one strand in this decentralized revolution happening from Athens to Babylon and in many places in between," whereby "aristocrats and monarchs across the Greek world began to found and fund libraries as part of the politics of elite benefaction, euergetism."

[8] Bagnall points to evidence for the new intellectual endeavors "supported by the Library's collections," including the compilation of critical editions as well as "many attempts to compile systematic information about different subjects"; "Alexandria: Library of Dreams," 361. The linkage of library and literature similarly underpins Whitmarsh's characterization of the Hellenistic age in terms of an archival impulse in *Ancient Greek Literature*, 122–138.

[9] Johnstone, "New History of Libraries," 349.

[10] This has led some Classicists to take the *Epistle of Aristeas*' account of the Library largely at face value, e.g., Blum, *Kallimachos*, 102–103; cf. Bagnall, "Alexandria: Library of Dreams," 349–354.

circles.[11] As Bagnall notes, "even if Pseudo-Aristeas's story of the creation
of the Septuagint is fictitious, it shows us that inclusion in the Library was
a kind of universally recognized validation to which people would
inspire."[12] No less significantly, for our purposes, it confirms that at least
some learned Jews both knew of this Library and recognized its ramifications for the politicization of books and knowledge.

Nor is the author of the *Epistle for Aristeas* alone in seeking to situate
Jews within the new *oikoumene* constituted by the empires of Alexander's
successors. Roughly around the same time, as we have seen, Pseudo-
Eupolemus, Artapanus, and others were writing in Greek to argue for
including Enoch, Abraham, and Moses among the ranks of those ancient
inventors and discoverers who shaped what "the Greeks" valued as
constituent of civilization.[13] Just as the *Epistle of Aristeas* proclaims the
inclusion of the Torah in the Ptolemaic archive of Greek literature, so
these and other Jewish authors preserved via Alexander Polyhistor culled
the pre-Sinaitic past for Jewish figures to include in globalizing Hellenistic
histories of knowledge as well. In the process, they argued for a place for
Israel, alongside Egypt and Babylonia, as among those most ancient
nations of "barbarians" who constituted the heritage of wisdom culled
in the name of the Greeks.[14]

---

[11] For a recent reassessment see Wright, "*Letter of Aristeas and the Question of Septuagint
Origins Redux*" – there stressing the shortcoming of studies that have conflated evidence
for the production and reception of Greek translations of the Torah and other Hebrew
scriptures (306) and concluding that the "*Letter of Aristeas*, which forges close associations
among royal patronage, independent scriptural status, and a product of literary and
philosophical character, does not offer a picture consistent with what we can observe in
the Septuagint itself, and thus we cannot rely on it for information about the translation's
original historical and socio-historical contexts … In the end, however, the *Letter of
Aristeas* tells us about the Septuagint in *Aristeas*' own time, not at the time of its
origin" (324).

[12] Bagnall, "Alexandria: Library of Dreams," 361. This is part of a broader pattern whereby
"already within a century or so of its founding the Library had become a *symbol* of
universality of intellectual inquiry and of the collection of written texts." Contrast
Seleucid imperial archives and their indigenous reception as discussed in Kosmin, *Time
and Its Adversaries*, 55–63.

[13] For the relevant texts with commentary, see Holladay, *Fragments from Hellenistic Jewish
Authors*, esp. 1:93–244. On Hellenistic-era competitive history and its Greek
ethnographical precedents see Sterling, *Historiography*, 20–136.

[14] See further Honigman, "Jews as the Best of All Greeks"; Sterling, *Historiography*,,
137–225; Reed, "Abraham as Chaldean," 136–145. Just as Egyptian and Babylonian
efforts of this sort often occur under the aegis of Ptolemaic and Seleucid patronage and
competition, so Jewish efforts in Alexandria, in particular, may be predicated on the partial
inclusion of Jews in Greekness. Honigman points to Ptolemaic administrative documents
that confirm the categorization of Egyptian Jews as "Greeks," thus suggesting – contrary to

Scholarship on Greek Jewish literature has charted some of the effects of the increased place of books and knowledge in the imperial pageantry and culture politics of the early Hellenistic age.[15] But what might we learn if we approach the Aramaic Jewish literature of the same centuries with an eye to these same dynamics? In recent research on Ptolemaic Egypt and Seleucid Babylonia, Demotic and Akkadian works have been reconsidered in light of some of the same cultural shifts and concerns so richly analyzed in Greek literature of the time.[16] Can our understanding of the Aramaic Jewish literature of the early Hellenistic age similarly benefit from more attention *both* to trends in Greek literature *and* to sources beyond the Greek language?

The previous chapter reread the angelology of the *Astronomical Book* in relation to cross-cultural trends toward repackaging received lunar and other technical knowledge in newly literary, pedagogical, and cosmographical forms, especially in the third century BCE. This chapter extends the experiment to the demonology of the *Book of the Watchers* (*1 Enoch* 1–36). Here too, a sense of the broader archival turn across the Hellenistic world might help us to draw out the reasoning and ramifications of its anthological impulse and redactional creativity – which, in this case, enables the construction of a systematized Jewish demonology out of the bricolage of "magical," biblical, and other Near Eastern traditions. Insofar as the *Book of the Watchers* does so with increased attention to Enoch himself, it draws our attention to the growing importance of exemplarity for this Jewish articulation of "archival sensibility": appeals to this antediluvian sage enable the integration of a diverse spectrum of different types of knowledge into Jewish scribal expertise while also

conventional modern assumptions about Jewish self-isolation – that "insofar as the ethnic labels used in the Ptolemaic administrative papyri correspond to genuine social categories and document a peculiar two-tiered construction of Greek ethnicity, there is no reason to doubt that the *Ioudaioi* settled in Alexandria, and in Egypt as a whole, in Ptolemaic times were defined by the royal administration as a sub-group within the immigrant community of the Greeks" (211–212, with special reference to *Ep.Ar.* 182).

[15] Recent research on relationships between Greek Jewish literary production and Alexandrian intellectual trends (e.g., Niehoff, *Jewish Exegesis and Homeric Scholarship in Alexandria*; Honigman, *Septuagint and Homeric Scholarship in Alexandria*) have looked especially to Hellenistic scholasticism on Homer to illumine the translation of the Torah into Greek. My suggestion here is that this celebrated connection may be one cluster in a bigger constellation of intersections of varying intensity.

[16] e.g., Moyer, *Egypt and the Limits*, 128–135; Haubold, *Greece and Mesopotamia*, 127–177.

grounding a claim for Jewish priority within the heurematography of the early Hellenistic age.[17]

Since J. T. Milik's publication of the Aramaic Enoch fragments from Qumran in 1976, scholarly attention to the *Book of the Watchers* has revolutionized the study of apocalypses.[18] This chapter builds upon these findings, albeit with a different aim and focus. Rather reading the *Book of the Watchers* in relation to the history of apocalyptic literature or ideology, I here attempt to situate it within its own time. Accordingly, I consider the microdynamics of the collection and combination of diverse materials within the *Book of the Watchers*, and I consider its extension of the angelology, cosmology, and scribal practices that shaped the earlier *Astronomical Book* and its resonance with references to demons in other Aramaic and pre-Maccabean writings, while attempting to avoid the retrojection of later ideas and developments. Special caution is taken not to read this work through the lens of Daniel and the Maccabean-era shifts in Enochic pseudepigraphy and apocalyptic literary production.[19] Instead, I focus on the anthological and other writing-practices that shaped what we might plausibly reconstruct as the pre-Maccabean forms of the *Book of the Watchers*, and I ask *why* this redactional activity intensified and coalesced *when* and *how* it did.

To the degree that past scholarship have sought to situate the demonology of the *Book of the Watchers* in historical context, it has been largely through hypotheses about which contemporary figures or controversies might lie *behind* its references to Watchers and Giants.[20] In this chapter, I look instead to the most dominant and defining element in the text itself – namely: its preoccupation with knowledge. In the process of exploring the

---

[17] Zhmud, *Origin of the History of Science*, 117–165; Thrade, "Erfinder II"; Kleingünter, "Protos Heuretes."

[18] Milik, *Books of Enoch*; Collins, "Towards the Morphology of a Genre."

[19] Elsewhere, I have also noted the scholarly tendency to conflate pre- and post-Maccabean Enochic apocalypses, perhaps in part because of the temptation to read them through the lens of the late antique compendium *1 Enoch*; see e.g. Reed, *Fallen Angels*, 58–83. The value of taking a similarly synchronic approach to Daniel, "Animal Apocalypse," and "Apocalypse of Weeks" – reading them together as Maccabean-era writings that respond to the specificities of Seleucid rule and can be compared to contemporaneous Babylonian and Iranian writings – has been demonstrated recently by Kosmin, *Time and Its Adversaries*. In my view, Kosmin's demonstration of their distinctive features (esp. in relation to time) is confirmed by the contrast with what is differently distinctive about their pre-Maccabean precedents for both apocalyptic literary production and Enochic pseudepigraphy; see further Chapter 5.

[20] Most influentially: Suter, "Fallen Angel, Fallen Priest," 132–135; Nickelsburg, "Apocalyptic and Myth in I Enoch 6–11."

function of its claims to knowledge – and its claims to knowledge about transmundane powers in particular – I ask what might be missed when such references are reduced to ciphers for specific historical figures or groups at the time of the *Book of the Watchers* or its sources.

What happens when we take seriously the *Book of the Watchers'* claims to knowledge about spirits and monsters as actually claims to knowledge about spirits and monsters? Such an approach – I suggest – follows the dominance of epistemological concerns within the *Book of the Watchers*, and it illumines their place within the textual formation and literary structure of the apocalypse. When we read the *Book of the Watchers* on its own terms, we encounter ample evidence for demonology as an intellectual project in its own right. Fallen angels, evil spirits, and archangels are here presented as components of the cosmos, participants in human history, and elements of lived experience – with no sense that they must be read merely or mainly as metaphors. Their concreteness, in fact, is what gives power to the scribal claim to know and write their names, their origins, their functions, and their fates. By collecting and consolidating knowledge about transmundane powers, the scribes responsible for the *Book of the Watchers* thus contribute to the broader process, discussed in Chapters 2 and 3, whereby the authority of the Jewish scribe and the scope of the Jewish archive become radically expanded in the early Hellenistic age.

When we pair our above insights from the *Astronomical Book* with analysis of the *Book of the Watchers*, we notice further points of intersection with translocal trends at the time toward totalization, textualization, and the re-ordering of local knowledge. Claims to epistemological mastery over demons – as we shall see – prove integral for the totalizing intellectual project of the *Book of the Watchers* whereby complete and concrete knowledge about the cosmos, its structure, its history, and its workings is placed first among Jewish scribes. And, just as the comprehensiveness of this project resonates with the cross-cultural competition sparked by the Ptolemaic politicization of books and knowledge, so its concreteness points also to the cultural work done by demonology in local and inner-Jewish contexts as well.

A sense of these local and inner-Jewish contexts is now newly possible to recover due to evidence from the Dead Sea Scrolls for practical efforts among ancient Jews to combat demonic forces in their everyday lives. This evidence includes some plausibly pre-sectarian materials in both Aramaic and Hebrew (e.g., 4Q560; 11Q11) as well as related materials composed within the Qumran community (e.g., *Songs of the Maskil*). In addition, it is intriguing that the two earliest known Jewish narratives about exorcism appear in other Aramaic texts from the early Hellenistic age: the Book of Tobit from the third century BCE and *Genesis Apocryphon* from the second century BCE.[21] Taken together, these sources serve to remind us of the local circulation of ideas about angels and demons outside of literary, elite, and exegetical contexts, while also pointing to new trends in their textualization, narrativization, and systemization – especially in Aramaic – in precisely the era in which the *Book of the Watchers* was taking form.[22]

The present chapter thus attempts a synchronic analysis of the *Book of the Watchers*, arguing for the importance of situating this work *both* within the translocal epistemic ferment of the early Hellenistic age *and* within a local continuum of Jewish commerce with transmundane powers in the practical domain of so-called magic.[23] Such an analysis helps us to pinpoint the innovation of the *Book of the Watchers* before and beyond the Maccabean-era development of historical apocalypses like Daniel. Its demonology is not a symbol-system in the service of *vaticinium ex eventu*. Rather, it is the product of scribal efforts to compile, order, organize, and narrativize received materials. This anthological impulse resonates with the archival sensibility and textualizing trends of the early Hellenistic age that

---

[21] One partial exception is 1 Sam 16:13–23; cf. *LAB* 60:2–3. On the reception of David as exorcist, see Mroczek, *Literary Imagination*.

[22] On the many connections between Tobit and *Genesis Apocryphon*, as well as the question of their representativeness vis-à-vis the Aramaic DSS, see Machiela and Perrin, "Tobit and the Genesis Apocryphon."

[23] There is no notion of "magic" *emic* to Second Temple Judaism, and no Hebrew or Aramaic terms functions quite like Greek *mageia* or *goêteia*; Bohak, *Ancient Jewish Magic*, 75–78. The assumption of an ontological difference between "magic" and "religion" is anachronistic and, as with "science" and "religion," reflects the post-Enlightenment European ordering of knowledge rather than any universal distinction (see further, e.g., Tambiah, *Magic, Science, Religion and the Scope of Rationality*). Accordingly, there is a lively scholarly debate about the heurism of the category within and across ancient cultures, on which see Stratton, *Naming the Witch*, 1–38. For the limited purposes of the present inquiry, I use the adjective "magical" sparingly for the heuristic purpose of countering the scholarly tendency to read ancient discussions about demons as if such traditions reflected *only* the theological musings of a literate elite. Here and below, "magical" is used to denote materials reflecting practical and context-specific rituals and invocations aimed at combatting the unwelcome intervention of otherworldly spirits in the lives and fates of individuals (notably: Jewish rituals to coerce or adjure lesser spirits for other aims – like love, revenge, power, or learning – were either rarer at this time or do not survive in writing). What proves helpful about the designation, for the present study, is its power to remind us that ancient Jewish beliefs about transmundane power were not limited to the pens, scrolls, and minds of learned scribes.

we discussed in Chapter 3 in relation to the *Astronomical Book*. In this case, the materials are perhaps even broader, spanning biblical and related traditions and Mesopotamian myth and scholasticism but also local and Near Eastern practices of exorcism and apotropaic prayer. What we finally find in the *Book of the Watchers*, then, is precisely what we had noted in Chapter 1 as so conspicuously absent in the Hebrew Bible – that is: the systemization of diverse demon-beliefs into demonology.

Accordingly, this chapter first argues against the tendency to explain away the traditions about otherworldly spirits in the *Book of the Watchers* and then explores their angelological and demonological ramifications in light of what we know of Jewish "magic," especially from the Dead Sea Scrolls. I then turn to situate its systemization of ideas about spirits in relation to the angelological concerns and anthological practices of the *Astronomical Book*, and I map the methods by which the *Book of the Watchers* imposes order on the unseen world – including but not limited to the naming, mapping, listing, and hierarchized abstraction of its inhabitants, on the one hand, and the narrative evocation of those with the expertise to know them, on the other. Finally, I situate its treatment of spirits, scribalism, and the antediluvian past against the background of broader intellectual trends in the early Hellenistic age, including the archival turn noted in the previous chapter but also the redeployment of Near Eastern scribal *Listenwissenschaft*.

In the process, I argue that the *Book of the Watchers* marks the beginnings of Jewish demonology but also a watershed moment for the reshaping of the very scope of the Jewish archive. Like the scribes responsible for the *Astronomical Book*, those responsible for the *Book of the Watchers* textualize received traditions about transmundane powers in newly literary forms. Here, however, the association with Enoch becomes more central: he is used to model the scribal mastery of an even broader range of topics of Jewish teaching, learning, and writing, and his exemplarity becomes the magnetized core of this newly expansive anthological impulse. If one can speak of an "Enochic discourse" akin to what Hindy Najman analyzes as the "Mosaic discourse" in works like Deuteronomy and *Jubilees*,[24] it is in relation to this impulse, whereby Near Eastern ideals of scribal education and expertise are redeployed by learned Jews to match and counter the newly globalizing purview of Greek *paideia*. The result is a startlingly capacious ideal of Jewish learning and literature,

---

[24] Najman, *Seconding Sinai*.

exemplified by its expansion to encompass knowledge about the divine abode in heaven, the structure and contents of the earth to its very ends, the winds and spirits that cross and connect them, and the fallen angels and evil spirits that impinge upon their order.

INTERPRETING EVIL SPIRITS IN THE *BOOK OF THE WATCHERS*

By all accounts, the *Book of the Watchers* marks the earliest attestation of any systematic Jewish discourse about demons. Within earlier biblical literature, one finds terms related to names associated with demons elsewhere in the Near East, and some angels and other figures – such as *ha-satan* – take on functions adversarial to Israel. Even as Biblicists debate the nature of the beliefs behind allusive passages about Azazel, Resheph, Deber, *ha-satan*, and *se'irim*, however, it is clear that those responsible for the Hebrew literature that comes down to us as "biblical" did not take demonology as a topic for concerted literary exploration, nor as a central element of the textualized history and memory of the Jewish past, nor as a primary domain of scribal pedagogy or scholastic expertise.[25] If anything, expertise in spirits is figured as foreign. As noted in Chapter 1, the only two references to *shedim* in the Hebrew Bible describe them as subjects of worship that is deemed dangerous due to the blurring of boundaries between Israel and other nations.[26] Furthermore, Israelite ritual practices that involve commerce with spirits – such as sorcery, divination, witchcraft, spell-binding, omens, and necromancy – are polemically presented in biblical literature as if paradigmatically non-Israelite (e.g., Deut 18:9–14).

Some biblical passages provide indirect data for practices that fell outside of the purview of priestly authority but nevertheless shaped ideas about transmundane powers current in ancient Israel.[27] What they do not

---

[25] Abusch, "Exorcism," 517–518; Blair, *De-Demonising*.

[26] I.e., in Psalm 106, it is asserted that attention to *shedim* came only because Israel "mingled with the nations and learned their ways" and "worshipped their idols" (vv. 34–41), while in Deuteronomy 32, *shedim* are similarly dismissed both as "no-gods" and as new to Israel (vv. 16–18); see further Chapter 1. This is partly a result of a pattern noted by Abusch whereby "ancient Israel did not transmit its magical expertise in writing," perhaps paralleling the situation in early periods of Mesopotamia, prior to the increased written record there beginning in the late second millennium BCE ("Exorcism," 517–518).

[27] Abusch, "Exorcism," 518–519; Schmitt, "Problem of Magic and Monotheism in the Book of Leviticus." Notably, Israelite women are sometimes associated with those types of ritual expertise and commerce with spirits that are rejected as counter to the will of Israel's God (Ezek 13:18–21; cf. Exod 22:17).

attest, however, is what we find expressed so unequivocally in the *Book of the Watchers* – namely, Jewish attempts to compile, organize, and textualize knowledge about demons in a concrete and systematic manner. The *Book of the Watchers* includes explanations of the origins, nature, and fate of "evil spirits" (Gr. πνεύματα πονηρά; Eth. *manfasa 'ekuya'*), and these explanations form part of a sophisticated and systematic account of transmundane powers, which outlines the proper roles and domains of "spirits" in contrast to "flesh" as well as mapping the spaces overseen by specific archangels and the places of the imprisonment of wayward angels and their eschatological judgment. This theorization is further achieved with a focus on angelic transgression and its consequences for the origin and spread of demons, as explored along both temporal and spatial axes. Its aetiological appeal to the past pivots on the tale of the earthly descent of 200 angels from the class "Watcher" (Aram. עיר; Eth. *teguh*), their desire for human women, their teachings of corrupting and civilizing arts, and their paternity of monstrous Giants who tormented humankind and polluted the earth – in hybrid flesh until the purification of the Flood and as demonic forces thereafter.[28] Its spatial ideology pivots on the claim to know the places of angelic descent, imprisonment, judgment, and punishment no less than the structure of the cosmos, God's heavenly abode, and the sites of the post-mortem and eschatological fates of humankind.

One finds hints of an antediluvian transgression of cosmic order already in the terse description of the "sons of God," "daughters of men," and *Nephilim* in Genesis 6:1–4. What is allusive and unexplained in Genesis, however, is expounded in spectacularly specific detail in the *Book of the Watchers*. In *1 Enoch* 6–16 alone, the "sons of God" are explicitly equated with angels; their class is specified as "Watchers," and their number, names, leader, and place and method of descent are all explained, together with their sexual and pedagogical transgression, their motives, and the proximate and ultimate results. The brief notice in Genesis veers abruptly to the assertion that "YHWH saw how great was humankind's wickedness on the earth, and how every plan devised by his mind was nothing but evil all the time" (Gen 6:5), followed by an extensive narrative about Noah and the Flood (6:6–8:14). By contrast, the *Book of the Watchers* explains every step of the connection between angelic descent and diluvian destruction. This apocalypse includes detailed accounts of the fallen angels' corrupting teachings of humankind, the violence and bloodshed wrought upon the

---

[28] On עיר as the name for a class of angel, see Dimant, "Fallen Angels," 32–33; Davidson, *Angels at Qumran*, 38–39, and compare Daniel 4.

earth by their gargantuan hybrid sons, and the earthly prayers and archangelic intercession that prompted God's watery purification of the earth and
the imprisonment of the Watchers. Not only is angelic descent here made
definitive of the decline of the antediluvian age, but it is also interwoven
with the biography of Enoch, serving simultaneously to explain how and
why this figure – mentioned only passingly in Genesis (5:18–24) – came to
"walk with God."[29]

   Much past research has focused on the possibility of recovering the older
myths or sources that might lie behind *1 Enoch* 6–16, particularly with the
aim of determining the precise relationship of these materials to the terse
treatment of Enoch in Genesis 5 and the passing references to "sons of God"
and *Nephilim* in Genesis 6.[30] To the degree that scholars have attended to
the contextualization of the formation of the *Book of the Watchers* in the
third century BCE, it has been largely through attempts to read the descriptions of Watchers and Giants therein as symbolic expressions of contemporary critiques or controversies. In an influential 1979 article, for instance,
David Suter posited a "paradigmatic" interpretation of fallen angels as
ciphers for wayward priests, thus locating the formation of the *Book of
the Watchers* among Jews who countered the leadership in the Jerusalem
Temple.[31] Writing soon thereafter, George Nickelsburg further suggested
that the violence of the Giants in *1 Enoch* 6–11 encoded the wars of the
Diadochi, and he adduced parallels between the corrupting teachings of the
fallen angel Asael in *1 Enoch* 8 and Greek traditions about Prometheus to
posit a critique of Hellenism.[32] Despite some notes of caution, symbolic
approaches of this sort have shaped the scholarly discussion of the historical
context of the *Book of the Watchers* for over three decades.[33]

---

[29] The contrast is notable even if the relationship between Genesis and the *Book of the
Watchers* cannot be reduced to exegesis; see further Reed, *Fallen Angels*, 52–57.

[30] For recent summaries of the source-critical debate see Bhayro, *Shemihazah and Asael
Narrative I Enoch 6–11*; Drawnel, "Knowledge Transmission in the Context of the
Watchers," 123–127.

[31] Suter, "Fallen Angel, Fallen Priest."

[32] Nickelsburg, "Apocalyptic and Myth"; Nickelsburg, "Enoch, Levi, and Peter" 584–587;
Nickelsburg, *1 Enoch 1*, 191–193. To be sure, these interpretations each resonate with
important themes in the *Book of the Watchers* (e.g., the defense of an ideal of purity, the
diagnosis of earthly ills of war and bloodshed, the ambivalence toward some types of
knowledge). What I would like to question here, however, is the modern scholarly
tendency to reduce its references to transmundane powers into symbols for
something else.

[33] e.g., Bartelemus, *Heroentum in Israel*, 161–166; Tigchelaar, *Prophets of Old*, 195–203;
Drawnel, "Professional Skills of Asael." Notably, older symbolic readings of Watchers
and Giants have also been revived in recent scholarly efforts to redescribe the corpus of

The reading strategy of interpreting transmundane powers as historical symbols dovetails with a common practice in modern scholarship on apocalyptic literature whereby such works are dated by deciphering historical allusions in the mythic or visionary material therein.[34] The parade example is Daniel 12, which uses symbols to recount an *ex eventu* prediction of the succession of empires from up until the rise of Antiochus IV Epiphanes. There, the correspondence is exact enough to enable dating of the work as a redacted whole to the time that this prediction ceases to describe history as we know it from other sources – in this case, the death of Antiochus IV and the success of the Maccabean Revolt.

If Daniel contains symbols that can be decoded, however, it is precisely because its authors and redactors explicitly engage in what Anathea Portier-Young has shown to be an "alternative symbol-making [that], like alternative syntax, disrupts the logic of imperial hegemony and introduces other ways of seeing and speaking the real."[35] Their sense of the symbol and knowledge, moreover, is self-consciously signaled. Within Daniel, visions are marked as encoding other meanings; not only are the animals and other symbols therein framed as objects and figures viewed in dreams, but their symbolic character is narratively conveyed by Daniel's own requests to angels to interpret them. If Portier-Young is correct that "their use of 'mythical images rich in symbolism' exposes and counters imperial mythologies, through a strategy of critical inversion that enables readers to reimagine a world governed not by empires but by God,"[36] it is by virtue of its representation of revealed knowledge as symbols in need of interpretation.

This sense of knowledge also shapes the depiction of Daniel himself. In Daniel 7, for instance, he is described as confused about the meanings of the imagery in his dream-visions. Yet he is quite certain that their imagery

---

apocalypses as "resistance literature" (e.g., Horsley, *Revolt of the Scribes*, 47–62; Portier-Young, *Apocalypse against Empire*, 15–21).

[34] Erho terms this approach to dating "historical-allusional," in the sense that it "operates by identifying instances of *vaticinia ex eventu* and matching them to their historical complements, with the latest thereof providing a *terminus a quo* representing the approximate date of writing" ("Historical-Allusional Dating," 506); he warns, however, that "while undeniably useful in realizing its intended purpose in many situations, the historical–allusional method is limited by the constraints of two parameters: the accuracy of any results derived from this process are dependent on the interrelationship between the quantity and quality of the evidence. Below a certain threshold, the equation ceases to rely on a sufficiently solid evidential foundation, and the attribution of a text to a particular historical event becomes heavily imbued with the suppositions of the scholar."

[35] Portier-Young, *Apocalypse against Empire*, 44.

[36] Portier-Young, *Apocalypse against Empire*, 44.

must be a veiled expression of some true meaning awaiting proper interpretation (i.e., *pesher*):

As for me Daniel, my spirit was disturbed within me, and the vision of my
mind (וחזוי ראשי) alarmed me. I approached one of the attendants and asked
him the true meaning of all this. And he gave me this interpretation of the matter
(ופשר מליא יהודענני) ... (Dan 7:15–16; JPS)

So too in Daniel 8:

While I, Daniel, was seeing the vision, and trying to understand it, behold, there
appeared before me one who looked like a man. And I heard a human voice from
the middle of Ulai, calling out, "Gabriel, make that man understand the vision"
(גבריאל הבן להלז את־המראה). He came near to where I stood, and as he came, I was
terrified, and fell upon my face. He said to me, "Understand, son of man, that the
vision refers to the time of the end." (Dan 8:15–17; JPS)

The narrative framing of the visions, then, conveys an understanding of
imagery within dreams as sets of symbols in need of decoding to discover
predictions of divinely-set events fated to unfold on the stage of human
history (cf. Gen 37:5–11; 40:5–41:57).[37]

As with Enoch in the *Astronomical Book*, Daniel is described in scribal
terms, and Jewish scribes are associated with skills and services also
attributed to angels.[38] There is, however, a striking difference. Daniel
dramatizes the power of revealed wisdom to expose mantic meanings that
would otherwise be obscure and inaccessible; the meanings of the predict-
ive dreams are there presented as beyond the normal bounds of human
education or understanding, but nevertheless accessible to Daniel by
virtue of God's granting of night-visions and angelic interpreters.[39] As

[37] Notably, within the narrative world of Daniel, this logic makes sense as well: the two
opening chapters describe Daniel as an exiled Jew in the Babylonian court who had
"understanding of visions and dreams of all kinds (1:17). When Nebuchadnezzar had a
troubling dream and commanded his court "to call for magicians, exorcists, sorcerers,
and Chaldeans to interpret for the king" (2:2), others failed to understand the meaning of
imagery therein but "to Daniel in a vision, which was at night, the mystery was revealed"
(2:19). The angel whom Daniel consults in chapters 7–8, thus, takes on a role akin to
Daniel himself in relation to the king in chapter 2.
[38] Daniel's own scribalism is doubled: he and his companions are said to have been taught
"the writings and the language of the Chaldeans" (ספר ולשון כשדים; Dan 1:4) in the
Babylonian court, but it is later stressed that the God of Israel also gave them "all
writing and wisdom" (בכל־ספר וחכמה; 1:17) – a pairing that recalls the scribal training
described in *Aramaic Levi*. The signaling of Aramaic as a language among mantic experts
in the Babylonian court (e.g., 2:4) makes these connections all the more intriguing.
[39] Notably, interpretation is a major concern throughout Daniel. "Of all Hellenistic Jewish
narratives," as Sanders notes, "Daniel is likely the most abundant in moments in which

we have seen in the previous chapter, however, Enoch and Uriel model a very different scribal epistemology. In the *Astronomical Book*, Jewish scribes are akin to angels in their capacity to understand everything, and scribal teaching is depicted as encompassing and conveying a grand and sweeping totality of knowledge. Whereas the confused Daniel awaits a God-given vision or angel to explain, the confident Enoch is akin to the angel Uriel in his ability to know and to teach. Daniel's acts of seeing are visionary; Enoch's acts of seeing are scientific and scribal.

The difference, in my view, cautions us against conflating the concerns of apocalypses from different eras – and especially against reading the earlier, pre-Maccabean *Book of the Watchers* retrospectively in terms of the later, Maccabean-era Daniel.[40] Even if Portier-Young is correct that "imperial resistance" was among the factors in the development of the genre of the apocalypse, it remains that different apocalypses took form at different times and in different imperial cultures.[41] If anything, as we have seen in the case of the *Astronomical Book*, synchronic approaches point to the notable differences in *how* pre-Maccabean and Maccabean-era writings reflect and engage their imperial settings – thus raising the possibility of distinctive responses to

revelation is explicitly interpreted, at the center of all but three of its 12 chapters"; "Daniel and the Origins." Also Henze, "Use of Scripture in the Book of Daniel."

[40] For the consensus argument along these lines for Daniel, the "Animal Apocalypse," and Similitudes of Enoch, e.g., see Collins, *Apocalyptic Imagination*, 67–72, 87–88, 178 – although, notably, Collins himself refrains from extending the pattern to all of Enochic traditions: "Like the *Book of the Watchers*, both the 'Apocalypse of Weeks' and the *Epistle* avoid explicit reference to historical figures and events, and so frustrate the desire to date them precisely" (62). Recent attempts to stretch these reading practices to other Enochic materials, however, include Angel, "Reading the Book of the Giants," 320–321, 326–341 – there drawing inspiration directly from Horsley's and Portier-Young's readings of both Enochic and Danielic apocalypses as "resistance literature." See, however, the concerns raised in Stuckenbruck, "Qumran Aramaic Today," 5–7; Ehro, "Historical-Allusional Dating"; Ehro, "Internal Dating Methodologies."

[41] Horsley goes so far as to posit that "*no* Second Temple Judean text classified as 'apocalyptic' has survived that does *not* focus on imperial rule and opposition to it" (*Revolt of the Scribes*, 3) and thus treats the *Book of the Watchers* as akin to the Book of Daniel in this regard, even despite its pre-Maccabean date (47–80). Similarly, Portier-Young argues for the "origins of the genre itself as a literature of resistance" in part by reading even earlier apocalypses as examples of how "apocalyptic writers used the power of symbol to counter imperial domination" (45, 198). I find Portier-Young's argument quite convincing for Daniel and the "Animal Apocalypse," but I am less convinced of her generalization of these points to apocalypses more broadly, especially in the case of the earlier *Book of the Watchers*.

Ptolemaic and Seleucid rule, perhaps corresponding to the particularities of each of these different empires.[42]

What I suggest, in what follows, is that the demonology of the *Book of the Watchers* may be best understood in relation to the angelology of the *Astronomical Book* – and, hence, as potentially shaped by aims other than "symbol-making." Not only do both predate Daniel and reflect a pre-Maccabean and likely Ptolemaic context, but both are marked by an appeal to Enoch that is couched in totalizing rhetoric celebrating the comprehensiveness and certainty of Jewish scribal knowledge. If anything, the pattern is even more pronounced in the *Book of the Watchers*. Even at the outset, the scribal is described as having learned everything taught and shown to him by angels:

I, Enoch, a righteous man whose eyes were opened by God, beholding the sight of the Holy One and of heaven (Gr^Pan: ἄνθρωπος δίκαιός ἐστιν, ᾧ ὅρασις ἐκ θεοῦ αὐτῷ ἀνεῳγμένη ἦν, ἔχων τὴν ὅρασιν τοῦ ἁγίου καὶ τοῦ οὐρανοῦ). He showed me (Ἔδειξέν μοι). And from the words of the Watchers and holy ones, I heard everything (Aram. שמעת אנה [כלה וקדישין [עירין] מלי ומן],[43] and as I heard everything from them, so I also understand what I saw (Gr^Pan: καὶ ὡς ἤκουσα παρ' αὐτῶν πάντα καὶ ἔγνων ἐγὼ θεωρῶν). (*1 En* 1:2)

Here, Enoch is placed at the head of a lineage of scribes, and he models their ability to understand for themselves in a manner akin to the angels. As with Uriel in the *Astronomical Book*, Enoch's angelic interlocutors in the *Book of the Watchers* function less as *angelus interpres* and more as teacher. Angels do not reveal secret meanings that the human scribe is otherwise unable to comprehend. Quite the contrary. It is stressed that Enoch's "eyes were opened by God,"[44] and that it was God Himself who "showed" him, such that he can learn "everything" and understand. Furthermore, throughout the *Book of the Watchers*, angels do not reveal secret or hidden meanings *per se*: they are teachers, and their didactic tasks of showing and teaching are paired with writing and reading as in the practice of scribal pedagogy on earth. It is here only fallen angels, in fact, who model more mantic acts (e.g., *1 En* 8:3).

---

[42] On the some of the differences between Ptolemaic and Seleucid imperial cultures, sketched with an eye to indigenous responses to the latter, see Kosmin, *Time and Its Adversaries*, 3–7, 57–58, 82–83, 88–90.

[43] Here following the fragmentary Aramaic of 4Q201 col. i line 3, as reconstructed in Milik, *Books of Enoch*, 142; Nickelsburg, *1 Enoch 1*, 137. The corresponding clause in Gr^Pan reads καὶ ἁγιολόγων ἁγίων ἤκουσα ἐγώ.

[44] Cf. *1 En* 90:6 [*Book of Dreams*]; 4Q268 1.7–8. For parallels to this metaphor of "opened eyes," see further Nickelsburg, *1 Enoch 1*, 380–381.

Rather than mysterious symbols in need of decoding, transmundane powers are presented in the *Book of the Watchers* as agents in the history of humankind's antediluvian past and its lineages of knowledge.[45] Their stories are told in third-person narrative prose in the course of a description of events before the Flood – first with no reference to Enoch at all (*1 En* 6–11) and then with him actively involved as a scribe whom wayward Watchers approach for aid in penning a petition and whom God commissions to rebuke them (*1 En* 12–16). Further information about these Watchers follows in the course of Enoch's journeys (*1 En* 17–36), when he visits the sites of their present binding and future punishment and learns about the evil spirits that sprung from the bodies of their hybrid sons. Far from ciphers to decode, Watchers and Giants are presented as part of the history and structure of the cosmos created by God, as known and mastered by Jewish scribes since Enoch.

To be sure, figures like Uriel, Shemihazah, and Asael might simultaneously serve as *exempla* for the pedagogical illustration of acts to emulate or avoid – an approach that is attested quite early in the reception-history of the *Book of the Watchers*, even if not yet unequivocally therein.[46] In this, however, these figures are akin to the men and women of Israel's history.[47] There is no indication that these figures are reduced to symbols or paradigms in any manner that blunts the claims to the concreteness of their claimed existence. Rather, knowledge about angels and demons is here presented as an integral part of knowledge about the workings of the cosmos and the conditions of human experience. Instead of denouncing such knowledge as foreign, feminine, popular, or polluting, the scribes responsible for the *Book of the Watchers* use some of the same epistemological and anthological strategies that we saw in the *Astronomical Book* to lay claim to demonology as a domain of Jewish scribal expertise. To understand how and why they did so, then, it might be less useful to look to Daniel than to begin with what we know of other concerns with demons among ancient Jews – especially in relation to so-called magic.

---

[45] Notably, this is the case even in the "Animal Apocalypse" – the Enochic work that most conforms to the Danielic model of presenting encoded meanings through symbols in dreams; when angels are there meant, for instance, stars, horses, shepherds, etc., are used to symbolize them.

[46] On the polyvalence of angelic descent, see Collins, "Methodological Issues"; on the Watchers as negative exempla, see Reed, *Fallen Angels*, esp. 98–116.

[47] Reed, "The Construction and Subversion of Patriarchal Perfection."

FROM JEWISH EXORCISM TO ENOCHIC SCRIBAL EXPERTISE

On the basis of the biblical avoidance of demons and condemnation of commerce with otherworldly spirits, it might be tempting to presume ancient Jewish disinterest in the demonic. Evidence from the Dead Sea Scrolls, however, offers a wealth of more personalized and practical materials pertaining to the manipulation of such intermediate spirits. As Esther Eshel has shown, these fall into two main types: [1] "incantations or spells, aimed to exorcize or drive out evil spirits or other evil forces" and [2] "apotropaic psalms which were intended for protection."[48] The former are addressed directly to demonic power(s), while the latter appeal to God and/or angels for protection against them. In the case of the former, we find the rhetoric of adjuration and, at times, appeals to the exorcistic efficacy of the divine Name. In the case of the latter, verbal patterns best known to us from Psalms (esp. Ps 91) are deployed in the service of demonic protection.[49] Both exorcistic and apotropaic materials thus presume the power of the spoken word to empower individuals to manage their everyday interactions with intermediate spirits.

Most relevant, for our purposes, are those materials which plausibly predate the foundation of the sectarian Qumran community and which might therefore offer some clues as to the views of otherworldly spirits that likely circulated among Jews in the third century BCE. Especially significant in this regard are 4Q560, which preserves what seems to have been an Aramaic "magic book,"[50] and 11Q11, which preserves what seems to have been a Hebrew exorcistic manual of probable pre-sectarian provenance.[51] Both sources exhibit interesting overlaps with the *Book of the Watchers* but also notable points of divergence.

Although 4Q560 is highly fragmentary, it conveys a poignant sense of the variety of Jewish beliefs about demons that circulated before and beyond concerted elite or literary attempts to systematize

---

[48] Eshel, "Genres of Magical Texts in the Dead Sea Scrolls," 396; Eshel, "Apotropaic Prayers in the Second Temple Period," 84–86.

[49] Frölich, "Magical Healing at Qumran (11Q11) and the Question of the Calendar," 44–46.

[50] Penney and Wise, "By the Power of Beelzebub"; Naveh, "Fragments of an Aramaic Magic Book."

[51] Frölich, e.g., reasons that the latter "manuscript was, in all probability, a library copy used as a manual for appointed days," in part because "the length and the form of 11Q11 do not allow for the possibility that the text could be stored inside an amulet worn on the body" and "the leather on which the text was written shows no traces of folding" ("Incantations in the Dead Sea Scrolls," 27).

them. Fragments of one column, for instance, preserve examples of direct first-person speech to a "spirit" (רוח) as the subject of adjuration (4Q560 1 11), while fragments of the other includes mention other different types of demons, including male and female shudder-demons (חלחלא דכרא חלחלא נקבתא) and male and female crumble-demons (פרך, פרכית; 4Q560 1 1).[52] In the latter, the danger of the demonic is linked in part to their ability to foster iniquity and transgression (1 4). Yet their power to infect is associated foremost with bodily ailments: not only do demons pose a threat to women during childbirth (4Q560 1 1), but they enter into the teeth and body, and they can cause "fever, chills and heart fever" (13–15).

In 11Q11, similar concerns are expressed through Hebrew apotropaic psalms and related incantations, albeit here framed in a more cosmic perspective and articulated in terms recalling both biblical and Enochic traditions.[53] Explicit references to *shedim* and *mal'akim* occur alongside references to David, Solomon, Israel, and YHWH.[54] Among the Hebrew incantations here preserved in fragmentary form is one "in the Name of the Lord" (11Q11 V 4; cf. 8Q5 frg. 1), directly addressing a demon as follows:

Who are you [the one who was born of] man and seed of the ho[ly ones]? Your face is a face of [delu]sion, and your horns are horns of disappearance. You are darkness not light, [injust]ice not justice. (11Q11 V 6–8)

The adjuration alludes to one demon's mixed parentage as the product of the mingling of humankind and "holy ones." The danger of the demonic is thus located in the pollution emblematized by the angelic–human hybrid. Although this allusion does not necessarily imply that all demons originated from one single instance of interspecies reproduction, scholars have often noted the parallel to the *Book of the Watchers'* aetiology of evil spirits from the union of the fallen Watchers and their human wives.[55]

At first sight, it might be tempting to interpret this parallel as an instance of the influence of the *Book of the Watchers*. It may be worth wondering, however, whether the relationship between 11Q11 and the

---

[52] Eshel, "Genres of Magical Texts," 396–398. This formula of male–female pairing, as Penny and Wise have noted, is characteristic enough of later Aramaic amulets and incantation bowls as to be "virtually diagnostic" ("By the Power of Beelzebub," 628).

[53] So Eshel, "Genres of Magical Texts," 401.

[54] On 11Q11 as part of the continuum of psalmic compilations at Qumran and beyond, see Mroczek, *Literary Imagination*.

[55] e.g., Alexander, "Wrestling against Wickedness in High Places," 329; Eshel, "Genres of Magical Texts," 404; Bohak, *Ancient Jewish Magic*, 109.

Book of the Watchers may be better understood on analogy to the relationship between the didactic list of 4Q208 and the narrativized forms of the *Astronomical Book* that we examined in Chapter 3. In both cases, we find two sets of materials with similar content, each framed in different forms to fit different aims, and the more context-specific forms may help us to recover a sense of the earlier received materials that were compiled and synthesized in the more abstractified and narrativized forms. In the case of 11Q11 and the *Book of the Watchers*, of course, the correspondence is far less precise. Nevertheless, even if 11Q11 postdates the *Book of the Watchers* and does not approximate any of its "sources," it may aid us in speculating about the practical, context-specific, and local rites that preceded and enabled Jewish scribal claims to map a systematic demonology – especially if read alongside 4Q560 and other examples of Jewish "magic" within and beyond the Dead Sea Scrolls.

As in the case of the *Astronomical Book*'s relationship to 4Q208 and 4Q209, then, it may be useful to reconsider the *Book of the Watchers'* relationship with this Qumran evidence for Jewish "magic" through the lens of David Carr's emphasis on the differing force of long-duration literature and context-specific writing.[56] The parallels between 11Q11 and the *Book of the Watchers*, in particular, provide a poignant example of how much the same content can be framed variously within context-bound and formalized modalities of writing. What is specific to the setting of a written script for direct speech to one demon in the former ("Who are you [the one who was born of] man and seed of the ho[ly ones]?"; 11Q11 v 6–8) is universalized into an aetiology of all evil spirits in the latter (esp. *1 En* 15) and integrated into a narrative about the early history of the cosmos and humankind (esp. *1 En* 6–16). In this sense, the *Book of the Watchers* exemplifies the power of long-duration literature to "formalize, generalize, and perpetuate features and intentions of language, cutting it loose from momentary and context-bound utterance."[57]

A similar pattern can be seen in later "magical" materials that attest the continued circulation and vitality of ideas about demons in practical settings and non-systemized forms, even after the systematizing demonological efforts of the *Book of the Watchers*. Hebrew prayers for protection composed by the Qumran community, for instance, include references to a class of demons called "spirits of the bastards" (רוחות ממזרים) or simply "bastards" (ממזרים) – a term also applied to the

---

[56] Carr, *Writing on the Tablet*, 10.   [57] Carr, *Writing on the Tablet*, 10.

Giants in the *Book of the Watchers* (1 *En* 10:9).[58] In the *Songs of the Maskil*, the list of demons against which the petitioner seeks protection includes "the spirits of the destroying angels (רוחי מלאכי חבל) and the spirits of the bastards, the demons" (4Q510, frg. 1, 5)[59] alongside other types of spirits with counterparts in Near Eastern and/or biblical traditions: "*lilith*, the howlers, and [the yelpers?], and those who strike suddenly to lead astray a spirit of understanding and to destroy their hearts" (5–6; cf. Isa 34:14). Some impact of the *Book of the Watchers* seems possible, particularly in light of our evidence for its popularity at Qumran.[60] Yet these "magical" traditions cannot be collapsed into their literary counterparts, nor their relationship reduced to an arithmetic of simple influence: transmundane powers are here deployed for more context-specific and individualized aims and, thus, in different forms, configurations, and settings shaped by the shifting purposes and practical needs at hand.

That ancient Jews continued to cultivate more context-specific and practical demon-beliefs, even after the development of systemized demonologies, is also clear from the corroborating evidence of late antique Aramaic incantation bowls. Parallels with 4Q560 were noticed already by Douglas Penney and Michael Wise.[61] More recently, Gideon Bohak and Siam Bhayro have pointed to parallels with 11Q11 as attesting some continuity in the traditions circulating within practical settings in which expertise in demons was deployed for the apotropaic protection of individuals.[62] Inasmuch as the "magical" materials from the Dead Sea Scrolls also exhibit some overlaps with earlier Mesopotamian traditions, they may provide a "missing link" of sorts, revealing a situation akin to what we discussed above in Chapter 3 in relation to calendrical astronomy.

---

[58] Milik, *Books of Enoch*, 175; Nitzan, *Qumran Prayer and Religious Poetry*, 227–272.

[59] I here follow the common rendering of the last term as the plural "demons" (i.e., שד אים as if שדים), although the term could also be read as a singular "fearsome demon"; Baillet, *Qumrân Grotte 4 III*, 216–217. The plural, in my view, makes more sense in the context of the list. See, however, Reimer, "Rescuing the Fallen Angels."

[60] Alexander, "The Demonology of the Dead Sea Scrolls," 333–334.

[61] See Penney and Wise, "By the Power of Beelzebub," 628–630, there noting parallels in formula of 4Q560 and later Aramaic amulets and incantation bowls and explaining them with an emphasis on how "amulets and incantation texts were conservative of tradition" (630).

[62] Bhayro synthesizes a number of findings so as to make the argument that "incantation bowls can serve as an important testimony for how no-longer extant first-millennium BCE Aramaic sources were themselves received and used by later scribes"; "Reception of Mesopotamian and Early Jewish Traditions," quote at 196. See already Bohak, "From Qumran to Cairo."

On the basis of his triangulation of Mesopotamian "magic," the Dead Sea Scrolls, and Aramaic incantation bowls, Bhayro proposes an "Aramaic cultural mediation" of Mesopotamian scholasticism in the case of exorcism, similar to what Jonathan Ben-Dov has posited on the basis of the *Astronomical Book* and other "scientific" Dead Sea Scrolls in the case of calendrical astronomy.[63] If Bhayro is correct, exorcistic expertise may have played some part in the Aramaic Jewish pedagogy of the early Hellenistic age. Just as knowledge about the moon, sun, and stars circulated in other forms and settings both before and after its integration into the narrativized forms of long-duration literature like the *Astronomical Book*, perhaps so too with the knowledge about transmundane powers integrated within the *Book of the Watchers*.

What is clear, in any case, is that our analysis of parallels with Jewish magical materials cannot be reduced to debates about the dependence of one on the other. To chart their relationship, rather, is to recover something of the vitality of the local and practical demon-belief that preceded, paralleled, and informed the beginnings of Jewish demonology, constituting the lived and local experiences that gave meaning and power to the claims of some scribes to know – and write – the origins, nature, names, types, and purpose of these and other transmundane powers.

Consequently, these data appear to fit a common pattern found in cross-cultural examples of demonology: beliefs about demons that spring from local, context-bound, and practical concerns (e.g., healing, protection) tend to precede and inform elite literary efforts to make sense of them.[64] Nor was such systemization either inevitable or conclusive. Rather, as Karel van der Toorn has emphasized, "scholarly" experts sometimes sought to resolve sets of demon-beliefs that quite readily coexisted in "popular" experience: the former "aimed for an order in which gods and demons had their proper place" *even though* "people can believe in an all-powerful God while fearing at the same time attack by demons."[65] The practice of systematizing transmundane powers often contributed to the authority of temples, ritual experts, or intellectuals. Nonetheless, "magical" discourses about demons tend to continue long after the rise of more "theological" explanations, often absorbing elements thereof but never wholly collapsed into them.

---

[63] I.e., in the sense that "ancient Babylonian science and literature was, in some form or another, received in Aramaic, which allowed their reception within Jewish circles"; Bhayro, "Reception of Mesopotamian and Early Jewish Traditions," 188.

[64] Frankfurter, *Evil Incarnate*, 13–30.   [65] Van der Toorn, "Theology of Demons," 62.

Likewise, data from the Dead Sea Scrolls for "magical" engagement with demons exhibit some overlaps with the *Book of the Watchers*, but their relationship resists reduction into any unidirectional arrow of "influence."[66] Rather than trying to draw any direct lines of literary dependence, or to trying construct one system to make seamless sense of both, then, it may be more useful to consider how varying modes and practices of writing inform their distinctive articulations of common ideas about the workings of a world in which humans and spirits inhabited the same landscapes. In the process, moreover, juxtaposition with "magical" materials may highlight dynamics in the *Book of the Watchers* neglected in the dominant scholarly focus on its relationship to Genesis and other literary materials.

Most basically, for instance, 11Q11 and the *Book of the Watchers* presume the same logic with respect to the mechanics of demonic control. Multiple incantations in 11Q11 coerce demons by means of voiced threats. In one case, a demon (שד) is to be warned that the "chief of the army of the Lord" (שר הצבא יהוה) will imprison it in the deep (11Q11 V 8–13). In another incantation, the threat to be made to the demon is that God will send "a powerful angel" (מלאך תקיף) to take the demon "down to the great abyss" to dwell in darkness (IV 5–9). The content of these threats is the much the same as what the *Book of the Watchers* describes when recounting the fate of the fallen angels. Binding, for instance, looms large in the account of God's acts of commissioning archangels to act on His behalf to cleanse the earth of antediluvian evils (*1 En* 10:4–14). Passing mention is made of Noah and the Flood in the context of the commission of Sariel to warn and save him (10:1–3). Here, however, much more attention is given to angelic acts of binding – with Raphael sent by God to "bind Asael hand and foot, and cast him into the darkness" (10:4–8) and Michael to "bind Shemihazah and the others with him who have united themselves with the daughters of men" (10:11–14). Later, Enoch himself claims to have visited the deep pits of bound stars (21:1–6) and the prison of angelic confinement near the abyss (21:7–10). Just as the scribes responsible for the *Book of the Watchers* seem to root their descriptions of the aetiology of evil spirits in ideas about some specific demons current in incantations circulating for

[66] I remain unconvinced by Alexander's attempt in "Demonology" to argue for a single and coherent demonology that was based on the *Book of the Watchers* and is expressed in the DSS. For other critiques of his approach, see Reimer, "Rescuing the Fallen Angels"; Stuckenbruck, "Origin of Evil," 103–104 nn. 34, 36.

practical use against them, so they seem also to ground the plausibility of their description of the punishment of the fallen angels in common notions of what angels could be called upon to do by individuals in the course of more practical efforts to combat the demons encountered in everyday life. In short, data from the Dead Sea Scrolls confirm that the *Book of the Watchers* took form in a milieu in which expertise about demons and their names circulated already in everyday efforts to combat them.

This point has important ramifications for our understanding of its much-discussed myth of the fallen angels. One prominent line of research on apocalyptic literature has read this myth as promoting one position in a purportedly dichotomous debate about theodicy. Paolo Sacchi and Gabriele Boccaccini, for instance, read Genesis 1–3 as exemplary of what they see as the position in the Hebrew Bible, central to what they call "Zadokite/Mosaic Judaism," which emphasizes human responsibility for the origins of evil, and they point to the chapters about the fallen angels in the *Book of the Watchers* (*1 En* 6–16) as exemplary of what they call "Enochic Judaism," which they reconstruct around the counter-claim that "supernatural" forces are responsible for earthly ills.[67] Elsewhere, I have questioned the logic whereby differing aetiologies of sin and suffering are extracted from such sources and imagined to have sufficed to splinter Judaism(s) in Second Temple times; as much as twentieth-century thinkers have been preoccupied with "origins," theodicy, and the "problem of evil," it is unclear whether such concerns were framed in quite the same fashion already by Jews in the early Hellenistic age.[68] Furthermore, "magical" materials like 4Q560 and 11Q11 corroborate what can be inferred from reading the *Book of the Watchers* on its own terms: its demonology cannot be reduced to rarefied theological reflection about evil. Rather, the *Book of the Watchers* draws much of its persuasive power from local ideas about otherworldly spirits that were current in contemporary efforts to combat their interventions in the lives of individuals.

Whereas scholars such as Sacchi and Boccaccini have approached the angelic descent myth as an important moment in the intellectual history of Second Temple Judaism, P. S. Alexander stresses how much we miss when

---

[67] e.g., Boccaccini, *Roots of Rabbinic Judaism*, 26–42, 89–102.
[68] Reed, "Interrogating Enochic Judaism." Even though Genesis 1–3 eventually came to be interpreted as an aetiology of evil, especially by Christians, it is not clear that this was how it was understood by Jews prior to the first century CE.

we disembody this myth from local landscapes vivified by beliefs about invisible forces with impact upon everyday life: "Faced almost certainly with a multiplicity and diversity of evil spirits in the religion of the day, the author or authors of this myth tried to bring order into the anarchic and chaotic demonic realm, and to integrate demons into their theological worldview."[69] Accordingly, Alexander calls for understanding its demonology "with utmost seriousness."[70]

Our analysis confirms Alexander's insight in this regard. But we might also push one step further. As we have seen, the *Book of the Watchers'* understanding of demons did not simply spring from exegesis or elite debate but also – and perhaps primarily – from an acutely felt and lived sense of malevolent forces as active in everyday life. Nevertheless, a desire for theological control over the entropic quotidian does not suffice to explain its innovative turn to demonology. The innovation, after all, is not just epistemological but also textual: the scribes responsible for the *Book of the Watchers* write order upon evil spirits, and in the process, they make claims for the power of scribal expertise vis-à-vis forces that were widely believed to intervene in the lives, fates, and bodies of individuals.

This positive appropriation of knowledge about demons marks a rather radical departure from the patterns in early biblical literature discussed in Chapter 1. Yet, as noted above, we do find some parallels in other Aramaic Jewish literature from the third and second centuries BCE. Both Tobit and *Genesis Apocryphon* preserve second-hand evidence for Jewish exorcism. In contrast to Deuteronomistic denunciations of commerce with demons and the spirits of the dead as exemplary of the "abhorrent practices of the nations" that Israel must abandon to be worthy of the Promised Land (e.g., Deut 18:9–14), both works include narratives that associate exorcistic efficacy with pious Jews with special access to angels (e.g., Tob 4:17; 6:13–17; 8:1–3; 1QapGen 20:28–29; cf. 1 Sam 16:14–23; Zech 3:1–2). Manipulation of demons is there assumed to be an appropriate domain of Jewish expertise: it is not framed or presented as a sign of corruption by "foreign" customs, but rather narratively represented as an extension of piety and a consequence of close commerce with the angels of the God of Israel. Taken together, this evidence suggests that knowledge about such matters was taking on

---

[69] Alexander, "Contextualising the Demonology," 338.
[70] Alexander, "Contextualising the Demonology," 338.

positive associations among some Jewish scribes in the early Hellenistic age. In associating Enoch with claims to knowledge about the origins and fate of wayward angels, evil spirits, and the spirits of the dead, the scribes responsible for the *Book of the Watchers* take up topics that are systematically excluded from the earlier Hebrew literary cultures that shaped the Bible. These and other Jews writing in Aramaic, in fact, may participate in a broader project of the scribal appropriation of such domains of expertise, emblematized by demonology no less than astronomy.

To what degree, then, does the *Book of the Watchers* collect, compile, and textualize known traditions about heavenly, wayward, and wicked spirits, and to what degree does it impose its own schemata or interpretations? Unfortunately, the surviving first-hand evidence for Jewish "magic" still remains sparser for the Second Temple period than for later eras.[71] Nor can we presume that all such materials voice a singular, static, or systematic view of otherworldly spirits. The relevant material that survives, however, does seem to share some basic assumptions. It is generally presumed, for instance, that multiple varieties of impure and malicious spirits, male and female, are active on the earth. Such spirits intervene in everyday human lives, sometimes in unwelcome ways. They sometimes induce illness and sometimes inspire iniquity. They penetrate tooth and flesh, but also sway the heart or mind. Accordingly, as in many ancient Mediterranean and Near Eastern cultures, healing, prayer, and exorcism are overlapping domains.[72]

Prominent in the surviving evidence from Second Temple Judaism, in particular, is a sense of the special power of the spoken word when deployed in incantations, petitions, and apotropaic prayers. The status of speech as the main medium for communication with the divine is well established already in ancient Israelite psalms, liturgy, and prophecy, and if anything, perhaps intensified with the growth of interest in prayer in Second Temple times.[73] Likewise, notions of the latent power of language as activated by oral performance are familiar from Jewish traditions surrounding the divine Name as well as from the ideal of Scripture as

---

[71] The best summary and synthesis of the relevant data remain Bohak, *Ancient Jewish Magic*, 70–142.

[72] See, e.g., Scurlock, "Physician, Exorcist, Conjurer, Magician" on *asû* and *āšipu* on ancient Mesopotamia.

[73] On prayer in this period see Newman, *Before the Bible*. On the centrality of the spoken word in premodern Jewish magic generally, see Harari, *Jewish Magic*, 176–190.

read from mouth to ear to memory. As we have seen, "magical" materials from the Dead Sea Scrolls presume the potentiate power in human speech to wield exorcistic or apotropaic power. Speech is figured as the main channel for people seeking to petition angels for aid and protection from demons, and it is also assumed to be efficacious for coercing demons through threats.

Notably, this sense is also present in the *Book of the Watchers* – and precisely in *1 Enoch* 10, the chapter that contains the greatest density of overlaps in theme and content with extant "magical" materials like 4Q510 and 11Q11. It is perhaps telling that the narrative context of this chapter is explicitly petitionary: *1 Enoch* 10 describes the divine and archangelic acts that answer human suffering at the hands of Watchers and Giants after the cries of perishing men went up to the heavens (8:4; 9:3; 9:10). The prior chapter had taken care to describe the precise mechanics: "the earth ... raises the voices of their cries to the gates of heaven," and "Michael, Sariel, and Raphael, and Gabriel looked down from the sanctuary of heaven upon the earth and saw much bloodshed" (9:1–2). Just as "to the holy ones of heaven, the souls of men make suit, saying 'Bring in our judgment to the Most High'" (9:3), so the archangels then approach God on their behalf, stressing how "the spirits of the souls of the men who have died make suit, and their groan and has come up to the gates of heaven" (9:10). It is in God's answer, commanding them to act, that we find the monstrous sons of the Watchers described in terms also familiar from materials like *Songs of the Maskil* – with Gabriel sent "to the bastards, to the half-breeds, to the sons of miscegenation" (10:9). The result is not just to "fill gaps" left by the inclusion of a terse description of the "sons of God," *Nephilim*, and *Gibborim* prior to the narrative about Noah and the Flood in Genesis (i.e., Gen 6:1–4), but also to evoke a paradigmatic past instance in which spoken words on earth had the power to petition God and His angels for protection against the demonic violence and corruption. A practice that would have been familiar to readers at the time – petitionary prayer against violence from transmundane powers – is here projected back in the distant past and recounted in terms that reveal how its earthly efficacy operates from the perspective of heaven.

Juxtaposition with "magical" materials helps to draw out some of the epistemological force of the assertion of self-consciously textualized knowledge about transmundane powers in the *Book of the Watchers*, whereby the shift from demon-belief to demonology serves to expand the very scope of the conceptual territory claimed for Jewish scribal expertise.[74] In 4Q560, 11Q11, and the *Songs of the Maskil,* writing functions foremost as script: they prescribe context-specific rites for individuals to counteract specific demons among a multiplicity assumed to be active on the earth, but it is through speech that this expertise is activated. The scribes responsible for the *Book of the Watchers,* by contrast, use scribal strategies of textualization and narrative to theorize at a level of abstraction, leaving the realm of lived practice to opine on the cosmos and the distant past. Their acts of writing invoke the power of speech, but they impose written order on the demonic by distinguishing and filiating different types of transmundane powers through scribal strategies of systemization such as listing, naming, aetiology, lineage, and hierarchy.[75] The *Book of the Watchers* does not just reflect or express widespread ideas or beliefs about demons. Rather, such ideas and beliefs provide the raw material for scribal practices of textualizing and ordering knowledge that also make meaning in their own right.

The "magical" materials from the Dead Sea Scrolls help us to recover something of what Frankfurter characterizes as the "rudimentary systematizing of demons [that] belongs to the oral, interactive domain of popular discussion, legend-telling, and the recommendation (or composition) of protective spells," wherein "it is neither relevant nor conceivable to contemplate the entire range of potentially malignant spirits or to integrate them with the formal theology of the dominant religious institution."[76] Attention to such sources can thus help us to pinpoint the innovation of the *Book of the Watchers,* not as the advent of Jewish

---

[74] Abusch notes how, even in Mesopotamia, one finds different periods marked by different degrees and modes of textualizing "magical" knowledge – whereby e.g., one finds transcribed prayers or incantations in the second millennium BCE but only rarely ritual instructions and handbooks, while the first millennium BCE is marked by "a growing tendency to transmit magical materials in writing, and once in written form to reorganize, systematize, and expand the corpus" ("Exorcism," 517). Although much earlier than the dynamics examined here, the parallel reminds us of the complexity of the relationship between "magic" and writing, as well as providing an interesting parallel for the process whereby "the absence of written magical prescriptions in ancient Israel" (518) eventually gave way to the transcription of incantations, the textualization of ritual manuals, and then the literary systemization of Jewish demonology.

[75] See further below. As for aetiology, lineage, and hierarchy, note that the Watchers are here the fathers of Giants, from whose bodies spring evil spirits and whose mothers become sirens. This differentiation, notably, is among the reasons why it is not plausible to read the incantations in 11Q11 as if they simply presume the same aetiology of evil spirits outlined in the *Book of the Watchers*: the latter differs notably in its systematic efforts to distinguish between Watchers and Giants/demons in their origins, sins, and punishment.

[76] Frankfurter, *Evil Incarnate,* 15.

interest or belief in demons, but rather as the beginnings of a scribal Jewish engagement in the more abstractified, second-tier practices of "collection, classification, and integration" of demon-belief into systematic demonology.[77] As evidence from the Dead Sea Scrolls and Aramaic incantation bowls makes clear, the demonology of the *Book of the Watchers* did not displace or replace practical and local demon-belief. What it did, however, was inaugurate an influential line of Jewish literary tradition whereby scribes, in particular, claimed authority over – and by – using technologies of textuality to organize knowledge about transmundane powers into broader theological and cosmological systems.[78]

It is in this sense that we might liken the *Book of the Watchers'* integration of demon-beliefs known from these "magical" materials to what we discussed above in Chapter 3 concerning the *Astronomical Book's* integration of lunar and other didactic lists into newly narrativized and systematized forms. But in the case of demonology, the source material bears one important difference – namely, its focus on the power of speech rather than the power of writing. Above, we noted how the lunar and other astronomical lists that preceded and informed the *Astronomical Book* seem to have been cultivated from within a setting of scribal teaching that seems to have involved the visual consultation of didactic texts. By contrast, the above-noted "magical" materials seem to presume a different sort of expertise, recorded in writing but ultimately predicated on oral performance. The *Book of the Watchers* not only textualizes and narrativizes such traditions: it simultaneously scribalizes them.

With 11Q11 and other "magical" materials from the Dead Sea Scrolls – as we have seen – the *Book of the Watchers* shares a sense of the power of spoken words of prayer and petition to traverse the divides between earth and heaven, persuading angels to act against demonic or monstrous forces on behalf of humankind. Indeed, the above-noted archangelic acts of binding are clearly described there as spurred into action by sound: it is "a groan ... come up to the gates of heaven," for instance, that conveys the petition of the "spirits of the souls of the men who have died" at the hands of the Giants (*1 En* 10:9–10). What the *Book of the Watchers*

---

[77] Frankfurter, *Evil Incarnate*, 13–15.

[78] In Chapter 5, we shall see how this process continues, especially in *Jubilees*, drawing further upon local practices of petitionary prayer while simultaneously extending the *Book of the Watchers'* systemization of angelic and demonic roles to speak also to the relationship of Israel and other nations.

depicts, unparalleled in contemporaneous Jewish "magical" materials, is the power of writing also to cross precisely these same divides.[79]

It is telling, for instance, that Enoch does not even enter the narrative world of the *Book of the Watchers* (i.e., *1 En* 6ff) until his scribal *technai* are needed to open a line of communication between earth and heaven. When first approached by heavenly Watchers to rebuke their fallen brethren, he is explicitly called by the title "scribe":

And look, the Watchers of the Great Holy One called me, Enoch the scribe, and said: "Enoch, righteous scribe (Gr^{Pan}: Ἐνώχ, ὁ γραμματεὺς τῆς δικαιοσύνης), go and say to the Watchers of heaven who forsook the highest heaven, the sanctuary of their eternal station, and defiled themselves with women. As the sons of earth do, so they did and took wives for themselves. And they worked great desolation on the earth—'You will have no peace or forgiveness.'" (*1 En* 12:3–4)

That his mediatory role is predicated on his scribal skills becomes clear when the fallen angels respond with a request for him to "write (γράψω) a memorandum of petition for them, that they might have forgiveness, and that I recite (ἀναγνῶ) the memorandum of petition for them in the presence of the Lord of heaven" (13:6). Writing and reading are here presented as among those acts that lead to his heavenly ascent (*1 En* 14). The content of this "memorandum of petition" (τὸ ὑπόμνημα τῆς ἐρωτήσεως) is described in some detail, thereby highlighting the specificity and precision of the requested scribal tasks (e.g., as including "requests concerning themselves, with regard to their deed individually, and concerning [their sons] for whom they were making request, that they might have forgiveness and longevity"; 13:6).

This shift marks a notable innovation. Explicit references to the power of writing may be common in our evidence for "magic" from other cultures of the time, as well as in later Jewish traditions, but they are notably absent from our Jewish evidence from the Second Temple period.[80] Even the most

---

[79] These materials, of course, are themselves written, which is how we are able to access them. Their textualization, however, is here for the sake of enabling oral performance, as is clear from the contrast with later materials: "in the earlier stage, exorcistic hymns were gathered into handbooks [i.e., like 11Q11], but their use was in a verbal fashion; in the later period, they were used both in a verbal and in a scribal manner" (Bohak, *Ancient Jewish Magic*, 302).

[80] Bohak, *Ancient Jewish Magic*, 137–138. Bohak stresses the "scribalization gap" between Second Temple and late antique Jewish magical materials; it is much later than in the PGM and other Greek materials, for instance, that writtenness figures so strongly in Aramaic and Hebrew materials (esp. 283–285).

closely related materials from the Dead Sea Scrolls have no counterpart to the triangulation of scribal expertise, claimed commerce with heavenly spirits, and mastery of knowledge about demons that is narrativized and textualized in the *Book of the Watchers*. Even the contemporaneous Aramaic narratives of Tobit and *Genesis Apocryphon* feature other technologies of demonic control; the former describes how the demon Asmodeus was expelled by the smoke made from burning the heart and liver of a particular fish (Tobit 6:8, 16–17; 8:2–3),[81] while the latter conveys the power of holy men like Abraham to drive away demons, even apart from special words, substances, or even direct acts of intervention by God or angels (1QapGen 20:28–29).[82] The innovation that we see the *Book of the Watchers*, then, may not just be limited to its impulse to systematize and categorize knowledge about transmundane powers: it may relate also to the very contention that mastery of knowledge about demons should belong to those educated in writing and other forms of scribal expertise – a notion with precedents in Mesopotamia but wholly unparalleled in earlier biblical materials.[83]

Scholars have tended to focus on the bold theological contentions of the authors and redactors of the *Book of the Watchers* to know and convey the true purpose of angels, the sins of fallen angels, and the origins of demons – not least since these are the elements of its angelology and demonology that became so influential in later centuries.[84] For understanding its departures from the literary practices that shaped earlier biblical literature, however, it may be no less significant that these claims are predicated on the power of with what Frankfurter has observed across the ancient Mediterranean world as the demonological efficacy of "writing, as a technology allowing both abstraction from local experience and the magical force of the inscribed name."[85]

---

[81] That this narrative detail may have had some counterpart in actual practice is suggested by Bohak on the basis of supplementary evidence for the ancient Jewish use of fumigation to dispel demons; see *Ancient Jewish Magic*, 89–94, citing as parallels in Josephus, *War* 7.180–185, Justin, *Dial.* 85.3, and *Pirqe de Rav Kahana* (ed. Mandelbaum, p. 74). Taken together, these data attest Jewish beliefs about the inherently anti-demonic properties of certain natural substances, which could be activated by rituals and which could be efficacious seemingly apart from direct divine or angelic involvement.

[82] Bohak, *Ancient Jewish Magic*, 94–97.   [83] See Chapter 1.

[84] See further Reed, *Fallen Angels*.   [85] Frankfurter, *Evil Incarnate*, 21.

ORDERING THE DEMONIC: EXEMPLARITY, AETIOLOGY, ANTHOLOGIZING

In the case of the demonology of the *Book of the Watchers*, the power of writtenness has further ramifications in relation to what we noted at the beginning of this chapter as the prestige and politicization of textuality in the early Hellenistic age. In the *Book of the Watchers*, claims to knowledge about demons prove critical for the articulation of a newly totalizing vision of Jewish scribal knowledge and expertise. It is in this sense – I suggest – that it takes up the anthological and archival project of the *Astronomical Book*. As we have seen in Chapter 3, the *Astronomical Book* claims exact, certain, and complete knowledge about certain celestial cycles, as learned and textualized directly from the teachings of the very angel responsible for leading and managing their orderly movement. The *Book of the Watchers'* appropriation of demonology as a domain of Jewish scribal expertise, however, emblematizes the even more audacious scope of its epistemological claims, which here encompass not just angels and the heavens, but also demons, the ends of the earth, and the fates and realms of the dead. Like the *Astronomical Book*, it thus resonates with broader cultural trends of the early Hellenistic period inasmuch as it consolidates and anthologizes received knowledge in newly literary forms that embody a "totalizing gesture" and "archival sensibility." Yet it goes even further in matching the globalizing epistemological claims of Greek *paideia* and Ptolemaic culture politics.

In the previous chapter, we have seen how the elevation of the scribe in the *Astronomical Book* is paired with an elevation of scribalism embodied by the text itself, by virtue of its literary showcasing of the didactic practices of Near Eastern scribal pedagogy. Might this also be the case with the *Book of the Watchers*? The surviving data make this question a bit trickier to answer. For the *Astronomical Book*, there are Aramaic fragments that enable us to reconstruct some of the process by which its long-duration literary tradition surrounding coalesced around didactic lists. For the *Book of the Watchers*, however, we lack any comparable range of manuscript evidence for the fluidity preceding its literary stabilization. There are four Aramaic manuscripts from Qumran that include the *Book of the Watchers* (i.e., 4Q201–202, 4Q204–205).[86] But these

---

[86] I.e., including fragments of what appear to be the *Book of the Watchers* copied by itself (4QEn^{a,b}) but also manuscripts attesting its anthologizing together with other Enochic writings beginning at least from the second century BCE (4QEn^{c-e}). I summarize the full

align more closely both with one another and with the surviving translations – which, in this case, include the Ge'ez version preserved in full as
the first thirty-six chapters of the Ethiopian compendium *1 Enoch* (chh.
1–36) as well as the intermediary Greek translation(s) attested in a fifth-/
sixth-century Egyptian manuscript (Codex Panopolitanus = Gr^Pan) and in
excerpts cited by the ninth-century Byzantine chronographer George
Syncellus (Gr^Syn).[87]

To the degree that we can reconstruct something of the process of the
literary formation of the *Book of the Watchers* and the scribal practices
that constituted it, then, we find ourselves more dependent on internal
criteria. On this basis, however, research on *1 Enoch* has come to a
consensus concerning the composite character of the *Book of the
Watchers*, with most scholars delineating at least five distinctive textual
units therein:

- *1 Enoch* 1–5: First-person introductory frame (ch. 1), attributed to
  Enoch, followed by Nature Poem (chapters 2–5). This section often
  considered the latest to be added to the work.
- *1 Enoch* 6–11: Anonymous third-person narratives interweaving different traditions about the descent of Watchers, their intercourse with
  human women, and the violence of their hybrid progeny (chapters
  6–8), including their names, their teachings, and the specific roles of
  different Watchers (esp. Asael vs. Shemihazah), followed by an
  account of the archangelic intervention (chapters 9–10) – but *not*
  including any reference to Enoch. This section often considered to be
  the earliest portion of the work and to interweave even more ancient
  independent traditions.[88]
- *1 Enoch* 12–16: First-person narratives asserting the connection
  between Enoch (cf. Gen 5:18–24) and the story of angelic descent
  (cf. Gen 6:1–4) through what is presented as his own account of his
  encounter with angels on earth (chapters 12–13) and his ascent to
  heaven and commission by God (chapters 14–16). This section is the

---

evidence for this work as copied by itself and collected with other works in Chart 1 of
Reed, "Textual Identity."

[87] Codex Panopolitanus (5th/6th c.) preserves *1 En* 1:1–32:6 + 19:3–21:9, while quotations
from Syncellus (9th c.) correspond to *1 En* 6:1–9:4; 8:4–10:14; 15:8–16:1. See further
Knibb, *Ethiopic Book of Enoch*, 2:1–46; Nickelsburg, *1 Enoch 1*, 9–21; Reed, "Textual
Identity."

[88] These chapters are the most discussed portion of the *Book of the Watchers*. For the
history of research and various theories about the sources behind them, see Bhayro,
Shemihazah and Asael Narrative.

literary pivot of the work and presumes knowledge of *1 Enoch* 6–11, which it interprets.[89]

- *1 Enoch* 17–19: First-person narratives about Enoch's tours to the ends of the earth with angels. This section is likely the earliest form of the tour material.[90]

- *1 Enoch* 20–36: More first-person narratives about Enoch's tours to the ends of the earth with angels, partially repetitive with *1 Enoch* 17–19 and likely presuming, extending, and interpreting it.[91]

Most research on the literary formation of the *Book of the Watchers* has focused on the sources of what is widely agreed to be the most ancient unit (i.e., *1 En* 6–11) and/or on the process by which other units came to be combined with this unit.[92] For understanding the systematizing strategies and scribal practices that shape its demonology, however, it is more useful to look to the orchestrating logics of the work as a whole, considering these source-critical insights in light of our above analysis of the form and formation of the *Astronomical Book*.

As in the *Astronomical Book*, for instance, first-person framing-notices mediate the narrativization of scribal pedagogy in the *Book of the Watchers*. Among what unites its redacted form, in fact, is an extension of this pattern toward an emphasis on the exemplarity of Enoch. Here too, first-person prose is paired with the rhetoric of seeing and showing. Furthermore, it is largely through first-person speech that the *Book of the Watchers* mounts totalizing claims to knowledge unparalleled within earlier biblical literature (e.g., *1 En* 1:2).[93] In the process, the *Book of the Watchers* develops two elements that seem to have emerged relatively

---

[89] For its literary function, see Reed, "Heavenly Ascent, Angelic Descent, and the Transmission of Knowledge" and references there. On its combination with the subunits concerning the fallen angels (i.e., *1 En* 6–11; 12–16), see Newsom, "Development of *1 Enoch* 6–19."

[90] On these chapters, see Coblentz Bautch, *Study of the Geography*.

[91] On *1 En* 20–36 as possibly a later reflection or expansion on *1 En* 17–19, see discussion and references in Coblentz Bautch, *Study of the Geography*, 13–23. For an attempt to make sense of the redacted form of *1 En* 17–36 as three journeys with a "coherent structure," see Stock-Hesketh, "Circles and Mirrors."

[92] See further Reed, "Heavenly Ascent"; Bhayro, *Shemihazah and Asael Narrative*.

[93] That this emphasis on completeness was already present in the Aramaic is clear from 4Q201 col. i line 3: [...]ומן מלי [עירין] וקדישין כלה[ן] [...]; compare Gr^Pan: Ἔδειξέν μοι, καὶ ἁγιολόγων ἁγίων ἤκουσα ἐγώ, καὶ ὡς ἤκουσα παρ' αὐτῶν πάντα καὶ ἔγνων ἐγὼ θεωρῶν. In support of the above reconstruction see Nickelsburg, *1 Enoch 1*, 137, and textual notes there. Note also the lack of totalizing rhetoric in Balaam's oracle in Num 24:15–17, which otherwise seems to have served as a model for this opening proclamation.

late within the redaction history of the *Astronomical Book* – namely: (1) the interest in Enoch himself and (2) the interpretation of the rhetoric of seeing and showing in terms of his otherworldly journeys.

Throughout the *Book of the Watchers*, claims to knowledge become more tightly connected to Enoch. The assertion of the text's totality and trustworthiness in transmitting knowledge is directly tied to the exemplarity of this antediluvian sage (e.g., *1 En* 19:3: "And I Enoch alone saw the sights, the extremities of all things, and no one has seen what I saw").[94] And whereas the early forms of the *Astronomical Book* do not make any explicit claim that Enoch himself traveled to heaven (cf. 81), the *Book of the Watchers* situate acts of seeing and showing within narratives about his voyages with angels up to heaven and out to the ends of the earth. Over half of the *Book of the Watchers* (14–36), in fact, consists of reports of what Enoch "saw" and "was shown" during and after his ascent to heaven, when he approached God's throne and heavenly "house," and journeyed with angels to and beyond the edges of the inhabited world.

Even as the *Book of the Watchers* makes parallel claims to preserve the teachings of angels, it thus extends the scope of Jewish scribal expertise beyond what is claimed in the *Astronomical Book*. The image of the scribal expertise exemplified by Enoch here encompasses the cosmos and its "supernatural" inhabitants – not limited to those angels associated with celestial cycles, but also encompassing those associated with other cosmological roles. Its broader scope of spatial and cosmological concern is thus matched by a broader variety of transmundane powers. Whereas the angels of the *Astronomical Book* are most often described as "leaders" (Eth. *marāḥeyān*) or "heads" (Aram. רושין) of celestial phenomena, for instance, the *Book of the Watchers* deploys a larger lexicon of labels for angelic classes and functions. It discusses "Watchers" (עירין) and "holy ones" (קדישין), both in the third-person narrative at the beginning of the work (*1 En* 6–11) and in the first-person account attributed to Enoch that it frames (*1 En* 14ff).[95] The label "sons of heaven" appears throughout (e.g., 13:8; 14:3). In addition, the *Book of the Watchers* integrates references, whether direct or indirect, to other transmundane powers also mentioned in earlier biblical literature (see

---

[94] Gr^{Pan} *1 En* 19:3: κἀγὼ Ἐνὼχ ἴδον τὰ θεωρήματα μόνος, τὰ πέρατα πάντων, καὶ οὐ μὴ ἴδῃ οὐδὲ εἷς ἀνθρώπων ὡς ἐγὼ ἴδον.

[95] Note, e.g., *1 En* 12:2 where it is summarily said that Enoch was with "Watchers" and "holy ones" during the time he was removed from the earth.

Chapter 1). When Enoch ascends to heaven, for instance, he sees "the holy ones of the Watchers who approached him" day and night, but also *cherubim* and a multitude ("10,000 times 10,000") surrounding God's throne (14:11; 14:18; 14:23). Similarly, the work begins with descriptions of the "army" and "mighty host from the heaven of heavens" with whom God appears (*1 En* 1:4), and it predicts that he will come "to execute judgment on all" with the "myriads of his holy ones" (*1 En* 1:9; cf. Deut 33:2).[96]

Interestingly, the surviving Aramaic includes no evidence for its mention of *mal'akim*. Later translations thereof attest their Greek and Ethiopic counterparts. Yet "Watchers" and "holy ones" are here associated with some of the same tasks that earlier biblical literature associates with *mal'akim*, functioning as tour-guides and teachers. And even if such terminology was present in the Aramaic, the *Book of the Watchers* does not adhere to the pattern that Michael Mach posits for the Septuagint, wherein *mal'akim/angeloi* becomes an umbrella category for a variety of intermediate figures.[97] The *Book of the Watchers* does make a similar classificatory move of its own, however, through its use of the term "spirit." In Chapter 1, we have seen how the wide variety of what we now call "angels" were named and described in early biblical literature in terms that emphasized their functions, largely sidestepping any harmonizing classificatory practice of angelology or demonology. In the *Book of the Watchers*, by contrast, "spirits" becomes an umbrella category delineated with reference to the ontological status of those varied figures thereby classified.[98]

Whereas what Mach suggests of *angeloi* in the Septuagint is largely tacit, moreover, the classificatory function of *ruah* in the *Book of the Watchers* is much more explicit. Not only is it theorized through a

---

[96] On this passage and its parallels with Deuteronomy 33 and other earlier theophanies, see Hartman, *Asking for a Meaning*, 23–24. That heavenly spirits are associated with judgment is further made clear from the detailed description of how four of the archangels were involved in punishing those of the Watchers who came to earth to marry the "daughters of men" (*1 En* 6–11).

[97] See Mach, *Entwicklungsstadien*, and Chapter 1.

[98] Whereas the biblical use of the term *mal'ak* allows for some blurring between men and angels who fulfill the same functions of service to God as messengers, etc., this Enochic redeployment of *ruah* activates its potential to blur "natural" and "supernatural": it encompasses the invisible but felt presence of the winds as well as the invisible population of the cosmos, angelic and demonic alike. Even as this blurring finds some precedent in earlier uses of *ruah*, what is new is its repurposing as an umbrella category that encompasses different sorts of transmundane powers.

developed contrast with the category of "flesh," but this explanation is framed as the first-person speech of none other than God Himself. The explanation appears in *1 Enoch* 15–16, occasioned by the problem of fallen angels: some "Watchers of heaven," who are described as belonging to this category of "spirit," transgressed in their desire to possess the prerogatives particular to "flesh." With respect to these Watchers, God stresses that "you were holy ones and spirits, living forever" (15:4) and that "you originally existed as spirits, living forever, and not dying for all the generations of eternity" (15:6). A contrast is thus drawn with men, who are "flesh and blood, who die and perish" and to whom "therefore I gave ... women, so that they might cast seed into them, and thus beget children by them, that nothing fail them upon the earth" (15:4–5). The siring of Giants by fallen angels is here framed, thus, as the transgression of an essential distinction between "spirit" and "flesh," as emblematized by the different modes of continuance proper to each (i.e., immortality vs. reproduction). The character of this distinction is further developed in spatial terms: "The spirits of heaven, in heaven is their dwelling" (15:7).

In effect, in *1 Enoch* 15–16, the transgression of the fallen angels becomes an opportunity to theorize the essential difference of "spirit" and "flesh," and this theorization bears an angelological force, functioning to categorize all the various types of angelic creatures mentioned in the *Book of the Watchers* (e.g., Watchers, holy ones, cherubim, sons of heaven) as subsets of one class. Significantly, it is also in the divine speech in *1 Enoch* 15–16 that we find the *Book of the Watchers'* aetiology of evil spirits, which similarly bears a demonological force. This aetiology is introduced as an explanation of the consequences of the transgression of the divinely set boundaries between "spirit" and "flesh":

But now the giants who were begotten by the spirits and the flesh—they will call them evil spirits on the earth, for their dwelling will be upon the earth. The spirits that have gone forth from the body of their flesh are evil spirits, for from humans they came into being, and from the holy watchers was the origin of their creation. Evil spirits they will be on the earth, and evil spirits they will be called. The spirits of heaven, in heaven is their dwelling, but the spirits begotten in the earth, on earth is their dwelling. And the spirits of the giants <lead astray>, do violence, make desolate, and attack and wrestle and hurl upon the earth and <cause illness>. They eat nothing, but abstain from food and are thirsty and smite. These spirits will rise up against the sons of men and against the women, for they have come forth from them. From the day of the slaughter and destruction and death of the giants, from the soul of whose flesh the spirits are proceeding, they are making desolate without (incurring) judgment. Thus they will make desolate until the day of the consummation of the great judgment, when the great age will be consummated..." (*1 En* 15:8–16:1)[99]

As Alexander has shown, this aetiology marks a major move in the making of Jewish demonology: the very act of declaring all demons "only one species of being involves a significant rationalization of the demonic world."[100] All the apparently diverse demons of the earth are here given a singular moment and story of origination, and the result is a significant theological systemization whereby aetiology is used to claim true knowledge of their relationships to God, angels, and humankind.[101]

Alexander is surely correct to draw our attention to aetiology as a major systematizing strategy shaping the demonology of the *Book of the Watchers*. And this is certainly that most influential and enduring aspect of the afterlife of this apocalypse, both within and beyond *1 Enoch*.[102] His insights, however, also push us to look more closely. What are the other ways that the *Book of the Watchers* meditates the shift from demon-belief to Jewish demonology? Might a synchronic focus allow us to notice some more of the microdynamics of this shift?

As in the case of the angelology and astronomy of the *Astronomical Book*, I suggest that it is useful to attend to the specific writing-practices that accompany the textualization of demonology in the *Book of the Watchers*. So far, we have focused on the famous passage, *1 Enoch* 15–16, which claims to report the direct speech of God Himself explaining the distinct domains, tasks, and fates proper to flesh and spirit as well as their transgression and its results. Yet it is worth noting that the *Book of the Watchers* preserves an alternative account wherein the archangels destroyed the bodies and spirits of the Giants already in the era of the Flood (10:9, 15).[103] And it also includes other passages about demonic figures that maintain their multiplicity. During Enoch's otherworldly journeys, for instance, he arrives at a place at "the edge of the earth,"

---

[99] On the textual issues involved in reconstructing this passage, see Nickelsburg, *1 Enoch 1*, 268, 272–273. On the possibility that a similar aetiology may be presumed in the (unfortunately quite fragmentary) *Book of the Giants*, see Stuckenbruck, *Book of the Giants*, 159–160; Stuckenbruck, "Origin of Evil," 108–109; and discussion below.

[100] Alexander, "Contextualising the Demonology," 339. And see now Wright, *Origin*.

[101] Alexander, "Contextualising the Demonology," 339.

[102] See further Wright, *Origin*.

[103] So too in the "Animal Apocalypse" in the *Book of Dreams* (*1 En* 89:6), as stressed by Stuckenbruck, "Origin of Evil," 110.

where "the heavens come to an end" and where there is a "great chasm among pillars of heavenly fire" (18:10–11). His angelic guide Uriel informs him:

> There, the angels who mingled with women (οἱ μιγέντες ἄγγελοι ταῖς γυναιξὶν) stand. And their spirits (τὰ πνεύματα αὐτῶν)—having assumed many forms—bring destruction upon men and lead them astray to sacrifice to demons (τοῖς δαιμονίοις; cf. LXX Deut 32:17) as to gods until the day of the great judgment, in which they will be judged with finality. And the wives of the transgressing angels will become sirens (σειρῆνας)." (*1 En* 19:1–2)

It is left unclear whether the *daimones* to whom people sacrifice are here meant to be understood as the same as the *pneumata* that sprung from the dying bodies of the Giants according to *1 Enoch* 15:8–16:1. In any case, the multiform spirits of the Watchers seem to be described as still active in the realms inhabited by humankind in the period between the Flood and the Eschaton. Even their wives are here added to the monstrous hosts of the demonic.[104]

It might be tempting to dismiss this variance as a relic of the composite character of the *Book of the Watchers*, which – as noted above – is widely acknowledged as having taken form through the redactional combination of different received traditions. For our purposes, however, its composite character is an important datum in its own right. If the different ideas about demons in the *Book of the Watchers* plausibly reflect the diversity of local demon-beliefs herein compiled, it is significant that the scribes responsible for this work chose to retain something of this heterogeneity. The archival and anthological impulse – to collect and textualize – remains an important concern in its own right, even despite the tension with the impulse to harmonize, systematize, and explain.

This variance in demon-beliefs has often inspired scholarly speculation about sources or traditions behind the *Book of the Watchers*. For our purposes, it is an invitation to look more closely at the orchestrating logics by which these and other received traditions have been redactionally coaxed into literary unity. As in the *Astronomical Book*, narrative framing is key. But in this case, what is evoked is not just a first-person voice, but also different perspectives on "spirits" – as variously represented in the speech attributed to God in *1 Enoch* 15–16 and in the teachings attributed to Enoch's archangelic travel guides in *1 Enoch*

---

[104] See further Coblentz Bautch, *Study of the Geography*, 131–132; Coblentz Bautch, "What Becomes of the Angels' 'Wives.'"

17–19 as well as in the narrative account of angelic descent as seen from the perspective of the earth in *1 Enoch* 6–11.[105]

The theorization of "spirits" in *1 Enoch* 15–16 is presented as ultimately determinative for the demonology of the *Book of the Watchers* by virtue of its divine source. What is evoked there is a sweepingly cosmic divine perspective, abstracted from everyday experiences of petition, prayer, or exorcism, but claiming to explain them. This framing, moreover, is notable for what it communicates about scribal expertise: God's speech is not framed as his proclamation directly to those Watchers who came to earth to take wives of the "daughters of men" (*1 En* 6–8; cf. Gen 6:1–4). Rather, it is presented as his instructions to Enoch, whom he addresses as "righteous man and scribe of truth" (15:1) and whom he commissions to rebuke these fallen angels (15:2). It is in the context of a one-on-one conversation between God and Enoch, in other words, that the *Book of the Watchers* claims to record God's own perspective and plan on the proper place of angels in His created cosmos as well as the origins of demons. Even as the propriety of petition is noted as rightly from human to angel ("you should petition on behalf of men, and not men on behalf of you!"; 15:2), Enoch is not chastised for breaking this pattern but rather sent by God to carry the answer to a petition that he wrote and read on behalf of these angels. What is modeled by Enoch, and depicted as divinely ratified, is the power of the scribe as a creature of flesh who can nevertheless act like an angel, privy to divine knowledge about the true order of the cosmos and the proper function of both spirits and flesh therein.

LISTENWISSENSCHAFT, DEMONOLOGY, AND SCRIBAL EXPERTISE

The *Book of the Watchers* is rightly famous for its use of yet another scribal strategy for systematizing demon-belief into demonology – namely, list-making. In Frankfurter's comparative study, for instance, it stands as a parade example of "demonology proper," due to its inclusion of two lists with the names of fallen angels (*1 En* 6:7–8; 8:3). In his view, the *Book of the Watchers* thus marks the "beginnings of demonology as a learned scribal effort to collect, speculate on, and control the cosmic sources of misfortune" precisely because "its abstracted lists of fallen

---

[105] See further Reed, "Heavenly Ascent."

angels assumed a special authority in literary society and scribal subcultures":[106]

...the list form serves to pluck social or cultural threats from their immediate circumstances of experience (a local ritual expert or a cosmetics seller at the market), to personify them as demons with a mythology, and to arrange them with other threats of the same class for further speculation: where did they come from? To what powers are they beholden? How are they opposed? What will happen to them? As the list form in the exorcistic spells functions to exert control —verbally then through the power of the written word—so in these apocalyptic demonologies the list defines and controls the experience of the demonic. These rudimentary demonological lists show, on the one hand, a continuing endeavor on the part of scribes to abstract and list negative experiences as a form of control, and on the other hand, the beginnings of a real demonological literature—a sort of canon, to which both amulets and later demonologies might refer. "Demonology" emerges in these texts as a literary-theological pursuit basically divorced from the local experience of spirits, yet it pretends to embrace and define that local experience.[107]

For Frankfurter, the systematizing power of these textualized lists forms part of continuum of demonological list-making. Initially, "demons and the illnesses they cause are not yet clearly distinguished, reflecting an ambiguity characteristic of popular discussions of misfortune and supernatural attack."[108] On the basis of comparative evidence, Frankfurter suggests that "the essential stage in drawing demons out of their particular 'lived' situations and oral discussion into a speculative system involves the list."[109] The making of lists, in such cases, signals an initial impulse "to capture and categorize malign effects and perpetrators in order to project control," prior to demonology but developing toward it.[110] Likewise, the more extensive use of lists – and written lists, in particular – is often critical to the further systematizing of demonology as a domain of learned expertise:

Popular demonological thinking is situation-specific, embedded in the world— part of the larger endeavor of an individual, family, or community to negotiate the immediate environment and its margins. To turn this *ad hoc* sense of demons into demonology proper, self-defined experts and institutions have taken to lists,

---

[106] Frankfurter, *Evil Incarnate*, 24 – there stressing, however, that "we must be extraordinarily careful not to infer from these texts and their descendants a uniform Jewish or Christian demonology, for in village culture misfortune would continue to be mapped according to landscape, fauna, time, and quite particular demonic personalities."

[107] Frankfurter, *Evil Incarnate*, 24.   [108] Frankfurter, *Evil Incarnate*, 22.

[109] Frankfurter, *Evil Incarnate*, 15.   [110] Frankfurter, *Evil Incarnate*, 22.

plucking local spirits from their embedded natures and combining them as members of a class, "demon." This activity... came about especially through the technology of writing. The enumeration of demons not only rendered ambivalent spirits demonic; it also claimed power over them—what is listed is thereby repelled.[111]

Our analysis above confirms Frankfurter's findings but also permits us to push them a bit further. In the case of the *Book of the Watchers*, we have considered its collection, ordering, and textualization of local traditions about transmundane powers as well as its abstractified and narrativized assertions about their origins and history. Not only is it the first known work thereby to textualize a claim to authority over demons as a domain of Jewish scribal knowledge and expertise, but it does so by collecting, textualizing, and redactionally anthologizing a repertoire of "magical" and other motifs, thereby offering influential models for the practice of organizing knowledge with and about transmundane powers for many centuries thereafter. When we also situate the lists in the *Book of the Watchers* in relation to this anthologizing, we notice the ramifications for remapping Jewish scribal authority as well: the scribes responsible for the *Book of the Watchers* use the form of the written list to order local knowledge about spirits, but they simultaneously repurpose the demonological power of the list to make new claims about the scribal art of *Listenwissenschaft* and the scope of its power to order knowledge about the world. Through such lists, knowledge about demons is claimed and marked as Jewish knowledge, and it is textualized as part of a literary heritage of writing about the Jewish past that is claimed to go back before the Flood – with consequences for the remaking of the very image of that past as well as its self-claimed scribal custodians.

To be sure, the precise place of lists in the literary formation of the *Book of the Watchers* is more difficult to recover than for the *Astronomical Book*. For the *Astronomical Book*, we have evidence for how some didactic lists initially circulated separately and how information of this sort was then integrated in part through first-person narrative framing-notices – in that case, perhaps, initially dramatizing the teachings of an unnamed scribe to his student and eventually associated with the angel Uriel and the antediluvian scribe Enoch. For the *Book of the Watchers*, we possess no surviving manuscript evidence akin to 4Q208, which in the case of the *Astronomical Book* attests the independent circulation of lists

---

[111] Frankfurter, *Evil Incarnate*, 30.

containing the information that is later compiled and narrativized in more literary forms (i.e., beginning already with 4Q209). Nevertheless, the patterns that we observed in the *Astronomical Book* draw our attention to the multiple lists embedded within the *Book of the Watchers*. Significantly, for our purposes, these are not limited to the two lists of the names of fallen angels but also include catalogues and itineraries of cosmological information and the enumeration of the names of heavenly angels and the domains associated with them. What is striking, in fact, is the degree to which the lists encapsulate the audaciously expansive scope of the knowledge here associated with Enoch and thereby claimed for Jewish scribalism – and thus the broader context of its demonology.

One such list occurs in an early unit about Enoch's tours of the cosmos (*1 En* 17–19) and may preserve an even earlier core thereof. It consists of a first-person itinerary recounting what Enoch saw during his travels with angels:[112]

I saw (Gr[Pan] ἴδον; Eth *re'iku*) the treasuries of all the winds.
I saw how through them he ordered all created things.
I saw the foundation of the earth and the cornerstone of the earth (cf. Job 38:4, 6).
I saw the four winds bearing the earth and the firmament of heaven.
I saw how the winds stretch out the height of heaven. They stand between earth and heaven; they are the pillars of heaven.
I saw the winds of heaven that turn and bring to setting the disk of the sun and all the stars.
I saw the winds on the earth bearing clouds.[113]
I saw at the ends of the earth the firmament of heaven above. (*1 En* 18:1–5)[114]

This list describes the sights at the edges of the earth, with an emphasis on the winds (Gr. ἄνεμοι; Eth. *nefasat*) that manage the cycles of the cosmos.

Inasmuch as it focuses on constituent elements of cosmological order that are either invisible to the human eye or too distant to encounter in the course of ordinary travels around the *oikoumene*, this list provides an interesting counterpart to the opening poem, also attributed to Enoch, which is structured around a catalogue of what he exhorts the reader/hearer "observe" and "contemplate" of those cycles of the cosmos that are visible in the course of daily life (e.g., celestial movements, signs of the

---

[112] Notably, the more detailed descriptions of Enoch's journeys later in the *Book of the Watchers* also include some passages with formal resonances with the subgenre of the itinerary list (e.g., *1 En* 28:1–32:2; 34–36).

[113] Ethiopic MSS here add "I saw the paths of the angels," a line with no counterpart here in Gr[Pan].

[114] Translation follows Nickelsburg, *1 Enoch 1*, 276 with some minor revisions.

seasons, flowing of seas and rivers; 2:1–5:3).[115] The catalogue of natural phenomena is used to emphasize the ethical aims of proper human inquiry into the cosmos:

> Contemplate all (his) works, and observe the works of heaven, how they do not alter their paths; and the luminaries <of> heaven, that they all rise and set, each one ordered in its appointed time; and they appear on feasts and do not transgress their own appointed order. Observe the earth, and contemplate the works that take place on it from the beginning until the consummation, that nothing on earth changes but all the works of God are manifest to you. (*1 En* 2:1-2)

The poem continues with calls to "observe" the signs of each of the seasons (2:3–5:1), culminating in the charge to "contemplate all these works, and understand that he who lives for all the ages made all these works ... and they all carry out their works for him, and their works do not alter, but they all carry out his word" (5:1-2) and, similarly, to "observe the sea and rivers," which "do not alter their works from his words" (5:3). Listing aspects of created world thus contributes to conveying its comprehensiveness in providing models for human obedience to God's laws – even convicting, by comparison, people who stray from the paths of righteousness (3:4; 5:4).[116]

If the poetic catalogue in *1 Enoch* 2–5 signals a point of continuity with the rhetoric of seeing and showing within the *Astronomical Book*, the list of sights and sites in *1 Enoch* 18 marks its extension into claims about Enoch's exceptionalism in having visited otherworldly realms. The latter is often cited as exemplary of what Michael E. Stone has identified as the subgenre of "lists of revealed things" within apocalyptic literature, whereby visionaries claim to know and/or reveal precisely what earlier sapiential literature enumerates as those elements of divine knowledge that lie outside of human comprehension. In Job 38–39, for instance, when God speaks to Job out of the whirlwind and questions his understanding, he cites his own unique knowledge of some of the same matters that Enoch here claims to see – including the earth's foundations, its cornerstone, the paths of the west and east winds, and movement of stars and clouds (38:4, 6, 31–34). In the redacted form of the *Book of the*

---

[115] See further Hartman, *Asking for a Meaning*, 17–21.

[116] Below, we shall see how much the same argument is made with reference to natural elements and cosmic cycles that lie beyond the inhabited world and everyday human experience. For similar notions in later literature, see *Wisdom of ben Sira* 16:26–28; *1 En* 100:10–11; 101:1–8 (*Epistle of Enoch*); *1 En* 41:5–8 (*Parables of Enoch*); *2 Baruch* 19:1–4; 48:9–10; *TNaphtali* 3:2–4:1; Nickelsburg, *1 Enoch 1*, 152–155; Stone, "Parabolic Use of Natural Order."

Watchers, however, the list in *1 Enoch* 18 is not juxtaposed with any claims about what humankind cannot know. Rather, it extends and underpins the exhortations of the opening poem's proclamation of what everyone can – and should – observe of the natural world around them. Enoch's visions of otherworldly sites are thus presented as an extension of the types of observation-based knowledge that are visible and accessible to everyone on earth.

Whereas Job 38–39 appeals also to various primordial waters and to the ways of animals, moreover, the itinerary list in *1 Enoch* 18 focuses more on the structure of the cosmos and its maintenance by winds. Here, we may glimpse a blurring of cosmology and angelology akin to what we have seen in the *Astronomical Book*. To be sure, in the Greek translation of the *Book of the Watchers* in Gr^{Pan}, there is a clear distinction between the "spirits" (πνεύματα) discussed in *1 Enoch* 15 and the cosmologically constitutive "winds" (ἄνεμοι) mentioned in the list of what Enoch sees *1 Enoch* 18. The two meanings, however, overlap in Hebrew *ruaḥ* (e.g., Pss 33:6; 104:4; 148:7–8) and its Aramaic cognate (e.g., Dan 2:35; 4:5).[117] Nor are the differences between spirit, wind, and breath consistently clear or marked in the choice of Ge'ez renderings of *nfas*, *manfas*, and related terms, which can also denote multiple senses of those invisible forces active in the cosmos and human body, spanning what modern thinkers habitually distinguish as "natural" and "supernatural."

The inextricable interpenetration of "natural" and "supernatural" is also evident in the most expansive summary of the cosmological order in the *Book of the Watchers* – which, perhaps tellingly, occurs in a list cataloguing the names and domains of the seven archangels:

These are the names of the angels of the powers (so Gr^{Pan} Ἄγγελοι τῶν δυνάμεων; cf. Eth. *qedusān malā'ekt*):

Uriel, one of the holy angels (ὁ εἷς τῶν ἁγίων ἀγγέλων), who is in charge of the world and Tartarus (cf. 19:1; 21:5, 9).

Raphael, one of the holy angels, who is in charge of the spirits of men (ὁ ἐπὶ τῶν πνευμάτων τῶν ἀνθρώπων; cf. 22:3, 6).[118]

Reuel, one of the holy angels, who is in charge of who takes vengeance on the world of the luminaries (cf. 23:4).

---

[117] Compare also, e.g., Gen 3:8; Num 5:14; Ezek 3:14; 11:1, 5, 24; 37:1–6; and see Chapter 1.

[118] This association, as Nickelsburg notes (*1 Enoch* 1, 20), departs from the healing-related tasks given to Raphael in Tobit (e.g., 3:17; cf. *1 En* 10:7) but resonates with *1 En* 22:3–6 and an understanding of רפא not in terms of the verb for healing but rather in terms of ghosts or shades (רפאים as in, e.g., Isa 14:9; 26:14).

Michael, one of the holy angels, who has been put in charge of the good ones of the people. (cf. 25:4–5)

Sariel, one of the holy angels, who is in charge of the spirits who sin against the spirit (ὁ ἐπὶ τῶν πνευμάτων οἵτινες ἐπὶ τῷ πνεύματι ἁμαρτάνουσιν; cf. 10:1–3; 27:2).

Gabriel, one of the holy angels, who is in charge of *pardes* and the serpents and the cherubim. (cf. 10:9–10; 32:6)

Remiel, one of the holy angels, whom God has put in charge of them that rise. The names of the seven archangels (ἀρχαγγέλων ὀνόματα ἑπτά). (*1 En* 20:1–8)[119]

This list marks a landmark in Jewish angelology: it is the oldest known catalogue of archangelic names. Inasmuch as *1 Enoch* 20 maps the cosmos into archangelic domains, it is also an early and important precedent for a common pattern in later Jewish "magic" and liturgy, including in Aramaic incantation bowls, wherein archangels become spatially associated with the cardinal directions.

When seen from a synchronic perspective, the archangelic list in *1 Enoch* 20 is also significant inasmuch as it conveys exact knowledge about certain named spirits, while simultaneously using knowledge about such spirits to organize other information about the cosmos – including, for Reuel and Remiel, the other spirits therein. It has a similar function, thus, to the *Astronomical Book*'s list of the names of celestial "leaders" (Eth. *marāḥəyān*) that we discussed above in Chapter 3 (i.e., 4Q209 frg. 28; cf. *1 En* 82:9–13). Here, however, the angelic status of the named figures is made more explicit, and they are used to map an even broader vision of the bounds of the cosmological knowledge known to – and textualized by – Enoch and his Jewish scribal heirs. The classification of the otherworldly population of the cosmos in the *Book of the Watchers* extends the use of lists in the *Astronomical Book* to organize knowledge about the cosmic cycles and forces that exemplify divine order.[120]

It is in this context – I suggest – that we should also understand the two lists of the names of fallen angels. As Nickelsburg notes, the fallen angel lists in *1 Enoch* 6 and 8 are inverted counterparts to the list of the names, number, and domains of the archangels in *1 Enoch* 20.[121] Taken together, they convey the completeness of the knowledge associated with Enoch: just as the *Book of the Watchers* includes lists of worldly and

[119] Revised from the translation at Nickelsburg, *1 Enoch 1*, 294.

[120] Some parallel to the inclusion of disorder can be found in the two chapters that appear to be later additions to the *Astronomical Book*, wherein the disorder of the stars is predicted, albeit there in eschatological terms and possibly postdating the *Book of the Watchers* (i.e., 80–81).

[121] Nickelsburg, *1 Enoch 1*, 294.

otherworldly cosmic phenomenon, so its cataloguing of the angelic agents of cosmic order is paired with the cataloguing of angelic causes of cosmic disorder as well.

Both lists of fallen angels are embedded within the only unit within the *Book of the Watchers* that lacks any reference to Enoch himself. Whereas most of the work is framed as the first-person speech of Enoch about his experiences, *1 Enoch* 6–11 consists of an anonymous third-person narrative about antediluvian angelic descent, likely preserving something of an early stage in the literary formation of the *Book of the Watchers* prior to the combination of the angelic descent myth with the biography of Enoch.[122] Whatever the precise origins of the oral and other mythemes that may lie behind this passage, it proves significant that the claimed knowledge about fallen angels is here given concreteness through names and numbers, pairing the potently "magical" power of naming with the paradigmatically scribal practice of *Listenwissenschaft*.

The list in *1 Enoch* 6 enumerates and names the 20 leaders of the 200 Watchers who are here said to have left their homes in heaven in the hopes of mating with human women, making an oath to descend together on Mount Hermon:

> And these were the names of their chiefs:
> Shemihazah – this one was their leader;
> Arteqoph, second to him;
> Remashel, third to him;
> Kokabel, fourth to him;
> <Armumahel>, fifth to him;
> Ramel, sixth to him;
> Daniel, seventh to him;
> Ziqel, eighth to him;
> Baraqel, ninth to him;
> Asael, tenth to him;
> Hermani, eleventh to him;
> Matarel, twelfth to him;
> Ananel, thirteenth to him;
> Setawel, fourteenth to him;
> Samshiel, fifteenth to him;
> Sahriel, sixteenth to him;
> <Tummiel>, seventeenth to him;

---

[122] Numerous studies have sought to disentangle the multiple earlier traditions about Watchers and Giants intricately interwoven therein and to speculate about their origins, especially in relation to Genesis 6:1–4; for a recent survey see Bhayro, *Shemihazah and Asael Narrative*.

Turiel, eighteenth to him;
Yamiel, nineteenth to him;
Yehadiel, twentieth to him.
These are their chiefs of ten. (*1 Enoch* 6:7–8; trans. Nickelsburg)

This list occurs in the course of the work's first retelling of the angelic descent myth (i.e., ch. 6–7), which emphasizes these Watchers' sexual defilement and pedagogical corruption of human women (7:1) as well as the great violence and bloodshed caused by the Giants who were born from this impure union (7:2–6). Apart from the aside for the leader Shemihazah, the list is skeletal, limited to names and numbers and thereby conveying the simple force of knowing – and writing – the proper names of these transmundane powers, apart from any need for any narrative or other elaboration.[123]

The second list of fallen angels follows from the subsequent assertion in *1 Enoch* 8 that one of the Watchers, Asael, taught civilized arts to humankind – including metal-working to make weapons and jewelry, the use of precious stones, and the manipulation of chemicals to create dyes and cosmetics (8:1). This list includes eight of the names in the other list, but it differs foremost in adding information about each of the figures, supplementing their names with notices about their teachings to humankind. Each is associated with pedagogical acts, and the dominant pattern is etymological, pairing most Watchers with auguries of celestial, meteorological, or other phenomena directly related to their names:

---

[123] I.e., following the insight from Robert Belknap's broad survey that both literary and pragmatic lists "are organized to display information," but that their "role is the creation of meaning, rather than the mere storage of it" (*List*, 3; see also Jeay, *Le Commerce des Mots*, 21–55). Also useful is his taxonomy whereby "a list of listings would include the catalogue, the inventory, the itinerary, and the lexicon. Lists differ from catalogues in presenting a simple series of units, without the descriptive enhancement a catalogue usually provides. The catalogue is more comprehensive, conveys more information, and is more amenable to digression than the list. In the inventory, words representing names or things are collected by a conceptual principle. In the itinerary, actions are ordered through time … In the lexicon, words are inventoried with their definitions, ordered and arrayed" (3–4). By this measure, this particular list is a list in the purest sense of the term, and its skeletal selectivity serves forcibly to convey the power in knowing and writing these names. It is interesting, thus, to juxtapose with the importance of naming (e.g., praying or adjuring "in the name of" [בשם] God and/or transmundane powers) across the apotropaic prayers, exorcistic incantations, etc., that we find from the DSS (e.g., 11Q11 v 4; cf. 4QShirShabb[e] frag. 2 line 2) to later Jewish amulets and bowls. The connection proves all the more poignant inasmuch some of these names – including the rather distinctive name "Shemihazah" – have very long afterlives within Jewish "magic"; for examples see Bohak, *Ancient Jewish Magic*, 166–167; Reed, *Fallen Angels*, 254–255.

Shemihazah taught (חלא) spells and the cutting of roots.
Hermani taught sorcery for the loosening of spells and magic and skill.
Baraqel taught the signs of the lightning flashes.
Kokabel taught the signs of the stars.
Ziqel taught the signs of the shooting stars.
Arteqoph taught the signs of the earth.
Shamshiel taught the signs of the sun.
Sahriel taught the signs of the moon ... (*1 En* 8:3)

Here too, the power of the list – to catalogue and thereby control and order knowledge – is coupled with the power of naming. Like its positive counterpart in *1 Enoch* 20, this list simultaneously claims knowledge about angels while also using angels to organize knowledge about the cosmos. In this case, knowledge of their names is claimed to expose the true lineages of some types of knowledge that have come to be common among humankind.

At first sight, the inclusion of knowledge related to celestial phenomena might seem to mark a departure from the *Astronomical Book*. After all, the first two Watchers in this list are associated with "magical" and medicinal topics,[124] while the other six are associated with signs that correspond to varying degrees to the celestial and meteorological phenomena associated with their names. With one exception (i.e., Arteqoph), the mantic teachings concern the meanings of "signs" that one sees in the skies, including occasional or irregular phenomenon (i.e., lightning, shooting stars) but also major celestial bodies (i.e., stars, sun, moon). To the degree that the cycles of the latter recall the concerns in the *Astronomical Book*, the listing of the names of these Watchers provides a poignant counterpart to the passage in the *Astronomical Book*, discussed above, which lists of the names of the "leaders" (*marāḥəyān*) who watch over the movement of celestial bodies and the separation of times (4Q209 frg. 28; *1 Enoch* 82).

That the *Book of the Watchers*' approach is not simply an inversion of the *Astronomical Book*, however, comes clear when we consider *1 Enoch* 8:3 in relation to the lists surveyed above. Whereas the list in *1 Enoch* 8 includes root-cutting, sorcery, and celestial auguries among the Watchers' teachings, for instance, the list in *1 Enoch* 20 uses the mapping of archangelic domains to express a far more capacious vision of angels

---

[124] *1 En* 7:1b: "And they began to go into them, and to defile themselves with them, and to teach them sorcery and charms, and to reveal to them the cutting of roots and plants." Even here, however, it is unclear whether this knowledge is meant to be associated only with women; Reed, "Gendering Heavenly Secrets."

and the cosmos, encompassing the inhabited world, spirits of humankind and places of their judgment, and transmundane powers like non-human spirits and cherubim. As a result, the *Book of Watchers* communicates an overarching positive linkage of angels and cosmological knowledge, to which the negative case of the teachings of the fallen angels becomes a specific exception. This is especially the case insofar as its redacted form also juxtaposes the list of corrupting mantic teachings of the fallen angels with its expansive vision of human knowledge of the cosmos, as conveyed both by the poetic catalogue of the visible cycles of the cosmos that Enoch exhorts the reader/hearer to "observe" in *1 Enoch* 2–5 and by the itinerary list of the otherworldly sites and cycles that he himself claims to have seen in *1 Enoch* 18.

The catalogue of fallen angels and their teachings in the *Book of the Watchers*, then, serves less to shed doubt on the value of cosmological inquiry in general, and more to embody the claims of comprehensiveness in the totalizing cosmological knowledge of Enoch – and hence of his Jewish scribal heirs. The naming and theorization of disorder caused by disobedience in the heavenly ranks here goes hand-in-hand with the naming of archangels and the theorization of their place in the cosmic order, and both contribute to their totalizing claims to know, name, describe, and write the precise role of spirits in the workings of the universe.

The knowing signaled by the naming of angels and fallen angels becomes further extended in the narrative material in the *Book of the Watchers*, wherein transmundane powers are granted their own individual motives, actions, and fates as well. Four of the listed archangels play specific roles in the narrative account of events surrounding the Flood, while six of them take Enoch on his tour and explain the sights that he sees. Two of the listed Watchers are described as interacting with Enoch and the archangels. The individuation of these spirits forms part of the broader Jewish scribal claim to knowledge about the precise place of spirits in the cosmos and human history. And it is in this sense that the approach to otherworldly spirits in the *Book of the Watchers* echoes and extends the same writing-practices that we have seen in the formation of the *Astronomical Book* – including the ordering of knowledge in written lists, the literary narrativization of such lists, the expansion of the scope of Jewish knowledge and teaching with appeal to angelic knowledge and teaching, and the association of such knowledge and teaching with the antediluvian scribal hero Enoch.

In its Mesopotamian contexts, as Ian Moyer notes, *Listenwissenschaft* can be defined as "a learned scribal habit in which the creation of lists or catalogs (of animals, plants, places, events, omens, etc.) elaborates a body of knowledge by referring particular items to each other, to a category, classification, or paradigm, or (in the case of historical events) to paradigmatic precedents," with such lists sometimes "expanded through the inclusion of exegetical comments on particular items."[125] Jonathan Z. Smith proclaimed *Listenwissenschaft*, in this sense, as the very "essence of scribal knowledge" in the Near East: "It depends on catalogues and classification; it progresses by establishing precedents, by observing patterns, similarities and conjunctions and by noting their repetitions."[126] Smith further posited a totalizing horizon for such scribal labors that "was nothing less than absolute perfection, the inclusion of *everything* within their catalogues."[127]

The totalizing horizon, as we have seen, marks the *Listenwissenschaft* of the *Book of the Watchers* – including, but not limited to, its treatment of transmundane powers. Whereas the literary form of the list is associated foremost with genealogy in the Torah/Pentateuch and other early biblical literature, the *Astronomical Book* and *Book of the Watchers* use lists to mount radically expansive claims for Jewish scribal expertise in relation to angels, demons, and other topics not treated in earlier biblical literature but commonly associated with scribes in Mesopotamian scholasticism. As we have seen in Chapter 3, the *Astronomical Book* does so mainly with lists of lunar and other celestial cycles, seemingly integrating earlier didactic lists from Aramaic scribal pedagogy into newly literary forms that angelify scenes of scribal teaching. The lists in the *Book of the Watchers* reflect its more extensive concern for cosmology as inclusive of both angelology and demonology. Even as its demonology is clearly connected to demon-beliefs current within local "magical" practices, its systemization of such beliefs through *Listenwissenschaft* results in a Jewish scribal claim to yet another domain of expertise long associated with Mesopotamian scholasticism. And here too, the practice of teaching with lists, common in Near Eastern scribalism, is presented as one of the means by which angels teach Enoch as well.

Just as the *Book of the Watchers* pairs angelology and demonology, so it may also extend the analogy of scribe and angel to encompass negative *exempla*. Henryk Drawnel, for instance, has suggested that the

---

[125] Moyer, *Egypt and the Limits*, 130, there following the lead of Smith, "Sacred Persistence."

[126] Smith, "Wisdom and Apocalyptic," 70–71.

[127] Smith, "Wisdom and Apocalyptic," 71.

association of divinatory knowledge with the fallen Watchers may be best understood in light of a "group of professional enchanters called in Akkadian *āšipu* or *mašmašu* ... a priestly group that was held in high esteem in Mesopotamian society because of its priestly, administrative, and scholarly status,"[128] and he speculates that Jews in Babylonia may have "reacted negatively [to them] for cultural and especially religious reasons."[129] If so, the appropriation of Mesopotamian models and materials within Jewish scribalism may have been accompanied by some internal critique: "The passage from Akkadian *ṭupšarrūtu* to Aramaic scribal craft ספר (or from Aramaic Babylonian ספר to Jewish priestly ספר) was preceded by the critique of those responsible for Akkadian knowledge and material culture closely related to the functioning of the Babylonian temple."[130]

Even if we remain wary of reducing the fallen angels only to symbols of Mesopotamian diviners, it is intriguing to wonder whether the discourse of likening scribe to angel – established in the *Astronomical Book* and there used in part to integrated Mesopotamian astronomy into Jewish scribal expertise – is expanded in the *Book of the Watchers* to include a potentially negative counterpart, using lists to telegraph lineages of knowledge and thereby marking divination, in particular, as dangerous. If so, we might here glimpse a glint of some self-conscious selectivity in the reception and redeployment of Mesopotamian scholasticism into Aramaic Jewish scribal pedagogy, paired perhaps with some self-consciousness about the dangers of knowledge and the importance of lineages of knowledge, as catalyzed precisely by new claims to possess its completeness.

CONCLUSION

Kelley Coblentz Bautch has richly shown how the geography of the *Book of the Watchers* combines biblical, Mesopotamian, and Greek elements – albeit to assert the priority of knowledge among Jewish scribes, as emblematized by Enoch.[131] We may see something similar at play at the beginnings of Jewish demonology in the *Book of the Watchers*. Just as the scribes responsible for the *Book of the Watchers* here repurpose both

---

[128] Drawnel, "Professional Skills of Asael," 521.
[129] Drawnel, "Professional Skills of Asael," 539.
[130] Drawnel, "Professional Skills of Asael," 539.
[131] Coblentz Bautch, *Study of the Geography*.

older modes of Near Eastern scribal *Listenwissenschaft* and anthological aggregation toward a totalizing horizon newly pressing in the Hellenistic age, so they do so also through claims for the antediluvian Enoch that resonate with both Mesopotamian traditions and Hellenistic concerns. As with the astronomy of the *Astronomy Book*, so too with the demonology of the *Book of the Watchers*: even as its content marks its continuity with older local, "magical," and Near Eastern traditions, its collection, textualization, and recontextualization of these traditions makes new meanings that make sense within its early Hellenistic context.[132]

To be sure, as F. W. Dobbs-Allsopp reminds us, "collecting is an old and venerable scribal practice with abundant examples from the pre-Hellenistic Near East," including the biblical books of Psalms and Proverbs, which "present themselves quite explicitly as collections," no less than Neo-Assyrian prophecy collections, which "gather short reports of prophetic activity from a plurality of prophets, presumably for royal archival purposes," Egyptian collections of love poetry, and "catalogues that list the incipits of a number of Akkadian love poems."[133] Across the variety of such efforts, Dobbs-Allsopp further notes that "writing is paramount" inasmuch as "all of these – collection on a singular (multi-column) tablet, catalogue, thematic organization by series – give expression to the chief modality of Mesopotamian scribal knowledge, *Listenwissenschaft*, in which aggregation serves primarily archival and intellectual ends."[134]

For understanding the Hellenistic-era redeployment of Near Eastern *Listenwissenschaft* in the demonology of the *Book of the Watchers*, however, there are also notable synchronic parallels – including the use of lists by Callimachus of Cyrene, a scholar and poet active in the Ptolemaic court in the third century BCE.[135] Tradition attributes to Callimachus works on natural phenomena (e.g., "On the rivers of the world," "On birds") but also – significantly for our purposes – catalogues claiming to list the totality of human cultural production. These include

---

[132] In this sense, we might fine-tune what J. Z. Smith famously suggests about the transformation of *Listenwissenschaft* among Near Eastern scribes in the wake of the demise of the native monarchies that once supported them (e.g., "Wisdom and Apocalyptic," 86) to include further attention to the specific cultural shifts in the wake of Alexander.

[133] Dobbs-Allsopp, *On Biblical Poetry*, 216–217.

[134] Dobbs-Allsopp, *On Biblical Poetry*, 217.

[135] I.e., under Ptolemy II Philadelphos, 285–246 BCE. For detailed discussion of his biography as presented in the *Suda* and elsewhere, see Blum, *Kallimachos*, 134–137.

his famous *Aetia*, a catalogue of aetiological tales, as well as his *Pinakes*, or "Tables of persons eminent in every branch of learning, together with a list of their writings." The latter is said to have spanned 120 books, divided by genre (e.g., Orators, Philosophers, Lyric Poets), with authors listed alphabetically with biographies, lists of composed works, and lines in each work.[136]

This Hellenistic-era interest in lists has attracted less scholarly attention among Classicists than the text-critical work enabled and diffused by the Library of Alexandria.[137] Nevertheless, as Andrew Erskine has shown, it was an important component of Ptolemaic efforts to use textuality as a means of "exerting their control over the Greek cultural heritage," while also helping to foster a newly expansive and unified sense of Greekness as centered on a common literary heritage.[138] So perhaps too for the *Listenwissenschaft*, totalizing horizon, and anthological temper of the *Book of the Watchers*: it makes sense in relation to the knowledge politics of the early Hellenistic age, even as it draws upon longstanding local and Near Eastern traditions.

At the beginning of this chapter, we noted how the *Epistle of Aristeas* argues for the inclusion of Jewish knowledge within the Ptolemaic epistemological enterprise. I suggest that the intensive concern for knowledge and textuality in the *Book of the Watchers* can be understood in the same context. To the degree that the scribes responsible for the *Book of the*

---

[136] Erskine, "Culture and Power," 45, there emphasizing the connection to Ptolemaic efforts to monopolize Greek culture: "there is something imperialist in the treatment of the books themselves – organizing them, cataloguing them, and editing them."

[137] To be sure, the celebrated character of such text-critical work results in part in the decisiveness of our surviving evidence for it. Even Bagnall, who takes a skeptical perspective, emphasizes the evidence that "the Library and Mouseion sustained for the first time a philological enterprise in which scholars tried to establish correct texts and to think about the art of doing so," stressing the "tangible results: In the literary papyri from Egypt, we can see the point – starting around 150 BCE – at which the messy, unstandardized tradition of Homer's text was replaced the standard text we owe to Aristarchos of Samos" ("Alexandria: Library of Dreams," 360).

[138] It is perhaps telling that "Callimachus' *Tables* are divided by genre, not by geography"; Erskine, "Culture and Power," 45. Something similar is achieved by his *Aetia*, which compiles tales about the origins of a seemingly random grouping of practices, rituals, names, etc. As Annette Harder notes, however, "the stories are from all parts of the Greek world, generally far from Alexandria, with a certain focus on areas which were colonized by the Greeks and thus draw attention to the notion of expansion," resulting in a "picture of the present as a world in which on the one hand the Greek expansion toward East and West still leaves its traces, but on the other hand also the important place on the mainland remind the readers of a shared past" ("Invention of the Past," 294–295).

Watchers partake in the broader trends of their time; however, it is in a manner more akin to what we have seen in the *Astronomical Book*. They do not argue for the inclusion of Jewish books in the Ptolemaic or other imperial archive, nor do they mount any claims to Greekness. Rather, they negotiate the relationship of local and imperial knowledge in the early Hellenistic age by radically centering their own local tradition while also radically globalizing its significance.

That the *Book of the Watchers* goes further than the *Astronomical Book* is clear from its demonological innovations: it does not only integrate earlier biblical and Mesopotamian scholastic traditions but also local "magical" materials. The effect is to claim even more completeness of knowledge for Enoch – and thus also for his Jewish scribal heirs. To reduce the *Book of the Watchers'* references to angels and demons to ciphers encoding historical realities, then, is to miss their crucial place within a radically expansive new vision of Jewish scribalism. If this apocalypse exhibits a surprisingly systematic demonology, it is in part because it models an integrative approach to the cosmos that encompasses mundane and transmundane forces, ordinary and extraordinary spaces, "natural" and "supernatural" *ruḥot*, and "scientific" and revealed scribal sights. The result is a newly totalizing vision of Jewish knowledge, built up from the bricolage of Israelite, Babylonian, and Greek ideas about mythic geography, together with traditions about spirits current in the local "magical" practices of the time as well as in earlier biblical literature and Mesopotamian scholasticism. Instead of inserting the Jews into a globalizing Greek archive or Hellenizing universal history, the scribes responsible for the *Book of the Watchers* conjure a no less totalizing and all-encompassing alternative of their own – rewriting the cosmos with the Land of Israel at its center and even its most distant peripheries brought into order by the scribes and spirits of Israel's God.

Much like what Berossus claims for the Babylonians through Oannes, the *Book of the Watchers* claims for Enoch. Conventionally, this emphasis has been read in terms of a claim to "authorship," antiquity, and authenticity. When we contextualize it in relation to anthologizing, *Listenwissenschaft*, and scribalism, however, it might be possible to sidestep this anachronism. Already in earlier Hebrew and Aramaic literature, after all, biography and anthology are already often paired. As Eva Mroczek notes for David, "linking texts and figures was sometimes less about filling a bibliographic gap than about expanding lore about a popular cultural figure" and celebrating his association with an evolving collection of psalms thus "let him inhabit a new literary home."[139] Likewise, in biblical books of prophecy associated with Amos, Isaiah, and Jeremiah, as Dobbs-Allsop notes, one also already finds self-conscious efforts at compilation achieved in Hebrew with the "technology of written prose narrative as a means for staging ... the individual oracles, visions, and like of a given prophet," at times with "attempts to situate prophetic utterance in light of a (remembered) prophetic biography."[140] These examples of what Mroczek calls "character-driven literary creativity" are matched, moreover, in Aramaic: "The fifth-century collection of Aramaic proverbs from Elephantine gathered in the name of Ahiqar is prefaced by a prose narrative that tells the story of this legendary scribe and wise man (TAD C1.1-5)."[141]

In each case, the association with an authorizing figure facilitates the act of collecting earlier materials and textualizing them into new literary forms. In the case of the *Book of the Watchers*, Enoch has an anthological function that is perhaps even more sweeping, enabling the collection of demonological and other diverse traditions under the unifying rubric of a totalizing claim to preserve their antediluvian if not originary attestation. Here too, attention to the broader Hellenistic cultural context may help to make sense of the timing: the Enochic discourse of the *Book of the Watchers* is anthological in a manner that extends Near Eastern scribal practices, but it does so in new ways that – as we have seen – resonate richly with Hellenistic-era concerns.

Whereas the *Astronomical Book* retains a closer connection to Mesopotamian scholasticism, the *Book of the Watchers* goes even further in mounting totalizing claims for Jewish scribal expertise that meet and answer contemporaneous claims for Greek *paideia*. Above, we noted its broader scope vis-à-vis transmundane powers. To this, we may add its broader scope in terms of cosmology, not least in terms of situating these powers within a spatial ideology. It is not just that the *Book of the Watchers* includes an explicit account of heavenly ascent: its detailed accounts of Enoch's journeys include his first-person claims to have seen the *pardes* of righteousness where angels still roam, the chasms beyond the ends of the earth where fallen angels are bound until the day of judgment, and the prisons of wayward stars as well as the distant caves where the spirits of the human dead await resurrection. Accordingly, the angelology of the *Book of the Watchers* is not just more extensive than

[139] Mroczek, *Literary Imagination*, 16.   [140] Dobbs-Allsopp, *On Biblical Poetry*, 218.
[141] Mroczek, *Literary Imagination*, 56; Dobbs-Allsopp, *On Biblical Poetry*, 218.

that of the *Astronomical Book* by virtue of its integration of an inter-twined demonology: it writes a cosmos in which people share spaces with the evil spirits who sprung from the slain bodies of the Giants, and it maps this cosmos to emphasize the totality of divine rule – and Jewish scribal knowledge about divine rule – as encompassing both inhabited center and demonic periphery.[142]

When we situate the formation of the *Book of the Watchers* in its pre-Maccabean Hellenistic contexts, we may thus learn something about how and why fallen angels and evil spirits were integrated – for the first known time – into the literary memorialization of the Jewish past. The answers may have less to do with theological debates about the problem of evil, and more to do with shifting ideas about Jewish knowledge and the role of the Jewish scribe. On the one hand, Enoch is elevated into an exemplar for Jewish scribalism who emblematizes claims for Jewish priority and exceptionalism in possessing earthly knowledge about the cosmos, its cycles, and its transmundane inhabitants, by virtue of special access to its God and His angels. On the other hand, his status as an antediluvian sage enables a capacious approach to collecting and textualizing know-ledge in his name – and thereby claiming that types of knowledge culti-vated and cherished also by non-Jews were first and foremost transmitted from heaven to earth in a line that leads from Enoch to later Jewish scribes. Enochic discourse may bear some exemplarity in its modeling of Jewish scribal expertise, but it is also and perhaps primarily an anthol-ogical discourse, enabling the textualization of a diverse array of received knowledge into new forms and formats, framed by an authorizing claim to extreme antiquity.

The ramifications for the beginnings of Jewish demonology are notable. Even if we cannot pinpoint the exact origins of the material organized by lists in the *Book of the Watchers*, or establish the circula-tion of such lists prior to their integration therein, it remains significant that they are used to posit demonology as part of Jewish scribal expert-ise. Whether arising in the same didactic settings in which astronomical lists were textualized and transmitted, or in later literary imitations of such lists, the formal parallel points to the extension of the *Listenwissenschaft* of Aramaic Jewish scribal pedagogy from astronomy to angelology to demonology. From a diachronic perspective, this move marks a striking departure from the early biblical literature treated in

---

[142] Compare the biblical view as described in Smith, *Memoirs*, 97–99.

246   *Demons, Angels, and Writing in Ancient Judaism*

Chapter 1, wherein the power of the written list was deployed foremost for lineage and with the structuring force of genealogy. It also represents a notable step of development from the didactic lists compiled by the *Astronomical Book*, wherein this paradigmatically scribal practice is put in the service of conveying knowledge about celestial cycles and their angelic leaders (and, hence, cosmic order). Whereas the *Astronomical Book* preserves didactic lists of lunar and other phenomena relevant for calendrical astronomy, the *Book of the Watchers* uses the paradigmatically scribal practice of *Listenwissenschaft* to catalogue knowledge about both heavenly and wayward spirits in a manner that emphasizes the comprehensiveness of Jewish knowledge about all of the forces of the cosmos – visible and invisible, mundane and otherworldly, "natural" and "supernatural" alike.

5

Rewriting Angels, Demons, and the Ancestral Archive of Jewish Knowledge

Within the study of Jews and Judaism, the early Hellenistic age has been largely seen through the lens of the momentous events in the wake of the ousting of the Ptolemies from the region by the rival Hellenistic kingdom of the Seleucids at the beginning of the second century BCE. The reigns of the Seleucid monarchs Antiochus III (r. 226–187 BCE) and Seleucus IV (r. 187–175 BCE) were marked by mounting tensions among Judaean priestly families vying for royal patronage, and during the reign of Antiochus IV Epiphanes (r. 175–164 BCE), some of the traditional privileges granted to Jews as a subject-people were revoked with respect to their practice of ancestral customs in the Land of Israel. The uprising that followed – the Maccabean Revolt (ca. 168–165 BCE) – brought Judaea and its environs under native rule for the first time in over four hundred years.

The period of Ptolemaic rule over the Land of Israel (ca. 301–200 BCE) had been an era of relative institutional stability. "Despite the violence in the world around it," as Seth Schwartz has shown, "Yehud/Judea experienced these centuries as unprecedented peaceful ones."[1] By contrast, as Paul Kosmin notes, the advent of Seleucid rule "brought swifter and more unsettling transformations – not only the desolating atrocities of

---

[1] Schwartz, *The Ancient Jews*, 30. See further *Imperialism*, 22–36, where Schwartz stresses the contrast with "the well-attested dynamism and disorder of the two and half centuries beginning in 170 BCE" and shows the long-standing scholarly habit of reading the entire period after Alexander in terms of tensions between Judaism and Hellenism to be ultimately ungrounded. It is largely without evidence, e.g., that Horsley asserts the "obvious impact" of hostilities elsewhere (*Revolt of the Scribes*, 22; cf. Portier-Young, *Apocalypse against Empire*, 215).

Antiochus IV Epiphanes's persecution in the mid-160's BCE, but also the more sustained interventions of the empire's fiscal regime, colonization, and temporal system."[2]

Responses, resistance, and reactions to Seleucid rule are richly attested in surviving Jewish literary sources from the Wisdom of ben Sira, Daniel, "Apocalypse of Weeks," and "Animal Apocalypse" to 1–2 Maccabees. As noted above, such sources have been central to the scholarly reconstruction of the encounter of "Judaism" with "Hellenism" more broadly. Much research has focused on debating the precise causes of the Revolt as well as mapping the many changes in its aftermath, which included the establishment of the Hasmonean dynasty, the emergence of the Qumran *yaḥad*, and the advent of the Jewish sectarianism so central for understanding Roman-era developments like the Jesus movement.[3] Furthermore, it is from around the time of the Revolt that Jewish scribes began to pen apocalypses that focus upon those topics that we have come to call "apocalyptic" – that is, the timetables and end of history.

Specialist studies of apocalypses have long noted the contrast between the interest in space, (e.g., cosmology, geography, ouranography) within pre-Maccabean examples of the genre like the *Book of the Watchers*, and the interest in time (e.g., history, eschatology) within Maccabean-era examples like Daniel, "Apocalypse of Weeks," and "Animal Apocalypse."[4] To explain the latter, scholars have tended to focus on the redeployment of the historical and theodical concerns of earlier biblical prophecy and/or to invoke the urgency of an acute situation of military crisis.[5] More recent research, however, has asked whether the shifts that we see within Maccabean-era apocalypse might also reflect their Seleucid contexts. Just as Anathea Portier-Young has countered the long-standing tendency toward isolationism within scholarship of this literature by demonstrating how Daniel and other Maccabean-era apocalypses respond to the distinctive structures and strategies of the Seleucid Empire, so Paul Kosmin has analyzed these apocalypses alongside Babylonian, Iranian, and other indigenous responses to its spread in the Near East as well.[6]

---

[2] Kosmin, *Time and Its Adversaries*, 10.

[3] For summaries of the scholarly discussion, see e.g., Grabbe, *Judaism from Cyrus to Hadrian*, 1:246–285; Baumgarten, *Flourishing*, 26–28, 83–91; VanderKam, *Calendars*, 15–33, 43–116.

[4] Reed, *Fallen Angels*, 71–72.   [5] Himmelfarb, *Apocalypse*, 31–48.

[6] Portier-Young, *Apocalypse against Empire*; Kosmin, *Time and Its Adversaries*.

Kosmin's findings confirm the value of a synchronic approach that situates ancient Jewish writings with reference to the specific empires within what scholars of Second Temple Judaism too often conflate as "the Greco-Roman world." Seen from a diachronic and inner-Jewish perspective, prophetic precedents might seem to suffice to explain the intensive preoccupation with history in Jewish apocalypses from around the Maccabean Revolt. Considered in synchronic perspective, however, the turn toward time in Daniel, "Animal Apocalypse," and "Apocalypse of Weeks" forms part of a broader trend in indigenous responses to Seleucid rule. Particularly after the innovation and promulgation of the Seleucid Era – as Kosmin has richly shown – temporality became an arena of both imperial power and indigenous contestation in the Seleucid Empire, and a number of local elites seem to have resisted its claims precisely by repurposing its numericalization of time and its conjuring of history in closure.[7]

Throughout this book, I have argued for treating pre-Maccabean materials on their own terms, rather than reading them retrospectively through the lens of later literature, and I have experimented with synchronic approaches to Jewish writings of probable Ptolemaic-era provenance. Kosmin's synchronic approach to later Seleucid- and Maccabean-era apocalypses further helps to highlight what is distinctive, in comparison, about Ptolemaic-era apocalypses like the *Astronomical Book* and the *Book of the Watchers*. To understand each set of materials on its own terms, moreover, is also to open the way for a richer sense of how Aramaic Jewish scribal pedagogy shifted under Seleucid rule as well as during and after the Maccabean Revolt.

In Chapters 3 and 4, we have seen how the capacious vision of Jewish scribal expertise of the *Astronomical Book* and *Book of the Watchers* resonates with the politicization of books and knowledge by early Ptolemies. But whereas the "*Book of the Watchers* ranges widely over topics from the origins of evil to the heavenly temple to the wonders of nature," as Martha Himmelfarb notes, "the focus of Daniel is much narrower."[8] In this sense, Daniel has more in common with other Seleucid-era scribal products – both Jewish and non-Jewish – which turn to focus on time and which depict history, books, and knowledge in terms that are bounded if not belated. These and other Jewish sources from the second century BCE form part of what Kosmin characterizes as a

---

[7] Kosmin, *Time and Its Adversaries*, 137–186.   [8] Himmelfarb, *Apocalypse*, 45.

"clustering and interrelation of responses among the various communities of empire [under the Seleucids], across regional difference, and beneath apparently contradictory attitudes," whereby one finds new expressions of "a historical positioning, apocalyptic eschatology, and anti-quarianism."[9] The appeal to the past in Aramaic Jewish literature of the early Hellenistic age resonates with Ptolemaic imperial concerns to assert unbroken access to the wisdom of the past through books and writing. By contrast, their Seleucid- and Maccabean-era counterparts conjure a "distanced, numericalized, and segmented past."[10]

Above, I argued that the Aramaic Dead Sea Scrolls expand our knowledge of Second Temple Judaism by virtue of shedding light upon the otherwise poorly attested centuries between the conquests of Alexander and the Maccabean Revolt – and thus also on the character of what have been traditionally generalized as "postexilic" changes, including but not limited to the beginnings of Jewish angelology and demonology. In the present chapter, I focus on demons, angels, and writing to show how understanding the Aramaic Jewish scribal pedagogy of the early Hellenistic age can also shed light on the much-studied period that follows.

Drawing on evidence from the Aramaic Dead Sea Scrolls, for instance, John J. Collins has charted several large shifts in Jewish literary production after the Revolt, including the increased use of Hebrew but also the explicit textualization of halakha:

It is remarkable that no halakhic works are preserved in Aramaic. Neither, I would argue, have we any works devoted primarily to halakha that date clearly to the time before the Maccabean revolt. Undoubtedly, halakhic exegesis went on from early times, and is often implicit in the Bible itself. Halakhic concerns are sometimes implicit in the wisdom texts from Qumran. There seems, however, to have been a great upsurge in interest in halakhic issues in the Hasmonean period, and they assume much greater prominence in the literature of that time.[11]

Building on the findings of Kosmin and Collins, this chapter looks to shifts in the textualization of transmundane powers. Much has been written about the *Book of the Watchers* and its reception within the apocalyptic tradition both by Daniel and by later Enochic writings, and much has also been written about its reception at Qumran. A focus on

---

[9] Kosmin, *Time and Its Adversaries*, 8. Note also his discussion of Seleucid archives and archival practices, which were noncultic in contrast to the previous pattern across the Near East and which evoked the utopian finitude of closed repositories (57–64).

[10] Kosmin, *Time and Its Adversaries*, 15.

[11] Collins, "Transformation of the Torah," 458.

angels and demons, however, opens up a broader purview, not limited to one genre or to a sectarian trajectory. If I am correct that the Aramaic Jewish literature of the early Hellenistic age incubated Jewish angelology and demonology, how did its innovations become so influential, even as much of this corpus itself came to be forgotten? How were the traditions therein mediated beyond this corpus and its scribal creators, and what was changed in the process?

In this chapter, I explore these questions through a focus on the *Book of Jubilees* – a Hebrew text from the mid-second century BCE (ca. 150s?) that features extensive treatments of angels, demons, writing, and the pre-Sinaitic past.[12] In these and other areas, *Jubilees* exhibits close connections to the Aramaic writings considered above. But it also exemplifies almost all of what Kosmin and Collins have noted as the major shifts in Jewish literature after the advent of Seleucid rule in the Land of Israel and after the Revolt. *Jubilees* take a numericalized approach to time, and is marked throughout by engagement with the Torah/Pentateuch and halakhic exegesis. Furthermore, it does not only use the Hebrew language: it explicitly elevates and promotes it. Even as *Jubilees* attests the rippling effects of the beginnings of Jewish angelology and demonology beyond the early Hellenistic age, the apocalyptic genre, and Enochic pseudepigraphy, it embodies and enables the process of its "translation" from Aramaic Jewish scribal pedagogy into Hebrew language and pentateuchal idiom.

Written in Hebrew, likely in Judaea, *Jubilees* claims to preserve angelic revelations to Moses on Mt. Sinai (1:1–2:1), which include accounts of events from the creation of the cosmos to the Israelites' Exodus from Egypt (*Jub* 2–49; cf. Genesis 1–Exodus 19). Both in its revelatory frame and in its narration of pre-Sinaitic events, references to angels and demons abound.[13] *Jubilees* explains the origins of different spirits, delineates the

---

[12] I here follow VanderKam, who dates *Jubilees* between 161 and 140 BCE (*Textual and Historical Studies*, 207–285), and Hanneken, who makes a case for the 150s BCE (*Subversion*, 272–284); cf. Himmelfarb, *Kingdom of Priests*, 72–74. For a comprehensive assessment of the evidence and range of past hypotheses see now VanderKam, *Jubilees: A Commentary in Two Volumes*, 1.25–38, demonstrating that the data necessitate a date sometime between the 170s and 125 BCE. Like VanderKam, I remain skeptical about the degree to which it is possible to extricate discrete sources from what we now have as the received form of *Jubilees*; past hypotheses have been relatively rare and less than convincing, and since most of the work only survives in Geʻez translation in medieval and early modern manuscripts, it is not clear as to the degree to which source-critical methods of the sort traditionally used on the Hebrew Bible, for instance, can be applied here.

[13] For a summary VanderKam, *Jubilees: A Commentary*, 1.47–53.

252 Demons, Angels, and Writing in Ancient Judaism

scope and mechanics of their power, and recounts their changing roles in human history. It purports to reveal heavenly knowledge both from and about angels, and it describes how the power and purpose of demons were perceived on earth at the time of the Flood, patriarchal age, and Exodus. Not only do angels and demons prove inextricable from *Jubilees'* distinctive literary structure, epistemology, and authority-claims, but traditions about them contribute to its cosmology, theology, theodicy, and ritual theory. Heavenly angels are here put in the service of promoting proper ritual and festal practice, and fallen angels and demons are used to articulate a schema of world-history that pivots on the articulation of the unique status of Israel in relation to other nations. And significantly, for our purposes, its discussion of such spirits is intertwined with explicit and extensive efforts to theorize and historicize Jewish books and writing.

Particularly since the discovery of Hebrew fragments of *Jubilees* at Qumran (1Q17–18; 2Q19–20; 3Q5; 4Q176 frgs. 21–23; 4Q216, 218–224; 11Q12), much research on this work has culled its evidence for early Jewish biblical exegesis.[14] In this chapter, I bring a different set of questions to *Jubilees* – shaped more by a concern for the afterlives of works like the *Astronomical Book, Book of the Watchers,* and *Aramaic Levi* than by concerns for the history of interpretation of Genesis and Exodus.[15] *Jubilees* may be most famous to modern readers as an exemplar of so-called biblical retelling,[16] but I argue that its sophisticated literature structure achieves much more – including but not limited to the consolidation of earlier Aramaic traditions and their "translation" into Hebrew. *Jubilees* is thus critical for understanding the eventual fate of the Aramaic Jewish scribal pedagogy that we have explored above: it marks its culmination, even as it heralds its demise and mediates its

---

[14] Although *Jubilees* is preserved in whole only in Geʿez, the surviving fragments suggest that its transmission was marked by much less textual fluidity than noted above in the case of the *Astronomical Book*; for a summary of the manuscript witnesses and textual situation with relevant references, see VanderKam, "The Manuscript Tradition of Jubilees." Major studies of its biblical exegesis include Endres, *Biblical Interpretation in the Book of Jubilees*; van Ruiten, *Primeval History Interpreted*; Kugel, *Walk through Jubilees.*

[15] Even in its choice to "retell" the pentateuchal past, *Jubilees* has a precedent in *Genesis Apocryphon*; VanderKam, "Some Thoughts."

[16] On what this labeling effaces, and for an analysis of its own native theory of textuality, see Mroczek, *Literary Imagination,* 139–155. "While much exegetical activity undoubtedly went into the composition of *Jubilees*," as Collins stresses, "it is not presented as an exegetical text"; "Genre of the Book of the Jubilees," 747.

diffusion. *Jubilees* embodies and enables the integration of many of its angelological and demonological innovations into the tradition at large. But what it takes from Aramaic Jewish scribal pedagogy is increasingly shorn of scholasticism and uncoupled from cosmopolitanism.

Just as many key elements that we have seen in the theorization of transmundane powers culminate in *Jubilees*, so too with the theorization of textuality. The work contains an unusual density of references to scribes, reading, writing, and books. Furthermore, it self-consciously situates its own production, not just through explicit statements grounding its origins-as-text in the authority of angelic revelation but also through references to a library of heavenly writings and an archive of pre-Sinaitic earthly records of angelic and human teaching.[17] The elevation of textuality that *Jubilees* expresses is embodied in its very form: its sophisticated structure draws richly from the period of literary experimentation that came before, embodying the creative interface between the anonymous and collective modes of textual production common in ancient Israelite and other Near Eastern cultures, on the one hand, and the models and practices of "authorship" from the Greek traditions imported into the region in the wake of the conquests of Alexander, on the other.

In this chapter, I first examine *Jubilees*' treatment of textuality in relation to its reception, transformation, and Hebrew repackaging of Aramaic Jewish scribal pedagogy, and I then turn to consider the consequences for its angelology and demonology. Throughout *Jubilees*, as we shall see, knowledge from and about angels serves to organize and inflect knowledge about other key issues – including the cosmos and demons but also halakha, foreign nations, and the history of Israel. In *Jubilees*, the history of writing is framed as the history of revelation by angels to a succession of chosen men in the line of Moses, in a manner that builds upon the scribalized lineage that we saw within *Aramaic Levi Document*, *Admonitions of Qahat*, and *Visions of Amram* in Chapter 2. Here, however, this lineage became recast in the image of a Hebrew literary culture projected back into the time of Abraham. And it is this recasting that enables *Jubilee*'s own self-authorizing claim to record what an angel of the presence told to Moses and read to him from the heavenly tablets, also in Hebrew.

For all its fascination with scribes and writing, however, what *Jubilees* conjures for its reader/hearer is the magic of the moment in which the

[17] Mroczek, *Literary Imagination*, 143.

words of a book are spoken aloud. What it claims to record in writing is an event of oral performance – the moment when the power of the written word gives way to the power of the voice, to renew the past and to render it present. With the soothsayer, medium, and necromancer, *Jubilees* shares the conviction that words have the power to invoke the other-worldly and to make the voices of unseen spirits heard upon the earth. In this case, the voice summoned is the voice of the angel of the presence who is here said to read and interpret the heavenly tablets for Moses on Sinai. *Jubilees'* angelology and demonology is thus predicated on this literary adjuration of angelic presence. It is this angelic voice that enables the harmonization of diverse traditions about angels and demons, emblematizing the text's own claim to continue the repetition and renewal of heavenly knowledge on earth.[18] It is through this voice, moreover, that *Jubilees* integrates much of angelology and demonology of earlier Aramaic Jewish scribal pedagogy, even as it severs their link to the textualization of Jewish knowledge in Aramaic.

BOOKS IN *JUBILEES* AND *JUBILEES* AS BOOK

Are there Jewish books older than the Torah/Pentateuch? Just how ancient is Israel's literary tradition, and how does it compare to the antiquity of other peoples? As noted above in Chapter 2, these are questions that are left unaddressed in the Torah/Pentateuch and other biblical literature but taken up in the Aramaic Jewish literature of the early Hellenistic age, concurrent with the growing prestige of books and libraries that we see elsewhere in the Mediterranean and Near East in the third century BCE. And it is here that *Jubilees'* debt to this literature comes clear: not only does it frame the pre-Sinaitic past as a literary heritage in scribal custodianship, but it does so with specific reference to Enoch and angels.[19]

In *Jubilees*, Enoch and his writings are described in terms that recall the *Astronomical Book*, *Book of the Watchers*, and other Aramaic writings associated with Enoch:[20]

---

[18] Notably, the theme of repetition and renewal in *Jubilees* is not limited to its concern for the transmission of knowledge but is also evident in its treatment of Sabbath and Shavuot.

[19] Mroczek, *Literary Imagination*, 139–155.

[20] On the basis of this passage, Grelot ("Hénoch et ses écritures," 484–488) proposed that the author of *Jubilees* was familiar with the *Astronomical Book* (cf. 4:17), *Book of the Watchers* (cf. 4:21–22), and *Book of Dreams* (cf. 4:19), and VanderKam (*Enoch,*

He was the first of humankind who were born on the earth who learned (the art of) writing, instruction, and wisdom and who wrote down in a book the signs of the sky in accord with the fixed patterns of their months so that humankind would know the seasons of the years according to the fixed patterns of each of their months. He was the first to write a testimony. He testified to humankind in the generations of the earth: The weeks of the jubilees he related, and made known the days of the years; the months he arranged, and related the sabbaths of the years, as we (i.e., the angels) had told him. While he slept he saw in a vision what has happened and what will occur – how things will happen for humankind during their history until the day of judgment. He saw everything and understood. He wrote a testimony for himself and placed it upon the earth against all humankind and for their history ... He was, moreover, with God's angels for six jubilees of years. They showed him everything on earth and in the heavens – the dominion of the sun – and he wrote down everything. He testified to the Watchers who had sinned with the daughters of men because these had begun to mix with earthly women so that they became defiled. Enoch testified against all of them (*Jubilees* 4:17-22; trans. VanderKam).[21]

Whether or not the author of *Jubilees* knew and used the *Astronomical Book*, *Book of Watchers*, and other Enochic writings in forms akin to those now known to us, he appeals to Enoch as the founder of the very Jewish literary tradition in which he also situates Moses.

In insisting on Enoch's status as "the first of humankind who were born on the earth who learned (the art of) writing," *Jubilees* asserts the priority of Israel in an arena valued by other cultures as an emblem of antiquity. In this heurematographical move, *Jubilees* finds some precedent in Pseudo-Eupolemus, as we noted in Chapter 2. But whereas Pseudo-Eupolemus claims Enoch as the discoverer of astronomy, *Jubilees* claims him as the first literate man and the first to write books. The antediluvian Enoch is here used, foremost, to claim the most ancient literary tradition in the world and, only secondarily, to gain the prestige of priority in the sciences of the stars. Furthermore, *Jubilees* pairs its globalizing epistemological claims with an emphasis on Jewish exemplarity: it is because of Enoch's acts of writing that "humankind would know the seasons of the years according to the fixed patterns of each of their months," but he is also the first to learn divine knowledge that would remain uniquely

---

114–117) further suggests possible knowledge of the *Epistle of Enoch* (cf. 4:18). See also Collins, *Seers*, 290–291; Nickelsburg, *1 Enoch 1*, 71–76; Reed, *Fallen Angels*, 87–89; Bergsma, "Relationship between *Jubilees*." For more skeptical readings see Dimant, "Fallen Angels," 92–103; van Ruiten, "A Literary Dependency of Jubilees on I Enoch," 90–93; Knibb, "Which Parts of 1 Enoch," 254–262.

[21] All quotations from *Jubilees* here and below follow VanderKam's 1989 edition and translation, with minor modifications to the latter.

cultivated by Israel, such as about "how things will happen for humankind during their history until the day of judgment" (4:17).

As in the *Astronomical Book* and *Book of the Watchers*, Enoch is here associated with the transmission and textualization of knowledge taught to him by angels. Here too, what is emphasized is the completeness of what was transmitted to and by Enoch. In *Jubilees*, however, the emphasis shifts from scribe to text. Whereas the *Book of the Watchers* stresses that Enoch understood everything that he was taught (*1 En* 1:2), *Jubilees* states that the angels "showed him everything on earth and in the heavens—the dominion of the sun—and he wrote down everything" (*Jub* 4:21). Even as Enoch's status as student of angels serves to set a pattern for the depiction of Moses, Enoch's acts of writing also provide a precedent both for the elevation of the Torah/Pentateuch and for the self-authorizing strategy of *Jubilees* itself, which is presented as a record of what was said and read to Moses by an angel of the presence.

In *Jubilees*, Enoch is the "first to write a testimony," and the content of this testimony is described as encompassing "the weeks of the jubilees . . . the days of the years . . . the months . . . the sabbaths of the years, as we [i.e., the angels] had told him" (4:18). In its preface, *Jubilees* similarly presents itself as a textualized record of "the words regarding the divisions of the times of the law and of the testimony, of the events of the years, of the weeks of their jubilees throughout all the years of eternity as he [i.e., an angel] related (them) to Moses on Mt. Sinai when he went up to receive the stone tablets—the law and the commandments—on the Lord's orders as he had told him that he should come up to the summit of the mountain."

The functions of the testimonies are parallel as well. Whereas *Jubilees* describes the purpose of Enoch's astronomical and calendrical writings in didactic terms (e.g., as teaching humankind about the cycles of time and the cosmos), it presents his testimony as serving another aim, more connected to the power of a text as archived record and material witness. When Enoch sleeps and dreams of the history and judgment of humankind, he has no need of an *angelus interpres* to understand the meaning of his vision, and he responds not by telling others in speech but rather by writing it down in a book that itself serves as an embodied warning: "he wrote a testimony for himself and placed it upon the earth against all humankind and for their history" (4:19; cf. 4:22). Here too, what is said for Enoch has echoes in earlier Aramaic writings but also in *Jubilees'* self-authorizing description of the function of Moses' writing within *Jubilees* itself (e.g., 23:32). Within *Jubilees*, then, Enoch's invention of writing is not just a claim of cross-cultural priority: it is also a claim of cultural continuity.

As in the lineage of scribalism in the *Aramaic Levi Document, Admonitions of Qahat,* and *Visions of Amram,* moreover, *Jubilees* here bundles "writing, instruction, and wisdom" (4:17). Among the results is an assertion of continuity that is similarly emblematized by the transmission of books. Just as these Aramaic proto-testaments focused upon the scribal line linking Levi to Moses, so *Jubilees* further fills in the gaps linking Levi back to Enoch. *Jubilees* includes ample references to how accruing teachings were transmitted by Israel's ancestors along a chosen line in the time between Enoch and Moses (11:16; 19:14; 47:9) but also traces how a growing library of books thus came to be passed on and preserved (10:14; 12:27; 45:16). "Fathers teach their sons the art of writing (cf. *Jub* 8:2; 11:16; 47:9)," as Jacques van Ruiten notes, and "in this way, the author of *Jubilees* creates a chain of tradition."[22] Enoch is said to have inaugurated Jewish literary production with astronomical, prophetic, and didactic texts. Reading, writing, and books are then associated with Noah, Shem, Abraham, Jacob, and Levi. As in the *Astronomical Book* and *Book of the Watchers,* what is evoked in *Jubilees* is thus the power of writing to survive historical disjuncture. Here, however, it is not just the Flood and Egyptian enslavement that are adduced as ruptures bridged by the textualization of knowledge in books: *Jubilees* extends and consolidates the accounts of the pre-Sinaitic past in these and other Aramaic writings to explain how an antediluvian literary heritage of Jewish knowledge came to be preserved "until this day" (45:16).

Scholars have long noted *Jubilees*' tendency to retroject Torah observance into the patriarchal period, recasting the pre-Sinaitic past in the light of the Sinaitic revelation, and Collins has more recently pointed to its explicit textualization of halakha as consonant with broader post-Maccabean shifts in Jewish literary production.[23] These innovations, however, also bear significant marks of continuity. Himmelfarb, for instance, notes a similar concern already in the "the law of the priesthood" that Isaac teaches to Levi in the *Aramaic Levi Document.*[24] In addition, the inclusion of halakha extends the epistemological project of the Aramaic Jewish scribal pedagogy even as it transforms it. *Jubilees*' imagined library largely matches the capacious vision of Jewish

---

[22] Van Ruiten, *Primaeval History Interpreted,* 316.
[23] Kugel, *Walk through Jubilees,* 7–8; Collins, "Transformation of the Torah," 458.
[24] Himmelfarb, "Earthly Sacrifice and Heavenly Incense."

knowledge that we see in the Aramaic literature of early Hellenistic age. And just as the *Book of the Watchers* expands upon the topics associated with the pre-Sinaitic past in the *Astronomical Book*, so *Jubilees'* extensive textualization of halakhic exegesis marks a further expansion of those types of knowledge newly textualized as foci of Jewish literary practice – and retrojected into the past in explicitly textualized forms as well.[25] Nor is *Jubilees'* inclusion of halakha a departure from the cosmological and angelological concerns of these earlier sources. In fact, as we shall see, its very point is to posit their inextricability: halakha is here asserted as a critical component of true knowledge about the cosmos and angels alike.

Likewise, *Jubilees* creates its comprehensive chain of tradition with references to figures already associated therein with books, writing, and/ or reading in earlier Aramaic sources. Noah, for instance, may be generally ignored or downplayed in the Aramaic Enochic literature, but he is associated with a book in the *Genesis Apocryphon* (1QapGen V–XVII) and perhaps also in the *Aramaic Levi Document* (cf. MS Athos, Koutlomoumous 39, fol. 206v).[26] *Jubilees* connects him with Enoch by describing how Noah adduces his teachings, as passed down to him from Lamech via Methuselah (7:38) and by depicting Noah as both reader and writer. Noah is said to possess a book recounting the division of land among his sons (8:11–12) and to write another book recording angelic revelations of "all the kinds of medicine" for protection against demons and disease (10:12–13). Much has been written about the possibility that the latter alludes to a lost "Book of Noah."[27] Whether or not this was the

[25] Throughout *Jubilees*, as Van Ruiten notes, "writing and reading are often connected with halakhic instruction of one type or another that is written down by the fathers in a book (4:17; 7:38–39; 10:13–14; 10:17; 12:27; 21:10; 39:6–7; 45:16)"; *Primaeval History*, 316–317.
[26] See further Peters, *Noah Traditions*, 31–51.
[27] Material that has been associated with the putative "Book of Noah" includes *1 En* 106–107, 1Q19/1QNoah, 4Q534–536, the Noah material in *Genesis Apocryphon* (1QapGen V–XVII), the beginning of the early medieval Hebrew medical work associated with Asaf ha-Rofe, and a reference to Noah's writing in the Levi material in MS Athos, Koutlomoumous 39 (fol. 206v: "That is what my father Abraham ordered me, because that is what he found in the writing of the book of Noah concerning the blood"). In my skepticism, I here follow Werman, "Qumran and the Book of Noah." Personally, I find it plausible that books attributed to Noah circulated in pre-modern times; what I find less convincing is the proposal that nearly all references that we now have to Noah must refer to the same book. For varying assessments, see García Martínez, *Qumran and Apocalyptic*, 1–44; Himmelfarb, "Some Echoes of Jubilees in Medieval Hebrew Literature," 127–136; Steiner, "The Heading of the Book of the Words of Noah"; Baxter, "Noachic Traditions and *The Book of Noah*." Notably, Abraham and Jacob are later associated with books as well (32:24; 39:6). In those cases, there are no surviving

case, *Jubilees'* references to Noah's writings remain significant, for our purposes, inasmuch as they illustrate its reception, consolidation, and transformation of received models and traditions from earlier Aramaic Jewish scribal pedagogy.

Within *Jubilees*, the connection of Enoch and Noah serves to signal the continuity in the Jewish literary tradition as crossing even the radical historical disjuncture of the Flood. In Chapter 3, we noted how such continuity was asserted through references to Methuselah in the *Astronomical Book*. *Jubilees* specifies the further links in this scribal lineage from Enoch (i.e., via Methuselah to Lamech to Noah to Shem; 7:38; 10:14). Whereas the antediluvian past functions to evoke a cosmopolitan horizon within the epistemology of the *Astronomical Book* and *Book of the Watchers,* its function in *Jubilees* is thus as the start of a story about Jewish textuality more specifically. It is stressed that Noah's library was passed along "to his oldest son Shem because he loved him much more than all his sons" (10:14). As a result of its transmission to Shem, moreover, ancestral books are later revealed to have been passed also to and by Abraham, Jacob, and Levi.

Enoch's acts of writing mark him as a culture hero. Noah's acts of writing are paired with copying, archiving, and preservation so as to establish the pattern in the transmission of knowledge in the generations that follow: fathers pass their own teachings to their sons, including in written form, but they also entrust them with a library of received knowledge as inheritance, together with skills of scribal literacy. Textualized knowledge is thus asserted to have traveled along an unbroken chain of tradition from Enoch onward, together with knowledge of how to read and study texts, how to copy texts, how to teach from texts, and how to textualize teachings to be passed forward as Israel's inheritance.

As with Enoch, the writings here associated with Noah span different kinds of works with different functions. The first book associated with Noah is geographical in character and is mentioned in the course of the description of his division of the earth among his sons (cf. Gen 10):

He (i.e., Noah) divided the earth into the lots which his three sons would occupy. They reached out their hands and took the book from the bosom of their father

sources that are both attributed to these figures and cover topics akin to the teachings here associated with them. Insofar as little is said about the actual content of Abrahamic and Jacobite books in *Jubilees*, it is possible that these references are merely meant to emphasize the continuity in Israel's ancient literary heritage (Najman, "Interpretation," 385–387).

Noah. In the book there emerged as Shem's lot the center of the earth which he would occupy as an inheritance for him and for his children throughout the history of eternity." (*Jubilees* 8:11–12)

From the passing reference, it is unclear what sort of book is meant – whether a scroll containing a map or a list of places, or perhaps a text more akin to legal documents pertaining to the inheritance of property. In any case, it remains that the decision determining the spread of the population of the earth is here represented as an act akin to bibliomancy. Perhaps tellingly, Noah's act here recalls the only type of divination described as licit and official across early biblical literature – that is, the casting of lots to determine divine will (e.g., 1 Sam 2:28; 14:18; 23:9–12; 30:7; Prov 18:18). But it thus proves all the more striking that the priestly vestments and Urim and Thurim of such biblical lot-casting are here replaced by a book.

Whereas the precise origin of the first book is left unstated, the second is described as having been written by Noah, transcribing knowledge taught to him by angels. In *Jubilees*, Noah is thus given a role akin to Enoch, as a student of angels who writes teachings in a manner to be preserved thereafter among his sons as books on earth:

We [the angels] told Noah all the medicines for their diseases with their deceptions so that he could cure (them) by means of the earth's plants. Noah wrote down in a book everything (just) as we had taught him regarding all the kinds of medicine, and the evil spirits were precluded from pursuing Noah's children. (*Jubilees* 10:12–13)

Medicine is here couched as a matter of protection against demons in a manner that recalls the traditions about exorcism noted in Chapter 4. Below, we will consider how *Jubilees* also attributes prayers for protection against demons to Noah and others, which also resonate with some "magical" and other traditions from the Dead Sea Scrolls. For now, it suffices to note that the ancient Jewish literary heritage evoked by *Jubilees* includes materials with both theoretical and practical orientations toward transmundane powers, possibly reflecting some knowledge of written forms of exorcistic incantations or even textual collections of spells.[28]

---

[28] From the evidence of this and other Second Temple Jewish references to ancient books containing instructions for exorcisms and other types of healing (e.g., Wisd 7:17–21; Josephus, *Ant.* 8.45–49; *War* 2.136), Bohak speculates that "books about the occult medical properties of various substances, pseudepigraphically attributed to angels or biblical ancestors ... were in circulation in the Second Temple period"; *Ancient Jewish Magic*, 93.

Inasmuch as both Enoch's and Noah's writings are depicted as passed along to later patriarchs, what is evoked as Israel's literary heritage is both ancient and expansive – including not just ethical and halakhic teachings but also astronomy and medicine.

In its bookishness, moreover, *Jubilees'* aetiology of medicine extends the scribalization of demonology in the *Book of the Watchers*. It goes even further, however, inasmuch as it recasts the dangers of demonic knowledge in terms of reading as well. Whereas the *Book of the Watchers* juxtaposes the teachings of the fallen angels with the writings of Enoch, *Jubilees* textualizes both, thereby conjuring two competing literary traditions from before the Flood. Enoch and Noah are the fountainheads of the angelically aligned Jewish scribal tradition. The fallen angels become the founders of a counter-tradition – textualized not in scrolls but on stone.

The reader/hearer first learns of this counter-tradition in an account of how Noah's great-grandson Kainan discovered one of these inscriptions:

When the boy grew up, his father taught him (the art of) writing. He went to look for a place of his own where he could possess his own city. He found an inscription which the ancients had incised in a rock. He read what was in it, copied it, and sinned on the basis of what was in it, since in it was the Watchers' teaching by which they used to observe the omens of the sun, moon, and stars and every heavenly sign. He wrote (it) down but told no one about it because he was afraid to tell Noah about it lest he become angry at him about it. (*Jubilees* 8:2–4)

On the one hand, the knowledge associated with fallen angels is dramatically diminished; whereas the *Book of the Watchers* credits them with teaching civilized arts like metallurgy alongside sorcery, root-cutting, and celestial divination (*1 En* 8:1–3), *Jubilees* limits them to "the omens of the sun, moon, and stars and every heavenly sign."[29] On the other hand, their teachings are here granted the continuity that comes with textualization; it is not just the angelically mediated knowledge of Enoch and Noah that survives the Flood but also that of the Watchers.

Within *Jubilees*, the era between Kainan and Abraham is characterized by the dominance of this counter-tradition, which is thus implied to be Abraham's initial education: *Jubilees* notes that Abraham was taught to read by his father Terah, whom *Jubilees* associates with idolatry (*Jub* 11:16). But it is also through reading that Abraham rejects the errors of his era. It is revealed that Abraham was also given books by his father in

---

[29] On the differences, see Reed, *Fallen Angels*.

Hebrew – a language that Terah himself could not read, because knowledge of Hebrew had become lost at the time. It is here where the power of textuality comes clear: the inscriptions of the Watchers may have survived the Flood, but so too with a library of Hebrew books, which circulated even after the language was lost with the fall of the Tower of Babel. And thus, the library bequeathed to Shem could be passed via Terah to Abraham even in an era when no one could read it. According to *Jubilees*, the words of Israel's ancestors once laid latent as if lost upon the earth, but by virtue of their textualization, they could be revived with the renewal of knowledge of Hebrew.

The renewal of Hebrew is here framed as an occasion of angelic revelation and teaching:

Then the Lord God said to me [i.e., the angel of the presence]: "Open his mouth and his ears to hear and speak with his tongue in the revealed language." For from the day of the collapse [i.e., of the Tower of Babel] it had disappeared from the mouth(s) of all humankind. I opened his mouth, ears, and lips and began to speak Hebrew with him – in the language of the creation. He took his fathers' books (they were written in Hebrew) and copied them. From that time he began to study them, while I was telling him everything that he was unable (to understand). He studied them throughout the six rainy months. (*Jubilees* 12:25-27)

In one sense, *Jubilees*' scribalization of Abraham echoes and explains the image that we find already in *Genesis Apocryphon* of Abraham as one who read from "the book of the words of Enoch." As with Enoch in the *Astronomical Book*, moreover, Abraham is here a student of angels, and his studies are described in terms of scribal didacticism: he reads books, for instance, but also copies them. Even as *Jubilees* thus adopts and extends the scribalization of angel revelation from Aramaic Jewish scribal pedagogy, however, it uses it to elevate Hebrew as the sole language of Jewish learning. *Jubilees* may liken Abraham to Enoch as scribal pupil of angelic teachings, but it does so primarily to assert that the patriarch learned Hebrew from the very same angel who later speaks to Moses.

This explicit elevation of Hebrew is among the innovations of *Jubilees*. Not only is it part of a renaissance of literary creativity in Hebrew beginning with ben Sira under Seleucid rule and flowering during the Maccabean Revolt and Hasmonean period,[30] but it is perhaps the first example of an explicit theorization of the centrality of Hebrew to Jewish collective identity: Hebrew is here lauded as the language of creation and

---

[30] See further Schwartz, "Language, Power, and Identity in Ancient Palestine."

revelation, lost to humankind in the time between the Tower and Terah but revived with Abraham. In effect, then, *Jubilees* rewrites the patriarchal past as a story about the revival of Hebrew, precisely in a historical age in which Hebrew was increasingly becoming adopted as a symbol of Jewish exemplarity.

What, then, was the language that Abraham learned from Terah? It is certainly intriguing to wonder, with Jonathan Ben-Dov, whether the reader/hearer is meant to assume that it is Aramaic – the very language of the pre-Maccabean Jewish literature that *Jubilees* here both integrates and displaces. It is left unspecified, however, and the narrative effect of this lack of specification is to emphasize the uniqueness of Hebrew in comparison to all other languages – a move that is particularly poignant in an era marked by the globalization of Greek. Accordingly, Aramaic is not so much rejected as relativized, reduced to yet another earthly language in contrast to the one holy, heavenly tongue.

Even this innovation, however, is couched in continuity. *Jubilees* elevates Hebrew in a manner indebted to the treatment of textuality in the Aramaic Jewish literature examined above. Early biblical literature, as noted in Chapter 2, often associates the physicality of a book with the danger of loss of teachings to remembrance, as in the case of the book of *torah* forgotten and later rediscovered in 2 Kings 22. By contrast, *Jubilees* presumes a firm trust in the physicality of books to preserve knowledge. Authors die, and entire languages can be lost upon the earth. But textuality enables the knowledge therein to become reactivated – whether with negative consequences, as for the writings of the Watchers discovered by Kainan after the Flood, or with positive consequences, as for the writings of Enoch and Noah as read and copied by Abraham.

That Abraham here marks the continuance of this line of transmitting books, as well as the revival of the Hebrew needed to read them, is further signaled by its description of Jacob's acts of reading and writing. The scribalization of Jacob finds some precedent in Aramaic Dead Sea Scrolls; 4Q537 includes a reference to a seemingly angelic command to Jacob to "take the tablets and read everything."[31] For *Jubilees* too, revelations to Jacob are couched in terms of angelic teaching on the model of scribal didacticism, albeit in a dream:

In a night vision he saw an angel coming down from heaven with seven tablets in his hands. He gave (them) to Jacob, and he read them. He read everything that

[31] Mroczek, *Literary Imagination*, 153–154.

was written in them – what would happen to him and his sons throughout all ages. After he had shown him everything that was written on the tablets, he said to him: "Do not build up this place, and do not make it an eternal temple. Do not live here because this is not the place. Go to the house of your father Abraham and live where your father Isaac is until the day of your father's death. For you will die peacefully in Egypt and be buried honorably in this land in the grave of your fathers – with Abraham and Isaac. Do not be afraid because everything will happen just as you have seen and read. Now you write down everything just as you have seen and read." Then Jacob said: "Lord, how shall I remember everything just as I have read and seen?" He said to him: "I will remind you of everything." When he had gone from him, he awakened and remembered everything that he had read and seen. He wrote down all the things that he had read and seen. (*Jubilees* 32:21–26)

The description of Jacob's scribalism recalls the totalizing rhetoric associated with angelic teaching of Enoch in the *Astronomical Book* and *Book of the Watchers*. Here too, the emphasis falls on the trustworthiness and completeness of what was transmitted to and by him: in a dream, he read everything on the heavenly tablets he was shown, and after waking, he remembered and wrote everything he had read and seen.

Jubilees conjures an imagined past in which the chosen line of Israel included a chain of scribes trained in the skills of reading and writing and, therefore, not dependent on others for their knowledge of the content of ancient books. Yet books and writing are assumed to be preciously rare; it is imagined, for example, that there was only one curator of the ancient literary heritage in each pre-Sinaitic generation – who, in turn, selected only one of his descendants to continue the task of literary preservation and cultivation (e.g., 10:14; 45:16).[32] Thus Jacob is significant in part because he passes the library on to Levi. And the lineage from Levi, in turn, is said to lead to the priesthood of the reader's present:

He [i.e., Jacob] gave all his books and the books of his fathers to his son Levi so that he could preserve then and renew them for his sons until today. (*Jubilees* 45:16)

Throughout *Jubilees*, such references to writing, reading, and books resonate with verisimilitude within a world of scribes. In this, it departs from the patterns that we noted within biblical literature in Chapter 2, wherein the agency of the scribe is effaced. Instead, *Jubilees* extends the

---

[32] I.e., Methuselah, Lamech, Noah, Shem, Terah, Abraham, Jacob, Levi. The line of transmission between Shem and Terah is not made explicit, even as allusions are made to the literacy of Serug and Nahor (*Jub* 11:8).

innovations within the Aramaic Jewish literature of the early Hellenistic age, wherein the continuity in Jewish tradition becomes reframed in explicitly textual terms. Israel's ancestors are granted scribal training, and many are depicted as writing and/or copying books as well.

The representation of reading in *Jubilees* spans a continuum from the oral recitation and aural reception common within the Torah/Pentateuch (see Chapter 2), to the visual consultation of written sources, akin to the scribal didacticism elevated in the *Astronomical Book* (see Chapter 3). Scenes of reading here include:

- the oral reading of a book in the context of teaching (e.g., 39:6)
- the oral reading of a book by one figure so that another can copy its contents in writing (e.g., 1:26–2:1)[33]
- the copying of books through visual consultation, as the first stage in studying their contents (e.g., 8:3; 12:27)
- the visual consultation of a book, the contents of which are later written down from memory (e.g., 32:21–25)

Just as the angel of the presence is here said to read aloud to Moses (1:26–2:1), so the angel gives Jacob books to read and helps him to remember their contents (32:21–25). Likewise, Joseph is later described as recalling lessons that he learned when Jacob read aloud to him from the books of Abraham (39:6). Even as figures like Abraham and Jacob engage in the visual consultation of written texts (e.g., seeing and reading), the fluidity between oral reading, aural learning, and textual transmission is evoked by references to the written transcription of oral teachings (e.g., 10:12–13) and the oral appeal to the authority of written teachings for pedagogical and exhortative aims (e.g., 20:10). Far from ignored or erased, scribal acts are here highlighted as part of the mechanisms of tradition that enable continuity between generations.

As in the Torah/Pentateuch, private reading is presented as the exception rather than the rule in *Jubilees*. The dangers of thus encountering knowledge without the presence of a teacher, for instance, is emblematized by Kainan (8:3). Yet *Jubilees* also points to the positive potential of private reading: Abraham is depicted as alone in his generation in knowing how to read Hebrew, living in an era marked by the demon-spurred spread of false teachings and practices (e.g., idolatry, divination; 12:27). And yet his access to books is what enables his revival of the truth.

---

[33] Notably, this is depicted as a one-on-one process of dictation and copying, rather than a *scriptorium*-style "factory" in which one person reads from a text to multiple copyists.

It is generally accepted that the author of *Jubilees* was most probably a scribe himself.[34] This consensus finds further confirmation in the intimate knowledge of earlier texts displayed throughout the work. For example, its verbatim repetition of portions of texts like Genesis is consistent with the visual consultation of manuscripts and/or specialized training in their written replication and/or oral recitation. So too with its treatment of traditions from texts like the *Book of the Watchers*. It is against this background that its reception and transformation of earlier traditions of Aramaic Jewish scribal pedagogy also makes sense. What we might glimpse here, in other words, are shifts in what Schwartz calls the "curatorial class" of Judaean culture during the Seleucid and Hasmonean periods.[35] *Jubilees* takes for granted the case made in pre-Maccabean Aramaic Jewish literature for trust in the power of writing, the importance of the scribe, and the association of Israel's ancestral knowledge with an archive of pre-Sinaitic books. But it reinterprets these contentions with an emphasis on the Hebrew language.

WRITING HEAVENLY AND EARTHLY PERSPECTIVES ON ANGELS AND DEMONS

As with its treatment of scribes, books, and reading, so *Jubilees'* angelology and demonology are marked by the reception, consolidation, and transformation of traditions from Aramaic Jewish scribal pedagogy. In the case of its treatment of transmundane powers, such traditions are interwoven and harmonized with pentateuchal and other traditions. This very interweaving and harmonization, moreover, is achieved by means of the extension of the archival impulse and literary experimentation of pre-Maccabean Jewish precedents like the *Astronomical Book* and *Book of the Watchers*. Even as *Jubilees* stands as a major exemplar of the vitality of what Hindy Najman calls "Mosaic discourse,"[36] it extends what we have seen of the anthological project of Enochic discourse.

---

[34] Notably, it is not the case that every "author" would necessarily also be a "scribe": in antiquity, books were often composed by oral dictation to a scribal secretary (e.g., Jer 36:4; Rom 16:22). With respect to *Jubilees*, Newsom similarly situates the author in the "knowledge industry" of Second Temple Judaism: the "common field of symbolic production" occupied by legists, apocalyptic scribes, and sapiential scribes (*The Self as Symbolic Space*, 50–51).

[35] Schwartz, "Language, Power," 29–30.   [36] Najman, *Seconding Sinai*.

A number of studies have drawn attention to the creative ways in which *Jubilees* combines elements of the Torah/Pentateuch and early Enochic literature.[37] Paulo Sacchi and Gabriele Boccaccini have gone so far, in fact, as to characterize this process as its negotiation of two conflicting "streams" of earlier Jewish tradition.[38] The literary data bear out their base insight: *Jubilees* has been meaningfully shaped by an impulse toward harmonization of earlier Hebrew and Aramaic materials. Far less convincing, in my view, is the retrospective reconstruction of a prior binary conflict that *Jubilees* purportedly resolves. Not only is the evidence for such a conflict slim and tenuous,[39] but parallels to *Jubilees'* traditions about angels and demons in the Dead Sea Scrolls and late antique Jewish sources shed doubt on the characterization of its harmonization solely in terms of the negotiation of any *two* different traditions. Rather, as we shall see, the references to angels and demons in *Jubilees* seem to reflect efforts to encompass, integrate, and systematize a variety of received traditions – hardly limited to two allegedly dichotomous "Judaisms."[40] For *Jubilees'* traditions about unseen powers, as we shall see, there are precedents and parallels in the Hebrew Bible and early Enochic literature but also apotropaic prayers, exorcistic incantations, and narrative descriptions of "magical" practices in and beyond the Aramaic Dead Sea Scrolls.

---

[37] e.g., Kvanvig, "Jubilees–Between Enoch and Moses"; Boccaccini and Ibba, *Enochic and the Mosaic Torah*.

[38] I.e., what they speculatively reconstruct as a prior split between "Enochic Judaism" and "Mosaic"/"Zadokite Judaism." Sacchi goes as far as to assert that "the author's aim in Jubilees is to unify the theologies of Enochism and Zadokism" ("History of the Earliest Enochic Texts," 404); see also Boccaccini, *Beyond the Essene Hypothesis*, 88–90. As Mroczek has shown, however, "the model of competing communities focused around a single figure is dependent on a projection of postcanonical thinking on precanonical Jewish culture"; *Literary Imagination*, 147. For the problems with this particular dichotomy, see also Reed, "Interrogating Enochic Judaism."

[39] I discuss this issue in more detail in Reed, "Enochic and Mosaic Tradition in *Jubilees*."

[40] Needless to say, *Jubilees* was not shaped by an "author" in our modern Western sense of the term. I choose to use the term nonetheless, primarily with the aim of drawing attention to the high degree of literary unity in its present form – a unity that stands in notable contrast to most other Jewish writings of the time. Although the work contains some internal contradictions, etc., these are no more than are found in single-authored texts like Josephus' *Antiquities*. Indeed, *Jubilees* may reflect a mode of "authorship" that is, in its own way, no less innovative than the Wisdom of ben Sira: it may be the product of a single composer, who eschewed Hellenistic modes of attributed "authorship" and who instead chose to mimic the forms of those earlier composite writings that he accepts as authoritative (e.g., Torah/Pentateuch, *Book of the Watchers*).

Jubilees achieves this harmonization through a sophisticated literary structure that is consistent both with its hyper-literate scribalism and with its many debts to pre-Maccabean Aramaic Jewish literature. Central to its structure is the nesting of different voices and perspectives – angelic and human, heavenly and earthly. As noted above, *Jubilees* begins with an anonymous third-person account of a conversation between Moses and God on Mount Sinai, set on the day after the giving of the Torah/Pentateuch (praef. + ch. 1). This conversation culminates with God's commission of an angel of the presence to reveal teachings from the heavenly tablets to Moses.[41] The rest of *Jubilees* (2:1ff) is presented as the words of this angel, in whose mouth is placed a chronological account of the important events from Creation to the Exodus from Egypt. As a result, *Jubilees* situates itself in two ways. Within chronological context of its story, its own production stands at the culmination of a history that begins with the creation of the cosmos and includes a series of earlier writings. Yet, within its cosmology, it frames itself as a record of angelic speech concerning human events.

In this, *Jubilees* adopts and extends both the use of first-person narration and its anthological application in framing-notices common in earlier Aramaic Jewish literature. First-person framing-notices are not limited to the beginning of *Jubilees*. Rather, there is a consistent use of the first-person plural ("we ...") to describe the deeds of angels, which serves to remind the reader/hearer of the angelic status of the putative narrator. Peppered throughout, moreover, are first-person-singular angelic asides ("I ...") and references to the heavenly tablets from which the angel of the presence is said to read. The claim of a Sinaitic setting also remains firmly in view. When *Jubilees* returns to this setting at the very end of the book (49–50), for instance, it is after a number of passages that reference the purportedly recent revelation of the Torah/Pentateuch. It is also after an account of the early life of the man here said to be

---

[41] On the heavenly tablets in *Jubilees* see García Martínez, "The Heavenly Tablets in the *Book of Jubilees*"; Himmelfarb, "Torah, Testimony, and Heavenly Tablets"; Najman, "Interpretation"; Werman, "The TWRH and the T'WDH." In the *Astronomical Book*, Uriel gives Enoch heavenly tablets to read (*1 En* 81:1). Even as the *Astronomical Book* purports to record the contents of Uriel's revelations to Enoch about the divine laws that govern astronomical cycles, the tablets are therein described as containing knowledge not preserved in the *Astronomical Book*. Enoch himself is said to read, for instance, from the heavenly book containing "all the actions of the people and of all humans who will be on the earth for the generations of the world" (*1 En* 81.2; cf. 72.1).

transcribing the teachings recorded in *Jubilees* itself – namely Moses, who is described in second-person address ("you ...").

In narratological terms, as Helge Kvanvig notes, *Jubilees* has both a "narrative" and a "story":

As a whole the book is a narrative, and in this narrative there is a story, chaining the events in a line. The narrative begins on Mt. Sinai and ends on Mt. Sinai (50,2). It organises the content as a revelation given there to Moses by the angel of presence. Throughout the book we are repeatedly reminded through the addresses by this angel to Moses that this is the setting (cf. 2:26.29; 6:11.13.19.20.32 etc.). We are in the narrative on Mt. Sinai all the time. The story line is different. The story starts with the creation, moves through the various stages of the history of the ancestors of Israel, and ends with Moses on Mt. Sinai, with the curious effect that Moses on the narrative level is revealed what happened to him on the story level ...[42]

It ends, moreover, at the very time and place when the framing "narrative" and chronological "story" dovetail, with Moses at Mount Sinai.

Jubilees' very form thus points to its continuity both with the "archival sensibility" of the early Hellenistic age and with the anthological temper of earlier Enochic discourse. It embodies a scribal perspective that is highly attuned to the creative power of acts like collection, textualization, framing, and narrativization to make new meanings out of received traditions. As much as can be learned about its views about angels and demons by extracting its traditions about them and considering their themes, thus, I would suggest that one cannot fully understand its angelology and demonology – or its debts to Aramaic Jewish pedagogy – without considering the literary contexts of its references to transmundane powers.

When *Jubilees* conveys information about such spirits, it does so from multiple voices and perspectives, which include:

1. first-person statements attributed to Moses and God in the anonymous third-person narrative that begins the text and establishes its setting (*Jub* 1);
2. first-person statements attributed to the angel of the presence who is said to narrate the rest of *Jubilees* (i.e., 2:1ff) – as sometimes framed in first-person plural as conveying an angelic perspective on human history and sometimes framed in first-person singular as his

---

[42] Kvanvig, "Jubilees," 246.

conversational asides to Moses in the course of reading aloud from heavenly tablets;

3. expository comments about important events in early human history, as framed explicitly or implicitly as the meaning of such events as recorded in the heavenly tablets from which the angel of the presence reads to Moses;

4. descriptions of the place of otherworldly spirits in its narration of the chronological "story" of early human history;

5. the prayers, testimonies, and blessings attributed in to human actors in this "story" (esp. patriarchs) and integrated therein as quotations of first-person direct speech.

In what follows, I will survey what *Jubilees* presents as angelic and heavenly perspectives on transmundane powers (#2, #3). Then, I will turn to consider what is here presented as the earthly purview on transmundane powers as seen and spoken from the perspective of the lived experiences of Israel's ancestors (#1, #5). Last, I will revisit their representation within its so-called biblical retelling (#4).

In highlighting this variance of voices and perspectives, I do not mean to suggest different sources or strata therein; like VanderKam, I remain unconvinced by recent attempts to posit large-scale contradictions in *Jubilees* that purportedly only make sense as the work of different authors with different aims.[43] To attend to *Jubilees'* literary sophistication, rather, is to see its debt to the anthological scribal practices of Aramaic Jewish scribal pedagogy, and it is also to highlight the orchestrating logics by which it deftly interweaves elements of its angelology and demonology with pentateuchal, "magical," and other traditions. It is through this variance of heavenly and earthly perspectives – as we shall see – that *Jubilees* integrates diverse earlier traditions, including but not limited to traditions best known from the Hebrew Bible and early Enochic literature. Elements of the angelology that we considered in Chapter 3 are here interwoven with a concern for halakha, and the parallel of angels and scribes is here expanded to include all Israel. Elements of the demonology that we considered in Chapter 4 are here integrated into a framework of the biblical past from the Torah/Pentateuch but also through the extension of a parallel correlation of demons with Gentiles. The result is a distinctive vision of angels, demons, and Jewish knowledge.

---

[43] VanderKam, *Jubilees: A Commentary*, 1.25–38; cf. Kugel, *Walk through Jubilees*.

ANGELIC AND HEAVENLY PERSPECTIVES ON ANGELS AND DEMONS IN *JUBILEES*

The first references to otherworldly spirits within *Jubilees* occur in the work's introductory frame-narrative about God and Moses (*Jubilees* 1).[44] It is here that we find its claim to convey textualized knowledge about angels as transcribed from the first-person voice of an actual angel. In the second chapter of *Jubilees*, the angel begins his revelations to Moses. As Najman has noted, the angel of the presence is thereafter placed in an authorial and authorizing position in relation to *Jubilees* itself, with Moses as his trustworthy scribe.[45]

The association of the angels with knowledge is signaled already in *Jub* 1:27–29, when the "angel of the presence" (מלאך הפנים)[46] is introduced into the narrative. This figure is the only angel granted a unique personality in *Jubilees*,[47] and his special connection with Israel is suggested by his identification as the one "who went before the camp of Israel" (1:29; cf. Exod 14:19; 23:20–23; 32:34; 33:2). It is this angel whom God orders to "dictate[48] (להכתיב) for Moses from the beginning of the creation until the time when My temple is built among them throughout the ages of eternity" (1:27; 4QJub[a] iv 6). The angel does so, taking up the heavenly tablets (1:29).[49] The rest of *Jubilees* is framed as the words of this angel to Moses, retelling and explaining events also described in Genesis and Exodus.

Inasmuch as most of the rest of *Jubilees* (2–50) is presented as the words of this angel, the veracity of its traditions about transmundane powers is rooted in the claim to record a heavenly perspective on them – as outlined, moreover, by one of their own: not only has the angel of the presence been privy to a heavenly vista upon the unfolding of human history, but he has access to heavenly tablets about this history and its

---

[44] See further VanderKam, "Studies on the Prologue and Jubilees I"; VanderKam, "The Scriptural Setting of the *Book of Jubilees*."

[45] Najman, "Interpretation as Primordial Writing," 389–400. VanderKam emphasizes the pentateuchal precedent for this depiction: in Exod 23:20–21, for instance, God states: "I am sending an angel before you [מלאך לפניך]" and commands the Jews to "pay heed to him [והשמר מפניו] and obey him [ושמע בקלו]"; "Demons in the Book of Jubilees," 385–387.

[46] See 4QJub[a] v 5 and discussion in VanderKam, "The Angel of the Presence in the *Book of Jubilees*," 382–384.

[47] Contrast the *Book of the Watchers*' inclusion of a great number of named angels, both fallen and heavenly (see Chapter 4).

[48] VanderKam, "Putative Author."

[49] See further García Martínez, "Heavenly Tablets"; Himmelfarb, "Torah, Testimony"; Najman, "Interpretation."

meaning as well. With respect to the place of transmundane powers therein – as for halakhic, calendrical, and other matters – the material framed as first-person angelic speech claims a privileged epistemological perspective. Yet, at the same time, the trope of angelic speech serves to convey *Jubilees'* understanding of the origins, power, and purpose of transmundane powers, on the one hand, and knowledge and writing, on the other. In effect, its notions of angels are expressed within the text but also through the text itself, which embodies the very claims that it makes concerning Israel's special access to knowledge from heaven.

Quite fittingly, the creation of the angels is among the very first revelations to Moses here presented in first-person angelic speech. On the first day of creation (cf. Gen 1:1–5), God made "every spirit (*man-fas*)[50] who serves before Him." What this category encompasses is then elaborated through a list:

the angels of the presence;
the angels of holiness (מלאכי הקו[דש]);
the angels of the spirits of fire;
the angels of the spirits of the winds;
the angels of the spirits of the clouds, of darkness, snow, hail, and frost;
and the angels of the sounds, the thunders, and the lightnings;
the angels of the spirits/winds[51] of cold and heat, of winter, spring, autumn, and
    summer, and of all the spirits (רוחות) of his creatures which are in the heavens,
    on the earth, and in every (place). (*Jub* 2:2; 4QJub[a] v 5–9)[52]

The list recalls the tiered cosmology conveyed by Enoch's ascent from earth to heaven in the *Book of the Watchers* (*1 En* 14). There, it is described in downward movement: from the highest heaven where angels serve God in a priest-like capacity (cf. *1 En* 14:23), to its fiery entrance (cf. *1 En* 14:9–10), to the winds on which celestial bodies travel (cf. *1 En* 18:4), through the earthly winds and other meteorological phenomena whose gates are directly below (cf. *1 En* 14:8; 18:5), and

---

[50] No Hebrew for this verse is extant. If Hebrew רוח here stands behind Ge'ez *manfas*, there may be an echo here of רוח אלהים in Gen 1:2; so VanderKam, "Genesis 1 in Jubilees 2," 307; van Ruiten, *Primeval History*, 25.

[51] A distinction between two sets of winds, celestial and earthly, is similarly presumed in *1 En* 18:4–5.

[52] On this passage and its parallels see VanderKam, "Genesis 1 in *Jubilees* 2"; Brooke, "Exegetical Strategies"; Sollamo, "The Creation of Angels and Natural Phenomena." Notable, for our present purposes, is Brooke's suggestion that *1 En* 6:7, 8:3–4, 60:12–22, and 69:2 point to the possible source of *Jubilees'* association of angels with natural phenomena.

all way down to earth.[53] The structure of the list of angels in *Jubilees* similarly conveys a hierarchy of angelic activity, albeit described from top down: it begins with the two highest classes of angels, elsewhere called the "two great kinds" (2:18),[54] and it ends on earth, with celestial elements in between.[55]

The association of lower classes of angels with weather, seasons, and the elements suggests that the author of *Jubilees* sees the function of angels as encompassing the governance of nature in a manner akin to the association of angels with the seasons in the *Astronomical Book* (1 En 82:13; cf. 75:3; 75:1; 80:1). Whereas the *Astronomical Book* privileged a nature-angel (i.e., Uriel) as Enoch's angelic teacher, however, the angelic narrator of *Jubilees* is distanced from the cycles of the natural world; he is of a class of spirits is associated with worship of God in heaven and with involvement in the history of Israel on earth.

Somewhat fittingly, the first-person discussion in *Jubilees* 2 contains a special wealth of information about the class of spirits to which the narrator belongs.[56] Not only are the angels of the presence asserted to have been the very first beings created by God, but their special function is conveyed by the first deed attributed to them: "we" bore witness to God's act of creation and praised Him (2:3). The association of angels and knowledge is thereby reinforced, and the angelic narrator of *Jubilees* is shown to be well suited for the task of revealing knowledge to Moses; after all, he belongs to the exalted class of angels who have witnessed and praised God's words and deeds from the very beginning.

That the angel of the presence is specially qualified for the task of revealer is further communicated through the association of his class of angels with Israel in *Jub* 2:17ff. In the course of *Jubilees'* account of the seventh day of creation, the angelic narrator reveals that Sabbath was made as a sign "for us" (2:17; cf. Gen 2:1–3; Exod 31:13, 17; 4QJub[a] vii 5) – or, more specifically, for the angels of the presence and the angels

---

[53] The *Astronomical Book*, as noted in Chapter 3, features angels governing the paths of the stars, seasons, etc. In *Jubilees*, stars are conspicuously absent.

[54] It is these angels who are said in *Jub* 2:17 to observe the Sabbath.

[55] Tacit in the assertion that all angels were created on the first day is the implication that the *satan* Mastema must have emerged at this time; for, as noted below, when this figure later appears, he is described an "angel of the spirits" (*mal'aka manāfest*; 10:8). This is not made explicit, however.

[56] As Dimant notes, most of the traditions about angels in *Jubilees* pertain specifically to this one class; "Sons of Heaven."

of holiness.[57] Together, these two classes of angels abstain from work every week to observe Sabbath with God (2:17–18; also 2:30).[58]

It is in the context of revealing the angelic observance of Sabbath that the narrator recounts God's decision to choose one earthly people:

> He said to us: "I will now separate a people for myself from among my nations. They, too, will keep Sabbath. I will sanctify the people for Myself and will bless them as I sanctified the Sabbath day. I will sanctify them for Myself; in this way I will bless them. They will become My people, and I will become their God."
>
> (*Jub* 2:19)[59]

This passage thus serves to concretize the association between Israel and God's angels. Not only is Israel likened to the Sabbath – sanctified as separate from other nations just as the Sabbath is distinct from other days (cf. Exod 31:13) – but the practice of Sabbath-observance is interpreted as a ritual marker of Israel's special status as God's own people, like unto the highest angels. Just as these angels are enjoined to keep Sabbath with God (*Jub* 2:18), so Jews are called to keep Sabbath with them (2:21; cf. Gen 2:2–3; Exod 31:17). Israel is the only nation on earth permitted to observe Sabbath (2:31), such that they alone have the potential to be "holy and blessed throughout all times" like the highest angels (2:28).[60] And, just as these angels see God's act of creation, bless Him, and praise Him (2:3), so Israel is commanded "to bless Him who has created all things" on the Sabbath (2:21).

For the authority-claims of *Jubilees*, the implication is striking: lest the reader/hearer doubt that any human being has access to heavenly secrets, we are assured that the angelic transmission of knowledge is a natural extension of the cosmic connection between angels and Israel, as actualized weekly through their parallel ritual and liturgical practices, in heaven and on earth. Just as Jews join on the Sabbath in the angelic praise of God through the observance of holy times, so the revelation of heavenly

---

[57] Doering, "The Concept of the Sabbath in the *Book of Jubilees*," 185. Skehan ("*Jubilees* and the Qumran Psalter") observes that the list of the nature-angels in *Jub* 2:2 bears intriguing similarities with the *Hymn to the Creator* (11QPs[a] 26.11–12). If so, it may prove all the more significant that the highest angels are so closely associated, in 2:17–18, with the Sabbath: the angelic role in ensuring the orderly functioning of the divinely created cosmos includes their participation in the orderly cycles of Israel's festivals – which are thereby shown to be just as natural, predetermined, and primordial as changes in weather and the cycles of the seasons.

[58] Doering, "Concept of the Sabbath," 185–188.

[59] The angels of the presence also often function in *Jubilees* as the audience for God's pronouncements concerning Israel; van Ruiten, *Primeval History Interpreted*, 149.

[60] Doering, "Concept of the Sabbath," 189–191.

knowledge to Moses enables them to participate in the angelic praise and remembrance of God's deeds through reading and writing as well.

Throughout *Jubilees*, further information about angels is conveyed in the first-person plural ("we ..."), consistent with the literary fiction of angelic speech. Insofar as such statements are integrated into its account of early human history, the first-person singular statements ("I ...") break the flow of the narrative and are presented as if conversational asides by the angelic narrator. From a literary perspective, the inclusion of angelic asides thus allows for the integration of self-conscious appeals that hail back to the frame, setting, and speaker of *Jubilees*. They repeatedly remind the reader/hearer of the text's claims to transcribe the teachings of an angel.

Furthermore, as VanderKam has shown, these angelic asides have been placed at critical moments in the work and mark points of special significance therein.[61] The first set of asides occurs in the context of the discussion of God's renewal of the covenant with Noah and the institution of the festival of Shavuot.[62] They serve to explain the festival, initially with an appeal to a statement in the heavenly tablets:

For this reason [i.e., in memory of God's renewal of the covenant with Noah] it has been ordained and written on the heavenly tablets that they should celebrate the Festival of Weeks during this month – once a year – to renew the covenant each and every year. (*Jub* 6:17–18)

This is followed by the assertion that "this entire festival had been celebrated in heaven from the time of creation until the days of Noah" (6:18). The result is a double etiology of Shavuot – namely: as an earthly event inaugurated in the days of Noah and as a festival celebrated in heaven, even prior to Noah. Whereas the angels observed Sabbath with God since Creation and still celebrate Sabbath with Israel (2:17–21), the heavenly practice of Shavuot seems to have ended with Noah's adoption of this observance. The implication is that Shavuot – and the covenant it memorializes (6:17) – now belong to Israel alone.

Rather aptly, it is the assertion of the heavenly celebration of Shavuot that occasions the angelic narrator's own comments on the issue, claiming for himself the task of having renewed its celebration through Sinaitic revelation:

---

[61] VanderKam, "Angel of the Presence," 381.
[62] This discussion occurs in the context of the account of God's renewal of the covenant with Noah (*Jub* 6:15–22; cf. Gen 9:8–17), on which see van Ruiten, *Primeval History Interpreted*, 247–250; van Ruiten, "The Covenant of Noah in *Jubilees*."

Abraham alone kept (Shavuot), and his sons Isaac and Jacob kept it under your lifetime. During your lifetime the Israelites had forgotten (it) until I renewed (it) for them on the mountain. (*Jub* 6:19)

A few verses later, the first-person-singular voice is used to suggest that his role in the revelation of the Torah/Pentateuch involved the act of writing:

For I have written (this) in the book of the first law in which I wrote for you that you should celebrate it at each of its times, one day in a year. I have told you about its sacrifices so that the Israelites may continue to remember and celebrate it throughout their generations during this month – one day in each year. (*Jub* 6:22)

Here, the angelic narrator makes asides in which he – somewhat fittingly! – emphasizes his own place in the history of Israel.

Is the implication that an angel, rather than God, revealed the Torah/Pentateuch to Moses?[63] To this question, we appear to find conflicting answers in *Jubilees* (cf. 1:1; 6:22; 30:12). The apparent conflict, however, may say more about our modern notions of what it means to say someone "wrote" something than about the premodern practices that would have been associated with writing in second-century BCE Judaea. In a modern context in which literacy typically combines reading and writing, the act of writing a book, etc., is usually conceived as the autonomous creative act of an individual who both conceives the content and records it in written form. In many premodern contexts, one finds a different understanding of "writing" – potentially denoting the "authorial" task of creating the content and/or speaking it in oral dictation to a scribe or secretary, and potentially denoting the task of transcribing and recording such words in written form. This more communal sense of writing – and the potential multiplicity of "authorship" – seems to be at play in the case of doubled authorial appeal in *Jubilees* itself: to the question of who precisely "wrote" *Jubilees*, the text answers with both the angel of the presence and Moses.[64] Accordingly, we should perhaps not be surprised that the "authorship" of the Torah/Pentateuch is also multiple, and its textual authority thus over-determined with appeal to God, Moses, and an angel. The inclusion of this angel, moreover, also serves to emphasize *Jubilees*' own harmony with the Torah/Pentateuch: its comments about Shavuot are presented as supplementing, rather than supplanting, Exodus

[63] See further VanderKam, "Angel of the Presence," 390–391.
[64] For this, e.g., we might also compare some models of "authorship" in late-biblical prophecy, where God is presented as the ultimate origin of oracles, the prophet as the conduit for their expression on earth through oral proclamation, and the scribe as the one who records them.

34:22.[65] The authority of *Jubilees* is simultaneously underlined inasmuch as it is credited to the very same angel who helped mediate the Torah/Pentateuch (cf. 1:1).

The next first-person-singular angelic statement occurs in the course of *Jubilees'* subsequent defense of the 364-day year as consistent with the divinely ordained course of the year (6:32–33).[66] Here, an angelic aside is used to emphasize the heavenly origins of the true calendar:

> For I know and from now on will inform you—not from my own mind because this is the way the book is written in front of me, and the divisions of times are ordained on the heavenly tablets—lest they forget the covenantal festivals and walk in the festivals of the nations ... (*Jub* 6:35)

Lest the reader/hearer imagine that the angel's revelations might be lesser or different from the eternal truths known to God, we are here assured that the angel does not merely speak "from my own mind." Rather, he recounts only what is contained in the heavenly books from which he reads. Interestingly, we may glimpse here some anxiety about the mechanics of revelation and the accuracy of transmission – here projected even into the heavens. In earlier works, like the *Astronomical Book* and *Book of the Watchers,* the literary trope of the angelic revealer is used without any sense of the problem of the potential gap between angelic words and divine truth – even despite the latter's inclusion of traditions about heavenly knowledge wrongly revealed by the Watchers. In *Jubilees,* this potential problem is averted, and their consonance made explicit – and precisely with appeal to a book.

In this context, the angelic narrator stresses the ultimate purpose of his own act of revelation – that is: to ensure Israel's remembrance of God and His commandments by making portions of the heavenly writings available on earth. After warning Moses again that the Jews will stray from the proper calendar (6:36–37), he states:

> For this reason I am commanding you and testifying to you so that you may testify to them because after your death your children will disturb (it) ... (*Jub* 6:38).

---

[65] I.e., the authorizing claims of *Jubilees* serve neither to subordinate the book to the Torah/Pentateuch nor to supplant it. Among the effects of the history of Jewish books and writing within *Jubilees,* however, is to depict the Torah/Pentateuch as the culmination of a long line of earthly books by which angelic teachings and heavenly knowledge have been made available on earth; Himmelfarb, "Torah, Testimony," 27; Najman, "Angels at Sinai," 317–318.

[66] For a survey of curripent scholarly discussions about *Jubilees'* calendar, see VanderKam, "Recent Scholarsh," 421–423.

By means of first-person angelic asides, *Jubilees* thus communicates the proper channel in the transmission of truths between heaven and earth – from the will of God, to heavenly tablets and angelic testimony, to human recipients of angelic revelations, to written testimonies that can survive the death of their human transcribers.[67]

Extensive first-person comments also occur in the discussion of the dangers of intermarriage and Levi's investiture as priest (30:5–23), directly following *Jubilees'* retelling of the rape of Dinah (30:1–4; cf. Gen 34).[68] Here too the angelic narrator references his own involvement in the Torah/Pentateuch:

For this reason I have written for you in the words of the Law everything that the Shechemites did to Dinah, and how the sons of Jacob said "We will not give our daughter to a man who has a foreskin because for us that would be a disgraceful thing." (cf. Gen 34:14) (*Jub* 30:13)

The angel's double act of revelation – through his penning of the Torah/Pentateuch and through the instruction to Moses in *Jubilees* – is again linked to the heavenly tablets:

For this reason I have ordered you: "Proclaim this testimony to Israel—'see how it turned out for the Shechemites and their children—how they were handed over to Jacob's two sons. They killed them in a painful way. It was a just act for them and was recorded as a just act for them.'" (*Jub* 30:17)

It is in the heavenly tablets – the reader/hearer here learns – that the deeds of Simeon and Levi are recorded as just (cf. 30:5, 9).

The positive assessment of Simeon and Levi's zealous acts is also affirmed in *Jub* 30:18, which describes the elevation of Levi to the priesthood (cf. 31:14–16; 32:1–9).[69] Significantly, for our purposes, this elevation is achieved through a first-person plural reference to angels: "Levi's descendants were chosen for the priesthood and as Levites to serve before the Lord as we do all the time" (30:18). *Jubilees* here expands its characterization of angels to include the task of officiating as priests in heaven. Inasmuch as it equates the role of priests with the role of the highest angels in heaven, priests serve to emblematize – and ritually to actualize – the association of Israel with the angels.

Consistent with the affinity between angels and priests, angels are also credited with remembering the righteous deeds through which Levi

---

[67] See *Jub* 4:18–19; 8:11; 10:13; 12:25–27; 21:10; 32:21–26; 45:16; Najman, "Angels at Sinai," 315–317.

[68] Werman, "Jubilees 30."   [69] Kugel, "Levi's Elevation to the Priesthood," 47–51.

proved his worthiness for this role. The recording of his deeds on the heavenly tablets is linked to the angelic memory of his deeds:

So blessing and justice before the God of all are entered for him as a testimony on the heavenly tablets. We ourselves remember the justice which the man performed during his lifetime at all times of the year... (*Jub* 30:19–20)

The angel of the presence's act of reading heavenly tablets to Moses is thus revealed to be harmoniously consonant, not just with the angelic task of witnessing God's words and deeds, but also with the angelic task of seeing and remembering human actions. In effect, *Jubilees* itself is presented as result and record of these angelic efforts, poignantly and powerfully combined for the sake of Israel's salvation. By reading and following the angelic revelations about the laws of God and the deeds of righteous men in *Jubilees*, the reader/hearer is assured that his/her name might also be inscribed in heavenly books (30:21–22).[70]

First-person statements by the angel of the presence are also prominent in the final chapter of *Jubilees* (50:1–13). As in *Jub* 2:17–31 and 6:17–38, the focus falls on holy times – and the Sabbath in particular. The history of humankind is recounted by its sabbaths and jubilees, and the angelic narrator describes an eschatological future in which "there will be no more *satan* or any evil one, and the land will be clear from that time forever more" (50:5; cf. 23:29). He ends by reciting the regulations pertaining to the weekly observance of the Sabbath (50:6–13); just as the Sabbath was linked with God, angels, and creation in *Jubilees* 2, so the end of the work parallels this weekly day of rest with the end of history and the total cessation of demonic influence on humankind.

The demonology sketched out in these materials is most readily understood as a development of Deuteronomistic understandings of divine justice, interpreted in terms of the association of demons and foreign peoples that we noted in Chapter 1 (cf. Deut 32:8–9; Ps 106:35–37). Much like "the nations" in Deuteronomistic and prophetic writings, demons here function to test Israel's faithfulness and to mediate God's punishment of their unfaithfulness. Furthermore, like the *satan* of Job 1, they are granted the divinely governed task of accusing the righteous before God.

---

[70] It is not made clear *who* precisely records these names; *Jubilees* leaves open the possibility that the books are penned by angelic scribes but also allows for the possibility that this aspect of the angelic task of witnessing was taken over by Enoch after he was led to Eden (4:23).

The approach to angelology, however, is largely unprecedented in the Torah/Pentateuch, and it even finds little echo in the *Book of the Watchers*. Rather, its depiction of angels falls closest to what we have seen in the *Astronomical Book*, wherein angels are associated primarily with the revelation of heavenly laws (*1 En* 82:7), the mediation of human access to heavenly tablets (81:1; 82:2), and the governance of the celestial, atmospheric, and meteorological phenomena whose order is mirrored by human calendrical and festal observances (72:1; 74:2; 75:1, 3; 79:6; 80:1; 82:13, 17), with little reference to eschatology.[71] Throughout *Jubilees*, the angelic narrator embodies what is depicted as the role of the highest angels in God's creation – namely: to witness the words and deeds of God, to praise Him, to witness and remember human deeds, and to mediate the transmission of knowledge from heaven to earth.

From a literary perspective, the first-person statements of the angel of the presence help to authenticate *Jubilees*, by purporting to verify the heavenly origins of the information therein and by making explicit its self-authorizing claims about the divinely-sanctioned nature of its revelation. In a manner akin to the *Astronomical Book*, where repeated references to Uriel's status as the angelic leader of the celestial bodies (*1 En* 72:1; 74:2; 79:6) serve to stress his aptness for the task of teaching Enoch about astronomical cycles, the presentation of angels in the frame-narrative and related first-person angelic speech within *Jubilees* mirror and match the self-authenticating claims and concerns of the work as a whole.

In addition, comments about angels and demons can be found in some of the expository comments that punctuate *Jubilees'* account of early human history, which are often framed as information recorded on the heavenly tablets from which the angelic narrator is said to read.[72] As in the frame-narrative proper, such comments sometimes occasion the inclusion of further details about the place of intermediate spirits in the cosmos and human history. *Jubilees'* account of Cain and Abel (4:1–4; cf. Gen

---

[71] On the question of *Jubilees'* use of the *Astronomical Book*, see also Bergsma, "Relationship Between Jubilees."

[72] Himmelfarb, "Torah, Testimony," 25–28. Himmelfarb proposes that the heavenly tablets are here understood as "an archive of divine knowledge" that encompassed far more than the Torah/Pentateuch and *Jubilees* (28). In this context, she suggests that the author sees the Torah/Pentateuch as תורה, reflecting those portions of the heavenly tablets that concern with laws, and *Jubilees* as תעודה, reflecting those portions of the heavenly tablets that concern the "division of all the times" (1:4, 29), with the latter encompassing calendar, festivals, and human history from the beginning to the end of time (21).

4:2–15),[73] for instance, is followed by the revelation of laws from the heavenly tablets condemning those who maliciously beat their companions and cursing those who see such violent acts without reporting them (4:5–6). The latter – we then learn – is witnessed by the angels:

For this reason we report, when we come before the Lord our God, all the sin which take place in heaven and on earth—what (happens) in light, in darkness, or in any place. (*Jub* 4:6)

The angelic task of witnessing is thus depicted both as a parallel to proper Israelite legal practice and as an important component of the workings of divine justice (cf. 5:13–16). Not only do angels watch humankind, but they also see everything and report everything to God (cf. *1 En* 98:6–8; 99:3).

After recounting God's command to Abraham to circumcise his sons (15:1–24; cf. Gen. 17.1–27), *Jubilees* similarly provides an explanation of circumcision as the sign that a man belongs to God (15:26). It is here that the reader/hearer learns that the two highest classes of angels were created circumcised:

For this is what the nature of all the angels of the presence and all the angels of holiness was like from the day of their creation. In front of the angels of the presence and the angels of sanctification He has sanctified Israel to be with Him and His holy angels. (*Jub* 15:27–28)

Just as angels were earlier credited with the heavenly observance of Sabbath and Shavuot, so circumcision is presented as a physical mark of Israel's association with the angels (15:28; cf. 2:19).

The point is made in part to assert the converse: according to *Jubilees,* any male Israelite who does not bear this mark is doomed to destruction, "destroyed from the earth" and "uprooted from the earth" (15:26). The dynamics of this destruction are explicated in the passage that directly follows, which outlines a central principle of *Jubilees'* angelology and demonology:

...For there are many nations and many peoples, and all belong to Him. He made spirits (Eth. *manāfesta*) rule over all in order to lead them astray from following Him. But over Israel He made no angel or spirit rule, because He alone is their ruler. He will guard them and require them for Himself from His angels, His spirits, and everyone so that He may guard and bless them and so that they may be His and He theirs from now and forever ... (*Jub* 15:31–32)

---

[73] Van Ruiten, *Primeval History Interpreted*, 138–149.

By virtue of the status of Jews as the children of God and akin to the angels, Israel is here presented as the only earthly nation not ruled by spirits. Angels act as mediators on God's behalf to Jews, but their mediation does not extend to the actual rule of Israel – the only people governed directly by God. Conversely, foreign nations are ruled by spirits that lead them astray. Inasmuch as "all the people of Beliar/*belial* (lit. worthlessness)[74] will leave their sons uncircumcised" (15:33), those Jews who are not circumcised risk joining them in being "removed and uprooted from the earth" (15:34), giving up the privilege of their direct rule by God.

This association of intermediate spirits with the rule of non-Jewish nations resonates with the textual tradition surrounding Deut 32:8–9 that we discussed in Chapter 1,[75] and it is also paralleled in the Enochic *Book of Dreams* (*1 En* 89:59–70), wherein God is depicted as commissioning seventy angels as earthly rulers of the nations after the Babylonian Exile.[76] Here, however, the term "angel" is not explicitly used of the rulers of non-Jewish nations. But neither are they demonized in any sense that might imply any sovereignty or agency independent from God. Rather, in a manner akin to the use of "spirits" as an umbrella category in the *Book of the Watchers*, *Jubilees* speaks here of the "spirits" (*manāfest*) who are placed over the nations and who are enjoined by God to mislead them. Because of this injunction to mislead, these spirits might seem from the perspective of humankind to be evil, and it is in this sense – as we shall see – that they are called "demons" ('*agānent*) and "wicked spirits" (*manāfest 'ekuyān*) elsewhere in *Jubilees* and/or associated with Beliar/*belial*, Moloch, and the *satan* Mastema.[77] The first-person speech of the angel of the presence, however, makes clear that all nations ultimately belong to God (15:31) and all spirits ultimately serve Him. Far from relegating most of the earth to the capricious reign of demons, *Jubilees* reveals their place within the orderly hierarchy of God's governance of the cosmos as a whole. Demons, like other spirits, have divinely set tasks and domains.

The ramifications for Israel are further explored in *Jub* 30:8–16. We noted how the rape of Dinah serves as an occasion for *Jubilees* to exalt the

[74] On this term, see below.
[75] VanderKam, "Demons in the Book of Jubilees," 352–354.
[76] For this tradition and its relationship to later ideas about the seventy rulers of Gentile nations, see Tiller, *Commentary*, 51–60.
[77] See further below.

priesthood through the alignment of Jewish priests and heavenly angels. In the same chapter, we find a condemnation of intermarriage – in this case, in a command said to be recorded in the heavenly tablets:

> For this is the way in which it has been ordained and written on the heavenly tablets regarding any descendant of Israel who defiles (it): "He is to die; he is to be stoned." The law has no temporal limit. There is no remission or any forgiveness; but rather the man who has defiled his daughter within all of Israel is to be eradicated because he has given one of his descendants to Molech and has sinned by defiling them. Now you, Moses, order the Israelites and testify to them that they are not to give any of their daughters to foreigners and that they are not to marry any foreign women because it is despicable before the Lord. (*Jub* 30:9–11; cf. Lev 20:2)

Jubilees here equates the act of giving one's offspring to Moloch with the act of marrying one's daughter to a foreigner – and by extension, with any type of intermarriage.[78] What *Jubilees* elsewhere describes as the problem of Israel "sacrifice[ing] their children to demons" (1:11; cf. Ps 106:37) is here clarified to mean the problem of Jews marrying non-Jews and thereby aligning themselves with the spirits who rule over foreign nations.

That the principle of God's sole rulership of Israel alone is determinative of *Jubilees'* angelology and demonology becomes clear when we consider the eschatology outlined in *Jub* 23:11–32.[79] This passage strikingly does not include any reference to angels. Yet, as Todd Hanneken has shown, we may learn much about *Jubilees'* view of angels from their complete absence here.[80] The absence is perhaps most poignant in *Jub* 23:24, when Jews "cry out and call and pray to be rescued from the sinful nations," only to have no one intervene. The language recalls the scene in the *Book of the Watchers* where the souls of the murdered cry out and are heard by archangels, who deliver their pleas to God and who are sent by God to bind and destroy those responsible through the Flood (*1 En* 9:1–11). In the eschatology of *Jubilees*, by contrast, God is the only supernatural agent of punishment (23:22) and reward (23:30–31) – and even He is said not to intervene to renew creation until after the Jews have saved themselves through their own piety (23:24–29).

---

[78] Werman ("*Jubilees* 30," 14) suggests that this interpretation may derive from exegetical reflection on the inclusion of the law about Molech in Lev 18:21 alongside laws about incest.

[79] Davenport, *The Eschatology of the Book of Jubilees*; Hanneken, "Angels and Demons," 22–23; cf. Kugel, "The *Jubilees* Apocalypse."

[80] Hanneken, "Angels and Demons," 13–14, 22–23.

In the *Book of the Watchers*, God is described as executing judgment together with his myriad angels (*1 En* 1:9), and archangelic involvement in the punishment of the wicked is suggested by the typological equation between Flood and Eschaton (esp. *1 En* 10). Likewise, "good and bad angels" – as Hanneken shows – "play significant roles in each of the three phases of crisis and restoration ... the climax of evil, the earthly struggle, and the cosmic judgment" in the "Animal Apocalypse" in the *Book of Dreams* (*1 En* 85–90).[81] At first sight, the *Epistle of Enoch* appears to provide a parallel for *Jubilees'* displacement of otherworldly spirits from the Eschaton; the *Epistle of Enoch*, after all, stresses human responsibility for sin and suffering (*1 En* 98:4), and it invokes angels primarily in their role as witnesses to human deeds (98:6–8; 99:3; 100:10–11; 104:1).[82] Even there, however, angels retain some role in eschatological judgment, gathering the wicked and protecting the righteous (*1 En* 100:4–5; 102:3).[83] By contrast, *Jubilees* presents the eschatological future as a time when God's sole rulership of Israel is dramatically demonstrated.

The only reference to transmundane powers in *Jubilees* 23 occurs in the promise that "there will neither be a *satan* nor any evil one who will destroy" when Israel finally repents (23:29; cf. 40:9; 46:2; 50:5).[84] In the end, according to *Jubilees*, Israel alone will bear the responsibility for finding a path to repentance (23:24–29), and God alone will answer their repentance with eschatological vengeance and renewal (23:30–31). The emphasis on human responsibility is so marked that God refrains from intervening to save the righteous until after Israel's own deeds have led to the cessation of demonic influence (23:24–29) and the lengthening of their lifetimes.[85] Spirits are nowhere to be found in *Jubilees'* account of how

---

[81] Hanneken, "Angels and Demons," 22.

[82] In the "Apocalypse of Weeks" in the *Epistle of Enoch* (*1 En* 93:1–10, 91:11–17), the only angels cited are the wicked ones who are punished (91:15). Most end-time events, however, are there described in the passive voice, such that the precise agents of punishment, etc., are not clear.

[83] The possibility that this shift represents a self-conscious departure from Enochic tradition is raised by *Jub* 5:10, which predicts the destruction of the Watchers at the Last Judgment. The inclusion of this detail is consonant with the many parallels with *1 En* 10 in *Jub* 5:6–11. Whereas the destruction of the Watchers is a central element in early Enochic depictions of the Eschaton (*1 En* 10; 90:21–25; 91:15), however, it is never mentioned again in *Jubilees*.

[84] Hanneken, "Angels and Demons," 22–23.

[85] Kugel, "Jubilees Apocalypse." To what degree – we might further ask – is human repentance here predicated on the divine transformation of human nature promised in *Jubilees* 1? Lambert ("Did Israel Believe," 645–646) characterizes *Jubilees* as deeming repentance as possible *only after* the transformation of Israel's nature to protect them

Israel will be captured, plundered, and devoured in the End Times; such tasks are relegated to the human realm and associated with Gentiles (23:22–24). In effect, the close association of demons and Gentiles throughout *Jubilees* is here used to transfer the eschatological function of the former onto the latter.

Together with the first-person angelic speech within *Jubilees*, the descriptions of what is written on the heavenly tablets convey the place of angels and demons in the cosmos as it appears when seen from the perspective of heaven. Angels are associated with Israel. Demons are associated with Gentiles. Whereas demons tempt Israel to sin and accuse them before God, angels witness God's words and deeds, praise him through writing and recitation, and participate in the orderly cycles – both natural and festal – of the divinely created cosmos. The expository comments associated with the heavenly tablets, however, are used to reveal some of the implications of these associations – as well as their limits: Israel is not ruled by any angel or spirit but is beholden only to God. It is insofar as other nations are ruled by spirits that those Jews who choose to affiliate themselves with Gentiles align themselves with demons. In the end, moreover, human choices remain determinative inasmuch as intermediate spirits are granted no part in eschatological judgment.

HUMAN AND EARTHLY PERSPECTIVES ON ANGELS AND DEMONS IN *JUBILEES*

Through the human prayers, vows, speeches, testimonies, and blessings embedded in its narrative, *Jubilees* also gives voice to earthly perspectives on these spirits as experienced by humankind.[86] The importance of this perspective is clear from the very first chapter of *Jubilees*, which features

---

from demons. In my view, however, *Jubilees* 1 and 23 – and the demonology of the text as a whole – do not subordinate human action to divine transformation in such a straightforward fashion. Indeed, as VanderKam stresses, "the 'returning' of the people in exile [in *Jubilees* 1] precedes the divine transformation of their nature, just as it does in Deut. 30.1–10" (425).

[86] For prayers and vows, see e.g. *Jub* 10:3; 22:7–9; 27:27; speeches and testimonies, e.g. 7:20–39; 12:2–5, 19–21; 20:2–10; 21:1–25; 25:1–3; 36:1–16; blessings, e.g. 7:11–12; 12:29; 19:17–29; 22:10–23, 27–30; 25:15–23; 26:23–4; 31:12–20. Of course, some precedent for this literary trope is readily found in the patriarchal narratives in Genesis (e.g., Gen 27:28–29; 48:15–16; 49:1–27), even as *Jubilees* extends the trope of first-person speech to enhance the element of transmission of wisdom from generation to generation (see further Lambert, "Last Testaments in the *Book of Jubilees*").

Moses speaking in this fashion in response to God. After recounting how
God revealed the Torah/Pentateuch to Moses on Mount Sinai (1:1–4;
cf. Exod 19:1; 24:12–18), *Jubilees* tells how he commanded Moses to
write his words, lest Jews forget his faithfulness to them (1:5–6; cf. Exod.
34:27–28). God then warns Moses that the people will stray from him
and, as a result, will suffer punishment at the hands of foreign nations
(1:7–14; cf. Deut 31:16–21) before eventually returning to him (1:15–18).
The divine prediction of Israel's rebellion is couched in terms of their
adoption of non-Jewish practices: as part of the divine speech foretelling
that Israel will abandon God's laws to "follow the nations, their impurities, and their shame" (1:9), it is here that it is asserted that Jews
will "sacrifice their children to demons (*'agānent*)" (1:11; cf. Ps 106:37;
1 En 19:1).[87]

Moses responds with a prayer of petition:

"Lord my God, do not allow your people and your heritage to go along in the
error of their minds, and do not deliver them into the control of the nations with
the result that they rule over them lest they make them sin against you. May your
mercy, Lord, be lifted over your people. Create for them a just spirit (*manfasa
ratu'a*). May the spirit of Belial not rule over them so as to bring charges against
them before you and to trap them away from every proper path so that they may
be destroyed from your presence. They are your people and your heritage whom
you have rescued from Egyptian control by your great power. Create for them a
pure mind and a holy spirit (*lebb neṣuḥ wa-manfasa qeddusa*). May they not be
trapped in their sins from now to eternity." (*Jub* 1:19–21)

In the speech attributed to God in *Jub* 1:5–18, the arithmetic of divine
justice is outlined in classically Deuteronomistic terms: Israel's abandonment of covenantal obligations will lead to foreign rule, while their
remembrance of God's laws will result in return, restoration, and recon-
ciliation.[88] The response attributed to Moses questions the tidiness of this
theodicy. Moses here points to the indirect consequences of God's puni-
tive deliverance of His people into the hands of foreign nations: inasmuch
as Gentiles would no doubt lead Jews into wickedness, the very experience of foreign rule stands in the way of Israel's repentance (1:19).[89]
Moses likens life under non-Jewish rule, thus, to life under the rule of
the "spirit of Beliar/*belial*" (cf. 15:31), which – he argues – will block Jews
from following paths of righteousness (1:20).

---

[87] In Ps 106:37, etc., Geʿez *gānēn* ("demon") renders Hebrew שד.
[88] Himmelfarb, "Torah, Testimony," 23–24.
[89] Lambert, "Did Israel Believe That Redemption Awaited Its Repentance."

The term בליעל is well attested in the Hebrew Bible, where it bears the sense of "worthlessness."[90] The reference to Beliar/*belial* in *Jub* 1:19 thus allows for multiple interpretations – as a proper name, as an appeal to a "worthless spirit" in the sense of a demon, or as a more abstract or internalized appeal to the "spirit of worthlessness" and people governed by it (in this case: Gentiles).[91] Whatever its precise sense, however, its function in Moses' speech is clear – that is, to associate demons with Gentiles.[92] Gentiles are here said to worship demons, and foreign rule is thus paralleled to demonic rule.[93]

Although *Jubilees'* pairing of Gentiles and demons has roots in Psalm 106 and Deuteronomy 32, it here raises a problem for the traditional Deuteronomistic understanding of foreign nations as tools for the divine punishment of Israel's wickedness. Non-Jewish rule may be a means to punish sin, but it can simultaneously be a cause of sin and an obstacle to repentance – precisely due to what *Jubilees* posits as the Gentile alignment with the demonic. The former position is here put in the mouth of God, while the latter concern is expressed by means of Moses. The latter culminates in a petition: Moses pleads with God to "create in them a pure mind and a holy spirit (*lebb neṣuḥ wa-manfasa qeddusa;* 1:21)." In response, God promises to do so, such that their minds and spirits can cleave to His commandments (1:22–25) even in the face of demonic *qua* Gentile influence. It is in this context that angels are introduced. The reader has just been told how Israel will be purified in mind, infused with holy spirit (*manfasa qeddusa*), and adopted as "the children of the living God" (1:23, 25). The special status of Israel is then sealed with the divine promise that "every angel and every spirit (*kʷellu malʾak wa-kʷellu manfas*) shall know ... that they are my children" (1:25; cf. 2:19).

The claim to preserve Moses' first-person perspective on the threat of demons proves all the more poignant due to its parallels with early Jewish traditions of penitential prayer, as richly analyzed by Bilhah Nitzan.[94]

---

[90] I.e., בלי + יעל; Deut 13:14; 15:9; Judg 19:22; 20:13; 1 Sam 1:16; 2:12; 10:27; 25:17, 25; 30:22; 2 Sam 16:7; 20:1; 22:5; 23:6; 1 Kgs 21:10, 13; Nah 1:11; 2:1; Pss 18:5; 41:9; Job 34:18; Prov 6:12; 16:27; 19:28; 2 Chron 13:7.

[91] The multiplicity of meanings is in keeping with the range of meanings of "spirit" (Eth. *manfas*) within *Jubilees* as well as its representation of the mechanisms of demonic influence and their effects on the human mind/heart (*lebb*).

[92] VanderKam, "Demons in the *Book of Jubilees*," 340–341, 350–354.

[93] The parallelism is underlined by the use of the same verb, *kʷannana*, to refer to rule of both "the nations" and the "spirit of Belial" over Israel. On the connection of Gentiles and demons see also VanderKam, "Demons in the *Book of Jubilees*," 350–354.

[94] Nitzan, "The Penitential Prayer of Moses in *Jubilees* I."

Such parallels open the possibility that *Jubilees'* angelology and demonology has been constructed, not just from threads of pentateuchal, Enochic, and other literary traditions, but also from traditions about demons and angels current in the lived practice of its time. It does so, moreover, in a manner even more extensive than what we noted of the *Book of the Watchers* in Chapter 4. Nitzan notes, for instance, that a plea "to prevent ensnaring by evil spirits that tempt human beings to sin is expressed in *11QPlea for Deliverance* (11QPs[a] 19:13–17); in *4QAramaic Prayer of Levi* (4Q213a), and in apotropaic rabbinic prayers—e.g., *b. Berakhot* 16b."[95] Read in this context, Moses' prayer in *Jubilees* 1 emerges as a poignant reflection on the perceived power of demons to lead astray and the feelings of powerlessness thus invoked even in the most righteous of people. Even as *Jubilees* assures its readers/hearers that demons can actually hold no real power over righteous Jews,[96] it acknowledges and integrates the affective perspective of the human fear of demons.

The prayer of Moses is also notable due to its resonances with the prayers that *Jubilees* elsewhere attributes to Noah and Abraham. As with Moses' prayer, for instance, Noah's prayer in *Jubilees* 10 is predicated on the perceived danger of demons to humankind and is focused on an appeal to God for protection:

"God of the spirits which are in all animate beings—you who have shown kindness to me, saved me and my sons from the flood waters, and did not make me perish as you did to the people (meant for) destruction—because your mercy for me has been large and your kindness to me has been great: may your mercy be lifted over the children of your children; and may the wicked spirits (*manāfest 'ekuyan*) not rule them in order to destroy them from the earth. Now you bless me and my children so that we may increase, become numerous, and fill the earth. You know how your Watchers, the fathers of these spirits, have acted during my lifetime. As for these spirits who have remained alive, imprison them and hold them captive in the place of judgment. May they not cause destruction among your servant's sons, my God, for they are savage and were created for the purpose of destroying. May they not rule the spirits of the living for you alone know their punishment; and may they not have power over the sons of the righteous from now and forevermore." (*Jub* 10:3–6)

Here too, the fear expressed is that demons will "rule over" those under the petitioner's protection. Also parallel are the results of the two prayers: God responds by commanding angels to reveal heavenly truths that can

---

[95] Nitzan, "Penitential Prayer of Moses."
[96] Bonneau and Duhaime, "Angélologie et légitimation Socio-Religieuse."

be recorded in earthly books (1:27–29; 10:10–14). Furthermore, just as the angel elsewhere warns Moses that Israel will stray into wickedness after his death (6:38), so the account of Noah's petition is followed by a description of the deterioration of humankind after his death: consistent with *Jubilees'* emphasis on human responsibility, Noah's sons suffer at the hands of demons as a result of their own wayward deeds – and particularly their transgression of commandments concerning blood (11:2–6).

Prior to his migration to Canaan, Abraham is similarly described as praying for protection against demons:

"Save me from the power of the wicked spirits who rule the thoughts of people's minds. May they not mislead me from following you, my God, do establish me and my posterity forever. May we not go astray from now until eternity." (*Jub* 12:20; cf. 11:17)

Whereas Noah wished the whole earth to be rid of demons, however, Abraham's plea is framed only in terms of himself and his "posterity." Furthermore, with Abraham, Noah's prayer is finally answered. Noah pleaded for "mercy (to) be lifted over the children of your children" so that "wicked spirits not rule them" (10:3), and Abraham is presented as the progenitor and exemplar of the one line of Noah's children that did indeed free itself from demonic rule (15:32) – not least because of his own self-motivated choice to embrace righteousness (e.g., 12:19). As in the eschatology of *Jubilees* 23, the implication is that prayer alone does not suffice to save; righteous actions are necessary as well.

Noah expresses his fear that demonic rule over his children will result in their destruction "from the earth," and he stresses their destructive power and purpose. Abraham, by contrast, fears the demons because of their power to "rule the thoughts of people's minds" and "mislead me from following you, my God" (12:20). The true danger of demons – Abraham here recognizes – is not a capacity to do bodily harm, but rather the ability to sway the human mind (*lebb*). This shift proves particularly striking, for our purposes, in light of the similar concerns expressed in the prayer attributed to Moses. Moses, as noted above, is said to ask God to protect His people from "the error of their minds" and to create for them "a pure mind and a holy spirit (*lebb neṣuḥ wa-manfasa qeddusa*)." Elsewhere, it is suggested that neglect of Sabbath and embrace of idolatry are both results of "the error of the mind" (2:29; 12:3, 5; also 1:19; 22:18). And, just as Noah was chosen for salvation from the Flood because "his mind was righteous in all his ways" (5:19), so Abraham was able to infer the singular divine control of the cosmos because "a voice came to his mind" (12:17). As with the many references to the demonic power and purpose of leading humankind astray, such statements point to an understanding of demons consonant with *Jubilees'* overarching emphasis on human choice and responsibility: demons may be able to wreak physical harm on the wicked by fomenting illness, famine, and war, but for the righteous their only real danger lies in their capacity to mislead.

Alongside these prayers, *Jubilees* also includes testimonies and blessings purporting to reflect the human transmission of teachings from generation to generation on earth, in a line of oral transmission parallel to the line in which ancestral books are also passed.[97] The first instance of a lengthy inclusion of direct speech of this sort is Noah's testimony to his sons (7:20–39). Here, reference is made to Watchers and Giants, in keeping with Noah's claim to base his words on the teachings of Enoch (7:38–39; cf. 4:22). Consistent with narrative setting of this speech, as Noah's speech to his children after the Flood, the focus falls on its moral lessons. Noah here explains to his children that the Flood was caused by fornication, impurity, and injustice – all of which he sees as precipitated by the Watchers. According to Noah, these fallen angels were the first to commit acts of impurity, and their lust lead to the violence of the Giants and its spread to all of the earth's creatures (7:20–24). Noah also alludes to the powers of demons, blaming them for the strife among his progeny (7:26–27).

Abraham's testimony to his children and grandchildren in *Jub* 20:1–10 similarly speaks of the Watchers and Giants. These figures are again fodder for moral exhortation, and their punishment is a warning for humans who sin through lust. To these negative exemplars, he adds another from his own lifetime – namely, the Sodomites. The reader/hearer can thus glimpse what *Jubilees* exalts as the ideal dynamics of tradition: Enoch's testimony against the Watchers is the basis for Noah's testimony, which in turn is integrated with Abraham's own life experiences into his own testimony.

Angels and demons also feature in some of the patriarchal blessings that *Jubilees* purports to record. In Abraham's blessing of Jacob, for instance, we find a reference to demons that appears to reflect the equation between chosenness and freedom from demonic rule:

---

[97] Lambert, "Last Testaments."

"May the spirits of Mastema not rule over you and your descendants to remove you from following the Lord who is your God from now and forever. May the Lord God become your father and you his first-born son and people for all time ..." (*Jub* 19:28–29)

Here, demons are deemed dangerous because of their power to tempt the chosen away from the God who chose them. But when Abraham later blesses Jacob again, while on his death-bed (22:10–24), he focuses instead on demons' association with Gentiles:

"Separate yourself from the nations, and do not eat with them. Do not act as they do, and do not become their companion, for their actions are something that is impure, and all their ways are defiled and something abominable and detestable. They offer their sacrifices to the dead. And they worship demons [*wa-la-'agānent yesaggedu*]." (*Jub* 22:16–17)

As in Moses' prayer in *Jubilees* 1, Gentiles and demons are here associated with one another and with the temptation of Jews to sin. Whereas Moses prays to God to protect Israel from demons, Abraham calls upon his descendants to listen to his warning and avoid all contact with Gentiles.[98]

Isaac's blessing of Levi expresses the corollary connection of Israel with the angels:[99]

"And may the Lord give you and your descendants extremely great honor; may He make you and your descendants (alone) out of humanity approach Him to serve in His temple like the angels of the presence and as the holy ones. The descendants of your sons will be like them in honor, greatness, and holiness ..." (*Jub* 31:14)

The blessing goes on to outline priestly duties: Levi's sons will be "princes, judges, and leaders," and they will "declare the word of the Lord," tell the rest of Israel about God's ways, and mediate divine blessing (31:15). Here, priests take on the role of angels, not just by serving God (30:18), but also by teaching. Perhaps tellingly, Levi soon after learns – in a dream unmediated by any angel – that he and his sons "had been appointed and

---

[98] This theme recurs throughout *Jubilees*. The tales of patriarchs' conflicts with Esau (26:1–35; 37:1–38.24) and Shechemites (30), e.g., are far more prominent than in Genesis (e.g. Gen 27:1–41; 33:17–34:31). *Jubilees* even describes a battle between Jacob and Esau, for which the latter's sons enlist Moabites, Ammonites, Philistines, Hurrians, and Kittim (37:9–10). To these struggles are added a military conflict with Amorites (34:1–9).

[99] In an interesting interplay between heavenly and earthly knowledge, Isaac receives a "spirit of prophecy" (*Jub* 31:12) and speaks the blessing. The blessing is said to be recorded, with his blessing of Judah, "as an eternal testimony unto them on the heavenly tablets" (31:32). *Jubilees*, presumably, is claiming to record the angel reading the blessing to Moses, who then writes it down.

made into the priesthood of the most high God forever" (32:1). As noted above, moreover, the books of his forefathers pass to him so that he can "preserve them and renew them for his sons until this day" (45:16).

The treatment of Levi thus points to a notable pattern in *Jubilees'* account of human history, whereby the task of teaching becomes progressively transferred from angels to Israel. Although angels appear at certain critical moments in postdiluvian history (e.g., Aqedah, Exodus, Sinai), the transmission of knowledge is a task taken on, more and more, by men. The writings and teachings of Enoch, Noah, Abraham, and Jacob are presented as sources for oral and written teaching (e.g., 7:39; 21:10; 45:16), and these earthly teachings are increasingly cited as the basis for the ethical actions of individuals (e.g., 25:7; 39:6; 41:28). Even as *Jubilees* appeals to the authority of an angelic narrator, it evokes a human tradition of transmitting knowledge, both orally and in writing.[100] Just as Moses stands in a long tradition of scribes, so the reader/hearer of *Jubilees* is thus placed in a long line of recipients of angelic revelations transmitted by humans on earth.

DEMONOLOGY, ANGELOLOGY, AND THE PENTATEUCHAL PAST IN *JUBILEES*

As is well known, the "story" portions of *Jubilees* 2–48 have the same basic content and chronology as Genesis and the beginning of Exodus.[101] Accordingly, much research on *Jubilees* has focused on comparing its treatment of figures and events with the corresponding passages in the Torah/Pentateuch. This scholarly reading practice has yielded many insights, but it has also been so dominant that it has distracted from other questions about this complex and multifaceted work. My question, here, is whether and how these accounts of human history concord with the angelological and demonological principles noted above – or, in other words, whether and how *Jubilees'* description of angels and demons in the prehistory of Israel fits with what it theorizes as their functions and purpose, as seen from the perspective of heaven, and/or what it describes as their ramifications, as experienced by people on earth.

In the portions of the Torah/Pentateuch that correspond to the "story" of *Jubilees* (i.e., Genesis 1–Exodus 19), there is no explicit reference to

---

[100] Lambert, "Last Testaments."
[101] e.g., Endres, *Biblical Interpretation*; van Ruiten, *Primeval History*.

demons, and references to angels cluster in the tales about God's interventions in the lives of Abraham, his family, and his descendants (Gen 12–36).[102] In *Jubilees*, by contrast, angels are prominent in primeval history (cf. Gen 1–11). For instance, angels bring the animals to Adam so he can name them (3:1; cf. Gen 2:19). They are also credited with helping Noah bring creatures onto the ark (5:23). Angels lead Adam and Eve, and later Enoch, into Eden (3:9, 12; 4:23; cf. Gen 2:8, 15; *1 En* 28:1–32:6). In addition, angels are witnesses: God speaks to them about His decision to make a woman for Adam (3:4; cf. Gen 2:18); they are the audience for His decision to go down to earth to confound the languages of those who build the Tower of Babel (10:22–24; cf. Gen 11:6–7); they are present at the dividing of the earth between Noah's sons (8:10; cf. Gen 10). Their role as teachers of Enoch and Abraham, noted above, is prefigured by their teaching Adam how to tend the Garden of Eden (3:15; cf. Gen 2:15). Furthermore, and perhaps as an extension of their priestly role in heaven (30:18), it is the angels, not God, who here accept Abel's offering and reject that of Cain (4:2; cf. Gen 4:4–5).

In *Jubilees*, angels perform some tasks attributed to God in Genesis 1–11,[103] some tasks for which Genesis specifies no supernatural involvement, and some tasks that have no explicit counterparts in Genesis 1–11 but ample and extensive parallels in the *Astronomical Book* and the *Book of the Watchers*. The significance of these traditions in *Jubilees*, however, cannot be fully explained either in terms of Genesis or in terms of Enochic literature. The references to angels in *Jubilees*' account of primeval history resonate more with what we have seen of its angelological schema. In particular, the depiction of angels in primeval history serves to set the stage for *Jubilees*' treatment of Abraham and the origins of Israel. In this

---

[102] Kökert, "Divine Messengers," 56–72.

[103] Bonneau and Duhaime, "Angélologie et légitimation." At times, there appear to be exegetical "hooks" for these traditions in the text of Genesis. For instance, an angelic presence at the Tower of Babel can be inferred from the use of the first-person plural in Gen 11:7 ("Let us …"; van Ruiten, *Primeval History Interpreted*, 355). Inasmuch as *Jubilees* links the dispersion of the human with the loss of the Hebrew language (12:25), however, the inclusion of angels simultaneously proves fitting within the angelology of *Jubilees*: it seems apt that angels of the presence might be involved in this event inasmuch as one of their kind is later said to re-reveal knowledge of Hebrew in the time of Abraham (12:26). Likewise, even in cases where it might be tempting to dismiss the inclusion of angels as attempts to fill narrative lacunae left by Genesis, angels are marshaled in the service of *Jubilees*' own broader aims. The angelic instruction of Adam, e.g., functions to provide a precedent for their instruction of Enoch, Noah, Abraham, Jacob, and Moses – and, by extension, for the image of the angel of the presence.

sense, it is consistent with the functions of angels in the frame-narrative, angelic asides, and expository comments in the text: angels are here significant primarily due to their relationship with Israel, whether as heavenly counterparts to Israel's priests and worship, as revealers and authorizers of knowledge revealed to its holy men, or as witnesses to their deeds. Angelology, in other words, is not pursued for its own sake but rather as a means to articulate Israel's chosenness covenantal obligations, and cosmic status.

Demons are wholly absent from its account of primeval history, consistent with its claim – following the *Book of the Watchers* – that such spirits did not arise upon earth after the descent of the Watchers (10:1–5).[104] These fallen angels are mentioned on six occasions, spread over five chapters.[105] Perhaps not surprisingly, *Jubilees'* representation of fallen angels is tightly tied to its representation of angels in general. For instance, when the reader/hearer first learns of the Watchers, they are associated with teaching. Contrary to both Genesis (6:1) and the *Book of the Watchers* (*1 En* 6:1–3), *Jubilees* specifies that God sent them to earth (4:15; 5:6). It is thus able to specify the appointed task from which these angels later deviate – namely, to instruct humankind and encourage righteousness. Far from revealing divine laws to Israel and observing commandments like the other angels, however, the Watchers end up defiling themselves with human women (4:22; 7:21–25). And far from reciting future events from the heavenly tablets or revealing knowledge about celestial cycles that can lead to proper calendrical and festal observance, they instruct humankind in the practice of divining the future through "omens of the sun, moon, and stars and every heavenly sign" (8:3–4; cf. *1 En* 8:3). Fallen angels, in other words, are here depicted as inverting precisely what *Jubilees* has outlined as the pattern of proper

---

[104] VanderKam, "Demons in the Book of Jubilees," 340–341.

[105] I.e., (1) In the context of the genealogical notice about Jared's birth in *Jub* 4:15 (cf. *1 En* 6:6); (2) in the summary of Enoch's life and writings in 4:16–26; (3) in the third-person narrative account of the Flood in chapter 5 (cf. Gen 6:1–8:7), occurring directly after the genealogical notice about the birth of Noah's sons (4:33); (4) in the record of Noah's testimony to his grandsons of "all the ordinances and commands and all the judgments which he knew" in 7:20–39; (5) in the context of the genealogical notice about Kainan in 8:3, noting how he discovered inscriptions containing the Watchers' teachings about divination (cf. *1 En* 7:3; 8:1–3); (6) in the record of Noah's prayer to God in 10:3–6, right after the division of the earth between Noah's sons (9:1–13), which is the first time the reader/hearer learn of any connection between Giants and demons (cf. *1 En* 15:8–9). I discuss these traditions in more detail in Reed, "Enochic and Mosaic Traditions in *Jubilees*."

angelic practice, as known to the highest angels, as inscribed on heavenly tablets, and as mirrored on earth by proper Jewish practice.

To be sure, *Jubilees'* traditions about the fallen angels echo the traditions about the fallen angels found in the *Book of the Watchers*. Through its literary choices of selection and arrangement, however, the meanings of such traditions have been transformed, and the ramifications of angelic descent are blunted. Betsy Halpern Amaru has shown that the Watchers are mentioned in the text at times when irregularities occur in human genealogies.[106] The result is to present the Watchers and Giants as paradigmatic of the dangers of exogamy, drawing attention to human deviance from proper marriage practices in the primeval age and thus setting the stage for *Jubilees'* condemnation of intermarriage.

Similarly significant may be the choice to forestall any reference to the Watchers' teachings until after the account of the Flood – a choice that arguably serves to downplay their illicit instruction, possibly in reaction to the centrality of this tradition within the *Book of the Watchers'* aetiology of earthly evils.[107] Likewise, Hanneken has shown how this information is mentioned only when it becomes relevant; by virtue of the persistent connection between Gentiles and demons in *Jubilees*, demons only become a concern when distinct nations emerge, in the wake of the division of the earth between Noah's sons.[108]

Significantly, for our purposes, the account of angelic descent also occasions the introduction of further details about the function of angels more broadly. In *Jub* 5:3–11, we encounter the first reference to the angelic binding of other spirits (cf. 48.15, 18): when God wishes to uproot the Watchers, their heavenly brethren "tie them up in the depths of the earth" (5:6).[109] Consistent with the dissociation of otherworldly spirits from eschatological judgment in *Jubilees* 23, however, angels here function as agents of divine punishment only in a limited fashion: angelic

---

[106] Halpern Amaru, *The Empowerment of Women in the Book of Jubilees*, 20–28.

[107] Reed, *Fallen Angels*, 27–51, 89–95. I.e., the *Book of the Watchers* presents the Watchers' teachings as a direct cause of the antediluvian deterioration of human ethics (*1 En* 7:1; 8:1–3; 9.6), and it credits the teachings of Asael, in particular, with fostering promiscuity and bloodshed (8:1–2); Reed, "Heavenly Ascent."

[108] Hanneken, "Angels and Demons," 18.

[109] Compare the *Book of the Watchers*, where Sariel is commanded by God to save Noah (*1 En* 10:1–3; cf. God in *Jub* 5:5, 21–23); Raphael to bind Asael (10:4–8; cf. angels in *Jub* 5:6, 10); Gabriel to destroy the bodies of the Giants by fomenting war between them (10:9–10; cf. the sword in *Jub* 5:7–9); and Michael to bind Shemihazah and the others, destroy the souls of the Giants, and cleanse the earth of impurity (10:11–22).

violence is strictly limited to the binding of other angels and spirits (5:6; 10:7; 48:15, 18).

This subtle yet significant shift is perhaps consonant with *Jubilees'* major departure from the *Book of the Watchers* – that is, its assessment of the after-effects of the sins of the Watchers. *Jubilees'* account of angelic descent ends with the Flood, when God is said to have destroyed all the wicked and to have "made a new and righteous nature for all his creatures so that they would not sin with their whole nature until eternity" (5:12). This assertion is followed by an assertion of the inerrancy of divine justice and the proclamation of Yom Kippur as granted to Israel alone as a path to repentance (5:13–18). Rather than embracing the *Book of the Watchers'* view that angelic descent was the root cause of subsequent human sin, *Jubilees* goes even further than Genesis in depicting the post-diluvian age as a new beginning – almost wholly free of the taint of the antediluvian deeds of Watchers and Giants.

The delimited scope of the postdiluvian influence of the fallen angels is underlined by *Jubilees'* account of the origins of demons. As in the *Book of the Watchers* (*1 En* 15:8–9), it seems to be assumed that the spirits of the Giants remained on earth as demons, after their bodies were destroyed, and the account of angelic descent thus contributes to the aetiology of demons.[110] But, as noted above, the reader/hearer only learns of any connection between Watchers and demons when Noah entreats God for protection from the latter. When "impure demons" (*'agānent rekusān*) begin to mislead and destroy Noah's grandchildren (10:1), he prays to God that "the wicked spirits (*manāfest 'ekuyān*) not rule them in order to destroy them from the earth" (10:3), and he asks God to imprison all the demons in the same prison as their fathers (10:5). That the Watchers are the fathers of demons, however, is revealed precisely at the moment of the rectification of this after-effect of angelic sin. God agrees with Noah's proposal, and the angels promptly bind these spirits too (10:7).

To this seemingly neat solution, however, *Jubilees* then introduces a caveat, by means of the figure of Mastema.[111] This figure is identified first as the "angel/messenger of the spirits" (*mal'aka manāfest*; 10:8) and then

---

[110] VanderKam, "Demons in the Book of Jubilees," 349–350.

[111] On this figure, see Bernstein, "Angels at the Aqedah," 266–269; VanderKam, *Book of Jubilees*, 128–129; Hanneken, "Angels and Demons," 20–22. In 4Q225 2 i 8–10, we similarly find a reference to the intervention of this figure (there called שר המשטמה) in the Aqedah.

as "the *satan*" (10:11). The former title implies his affiliation with the angels (*malā'ekt*) who do God's bidding, while the latter suggests his specific role as a spirit appointed with the specific tasks of testing the righteous and punishing the wicked (cf. Job 1:6–12). Accordingly, Mastema comes to God with a counter-request: God should leave some of the demons unbound and put them under his rule (10:8). God agrees, allowing one-tenth of them to remain unbound (10:9). In effect, *Jubilees'* account of the origins of demons is paired with a detailed description of their demarcated role – as otherworldly spirits under the control of Mastema and consequently in service of divine will. As in the account of classes and domains of angels in *Jubilees* 2, the text here evokes an orderly and hierarchical system of transmundane powers in which even demons have clear-cut tasks and domains as well as an overseer who reports directly to God.

Lest the demons fight unfairly, God orders the angels to help Noah counteract them by revealing heavenly knowledge (10:10). As noted above, Noah thus receives medicinal teachings that he writes in a book (10:10–14). This revealed medicinal knowledge is said to have protected all of Noah's children from demonic harm during his lifetime. Upon his death, however, all of Noah's books are passed solely to Shem (10:14). The reader/hearer thus gets an initial glimpse at some of the mechanics of Israel's freedom from demonic rule: even before the reader/hearer has learned that Israel is ruled and guarded by God (15:32), we hear how the line of Shem has angelically mediated books that protect from demons.

Despite these books of medicine and despite the creation of a "new and righteous nature" for humankind, however, it is in the generations following the death of Noah that *Jubilees* describes demons as having the most influence on human life. Elements of this account echo the description of the earthly chaos in the wake of the Watcher's descent and the birth of the Giants (5:2–3). Strikingly, however, this account is notably more detailed – marked also by war, sickness, sin, idolatry, pollution, and divination. During these difficult years, people invented idolatry, under the influence of the demons who "were helping and misleading (them) so that they would commit sins, impurities, and transgressions" (11:4). Mastema and his spirits were able to rule all humankind:

Prince Mastema was exerting his power in effecting all these actions and, by means of the spirits, he was sending to those who were placed under his control (the ability) to commit every (kind of) error and sin and every (kind) of transgression; to corrupt, to destroy, and to shed blood upon the earth. (*Jub* 11:5)

Mastema even sends ravens to eat the seeds in their fields (11:11–13) – thereby suggesting an association of demons with famine as well.

The reader/hearer only later learns the reason: Enoch's testimony and Noah's protective knowledge were inaccessible during these years, due to the human loss of the Hebrew language (12:25–27). It seems, however, that the Watchers' divinatory teachings continued to be transmitted, inasmuch as Nahor learned from his father how "to practice divination and to augur by the signs of the skies" (11:9). Taken together, the spread of demonic control and the loss of revealed wisdom thus serves to set the stage for the righteousness of Abraham, who can thus be depicted – in stark contrast to his immediate predecessors and contemporaries – as turning to God without any external aid, even in the midst of a situation of degradation dominated by demons and Gentiles.

At the beginning of the account of Abraham's life, demons remain prominent, but angels are perhaps most notable for what they do not do. By this point in *Jubilees*, the pattern of angelic–human interaction is well established: angels reveal knowledge to righteous men who write books for their progeny. When Abraham is first introduced, however, it is stressed that he recognizes the errors of his time by himself (11:16–17) – even as a child and even apart from any ancient book or angelic revelation. Abraham thus arises as the first example of the power of God's purification of the human spirit into a "new and righteous nature" (5:12). His capacity for resisting demons, for instance, is suggested by his act of driving away the ravens sent by Mastema (11:18–22).[112] Whereas Enoch, Noah, and Moses are said to teach others what the angels had taught them or their ancestors, Abraham is able to know and teach apart from any contact with angels or heavenly knowledge. On his own, he infers the errors of idolatry (12:1–5, 12), the witness of celestial and meteorological cycles to the oneness of God (12:16–18), and the influence of demons on the minds of his contemporaries (12:20).

It is as a result that Abraham prays to God to save him from the demons and to choose him and his progeny for special protection against them (12:19–20); in effect, he is said to have chosen God (12:19) and to have prayed, in turn, to be chosen by Him. Whereas the angels were

---

[112] In this regard, the agricultural context and contents of Abraham's teaching proves particularly suggestive, evoking what *Jubilees* presents as the very first occasion of angelic instruction in human history – namely, their instruction of Adam concerning how to tend the Garden of Eden and guard it from birds and animals (on which see below).

created to serve God (2:2), Abraham is here depicted as deciding to do so. Above, we noted how *Jubilees* characterizes the heavenly perspective on chosenness whereby God chose Israel with angels and spirits as witnesses (2:19). In its account of Abraham's life, the reader/hearer gets the other side of the story – the tale of the earthly actualization of this chosenness, when Israel's forefather chose God, on his own accord, apart from any angelic influence and in bold resistance to the demonic influence all around him.

Interestingly, it is at this point in the "story" of *Jubilees* that the angelic narrator first takes part in human history.[113] The angel of the presence delivers a "word of the Lord" to Abraham telling him to leave his homeland and promising to make him a great people (12:22–24).[114] The angel then teaches Abraham how to speak Hebrew, the "revealed language" and the "language of creation" (12:25–26). Here again, angels are characterized as teachers of humankind, and their teachings are associated with books. In case of Abraham, however, the knowledge that they teach serves mainly to confirm, supplement, and extend what he has already figured out on his own. Abraham is presented as paradigmatic of the possibility that humankind can transcend demonic deception and the corruption of foreign cultures to find their way back to God and righteousness – even apart from angelic teaching or divine intervention. As in the eschatological scenario outlined in *Jubilees* 23, human agency is here depicted as precipitating divine aid and blessing.

In the rest of *Jubilees'* account of patriarchal history, angels take on variations of the same roles granted to them in Genesis 12–50. Most notably, they deliver divine messages and save the righteous from destruction. Hence, for instance, angels come to Abraham to announce the birth of Isaac (16:1–3; cf. Gen 18:1–15), and they save Lot (16:7; cf. Gen 19:15–22). In *Jubilees*, however, they also a visit to Sarah to announce Isaac's future deeds and fate (16:15–19; cf. Gen 18:10). Significantly, for our purposes, this visit provides an occasion to make explicit the non-chosen status of the rest of Abraham's progeny and to stress that only the children of Isaac will become "a kingdom and priests and a holy nation"

---

[113] Dimant, "Sons of Heaven," 107

[114] This angel, in other words, plays the role of revealer taken by God in Gen 12:1–9. Here too, deeds attributed to God in Genesis are attributed to angels in *Jubilees*. Perhaps the most striking example is 14:20, where angels are said to have made the covenants with Noah and Abraham.

(16:18–19).[115] For instance, when Abraham then celebrates the first Sukkot (16:20–22), it is stressed that no Gentiles were present (16:25), and angels are described as blessing him for his piety (16:28).

Above, we noted how demons are often mentioned in the prayers and testimonies of patriarchs. Interestingly, however, these spirits play little role in the "story" of the lives about Abraham, Isaac, and Jacob. The one major exception to this pattern is the inclusion of Mastema in *Jubilees'* account of the binding of Isaac (17:16–18:16; cf. Gen 22). *Jubilees* presents the Aqedah as part of a broader divine project whereby God "tested him (*'amakkaro*)" so as to prove him faithful (*mahāymen*) (17:7–18), including with the aid of angels (19:3). In the case of the Aqedah, Mastema proposes the test, and he is in conflict with the angel of the presence, who ultimately stays Abraham's hand (cf. Gen 22:11–12). Even as *Jubilees'* version of the Aqedah integrates the tropes of angelic accusation of humankind and angelic–demonic conflict that become common in later Rabbinic midrashim,[116] the text thus subordinates these themes to its overarching conceptualization of spirits as only capable of acting in accordance with God's will. In the end, the emphasis falls, once again, on Mastema's role as an agent of divine justice who acts against humankind only with divine permission (10:8–9).

When the "story" of *Jubilees* turns to Jacob and his sons, demons are absent, and angels appear only in dreams. Jacob dreams that he sees angels ascending and descending on a ladder (27:21), but the angels here are no more prominent than in Gen 28:10–15. When *Jubilees* describes Jacob's return to Bethel, however, it credits him with the "vision of the night" discussed above (32:21–24). Accordingly, the angel is here associated with a function already familiar from *Jubilees'* accounts of Enoch, Noah, Abraham, and Moses: he mediates revelations of heavenly knowledge to a man in the chosen line, who writes them down in books. The only new element is the means through which this mediation takes place – namely, through dreams.[117]

---

[115] In *Jub* 17:11–12, one of the holy angels is said to have appeared to Hagar when she was banished from Abraham's house. Here, *Jubilees'* account follows Gen 21:17–18 closely. Yet, consistent with its elevation of Isaac over Ishmael, relatively little emphasis is placed on this angelophany. Furthermore, it is specified that the angel who appears to Hagar is one of the second class of angels, rather than the angel of the presence. See further VanderKam, "Angel of the Presence," 389–390.

[116] Bernstein, "Angels at the Aqedah."

[117] For the ample Aramaic precedents, Perrin, *Dynamics of Dream-Vision*.

At first sight, it might seem that human contact with the divine is depicted as progressively more mediated in *Jubilees*. After all, God speaks directly with humans before Flood, but thereafter he increasingly sends angelic messengers, first in form and later in dreams.[118] But another interpretation is also possible: inasmuch as Israel is not ruled by either angels or demons (15:32), its historical emergence – with Abraham, Isaac, Jacob, and his twelve sons – is accompanied by a decline in the significance of spirits. Consistent with the association of Israel with angels, for instance, Abraham and the chosen line progressively take on the roles earlier served by angels, such as observing festivals, writing and delivering testimonies, officiating as priests, and revealing the truths that they learned from their forefathers' books. There is a shift away from the angelic micromanagement of human affairs in the primordial age, and this shift may thus be positive in valence, serving to convey the increasing independence of the chosen line of humankind and their developing capacity to take on angelic roles (e.g., witnesses, teachers, priests). If so, revelatory dreams may not communicate divine distance as much as exemplifying the internalization of the mechanisms of revelation within the "minds" (*'albāb*) and "spirits" (*manāfest*) of righteous men.

Consistent with *Jubilees'* depiction of demonic rule on earth as only effective over Gentile nations, moreover, the period in which the patriarchs dwell in the Land of Israel is an age relatively free from demonic influence. Mastema may foment bloodshed, idolatry, and famine in Chaldea. After Abraham's migration, however, his actions against him are strictly limited to those of a *satan*.

The connection between Gentile rulership and demonic influence is even clearer in the case of Joseph. When this patriarch ruled Egypt (40:6), it is stressed that "there was no *satan* and no evil" (40:9; 46:2) – a situation akin to what is promised of the eschatological future. After Joseph's death, however, demons are depicted as returning to prominence in Egypt. Most notably, a "prince of Mastema"[119] here features in the account of Israel's servitude in Egypt and deliverance by God (46:11–48:19; cf. Exodus 2–14). Consistent with *Jubilees'* principle that Gentile nations are ruled by spirits (15:31), this demon is depicted as motivated by the desire to protect the Egyptians, the people over whom he

---

[118] Dimant, "Sons of Heaven," 106.
[119] On the title here rendered "prince of Mastema" see VanderKam, *The Book of Jubilees*, 128. Note that the name may well be interchangeable with "Mastema" and/or bear the literal sense of "the prince of animosity."

rules (48:3–4). The angel of the presence tells Moses, for instance, that when he was returning to Egypt from Sinai (48:2–4; cf. Horeb in Exodus 3–4), it was the demon who tried to kill him and the angel who saved him (cf. the Lord and Zipporah in Exodus 4:24–25). Likewise, the military conflict between Israel and Egypt (48:12–13; cf. Num 20:16) is here told in part as a struggle between angels and demons.[120] Demonic influence is also cited to explain how Egyptian magicians were able to replicate some of the signs and wonders attributed in the Torah/Pentateuch to Aaron and Moses (cf. Exod 7:11–12, 22; 8:3) and in *Jubilees* to Moses alone.[121]

Nevertheless, demonic subservience to God remains emphasized throughout. When the "prince of Mastema ... hardens their hearts" (cf. Exod 14:8), it is following a divine plan (48:17–18). And when the time comes for the Passover, the first-born sons of Egypt are killed by "all the forces of Mastema" (49:2; cf. "the destroyer" in Exod 12:23). In the end, moreover, what is emphasized is how God Himself intervenes to act on the behalf of Israel: He parts the sea, lets His chosen people flee, and casts the Egyptian armies into the river (48:13–14).

CONCLUSION

In its depiction of its own origins-as-text, *Jubilees* evokes a paradigmatically scribal setting – the dictation of the angel of the presence to Moses. In this sense, its authorizing strategies stand in notable continuity with the angelification of Jewish scribal pedagogy inaugurated in the *Astronomical Book*. Whereas biblical literature effaces the agency of scribes (and modern scholars sometimes similarly dismiss their role as if merely cogs in the machine of rote reproduction),[122] *Jubilees* follows the precedent of the Aramaic Jewish literature of the early Hellenistic age in elevating the mundane cycles of scribal life to the status of the revelatory, not least by mapping them onto the imagination of heaven and its angels. Practices of copying, reading, and writing books are here placed at the very heart of the transmission and preservation of cosmic truths, on earth, in heaven, and between them. By focusing on the moment that speech becomes writing,

---

[120] In addition, angels repeatedly bind the demon so he cannot accuse the Israelites, then release him again so he inspires the Egyptians to pursue the Jews (*Jub* 48:15–18).

[121] Interestingly, it is stressed that the angels permit these spells to work – albeit only to a degree (*Jub* 48:9–11; cf. Exod 8:4, 14–15).

[122] Contrast also the denigration of the copyist in Greco-Roman culture; Haines-Eitzen, *Guardians of Letters*, 17, 53–55.

however, *Jubilees* shifts the focus from scribal expertise and the power of sight, to the vitality of reading as speech act and the power of writing for ensuring remembrance.[123] The angelic narrator in *Jubilees* functions less to elevate Jewish scribalism or to inaugurate Jewish angelology than to authorize a work in which the power of writing, elevation of scribes, and the cosmological significance of angels are assumed throughout – and put to the use of articulating a new vision of Israel as a whole.

Central, in this regard, is perhaps its most striking departure from the Enochic and other Aramaic writings surveyed above – that is: a preoccupation with Jewish/Gentile difference. "*Jubilees*," as Hanneken shows, "maintains a radical agenda of separation from the Gentiles," and this agenda shapes its halakha, exegesis, and historiography but also its angelology and demonology.[124] To be sure, this concern too finds some precedent in Aramaic Dead Sea Scrolls; Daniel Machiela notes the recurrence therein of "challenging scenarios in which the protagonists face the temptation of embracing foreign impiety," as exemplified by Qahat's insistence in the *Admonitions to Qahat* that his sons should be careful "not to give your inheritance to foreigners ... for they will treat you with disdain ... and be your rulers."[125] *Jubilees* goes even further, dramatically retheorizing Jewish/Gentile difference in cosmological, angelological, and demonological terms.

Whereas the *Astronomical Book* and other pre-Maccabean Aramaic Jewish writings appeal to angels, demons, and writing to defend the relevance of the knowledge of the Near Eastern scribe in the wake of the rise of new Hellenistic empires, *Jubilees* puts much of what it takes from Aramaic Jewish scribal pedagogy to the use of asserting the exemplarity of Israel and its contrast with all other nations. In its intensification of concern for the separation of Jews from others, it fits well with what we know about the shifts in the articulation of Jewishness during and after the Maccabean Revolt as well as the renewed significance of the Hebrew language and Torah/Pentateuch for expressing it.[126] Accordingly, it makes sense that *Jubilees* might abandon the cosmopolitanism of the earlier Aramaic Jewish scribal pedagogy on which it otherwise so heavily draws – including the very use of Aramaic.

---

[123] Cf. the notion of inspired dictation in Jaffee, *Torah in the Mouth*, 26
[124] Hanneken, "The Sin of the Gentiles," 1.
[125] Machiela, "Situating the Aramaic Texts," 94–97.
[126] Cohen, *Beginnings of Jewishness*; Collins, "Transformation of Torah"; Schwartz, "Language, Power."

Even as *Jubilees* embraces the *Book of the Watchers'* expansion of Jewish scribal expertise to encompass demonology, for instance, it puts this expertise newly to the purpose of theorizing Jewish/Gentile difference. Much of *Jubilees'* treatment of fallen angels and demons finds precedent in the *Book of the Watchers* – including in its understanding of the origins of demons from the spirits of the Giants (15:8–9). But whereas the *Book of the Watchers* presents the demonic terrorization of humankind as definitive of postdiluvian history, *Jubilees* emphasizes that they are part of God's plan, subordinated to the *satan* Mastema and assigned the task of ruling over non-Jewish nations. In some of the prayers that *Jubilees* attributes to Israel's ancestors, one finds a poignant awareness of the powerless that some of its readers/hearers might feel in the face of demonic power. Lest anyone imagine Mastema and his demons as the dark side of a cosmic dualism and/or as evil forces outside of divine control, however, *Jubilees* emphasizes that "there is no injustice" (5:13). Demons may cause suffering, but their actions are part of an unerringly fair system of divine justice that encompasses everything "in heaven or on the earth, in the light, the darkness, Sheol, the deep, or in the dark place" (5:14).

Even as the power granted to demons is diminished in *Jubilees*, however, demonization is dramatically expanded. As we have seen, *Jubilees* parallels demons and Gentiles to an unprecedented degree.[127] Demons are depicted as the objects of Gentile worship (1:11; 11:4), and they are also the rulers of these nations (15:31; 48) and the forces behind the efficacy of their "magic" (48:9–11). When Israel and its ancestors live under foreign rule (e.g., 1:20; 11:18–22; 48), they are said to be affected by the strife, bloodshed, famine, and disease that demons cause. Conversely, when Israel's enemies will be finally destroyed from the earth, demonic influence will disappear – in a manner akin to when Joseph ruled Egypt (23:29; 40:9; 46:2; 50:5). After all, according to *Jubilees*, demons ultimately have no control over Jews (15:32). Foreign nations may be ruled by demons, but they are not forces of independent evil; all nations belong to God, who rules directly over his chosen Israel (15:31). Consistent with the Deuteronomistic principle and its expansion in biblical prophecy, then, the nations can overtake Israel only when God commands – and so too with demons (e.g., 1:13; 23:23).

This emphasis on Jewish exemplarity also shapes *Jubilees'* angelology, wherein the scribalization of angels and the angelification of scribes in

---

[127] VanderKam, "Demons in the Book of Jubilees," 353–354.

Aramaic Jewish scribal pedagogy is repurposed to elevate all Israel as a nation like unto the angels. Angels are granted features akin to scribes and priests but also characteristics that parallel what sets Israel, as a whole, apart from other peoples (e.g., circumcision; Sabbath; festivals; 2:17–21; 15:27). In a manner presaging Rabbinic treatments of the rivalry of angels and humankind,[128] moreover, *Jubilees* presents angels as ultimately inferior to Israel inasmuch as they do not serve God by choice (cf. 12:19) and insofar as they have no path to atonement if they sin (cf. 5:17). And, as we have seen, their significance thus diminishes after Abraham and Jacob, as their roles as teachers, etc., increasingly shifts to Israel. As much as *Jubilees* brims with details about angels, it ultimately places them outside of God's special relationship to Israel, as evident both in His direct rule of the one nation (15:32) and in His sole involvement in their eschatological punishment and redemption (23:30–31).

It is perhaps not coincidental that *Jubilees'* extension and transformation of the angelology and demonology of earlier Aramaic Jewish literature that find parallels in Rabbinic and other later Jewish literature. Not only does *Jubilees* lay the groundwork for the harmonization of its angelology and demonology with understandings of Israel and the pre-Sinaitic past in the Torah/Pentateuch, but it also undercuts the scholasticism of the Aramaic Jewish scribal pedagogy of the early Hellenistic age in a manner that facilitates the broader diffusion of its angelological, demonological, and other innovations. Here too, angels are associated with books and teaching, and they are used to assert the ancient heritage of Jewish knowledge as a textual heritage encompassing cosmology, astronomy, demonology, medicine, eschatology, and the theorization of writing. But the association of angels and knowledge is also put to the purpose of commenting on halakhic issues central to Exodus and Leviticus, like ritual and festal practice, and on themes especially prominent in Deuteronomy, such as the meanings of the chosenness of Israel and the differences between Israel and other nations. In the process, the scribalized image of the pre-Sinaitic past in the Aramaic Jewish literature of the early Hellenistic age is recast with an eye to the *telos* of the chosenness of Israel, extending the angel-like profile and prerogatives of scribes more broadly to Israel as a whole.

Far from elevating only the Jewish scribe, *Jubilees* depicts all Israel as pure and unified – so much so, in fact, the sins of individuals can defile the

[128] Schäfer, *Rivalität*.

whole. The only Jews whom it actively excludes from the bounds of Israel, in fact, are those who exclude themselves by choosing to abandon the marks of Jewish distinctiveness (e.g., circumcision, Sabbath, endogamy). Like angels who stayed too long on earth, some of the author's contemporaries may have found themselves tempted to join non-Jews in meals, marriage, festivals, and friendship (cf. 1 Macc 1:11–15). To them, *Jubilees* reveals the cosmic ramifications of such seemingly mundane acts: to follow "the ways of the nations" is to trade away the status of angels for the rule of demons. Speaking from a heavenly perspective, its angelic narrator argues that when Jews adopt foreign worship and festivals, marry Gentiles, or refrain from circumcising their sons, they are committing sins with dire consequences: they are aligning themselves with Gentiles, thereby placing themselves under the rule of demons, dooming their children to destruction, and exempting themselves and their children from the special angel-like status granted to Israel alone.[129]

To be sure, *Jubilees* does not so much jettison this pre-Maccabean Aramaic Jewish heritage of scribalism as much as recast it with an eye to new concerns – including some concerns that we see across Seleucid-era materials, such as an interest in history, calendar, and the numericalization of time, and some concerns that we see in other post-Maccabean Jewish sources, such as an interest in halakhic exegesis, Hebrew language, and the theorization of Jewish/Gentile difference. In its reception and transformation of the Aramaic Jewish literature of the early Hellenistic age, we thus see patterns in *Jubilees* that mirror what we see within Seleucid- and Maccabean-era apocalypses as well as in the literature of the Qumran community that continued to cultivate this corpus.[130] What is no less significant, but especially salient in *Jubilees*, is the reordering of

---

[129] *Jubilees'* zealous warnings against the abandonment of Sabbath-observance (2:25–27; 50:8–9, 12–13), circumcision (15:14, 25–26, 33–34), and endogamy (22:20–21; 30:10–16, 22) further suggests that its special concern for Jews who were tempted to abandon the practices that most differentiated them from non-Jews. In the case of circumcision, the uncircumcised son of Jews is no longer part of Israel; he automatically belongs to Belial and is counted among the nations. In the case of intermarriage, the perpetrators must similarly be excluded from Israel (30:10), lest the entire nation be polluted and suffer (30:15); what was holy seed, after all, has been defiled and now belongs to Moloch. Likewise, following the logic of *Jubilees'* purity regulations (Himmelfarb, *Kingdom of Priests*, 61–72), intermarriage threatens all of Israel and defiles the Land and sanctuary.

[130] These continuities have been much discussed in relation to the influence of the *Book of the Watchers* in particular; see Davidson, *Angels at Qumran*; Reed, *Fallen Angels*; Alexander, "Contextualizing the Demonology."

the received knowledge from this corpus into a new form that claims to speak to and about all Israel. On the one hand, the result is a model for rendering their above-noted innovations in textuality, angelology, and demonology potentially relevant not just to scribes but to Jews more generally. But, on the other hand, its very integration of elements thereof into the broader Jewish tradition signals the obsolescence of this tradition of Aramaic literary production – at least as a cosmopolitan mode of Jewish scholasticism.

To the degree its Hebrew "translation" of elements of Aramaic Jewish scribal pedagogy marks a moment in the decline of a scholastic tradition with a distinct scribal culture, corpus, and archive, moreover, *Jubilees* rewrites its remembrance for posterity as an imagined library – projected far back into the past and up into the heavens. It is this "imagined library," as Mroczek shows, that *Jubilees* asserts as emblematic of its claim that "God has been communicating with Israel in writing since the beginning of the world and continuously through the ages."[131] In this sense, she suggests that its claims can be placed in counterpoint and conversation with the claims made for the Library of Alexandria to have collected "all the books in the known world" (*Ep.Ar.* 9).[132] If so, the ramifications are striking. Even as *Jubilees* marks a turn away from the cosmopolitanism of earlier Aramaic Jewish pedagogy to a localism focusing on Israel, it does so in a manner that resonates no less with the translocal Hellenistic-era trends that we noted in Chapters 3 and 4.

Mroczek proposes that "one of the many kinds of work that *Jubilees* does is the work of bibliography – listing and describing all the written texts that might be relevant to the author's subject matter," and "it seems that one of this author's goals is to gather, put in order, and describe all the written texts he knows, has heard of, or imagines must have once existed."[133] In this sense, we might parallel its project in part to that of Callimachus' *Pinakes*, which we noted in the previous chapter. To the degree that *Jubilees* evokes an "imagined library," its very act of imagining can also be likened to the Greek discourse surrounding the Library of Alexandria – the influence of which, as Roger Bagnall has stressed, lay just as much in its sway on the imagination than in the actual scope and

---

[131] Mroczek, *Literary Imagination*, 143, 155. I.e., "far from presuming or asserting any closed "canon" or delimited "Bible," what *Jubilees* evokes is a "bibliographically enchanted world … full of writing that proves God's constant, multiform, and renewing communication."

[132] Mroczek, *Literary Imagination*, 114–115.   [133] Mroczek, *Literary Imagination*, 143.

collection of its textual collection.[134] Perhaps even more so than the *Astronomical Book*, *Book of the Watchers*, and proto-testamentary materials among the Aramaic Dead Sea Scrolls, *Jubilees* matches such Hellenistic claims with Jewish counter-claims. Seen from this perspective, moreover, it can be set in the context of what Steve Johnstone calls the "decentralized revolution happening from Athens to Babylon and in many places in between" in the second century BCE, that resulted in the "invention of the library" as a new cross-cultural emblem of prestige across the Mediterranean world.[135] Even as *Jubilees* abandons one emblem of cosmopolitanism – that is, the Aramaic language – it thus adopts and extends another, drawing upon this earlier archive of textualized knowledge to mount a claim that Israel possesses, not only the oldest library of all, but also unique access to the archive in heaven above, written and read by the angels.

[134] Bagnall, "Alexandria: Library of Dreams."
[135] Johnstone, "New History of Libraries," 349 – there noting, e.g., how despite the conventional focus on more famous cases like the Library of Alexandria, what is perhaps more striking is how "aristocrats and monarchs across the Greek world began to found and fund libraries as part of the politics of elite benefaction, euergetism," during the second century BCE in particular.

Conclusion

Whether or not Peter Berger is correct to suggest that those who believe in demons and angels make up the "cognitive minority" in today's secular societies, it is certainly the case that angelology and demonology have been marginalized from the settings that have most shaped modern Western scholarship.[1] Partly as a result, even historians of religion tend to assume that any "real" interest in demons must have been popular or sectarian, rather than elite or mainstream, and that any literary claim to commerce with angels must signal a work's allegorical, esoteric, or mystical character. When confronted with premodern references to angels and demons by learned elites, it is common to presume that they must be symbols or ciphers for something else.

Bruce Lincoln, however, reminds us of the deleterious effects of these anachronistic assumptions and the scholarly reading-practices that they engender:

---

[1] Berger, *Rumor of Angels*, 2. According to recent polls (e.g., http://www.pewforum.org/2008/06/01/u-s-religious-landscape-survey-religious-beliefs-and-practices/), many Americans admit some degree of agreement with the statement that "angels and demons are active in the world." For our purposes, however, it is significant that such belief tends to be compartmentalized from scientific and other rationalizing discourses about nature and/or to flourish in explicit resistance to them; it is in this sense that Berger may be correct. Among the challenges of trying to comprehend ancient perspectives, then, is not just understanding this or that ancient text but also grappling with their formation from within different notions of what even counts as *knowledge* – prior to, and problematizing, the post-Enlightenment bifurcation of "natural" and "supernatural" that has been central within contemporary academic discourse in particular. See further Reed, "Knowing our Demons."

For all that demonology was a major part of many theological systems, the topic has received relatively little serious attention. The claims made by demonological discourse having been conclusively discredited in the European Enlightenment, it is as if the topic had been drained of all but antiquarian interest. While mild curiosity about the benighted beliefs of distant others may still be permitted, until recently most research remained distanced, condescending, and superficial... As the result of such skittishness, our understanding of many religions is impoverished, for some of the most serious issues of ethics, cosmology, anthropology, and soteriology were – and still are – regularly engaged via demonology. Though we may now reject the foundational assumptions of that discourse, this does not force the conclusion that beliefs about demons were of necessity naïve, ridiculous, or infantile. As a working hypothesis, it seems preferable to assume that the demonological components of any religion are no less intelligent, complex, or profound.[2]

Lincoln makes this point using examples from pre-Islamic Persia, wherein demonology could "stretch ... into physics, metaphysics, cosmology, and ontology" and even "constitute something like a unified field theory of what we treat separately under the rubrics of bacteriology, epidemiology, toxicology, teratology, criminology, Marxism, psychoanalysis, and others."[3]

In this book, I have proposed that angelology and demonology are no less informative for understanding Second Temple Judaism. The angels and demons of ancient Jewish literature often cross the lines of what modern thinkers often distinguish as "natural" and "supernatural," on the one hand, and "religious," "scientific," and "magical," on the other. And especially at its inception, the practice of Jewish angelology and demonology functioned as a knowledge-practice akin to – and closely connected with – cosmology and astronomy no less than theology.

Traditionally, the tale of the beginnings of Jewish angelology and demonology has been told either as a footnote to the origins of apocalyptic literature or as part of a supposed trajectory of "post-exilic" theological decline.[4] A different picture emerges, however, when we take angelology and demonology seriously and attend to their specific forms and functions within the earliest known Jewish texts that systematically textualize knowledge about transmundane powers. When explicit and extensive writing about angels and demons emerges within Judaism, it is as a means to order Jewish knowledge, model scribal expertise, and theorize textuality and cosmology alike. For this, moreover, the timing is telling – and thus well worth situating, not just

---

[2] Lincoln, "Cesmag, the Lie," 45.   [3] Lincoln, *Gods and Demons*, 31.
[4] Dimant, "Qumran Aramaic Texts," 197–198.

in relation to sweeping generalizations about "post-exilic" trends, but rather in relation what else we know of scribalism, textuality, cosmology, and the ordering of knowledge in the early Hellenistic age, both within and beyond Judaism.

Some connection between an increased interest in angels and the textualization of revelation can be glimpsed already in late biblical prophecy.[5] Both, however, develop dramatically around the third century BCE, alongside a new concern for demons. Enochic and other Aramaic sources from the time are marked by a striking self-consciousness about their own status as textual deposits of information about seen and unseen world, and much of what they claim to preserve in writing concerns what angels spoke, taught, and read – sometimes directly from heavenly books. Through reflections on fallen angels and the disembodied spirits of their sons, such sources also contribute to what David Frankfurter describes as "demonology's efflorescence" across the diverse cultures of the Mediterranean world in the periods of Hellenistic and Roman rule. And, here as elsewhere, the impulse to order and systemize "magical" and other local traditions about unseen forces is predicated on an understanding of "writing, as a technology allowing both abstraction from local experience and the magical force of the inscribed name."[6]

To consider the emergence of systematic reflection on transmundane powers in the Jewish literature of the early Hellenistic age, then, is also to recover something of the process by which the scope and forms of Jewish writing were radically expanded, concurrent with an elevation of scribalism perhaps unparalleled within Judaism before or after. The third century BCE, as we have seen, was marked by a remarkable efflorescence of Jewish literary production in Aramaic, newly embracing a number of topics downplayed or neglected in earlier biblical literature (e.g., angels, demons, astronomy, calendar, cosmology, protology, eschatology, the afterlife, heavenly ascent). Such topics were addressed, moreover, through experimentation with new literary forms, including but not limited to those that would come to coalesce into new Second Temple genres like the apocalypse and the testament. Contemporaneous Jewish literature penned in Greek similarly attests the adoption and adaptation of elements of Hellenistic literary genres – ranging from epic poetry to novelistic

---

[5] Davis, *Swallowing the Scroll*; Schaper, "Death of the Prophet"; Himmelfarb, *Ascent to Heaven*, 99–102; Najman, "Symbolic Significance."
[6] Frankfurter, *Evil Incarnate*, 19–21.

romance.[7] And in both Aramaic and Greek Jewish literature from the early Hellenistic age, one finds a newly self-conscious textuality, marked by the negotiation of older anonymous and collective modes of ancient Israelite and Near Eastern textual production with Greek notions of "authorship."

The adoption of Greek, of course, makes sense. But why would Jewish scribes in the Hellenistic period choose to write in Aramaic? Above, we have explored this question from several avenues, considering this choice as an example of the reordering of local and imperial knowledge in the Hellenistic Near East and as a sort of subversive counter-*paideia* invoking the cosmopolitanism of pre-Hellenistic Near Eastern scribalism. In addition, however, we might add that the Hellenistic-era corpus of Aramaic Jewish literature preserves something of the earlier importance of Aramaic – as a translocal, imperial, and globalizing language that did indeed rival the later spread of Greek.[8]

Across the Near East during the first millennium BCE, countless scribes were trained in the use of Aramaic. Under the Assyrian and Achaemenid empires, Aramaic served as the primary administrative language, and its spoken and written use continued into the Hellenistic period and long afterwards, both in and beyond the Near East. Seen from this perspective, what is surprising is not that some Jewish scribes chose to write in Aramaic. It is that we have so few surviving other examples. As much can be said of ancient libraries and collections of cuneiform and Greek literature – as Alan Millard notes – the investigation of their Aramaic counterparts concerns "what does not exist as much as what does":

Archives of Aramaic documents from the ninth to fourth centuries BCE are few and some of them very meagre ... The geographical span is large, from Iran to Egypt, and so much of the material comes from bilingual or polyglot societies. In fact, there are no indigenous Aramaic archives.[9]

---

[7] E.g., as evinced by the fragments of Greek Jewish writings preserved via Alexander Polyhistor, including Pseudo-Eupolemus, examined above, but also Ezekiel the Tragedian, Theodotus, and Philo the Epic Poet; Gruen, *Heritage and Hellenism*, 120–135. In relation to Hebrew as well as Aramaic and Greek sources, Wills posits a flourishing of a "novelistic impulse" concurrent with an increase in literacy in the Hellenistic age, which spurred efforts to give written expression to oral tales (e.g., Daniel, Tobit, Esther, Judith), and he proposes that the second century BCE was a critical moment for this development in Jewish literary culture in particular; *Jewish Novel in the Ancient World*, 4–10.

[8] Sanders, *From Adapa*; Machiela, "Situating the Aramaic Texts," 100.

[9] Millard, "Assyrian and Achaemenid Documents in Aramaic," 230.

The Aramaic tablets in the Fortification Archive in Persepolis, the *bullae* that mark the loss of perishable writing materials in Turkey and the Levant, the papyri and ostraca from Egyptian Jewish and Aramean settlements in Elephantine and Aswan, the scattered remnants of Aramaic epistolography preserved in hoards of papyri and in excerpts as in Ezra – "these are humble relics of an extensive bureaucracy devouring metres of papyrus monthly, all now lost."[10] The recovery of a corpus of Aramaic Jewish literature from the early Hellenistic age is thus highly consequential. It has much to tell us about Judaism, as we have seen above. But it may also have something to tell us about the *Nachleben* of the lost worlds of those whom Seth Sanders calls "Aramaic parchment scribes" in the wake of the fall of the Achaemenid empire to Alexander.[11]

In this book, I have drawn upon the Aramaic Dead Sea Scrolls to illumine the beginnings of Jewish angelology and demonology. Critical, in this regard, has been the integration of these new data into our understanding of previously known works, such as the writings now collected in *1 Enoch*; not only do the Dead Sea Scrolls include manuscripts witnessing the Aramaic forms of early Enochic literature, prior to their translation into Greek and Geʿez, but they also preserve fragments of what we now know to be the larger corpus of Aramaic Jewish sources to which they belong.[12] There is much to be done to understand these materials and to integrate them more fully into our understanding of ancient Jewish history and literature, but I hope that this book has contributed to that broader endeavor – at the very least by signaling some of what is at stake.

My contention, here, has been that these sources may permit new insights into Jewish life during the period of Ptolemaic rule over the Land of Israel – which otherwise, as Paul Kosmin notes, "remains something of a historical dark age."[13] Inasmuch as many of the relevant Aramaic sources are pre-Maccabean, and some plausibly from the period of Ptolemaic rule, they shed light on this puzzling yet pivotal period of Jewish intellectual history, and they make possible a synchronic approach to understanding the many innovations therein.

In research on Second Temple Judaism, it has been conventional to examine the experiences of Jews in the Land of Israel under Hellenistic rule in relative isolation from research on the rest of the Mediterranean world. The possibility that I have explored in this book is that a new sense

[10] Millard, "Assyrian and Achaemenid Documents in Aramaic," 233–236, quote on 236.
[11] Sanders, *From Adapa*, 196. [12] Dimant, "Qumran Aramaic Texts," 197–198.
[13] Kosmin, *Time and Its Adversaries*, 10.

of the Ptolemaic and/or pre-Maccabean settings of the earliest
"pseudepigrapha" and related Aramaic Dead Sea Scrolls might enable
their contextualization in conversation with recent research in Classics on
the cultural history of the Hellenistic period. The salient concerns of the
Aramaic Jewish literature of the early Hellenistic age resonate, for
instance, with what Tim Whitmarsh and Johannes Haubold characterize
as the "archival culture" of the time, wherein imperial patronage of
scholars and books catalyzed intensive efforts to consolidate, reconfigure,
and rewrite local knowledge.[14] Precisely by virtue of their preoccupation
with knowledge, writing, and books, Enochic and related Aramaic Jewish
literature may help us to recover the participation of some learned Jews in
parallel or intersecting endeavors.

Within the earliest "pseudepigrapha" and related Aramaic Dead Sea
Scrolls, as we have seen, the translocal is made local, in the sense that the
Aramaic language and Mesopotamian scholasticism become claimed as a
primeval heritage of textualized Jewish knowledge. But the local is also
made translocal, in the sense that this knowledge is claimed to be totalizing in scope and significance. In this manner, ancient Jewish scribes were
able to collect and organize knowledge about demons and angels from
both local landscapes and received Near Eastern lore, while simultaneously using such spirits to claim a uniquely comprehensive understanding of the cosmos, as encompassing the written deposit of angelic
teachings uniquely granted to the Jews.

Just as attention to the Hellenistic-era consolidation and spread of
Greek *paideia* may help to contextualize the intensification of explicitly
didactic concerns in much of the Jewish literature of this time, so attention
to the "power-knowledge complex" of Hellenistic imperial ideologies
may also aid us in making sense of the intensive preoccupation with
knowledge in those sources that most extensively attest the rise of Jewish
literary interest in angels and demons. From Alexandria to Babylon, we
find elites engaged in the written collection and consolidation of older
knowledge in newly totalizing terms and through claims to the origins of
local identities in a mythic past with prestige beyond local boundaries –
whether in the Golden Age or the time of heroes or at the very beginnings
of human culture before the Flood.[15] Of course, specific claims remain
distinctive to specific locales. But we find many of the same questions

---

[14] Whitmarsh, *Ancient Greek Literature*, 122–138; Haubold, *Greece and Mesopotamia*,
   127–177.
[15] Strootman, "Dawning of a Golden Age."

asked and answered, and many of the same strategies mobilized to do so – sometimes with a startlingly self-consciousness about the interconnectivity of cross-cultural lineages of knowledge.

This book has suggested that broader shifts of this sort might shed light on the turn to transmundane powers, the cosmos, and the pre-Sinaitic past in Aramaic Jewish literature of the early Hellenistic age, wherein – with the aid of angels – the archive of Jewish knowledge was reconfigured to encompass a broad array of topics and traditions unparalleled in earlier biblical literature but thereafter commonly addressed. Aramaic Jewish scribal pedagogy laid claim to much of the cosmopolitan intellectualism of the Near East, reframing elements of Mesopotamian scholasticism as among the ancient wisdom first and best known to the Jews. The beginnings of Jewish angelology and demonology are one product of this process, but also part of what makes it possible: it is the assertion of a special relationship of Israel and the angels, after all, that undergirds the claims to the unique antiquity and totality of Jewish access to knowledge about the cosmos more broadly.

In experimenting with synchronic approaches to the beginnings of Jewish angelology and demonology, I have attempted to sidestep the distortions caused by seeing this development through the retrospective lenses of post-70 Jewish and Christian perspectives on exile and "the Bible," on the one hand, and anachronistically modern notions of monotheism and "Old Testament Pseudepigrapha," on the other. In this, I hope to contribute to the broader task whereby scholars such as Eva Mroczek have pushed for using data from the Dead Sea Scrolls to counter and correct anachronistic readings of precanonical cultural contexts, resisting the old habit of reading our sources "hierarchically with the (proto)biblical at the top or center of the literary world" of Second Temple Judaism.[16] To experiment with other approaches – I suggest – is not just to be able to read Second Temple sources on their own terms; it is also to open the way for a more fine-grained approach to explaining the changes that we see within Jewish history and literature, both in terms of local and inner-Jewish shifts and in terms of broader cross-cultural and imperial trends.

If I am correct about the character of pre-Maccabean Aramaic Jewish scribal pedagogy, much remains to be done to consider its fate – including the patterns of continuity and change in the reception of its angelology

---

[16] Mroczek, *Literary Imagination*, 122.

and demonology. Above, we considered this issue through the lens of *Jubilees*. It might be worth also reconsidering their reception within Maccabean-era apocalypses and the sectarian literature of the Qumran community. In the Enochic *Book of Dreams* and *Epistle of Enoch*, for instance, angels serve similar roles as in the *Astronomical Book* and *Book of the Watchers*, but references to their activities reflect a sharpened concern for events on earth.[17] The *Epistle of Enoch* expands their association with the task of witnessing, consistent with its exhortative aims, while the *Book of Dreams* extends earlier views of their involvement in the history of Israel, consistent with its interest in the timelines of human history and its end. Whereas *Jubilees* integrates the angelology and demonology of the *Astronomical Book* and *Book of the Watchers* further into the remembrance of the pre-Sinaitic past in conversation with the Torah/Pentateuch, moreover, these second-century BCE Enochic writings mediate their integration into the imagining of the historical and eschatological future. If the reception of the angelology and demonology of earlier Enochic writings by *Jubilees* sets the stage for much of what we later see in Rabbinic midrashim, it might be worth exploring how Maccabean-era apocalypses also shaped their reception elsewhere, such as in later Second Temple "pseudepigrapha," New Testament literature, and early Christianity. Much remains to be done here too, but what is clear is that the marking of an end of sorts for what we have seen of the Aramaic Jewish scribal pedagogy of the early Hellenistic age is also the heralding of yet another new beginning in the sense noted by Edward Said – "an activity which ultimately implies return and repetition rather than simple linear accomplishment . . . making or producing difference . . . which is the result of combining the already-familiar with the fertile novelty of human work in language.[18]

In the case of Jewish angelology and demonology, these "beginnings" may well have been incubated within a small hyper-literate stratum of Judaean society. Edward Cook, for instance, concludes on the basis of linguistic analysis of the Aramaic Dead Sea Scrolls that it is "a generally uniform synchronic corpus, consisting of a small selection of partially preserved didactic-religious texts written in a formal or literary register."[19] Considering the significant clusters of thematic concerns therein, Andrew Perrin similarly posits the cultivation of this corpus within

[17] Collins, *Apocalyptic Imagination*, 62–70; Reed, *Fallen Angels*, 72–80.
[18] Said, *Beginnings*, xvii.   [19] Cook, "Qumran Aramaic," 363.

"close-knit scribal circles in the fourth to second centuries BCE."[20] If so, however, these were far from isolated "conventicles." Rather, they seem to have served as a crucible for Jewish cultural, intellectual, and textual change, with a highly learned set of scribes fostering the curation, collection, and reframing of diverse received traditions to make sense of the new cultural landscapes of the Hellenistic Near East and the place of Jews and Judaism therein.

Even if this particular mode of Aramaic pedagogy and literary production might not have continued in its initial form for long after the Maccabean Revolt, moreover, its innovations had lasting effects. We have seen how it served to expand the scope of Jewish literary concern thereafter. In addition, it is to the Aramaic Jewish scribal pedagogy of the early Hellenistic age that we owe the nascence of the literary genres of the apocalypse and the testament. It was a crucible for the cultivation of these and other first-person and parabiblical forms of textual discourse that reshaped the memory of pre-Sinaitic past and influenced Jewish writing practices throughout the Second Temple period. And it is also to this context that we owe the recovery and redeployment of many older Mesopotamian traditions in new Jewish forms, as well as the integration of many Mesopotamian and Hellenistic models for pedagogy.

Entwined with many of these developments – as we have seen – were the beginnings of Jewish angelology and demonology, and the resultant initiation of newly explicit, systematic, and totalizing modes of written reflection on transmundane powers would come to shape the imagining of the otherworld in Judaism, Christianity, and Western culture alike. Many of the pre-Maccabean practices and products of Aramaic Jewish pedagogy came to be abandoned, forgotten, and overwritten by later Jews and Christians. But to recover their innovations in angelology and demonology, thus, is also to recover a more integrative understanding of Jewish cultural and literary history. In the process, moreover, we may catch glimpses of a lost world – in which demons roamed the earth, angels sang in the skies, and human acts of writing could have cosmic consequences.

---

[20] Perrin, *Dynamics of Dream-Vision Revelation*, 230.

Bibliography

Abegg, M., P. Flint, and E. Ulrich. *The Dead Sea Scrolls Bible*. San Francisco, 1999.

Abusch, T. "Exorcism. I. Ancient Near East and Hebrew Bible/Old Testament." In *The Encyclopedia of the Bible and Its Reception*, ed. D. Allison et al., 8.513–519. Berlin, 2014.

Acosta-Hughes, B. and S. A. Stephens. *Callimachus in Context: From Plato to the Augustan Poets*. Cambridge, 2012.

Ahuvia, M. "Israel Among the Angels: A Study of Angels in Jewish Texts from the Fourth to Eighth Century CE." PhD diss., Princeton University, 2014.

Albani, M. *Astronomie und Schöpfungsglaube: Untersuchungen zum astronomischen Henochbuch*. Neukirchen-Vluyn, 1994.

Albani, M., J. Frey, and A. Lange, eds. *Studies in the Book of Jubilees*. TSAJ 65. Tübingen, 1997.

Albinus, L. "The Greek δαίμων between Mythos and Logos." In *Die Dämonen*, ed. Lange and Lichtenberger, 425–446.

Alcock, S. "The Heroic Past in a Hellenistic Present." In *Hellenistic Constructs: Essays in Culture, History, and Historiography*, ed. P. Cartledge, P. Garnsey and E. S. Gruen, 20–34. Berkeley, 1997.

Alexander, E. S. *Transmitting Mishnah: The Shaping Influence of Oral Tradition*. Cambridge, 2006.

Alexander, P. S. "Contextualizing the Demonology of the Testament of Solomon." In *Die Dämonen*, ed. Lange and Lichtenberger, 613–635.

"The Demonology of the Dead Sea Scrolls." In *Dead Sea Scrolls after Fifty Years*, ed. P. W. Flint and J. C. VanderKam, 2:331–353. 2 vols. Leiden, 1999.

"Enoch and the Beginnings of Jewish Interest in Natural Science." In *The Wisdom Texts from Qumran and the Development of Sapiential Thought*, ed. C. Hempel, A. Lange, and H. Lichtenberger, 223–244. Leuven, 2002.

"Physiognomy, Initiation, and Rank in the Qumran Community." In *Geschichte—Tradition—Reflexion: Festschrift fur Martin Hengel zum 70.*

Geburtstag, ed. H. Cancik, H. Lichtenberger, and P. Schäfer, 385–394. Tübingen, 1996.

"Pre-Emptive Exegesis: Genesis Rabba's Reading of the Story of Creation." *JJS* 43 (1992): 230–245.

"What Happened to the Jewish Priesthood After 70?" In *A Wandering Galilean: Essays in Honour of Seán Freyne*, ed. Z. Rodgers, M. Daly-Denton, and A. Fitzpatrick McKinley, 3–34. JSJSup 132. Leiden, 2009.

"Wrestling against Wickedness in High Places': Magic in the Worldview of the Qumran Community." In *The Scrolls and the Scriptures: Qumran Fifty Years After*, ed. S. E. Porter and C. A. Evans, 318–337. JSPSup 26. Sheffield, 1997.

Angel, J. L. "Reading the Book of Giants in Literary and Historical Context." *DSD* 21 (2014): 313–346.

Athanassiadi, P., and M. Frede, eds. *Pagan Monotheism in Late Antiquity*. Oxford, 1999.

Bachmann, V. *Die Welt im Ausnahmezustand: Eine Untersuchung zu Aussagegehalt und Theologie des Wächterbuches (1 Hen 1–36)*. Berlin, 2009.

"Wenn Engel gegen Gott freveln – und Menschen mittun: Das Wächterbuch (1 Hen 1–36) als frühhellenistischer Diskussionsbeitrag zum 'Bösen.'" In *Das Böse: Jahrbuch für biblische Theologie 2011*, ed. M. Ebner et al., 85–114. Neukirchen-Vluyn, 2012.

Baden, J. S. *The Composition of the Pentateuch: Renewing the Documentary Hypothesis*. New Haven, 2012.

Bagnall, R. S. *The Administration of the Ptolemaic Possessions Outside Egypt*. Leiden, 1976.

"Alexandria: Library of Dreams." *Proceedings of the American Philosophical Society* 146 (2002): 348–362.

Baillet, M., ed. *Qumrân Grotte 4 III (4Q482–4Q520)*. DJD 7. Oxford, 1982.

Barker, M. *The Great Angel: A Study of Israel's Second God*. London, 1992.

Bartelemus, *Heroentum in Israel und seine Umwelt: Eine traditionsgeschichtliche Untersuchung zu Gen 6, 1–4 und verwandten Texten im Alten Testament und der altorientalischen Literatur*. ATANT 65. Zürich, 1979.

Baumgarten, A. *The Flourishing of Jewish Sects in the Maccabean Era: An Interpretation*. Leiden, 1997.

Baxter, W. "Noachic Traditions and the Book of Noah." *JSP* 15 (2006): 179–194.

Beck, R. *A Brief History of Ancient Astrology*. Malden, 2008.

Belknap, R. E. *The List: The Uses and Pleasures of Cataloguing*. New Haven, 2004.

Ben-Amos, D. "On Demons." In *Creation and Re-Creation in Jewish Thought: Festschrift in Honor of Joseph Dan on the Occasion of His Seventieth Birthday*, ed. R. Elior and P. Schäfer, 27–37. Tübingen, 2005.

Ben-Dov, J. *Head of All Years: Astronomy and Calendars at Qumran in Their Ancient Context*. STDJ 78. Leiden, 2008.

"Ideals of Science: The Infrastructure of Scientific Activity in Apocalyptic Literature and in the *Yaḥad*." In *Ancient Jewish Sciences*, ed. Ben-Dov and Sanders, 109–152.

"Scientific Writings in Aramaic and Hebrew at Qumran: Translation and Concealment." In *Aramaica Qumranica*, ed. Berthelot and Stökl ben Ezra, 379–402.

Ben-Dov, J. and S. Sanders, eds. *Ancient Jewish Sciences and the History of Knowledge in Second Temple Literature.* New York, 2014.

Berger, P. L. *A Rumor of Angels.* New York, 1990.

Bergsma, J. "The Relationship between Jubilees and the Early Enochic Books (Astronomical Book and Book of the Watchers)." In *Enoch and the Mosaic Torah*, ed. Boccaccini and Ibba, 36–51.

Berman, N. *Divine and Demonic in the Poetic Mythology of the Zohar.* Leiden, 2018.

Bernstein, M. J. "Angels at the Aqedah: A Study in the Development of a Midrashic Motif." *DSD* 7 (2000): 263–291.

"'Rewritten Bible': A Generic Category Which Has Outlived Its Usefulness?" *Textus* 22 (2005): 169–196.

Berthelot, K., and D. Stökl ben Ezra, eds. *Aramaica Qumranica: The Aix-en-Provence Colloquium on the Aramaic Dead Sea Scrolls.* STDJ 94. Leiden, 2010.

Bhayro, S. "Reception of Mesopotamian and Early Jewish Traditions in the Aramaic Incantation Bowls." *Aramaic Studies* 11 (2013): 187–196.

The Shemihazah and Asael Narrative of 1 Enoch 6-11: Introduction, Text, Translation and Commentary with Reference to Ancient Near Eastern and Biblical Antecedents. Münster, 2005.

Black, M. *The Book of Enoch: A New English Edition.* SVTP 7. Leiden, 1985.

"The Twenty Angel Dekadarchs at I Enoch 6.7 and 69." *JJS* 33 (1982): 227–235.

Blair, J. M. *De-Demonising the Old Testament: An Investigation of Azazel, Lilith, Deber, Qeteb, and Reshef in the Hebrew Bible.* FAT 2.37. Tübingen, 2009.

Blum, R. *Kallimachos: The Alexandrian Library and the Origins of Bibliography.* Trans. H. H. Wellisch. Madison, 1991.

Boccaccini, G. *Beyond the Essene Hypothesis: The Parting of the Ways between Qumran and Enochic Judaism.* Grand Rapids, MI, 1998.

Roots of Rabbinic Judaism: An Intellectual History from Ezekiel to Daniel. Grand Rapids, MI, 2002.

Boccaccini, G., and G. Ibba, eds. *Enoch and the Mosaic Torah: The Evidence of Jubilees.* Grand Rapids, MI, 2009.

Bohak, G. *Ancient Jewish Magic: A History.* Cambridge, 2008.

"From Qumran to Cairo: The Lives and Times of a Jewish Exorcistic Formula (with an Appendix by Shaul Shaked)." In *Ritual Healing: Magic, Ritual and Medical Therapy from Antiquity until the Early Modern Period*, ed. I. Csepregi and C. S. F. Burnett, 31–52. Florence, 2012.

Bonneau, G. and J. Duhaime. "Angélologie et légitimation socio-religieuse dans le livre des Jubilés." *Eglise et théologie* 27 (1996): 335–349.

Bousset, W. *Die Religion des Judentums im neutestamentlichen Zeitalter.* Berlin, 1926 [1903].

Boustan, R. S. "Rabbinization and the Making of Early Jewish Mysticism." *JQR* 101.4 (2011): 482–501.

Boyarin, D. "Placing Reading: Ancient Israel and Medieval Europe." In *The Ethnography of Reading*, ed. J. Boyarin, 10–37. Berkeley, 1993.

Brakke, D. *Demons and the Making of the Monk: Spiritual Combat in Early Christianity.* Cambridge, MA, 2006.

Brand, M. T. *Evil Within and Without: The Source of Sin and Its Nature as Portrayed in Second Temple Literature.* Göttingen, 2013.

Brennan, A. "The Birth of Modern Science: Culture, Mentalities, and Scientific Innovation." *Studies in History and Philosophy of Science* 35 (2004): 199–225.

Brisson, L., S. O'Neill, and A. Timotin, eds. *Neoplatonic Demons and Angels.* Leiden, 2018.

Brooke, A. E., and N. McLean. *The Old Testament in Greek According to the Text of Codex Vaticanus Supplemented from Other Uncial Manuscripts with a Critical Apparatus Containing the Variants of the Chief Ancient Authorities for the Text of the LXX.* Cambridge, 1906–1940.

Brooke, G. J. "Exegetical Strategies in Jubilees 1–2." In *Studies in the Book of Jubilees,* ed. Albani, Frey and Lange, 39–57.

Brown, D. R. "The Devil in the Details: A Survey of Research on Satan in Biblical Studies." *CBR* 9 (2011): 200–227.

Brown, P. *Poverty and Leadership in the Later Roman Empire.* Hanover, NH, 2002.

Rise of Western Christendom: Triumph and Diversity, AD 200–1000. Malden, MA, 1996.

Burkes, S. *God, Self, and Death: The Shape of Religious Transformation in the Second Temple Period.* JSJSup 79. Leiden, 2003.

Burkert, W. *Greek Religion.* Trans. J. Raffan. Cambridge, MA, 1985.

Calduch-Benages, N. "The Hymn to the Creation (Sir 42:15–43:33): A Polemic Text?" In *The Wisdom of Ben Sira: Studies on Tradition, Redaction, and Theology,* ed. A. Passaro and G. Bellia, 119–138. Deuterocanonical and Cognate Literature Studies 1. Berlin, 2008.

Cancik, H. "Römische Dämonologie (Varro, Apuleius, Tertullian)." In *Die Dämonen,* ed. Lange and Lichtenberger, 447–460.

Carr, D. M. *The Formation of the Hebrew Bible: A New Reconstruction.* Oxford, 2011.

"Torah on the Heart: Literary Jewish Textuality within Its Ancient Near Eastern Context." *Oral Tradition* 25 (2010): 17–40.

Writing on the Tablet of the Heart: Origins of Scripture and Literature. Oxford, 2005.

Carruthers, M. *Book of Memory: A Study of Memory in Medieval Culture.* Cambridge, 2008.

Chambers, D. W. and R. Gillespie. "Locality in the History of Science: Colonial Science, Technoscience, and Indigenous Knowledge." *Osiris* 15 (2000): 221–240.

Charles, R. H. *The Book of Enoch.* Oxford, 1893.

Chesnutt, R. "Oxyrhynchus Papyrus 2069 and the Compositional History of *1 Enoch.*" *JBL* 129 (2010): 485–505.

Cline, R. *Ancient Angels: Conceptualizing Angeloi in the Roman Empire.* Leiden, 2011.

Coblentz Bautch, K. *A Study of the Geography of 1 Enoch 17–19: "No One Has Seen What I Have Seen."* JSJSup 81. Leiden, 2003.

"What Becomes of the Angels' 'Wives'? A Text-Critical Study of *1 Enoch* 19:2." *JBL* 125 (2006): 766–780.

Collins, J. J. *The Apocalyptic Imagination: An Introduction to Jewish Apocalyptic Literature.* Grand Rapids, MI, 1998.

"The Apocalyptic Technique: Setting and Function in the Book of Watchers." *CBQ* 44 (1982): 91–111.

"The Aramaic Texts from Qumran: Conclusions and Perspectives." In *Aramaica Qumranica* ed. Berthelot and Stökl Ben Ezra, 547–562. Leiden, 2010.

"The Genre of the Book of Jubilees." In *A Teacher for All Generations: Essays in Honor of James C. VanderKam*, ed. E. Mason, 737–755. Leiden, 2012.

"The Jewish Apocalypses." *Semeia* 14 (1979): 21–60.

"Jewish Apocalyptic against Its Hellenistic Near Eastern Environment." *BASOR* 220 (1975): 27–36.

"Methodological Issues in the Study of 1 Enoch: Reflections on the Articles of Paul D. Hanson and George W. Nickelsburg." *Society of Biblical Literature Seminar Papers* 18 (1978): 315–322.

Seers, Sybils, and Sages in Hellenistic-Roman Judaism. JSJSup 54. Leiden, 1997.

"Testaments." In *Jewish Writings of the Second Temple Period: Apocrypha, Pseudepigrapha, Qumran Sectarian Writings, Philo, Josephus*, ed. M. E. Stone, 325–355. Minneapolis, 1984.

"Towards the Morphology of a Genre." *Semeia* 14 (1979): 1–20.

"The Transformation of the Torah in Second Temple Judaism." *JSJ* 43 (2012): 455–474.

Cook, E. M. "Qumran Aramaic, Corpus Linguistics, and Aramaic Retroversion." *DSD* 21 (2014): 356–384.

Crawford, C. D. "On the Exegetical Function of the Abraham/Ravens Traditions in *Jubilees* 11." *HTR* 97 (2004): 91–97.

Crawford, S. W. and C. Wassen, eds. *Apocalyptic Thinking in Early Judaism.* Leiden, 2018.

Crawford, S. W. "Reading Deuteronomy in the Second Temple Period." In *Reading the Present in the Qumran Library: The Perception of the Contemporary by Means of Scriptural Interpretations*, ed. K. de Troyer and A. Lange, 127–140. Atlanta, 2005.

Rewriting Scripture in Second Temple Times. Grand Rapids. MI, 2008.

Cribiore, R. *Gymnastics of the Mind: Greek Education in Hellenistic and Roman Egypt.* Princeton, 2001.

Cuomo, S. *Technology and Culture in Greek and Roman Antiquity.* Cambridge, 2007.

Dalton, J. P. *Taming of the Demons: Violence and Liberation in Tibetan Buddhism.* New Haven, 2011.

Davenport, G. *The Eschatology of the Book of Jubilees.* Leiden, 1971.

Davidson, M. *Angels at Qumran: A Comparative Study of 1 Enoch 1–36, 72–108, and Sectarian Writings from Qumran.* JSPSup 11. Sheffield, 1992.

Davies, P. R. *In Search of "Ancient Israel": A Study in Biblical Origins.* Sheffield, 1992.

Davis, E. F. *Swallowing the Scroll: Textuality and the Dynamics of Discourse in Ezekiel's Prophecy.* JSOTSup 78. Sheffield, 1989.

Day, J. *Yahweh and the Gods and Goddesses of Canaan*. JSOTSup 265. Sheffield, 2000.

Day, P. L. *An Adversary in Heaven: Śāṭān in the Hebrew Bible*. Atlanta, 1988.

Dear, P. "What Is the History of Science the History Of? Early Modern Roots of the Ideology of Modern Science." *Isis* 96 (2005): 390–406.

Delcor, M. "Le mythe de la chute des anges et de l'origine des géants comme explication du mal dans le monde dans l'apocalyptique juive: Histoire des traditions." *RHR* 190 (1976): 3–53.

Deleuze, G. and F. Guattari. *A Thousand Plateaus: Capitalism and Schizophrenia*. Minneapolis, 1987.

Delia, D. "From Romance to Rhetoric: The Alexandrian Library in Classical and Islamic Traditions." *American Historical Review* 97 (1992): 1449–1467.

Denzey, N. F. *Cosmology and Fate in Gnosticism and Graeco-Roman Antiquity: Under Pitiless Skies*. Leiden, 2013.

Deutsch, N. *Guardians of the Gate: Angelic Vice Regency in Late Antiquity*. Leiden, 1999.

Dever, W. G. "Histories and Non-Histories of Ancient Israel: The Question of the United Monarchy." In *In Search of Pre-exilic Israel*, ed. J. Day, 65–94. JSOTSup 406. London, 2004.

Dillon, J. M. *The Middle Platonists: A Study of Platonism, 80 BC to AD 220*. London, 1977.

Dimant, D. "The Biography of Enoch and the Books of Enoch." *VT* 33 (1983): 14–29.

"The Fallen Angels in the Dead Sea Scrolls and in the Apocryphal and Pseudepigraphic Books Related to Them" [Hebrew]. PhD diss., Hebrew University, 1974.

"*1 Enoch* 6–11: A Fragment of a Parabiblical Work." *JJS* 53 (2002): 223–237.

"Between Qumran Sectarian and Non-Sectarian Texts: The Case of Belial and Mastema." In *The Dead Sea Scrolls and Contemporary Culture*, ed. Roitman, Schiffman, and Tzoref, 235–256.

"The Qumran Aramaic Texts and the Qumran Community." In *Flores Florentino: Dead Sea Scrolls and Other Early Jewish Studies in Honour of Florentino García Martínez*, ed. A. Hilhorst, É. Puech, and E. J. C. Tigchelaar, 197–206. JSJSup 122. Leiden, 2007.

"The Sons of Heaven: The Theory of the Angels in the Book of Jubilees in Light of the Writings of the Qumran Community" [Hebrew]. In *Tribute to Sara: Studies in Jewish Philosophy and Kabbala*, ed. M. Idel, D. Dimant, and S. Rosenberg, 97–118. Jerusalem, 1994.

"Themes and Genres in the Aramaic Texts from Qumran." In *Aramaica Qumranica*, ed. Berthelot and Stökl ben Ezra, 16–45.

"Tobit and the Qumran Aramaic Texts." In *Is There a Text in This Cave? Studies in the Textuality of the Dead Sea Scrolls in Honour of George J. Brooke*, ed. A. Feldman, M. Cioată, and C. Hempel, 385–406. STDJ 119. Leiden, 2017.

"Two 'Scientific' Fictions: The So-Called Book of Noah and the Alleged Quotation of Jubilees in CD 16:3–4." In *Studies in the Hebrew Bible, Qumran, and Septuagint Presented to Eugene Ulrich*, ed. E. C. Ulrich, P. W. Flint, and J. C. VanderKam, 230–49. VTSup 101. Leiden, 2006.

Dobbs-Allsop, F. W. *On Biblical Poetry*. Oxford, 2015.

Doering, L. "The Concept of the Sabbath in the Book of Jubilees." In *Studies in the Book of Jubilees*, ed. Albani, Frey, and Lange, 179–206.

Dozeman, T. B. and K. Schmid. *A Farewell to the Yahwist?: The Composition of the Pentateuch in Recent European Interpretation*. Atlanta, GA, 2006.

Drawnel, H. *The Aramaic Astronomical Book from Qumran: Text, Translation, and Commentary*. Oxford, 2011.

——— *An Aramaic Wisdom Text from Qumran: A New Interpretation of the Levi Document*. JSJSup 86. Leiden, 2004.

——— "Between Akkadian tupšarrūtu and Aramaic SPR: Some Notes on the Social Context of the Early Enochic Literature." *RevQ* 24 (2010): 373–403.

——— "Knowledge Transmission in the Context of the Watchers' Sexual Sin with the Women in *1 Enoch* 6–11." *The Biblical Annals* 2 (2012): 123–151.

——— "Priestly Education in the Aramaic Levi Document (Visions of Levi) and Aramaic *Astronomical Book* (4Q208–211)." *RevQ* 22 (2006): 547–574.

——— "Professional Skills of Asael (1 En. 8:1) and Their Mesopotamian Background." *RB* 119 (2012): 518–542.

——— "Some Notes on Scribal Craft and the Origins of the Enochic Literature." *Henoch* 31 (2009): 66–72.

——— "The Initial Narrative of the 'Visions of Amram' and Its Literary Characteristics." *Revue de Qumrân* 24 (2010): 517–554.

——— "The Literary Form and Didactic Content of the 'Admonitions (Testament) of Qahat.'" In *From 4QMMT to Resurrection: Mélanges qumraniens en hommage à Émile Puech*, ed. F. García Martínez, A. Steudel, and E. J. C. Tigchelaar, 55–73. STDJ 61. Leiden, 2006.

Duke, D., and M. Goff. "The Astronomy of the Qumran Fragments 4Q208 and 4Q209." *DSD* 21 (2014): 176–210.

Duke, R. R. *The Social Location of the Visions of Amram (4Q543–547)*. New York, 2010.

Edwards, M. J. "Quoting Aratus: Acts 17, 28." *Zeitschrift für die neutestamentliche Wissenschaft und die Kunde der älteren Kirche* 83 (1992): 266–269.

Ego, B. "'Denn er Liebt Sie' (Tob 6, 15, Ms. 319): Zur Rolle des Damons Asmodaus in der Tobit-Erzahlung." 309–317. Tübingen, 2003.

Elior, R. *The Three Temples: On the Emergence of Jewish Mysticism*. Oxford, 2004.

Elshakry, M. "When Science Became Western: Historiographical Reflections." *Isis* 101 (2010): 98–109.

Endres, J. *Biblical Interpretation in the Book of Jubilees*. CBQMS 18. Washington, DC, 1987.

Erho, T. "Historical-Allusional Dating and the Similitudes of Enoch." *JBL* 130 (2011): 493–511.

——— "Internal Dating Methodologies and the Problem Posed by the Similitudes of Enoch." *JSP* 20 (2010): 83–103.

Erskine, A. "Culture and Power in Ptolemaic Egypt: The Museum and Library of Alexandria." *Greece and Rome* 42 (1995): 38–48.

Eshel, E. "Apotropaic Prayers in the Second Temple Period." In *Liturgical Perspectives: Prayer and Poetry in Light of the Dead Sea Scrolls*, ed. E. G.

Chazon with the collaboration of R. A. Clements and A. Pinnick, 69–88. STDJ 48. Leiden, 2000.

"Demonology in Palestine during the Second Temple Period." PhD diss., Hebrew University, 1999.

"Genres of Magical Texts in the Dead Sea Scrolls." In *Die Dämonen*, ed. Lange and Lichtenberger, 394–415.

Falcon, A. *Aristotle and the Science of Nature: Unity Without Uniformity*. Cambridge, 2005.

Fishbane, M. *Biblical Interpretation in Ancient Israel*. Oxford, 1985.

Fleming, C. and O'Carroll, J. "Revolution, Rupture, Rhetoric." *Philosophy and Social Criticism* 38 (2012): 39–57.

Flint, P. W. "Noncanonical Writings in the Dead Sea Scrolls: Apocrypha, Other Previously Known Writings, Pseudepigrapha." In *The Bible at Qumran: Text, Shape, and Interpretation*, ed. P. W. Flint, 80–127. Grand Rapids, MI, 2001.

Floyd, M. H. "'Write the Revelation!' (Hab 2:2): Re-imagining the Cultural History of Prophecy." In *Writings and Speech in Israelite and Ancient Near Eastern Prophecy*, ed. E. Ben Zvi and M. H. Floyd, 103–143. Atlanta, GA, 2000.

Fossum, J. E. *The Name of God and the Angel of the Lord: Samaritan and Jewish Concepts of Intermediation and the Origin of Gnosticism*. WUNT 36. Tübingen, 1985.

Foucault, M. *The Archaeology of Knowledge*. Trans. A. M. Sheridan Smith. New York, 1972.

Frankfurter, D. *Evil Incarnate: Rumors of Demonic Conspiracy and Satanic Abuse in History*. Princeton, 2006.

"Master-Demons, Local Spirits, and Demonology in the Roman Mediterranean World: An Afterword to Rita Lucarelli." *JANES* 11 (2011): 126–131.

Freudenthal, J. *Alexander Polyhistor und die von ihm erhaltenen Reste jüdischer und samaritanischer Geschichtswerke*. Breslau, 1874.

Fröhlich, I. "Demons, Scribes, and Exorcists in Qumran." In *Essays in Honour of Alexander Fodor on His Sixtieth Birthday*, ed. K. Devenyi and T. Ivanyi. Budapest, 2001.

"Invoke at Any Time. . .: Apotropaic Texts and Belief in Demons in the Literature of the Qumran Community." *Biblische Notizen* 137 (2008): 41–74.

"Magical Healing at Qumran (11Q11) and the Question of the Calendar." In *Studies on Magic and Divination in the Biblical World*, ed. H. R. Jacobus, A. K. de Hemmer Gudme, and P. Guillaume, 39–50. Biblical Intersections 11. Piscataway, 2013.

Gamble, H. Y. *Books and Readers in the Early Church: A History of Early Christian Texts*. New Haven, 1995.

Gammie, J. G. "The Angelology and Demonology in the Septuagint of the Book of Job." *HUCA* 56 (1985): 1–19.

García Martínez, F. *Qumran and Apocalyptic: Studies on the Aramaic Texts from Qumran*. STDJ 9. Leiden, 1992.

"Scribal Practices in the Aramaic Literary Texts from Qumran." In *Myths, Martyrs, and Modernity: Studies in the History of Religions in Honor of*

Jan N. Bremmer, ed. J. Dijkstra, J. Kroesen, and Y. Kuiper, 329–341. Leiden, 2010.

"The Heavenly Tablets in the Book of Jubilees." In *Studies in the Book of Jubilees*, ed. Albani, Frey, and Lange, 243–260.

Gee, E. *Aratus and the Astronomical Tradition*. Oxford, 2013.

Geller, M. "Berossos on Kos from the View of Common Sense Geography." In *Common Sense Geography and Mental Modelling: A Tribute to Cyrus H. Gordon*, ed. K. Geus and M. Thiering, 101–109. Berlin, 2012.

"New Documents from the Dead Sea: Babylonian Science in Aramaic." In *Boundaries of the Ancient Near Eastern World: A Tribute to Cyrus H. Gordon*, ed. M. Lubetski, C. Gottlieb, and S. Keller, 224–229. JSOTSup 273. Sheffield, 1998.

Gerhardsson, B. *Memory and Manuscript: Oral Tradition and Written Transmission in Rabbinic Judaism and Early Christianity*. Trans. E. Sharpe. Uppsala, 1961.

Gieschen, C. A. *Angelomorphic Christology: Antecedents and Early Evidence*. Leiden, 1998.

Ginzberg, L. *The Legends of the Jews*. Trans. H. Szold. 7 vols. Repr. ed. Baltimore, 1998.

Gnuse, R. K. *No Other Gods: Emergent Monotheism in Israel*. JSOTSup 241. Sheffield, 1997.

Goody, J. *The Logic of Writing and the Organisation of Society*. Cambridge, 1986

The Power of the Written Tradition. Washington, DC, 2000.

Grabbe, L. L. *Judaism from Cyrus to Hadrian*, Vol 1: *The Persian and Greek Periods*. Minneapolis, 1992.

"The Seleucid and Hasmonean Periods and the Apocalyptic Worldview: An Introduction." In *The Seleucid and Hasmonean Periods and the Apocalyptic Worldview*, ed. L. L. Grabbe, G. Boccaccini, and J. Zurawski, 11–32. London, 2016.

Graf, F. *Magic in the Ancient World*. Cambridge, MA, 1997.

"Mythical Production: Aspects of Myth and Technology in Antiquity." In *From Myth to Reason? Studies in the Development of Greek Thought*, ed. R. Buxton, 317–328. Oxford, 1999.

Graff, H. J. *The Labyrinths of Literacy: Reflections on Literacy Past and Present*. London, 1987.

The Legacies of Literacy: Continuities and Contradictions in Western Culture and Society. Bloomington, 1987.

Greenfield, J. C., and M. E. Stone. "The Books of Enoch and the Traditions of Enoch." *Numen* 26 (1979): 89–102.

Greenfield, J. C., M. E. Stone and E. Eshel, eds. *The Aramaic Levi Document: Edition, Translation, Commentary*. Leiden, 2004.

Grelot, P. "Hénoch et ses écritures." *RB* 82 (1975): 481–500.

Gruen, E. S. *Heritage and Hellenism: The Reinvention of Jewish Tradition*. Berkeley, 1998.

"Jews and Greeks as Philosophers: A Challenge to Otherness." In *The "Other" in Second Temple Judaism: Essays in Honor of John J. Collins*, ed. D. C. Harlow, 402–422. Grand Rapids, MI, 2011.

Haines-Eitzen, K. *Guardians of Letters: Literacy, Power, and the Transmitters of Early Christian Literature.* Oxford, 2000.

Halpern Amaru, B. *The Empowerment of Women in the Book of Jubilees.* JSJSup 60. Leiden, 1999.

Halpern, B. *From Gods to God.* FAT 63. Tübingen, 2009.

"Sybil, or the Two Nations? Archaism, Kinship, Alienation, and the Elite Redefinition of Traditional Culture in Judah in the 8th–7th Centuries BCE." In *The Study of the Ancient Near East in the Twenty-First Century: The William Foxwell Albright Centennial Conference,* ed. J. S. Cooper and G. M. Schwartz, 291–338. Winona Lake, 1996.

Hamori, E. J. "The Spirit of Falsehood." *CBQ* 72 (2010): 15–30.

"When Gods Were Men": The Embodied God in Biblical and Near Eastern Literature. Berlin, 2008.

Hanneken, T. R. "Angels and Demons in the *Book of Jubilees* and Contemporary Apocalypses." *Henoch* 28 (2006): 14–18.

"The Sin of the Gentiles: The Prohibition of Eating Blood in the *Book of Jubilees.*" *JSJ* 46 (2015): 1–27.

The Subversion of Apocalypses in the Book of Jubilees. Atlanta, 2012.

Hanson, P. *The Dawn of Apocalyptic.* Philadelphia, 1975.

Harari, Y. *Jewish Magic before the Rise of Kabbalah.* Detroit, 2017.

Harder, A. "From Text to Test: The Impact of the Alexandria Library on the Work of Hellenistic Poets." In *Ancient Libraries,* ed. J. König, K. Oikonomopoulou, and G. Woolf, 96–108. Cambridge, 2013.

"The Invention of the Past, Present and Future in Callimachus' Aetia." *Hermes* 131: 290–306.

Harris, W. V. *Ancient Literacy.* Cambridge, 1989.

Hartenstein, F. "Cherubim and Seraphim in the Bible and in the Light of Ancient Near Eastern Sources." In *Angels,* ed. Reiterer, Nicklas, and Schöpflin, 155–188.

Hashiba, Y. "Andron of Alexandria." In *Brill's New Jacoby,* ed. I. Worthington, 246. Leiden, 2007. Available at: http://brillonline.nl

Haubold, J. *Greece and Mesopotamia: Dialogues in Literature.* Cambridge, 2013.

Hendel, R. *Remembering Abraham: Culture, Memory, and History in the Hebrew Bible.* Oxford, 2005.

Hengel, M. *Judaism and Hellenism: Studies in their Encounter in Palestine during the Early Hellenistic Period.* Trans. J. Bowden. 2 vols. Philadelphia, 1974.

Henze, M. "The Use of Scripture in the Book of Daniel." In *A Companion to Biblical Interpretation in Early Judaism,* ed. M. Henze, 279–307. Grand Rapids, MI, 2011.

Hezser, C. *Jewish Literacy in Roman Palestine.* TSAJ 81. Tübingen, 2001.

Himmelfarb, M. *The Apocalypse: A Brief History.* Malden, 2010.

Ascent to Heaven in Jewish and Christian Apocalypses. Oxford, 1993.

"Earthly Sacrifice and Heavenly Incense: The Law of the Priesthood in Aramaic Levi and Jubilees." In *Heavenly Realms and Earthly Realities in Late Antique Religions,* ed. R. Boustan and A. Y. Reed , 103–122. Cambridge, 2004.

"Heavenly Ascent and the Relationship of the Apocalypses and the Hekhalot Literature." *HUCA* 59 (1988): 73–100.

"Judaism and Hellenism in 2 Maccabees." *Poetics Today* 19 (1998): 19–40.
A Kingdom of Priests: Ancestry and Merit in Ancient Judaism. Philadelphia, 2006.
"Merkavah Mysticism since Scholem: Rachel Elior's The Three Temples." In *Wege mystischer Gotteserfahrung: Judentum, Christentum und Islam*, ed. P. Schäfer, 19–36. Oldenbourg, 2006.
"Some Echoes of Jubilees in Medieval Hebrew Literature." In *Tracing the Threads: Studies in the Vitality of Jewish Pseudepigrapha*, ed. J. C. Reeves, 127–136. Atlanta, GA, 1994.
"Torah, Testimony, and Heavenly Tablets: The Claim to Authority of the Book of Jubilees." In *A Multiform Heritage: Studies on Early Judaism and Christianity in Honor of Robert A. Kraft*, ed. B. G. Wright, 19–29. Atlanta, GA, 1999.
Hodges, J. H. "Gnostic Liberation from Astrological Determinism: Hipparchan 'Trepidation' and the Breaking of Fate." *VC* 51 (1997): 359–373.
Holladay, C. R. *Fragments from Hellenistic Jewish Authors*. 4 vols. Atlanta, 1983–1998,
Honigman, S. "'Jews as the Best of All Greeks': Cultural Competition in the Literary Works of Alexandrian Judaeans of the Hellenistic Period." In *Shifting Social Imaginaries in the Hellenistic Period: Narrations, Practices, and Images*, ed. E. Stavrianopoulou, 207–231. Leiden, 2013.
Septuagint and Homeric Scholarship in Alexandria: A Study in the Narrative of the Letter of Aristeas. London, 2003.
Horsley, R. A. *Revolt of the Scribes: Resistance and Apocalyptic Origins*. Minneapolis, 2010.
Hundley, M. "Divine Fluidity? The Priestly Texts in Their Ancient Near Eastern Contexts." In *Text, Time and Temple: Literary, Historical and Ritual Studies in Leviticus*, ed. L. Trevaskis, F. Landy, and B. Bibb, 16–40. Sheffield, 2014.
Hunter, R. L. "Written in the Stars: Poetry and Philosophy in Aratus' *Phaenomena*." *Arachnion* 2 (1995): 1–34.
Hurtado, L. W. *One God, One Lord: Early Christian Devotion and Ancient Jewish Monotheism*. 2nd ed. Edinburgh, 1998.
Hutter, M. "Demons and Benevolent Spirits in the Ancient Near East." In *Angels*, ed. Reiterer, Nicklas, and Schöpflin, 21–34.
Jacques, J.-M. "Sur un acrostiche d'Aratos ('Phén.' 783–787)." *REA* 62 (1960): 48–61.
Jaffee, M. S. *Torah in the Mouth: Writing and Oral Tradition in Palestinian Judaism 200 BCE to 400 CE*. Oxford, 2001.
Japhet, S. *I & II Chronicles: A Commentary*. Louisville, 1993.
"Postexilic Historiography: How and Why?" In *Israel Constructs Its History: Deuteronomistic Historiography in Recent Research*, ed. A. de Pury, T. Romer, and J.-D. Macchi, 144–173. JSOTSup 306. Sheffield, 2000.
Jeay, M. *Le commerce des mots: L'usage des listes dans la littérature médiévale (XIIe–XVe siècles)*. Geneva, 2006.
Johnston, S. I., ed. *Religions of the Ancient World: A Guide*. Cambridge, MA, 2004.

Johnstone, S. "A New History of Libraries and Books in the Hellenistic Period." *Classical Antiquity* 33 (2014): 347–393.

Kalleres, D. S. *City of Demons: Violence, Ritual, and Christian Power in Late Antiquity*. Berkeley, 2013.

Kelber, W. H. *The Oral and the Written Gospel: The Hermeneutics of Speaking and Writing in the Synoptic Tradition*. Philadelphia, 1983.

Kidd, D., ed. *Aratus: Phaenomena*. Cambridge, 2004.

Kleingünter, A. *Protos Heuretes: Untersuchungen zur Geschichte einer Fragestellung*. Leipzig, 1933.

Knibb, M. A. "The Book of Enoch or Books of Enoch? The Textual Evidence for 1 Enoch." Repr. in Knibb, *Essays on the Book of Enoch and Other Early Jewish Texts and Traditions*, 36–55. SVTP 22. Leiden, 2009.

Ethiopic Book of Enoch: Text and Apparatus. 2 vols. London, 1978.

"Which Parts of 1 Enoch were Known to Jubilees? A Note on the Interpretation of Jubilees 4.16–25." In *Readings from Right to Left: Essays on the Hebrew Bible in Honour of David J. A. Clines*, ed. J. C. Exum and H. G. M. Williamson, 254–262. JSOTSup 373. London, 2003.

Koch, K. "The Astral Laws as the Basis of Time, Universal History, and the Eschatological Turn in the Astronomical Book and the Animal Apocalypse of 1 Enoch." In *The Early Enoch Literature*, ed. G. Boccaccini and J. J. Collins, 119–137. JSJSup 121. Leiden, 2007.

Köckert, M. "Divine Messengers and Mysterious Men in the Patriarchal Narratives of the Book of Genesis." In *Angels*, ed. Reiterer, Nicklas, and Schöpflin, 51–78.

König, J. and T. Whitmarsh. *Ordering Knowledge in the Roman Empire*. Cambridge, 2007.

Kosmin, P. J. *The Land of the Elephant Kings*. Cambridge, MA, 2014.

Time and Its Adversaries in the Seleucid Empire. Cambridge, MA, 2018.

Kraft, R. A. "Para-mania: Beside, Before and Beyond Bible Studies." *JBL* 126 (2007): 3–27.

Kugel, J. *The Bible As It Was*. Cambridge, MA, 1997.

The God of Old: Inside the Lost World of the Bible. New York, 2003.

"The *Jubilees* Apocalypse." *DSD* 1 (1994): 322–337.

"Levi's Elevation to the Priesthood in Second Temple Writings." *HTR* 86 (1993): 1–64.

Traditions of the Bible. Cambridge, MA, 1998.

A Walk through Jubilees: Studies in the Book of Jubilees and the World of Its Creation. JSJSup 156. Leiden, 2012.

Kuhn, T. S. *The Structure of Scientific Revolutions*. 3d ed. Chicago, 1996 [1962].

Kuhrt, A. and S. Sherwin-White. *From Samarkhand to Sardis: A New Approach to the Seleucid Empire*. 3rd ed. Berkeley, CA. 1993.

Kvanvig, H. S. "*Jubilees* – Between Enoch and Moses: A Narrative Reading." *JSJ* 35 (2004): 243–261.

Roots of Apocalyptic: The Mesopotamian Background of the Enoch Figure and of the Son of Man. Neukirchen-Vluyn, 1988.

Lambert, D. "Did Israel Believe That Redemption Awaited Its Repentance? The Case of *Jubilees* 1." *CBQ* 68 (2006): 631–650.

"Last Testaments in the *Book of Jubilees*." *DSD* 11 (2004): 82–107.

Lange, A. "Considerations Concerning the 'Spirit of Impurity' in Zech 13.2." In *Die Dämonen*, ed. Lange and Lichtenberger, 254–268.

"Pre-Maccabean Literature from the Qumran Library and the Hebrew Bible." *DSD* 13 (2006): 277–305.

Lange, A. and H. Lichtenberger, eds. *Die Dämonen: Die Dämonologie der israelitisch-jüdischen und frühchristlichen Literatur im Kontext ihrer*. Tübingen, 2003.

Langermann, Y. T. "On the Beginnings of Hebrew Scientific Literature and on Studying History through *Maqbilot* (Parallels)." *Aleph* 2 (2002): 169–190.

Lehoux, D. *What Did the Romans Know?: An Inquiry Into Science and World-making*. Chicago, 2012.

Lemche, N. P. *The Israelites in History and Tradition*. Louisville, 1998.

Levinson, B. M. *Deuteronomy and the Hermeneutics of Legal Innovation*. New York, 1997.

Legal Revision and Religious Renewal in Ancient Israel. Cambridge, 2010.

"The Reconceptualization of Kingship in Deuteronomy and the Deuteronomistic History's Transformation of Torah." *VT* 51 (2001): 511–534.

Lincoln, B. "Cesmag, the Lie, and the Logic of Zoroastrian Demonology." *JAOS* 129 (2009): 45–55.

Gods and Demons, Priests and Scholars. Chicago, 2012.

Losekam, C. *Die Sünde der Engel: Die Engelfalltradition in frühjüdischen und gnostischen Texten*. Tübingen, 2010.

Lovejoy, C. and Boas, G. *Primitivism and Related Ideas in Antiquity*. New York, 1965.

Lucarelli, R. "Demonology during the Late Pharaonic and Greco-Roman Periods in Egypt." *JANER* 11 (2011): 109–125.

Luck, G. *Arcana Mundi: Magic and the Occult in the Greek and Roman Worlds: A Collection of Ancient Texts*. Baltimore, 2006.

MacDonald, N. *Deuteronomy and the Meaning of "Monotheism."* FAT 2/1. Tübingen, 2012.

Mach, M. *Entwicklungsstadien des jüdischen Engelglaubens in vorrabbinischer Zeit*. TSAJ 34. Tübingen, 1992.

Machiela, D. "The Aramaic Dead Sea Scrolls: Hellenistic Period Witnesses to Jewish Apocalyptic Thought." In *The Seleucid and Hasmonean Periods and the Apocalyptic Worldview*, ed. L. L. Grabbe et al., 147–156. LSTS 88. London, 2016.

"Aramaic Writings of the Second Temple Period and the Growth of Apocalyptic Thought: Another Survey of the Texts." *Judaïsme ancien/Ancient Judaism* 2 (2014): 113–134.

The Dead Sea Genesis Apocryphon: A New Text and Translation with Introduction and Special Treatment of Columns 13–17. STDJ 79. Leiden, 2009.

"Situating the Aramaic Texts from Qumran: Reconsidering Their Language and Socio-Historical Settings." In *Apocalyptic Thinking in Early Judaism*, ed. Crawford and Wassen, 88–110.

Machiela, D. and A. B. Perrin. "Tobit and the Genesis Apocryphon: Toward a Family Portrait." *JBL* 133 (2014): 111–132.

Macumber, H. "Angelic Intermediaries: The Development of a Revelatory Tradition." PhD diss., University of Toronto, 2012.

Maehler, M. "Der 'Wertlose' Aratkodex P. Berol. Inv. 5865." *Archiv für Papyrusforschung und verwandte Gebiete* 27 (1980): 19–32.

Martin, D. M. *Inventing Superstition: From the Hippocratics to the Christians.* Cambridge, MA, 2004.

"When Did Angels Become Demons?" *JBL* 129 (2010): 657–677.

Masuzawa, T. *In Search of Dreamtime: The Quest for the Origin of Religion.* Chicago, 1993.

McCants, W. F. *Founding Gods, Inventing Nations: Conquest and Culture Myths from Antiquity to Islam.* Princeton, 2011.

McDonald, L. M. *Forgotten Scriptures: The Selection and Rejection of Early Religious Writings.* Louisville, 2009.

Meier, S. A. "Angel 1." In *Dictionary of Deities and Demons in the Bible*, ed. K. van der Toornritz, B. Becking, and P. W. van der Hoorst. 2nd ed., 39. Leiden, 1999.

The Messenger in the Ancient Semitic World. Harvard Semitic Monographs 45. Atlanta, 1988.

Melvin, D. P. *The Interpreting Angel Motif in Prophetic and Apocalyptic Literature.* Minneapolis, 2013.

Miguélez-Cavero, L. *Poems in Context: Greek Poetry in the Egyptian Thebaid 200–600 AD.* Berlin, 2008.

Milgrom, J. *Leviticus 1–16: A New Translation with Introduction and Commentary.*

Milik, J. T. *The Books of Enoch: Aramaic Fragments of Qumrân Cave 4.* Oxford, 1976.

"Fragments grecs du livre d'Hénoch [P. Oxy. XVII 2069]." *Chronique d'Égypte* 46 (1971): 321–348.

Millard, A. R. "Aramaic Documents of the Assyrian and Achaemenid Periods." In *Ancient Archives and Archival Traditions: Concepts of Record-Keeping in the Ancient World*, ed. M. Brosius, 230–240. Oxford, 2003.

Momigliano, A. *Alien Wisdom: The Limits of Hellenization.* Cambridge, 1975.

Monson, A. *From the Ptolemies to the Romans: Political and Economic Change in Egypt.* Cambridge, 2012.

Moore, G. F. "Christian Writers on Judaism." *HTR* 14 (1921): 197–254.

"Intermediaries in Jewish Theology: Memra, Shekinah, Metatron." *HTR* 15 (1922): 41–85.

Morgan, T. *Literate Education in the Hellenistic and Roman Worlds.* Cambridge, 1998.

Moss, C. R. *The Other Christs: Imitating Jesus in Ancient Christian Ideologies of Martyrdom.* Oxford, 2010.

Moyer, I. S. *Egypt and the Limits of Hellenism.* Cambridge, 2011.

Mroczek, E. *The Literary Imagination in Jewish Antiquity.* Oxford, 2016.

Muehlberger, E. *Angels in Late Ancient Christianity.* Oxford, 2013.

Münnich, M. M. *The God Resheph in the Ancient Near East.* ORA 11. Tübingen, 2013.

Murphy, T. M. *Pliny the Elder's Natural History: The Empire in the Encyclopedia.* Oxford, 2004.

Na'aman, N. "Sources and Composition in the History of David." In *The Origins of the Ancient Israelite States*, ed. V. Fritz and P. R. Davies, JSOTSup 228, 170–186. Sheffield, 1996.

Najman, H. "Angels at Sinai: Exegesis, Theology and Interpretive Authority." *DSD* 7 (2000): 313–319.

——— "Interpretation as Primordial Writing: *Jubilees* and Its Authority Conferring Strategies." *JSJ* 30 (1999): 389–400.

——— *Losing the Temple and Recovering the Future.* Cambridge, 2014.

——— *Past Renewals: Interpretative Authority, Renewed Revelation, and the Quest for Perfection in Jewish Antiquity.* JSJSup 53. Leiden, 2010.

——— *Seconding Sinai: The Development of Mosaic Discourse in Second Temple Judaism.* JSJSup 77. Leiden, 2003.

——— "The Symbolic Significance of Writing in Ancient Judaism." In *The Idea of Biblical Interpretation: Essays in Honor of James L. Kugel*, ed. H. Najman and J. H. Newman, 139–73. JSJSup 83. Leiden, 2004.

Naveh, J. "Fragments of an Aramaic Magic Book from Qumran." *IEJ* 48 (1998): 252–261.

Neugebauer, O. "The 'Astronomical Chapters' of the Ethiopic Book of Enoch (72 to 82)." In *The Book of Enoch or I Enoch: A New English Edition*, ed. M. Black and J. C. VanderKam, 386–414. Leiden, 1985.

——— "The Survival of Babylonian Methods in the Exact Sciences of Antiquity and Middle Ages." In *Proceedings of the American Philosophical Society* 107 (1963): 528–535.

Newman, J. *Before the Bible: The Liturgical Body and the Formation of Scriptures in Early Judaism.* Oxford, 2018.

Newsom, C. A. "The Development of I Enoch 6–19: Cosmology and Judgment." *CBQ* 42 (1980): 310–329.

——— *The Self as Symbolic Space: Constructing Identity and Community at Qumran.* STDJ 52. Leiden, 2004.

Nicholson, E. "Current 'Revisionism' and the Literature of the Old Testament." In *In Search of Pre-Exilic Israel*, ed. J. Day, 1–22. JSOTSup 406. London, 2004.

Nickelsburg, G. W. E. "Apocalyptic and Myth in I Enoch 6–11." *JBL* 96 (1977): 389–391.

——— "The Books of Enoch at Qumran: What We Know and What We Need to Think about." In *Antikes Judentum und frühes Christentum: Festschrift für Hartmut Stegemann zum 65. Geburtstag*, ed. B. Kollmann, W. Reinbold, and A. Steudel, 99–113. BZNW 97. Berlin, 1999.

——— "Enoch, Levi, and Peter: Recipients of Revelation in Upper Galilee." *JBL* 100 (1981): 575–600.

——— *1 Enoch 1: A Commentary on the Book of 1 Enoch: Chapters 1–36; 81–108.* Minneapolis, 2001.

Niditch, S. *Oral World and Written Word: Ancient Israelite Literature.* Louisville, 1996.

Niehoff, M. R. *Jewish Exegesis and Homeric Scholarship in Alexandria.* Cambridge, 2011.

Nitzan, B. "The Penitential Prayer of Moses in *Jubilees* 1 and Its Relation to the Penitential Tradition of the Post-Exilic Judaism." *Henoch* 31 (2009): 35–41.

Nowell, I. "The 'Work' of the Angel Raphael." In *Angels*, ed. Reiterer, Niklas, and Schöpflin, 227–238.

Ogden, D. *Greek and Roman Necromancy*. Princeton, 2004.

Olson, D. *Enoch: A New Translation: The Ethiopic Book of Enoch, or 1 Enoch*. North Richland Hills, TX, 2004.

Olyan, S. M. *A Thousand Thousands Served Him*. TSAJ 36. Tübingen, 1993.

Ong, W. J. *Orality and Literacy: The Technologising of the Word*. New York, 2002 [1982].

Orlov, A. A. *Dark Mirrors: Azazel and Satanael in Early Jewish Demonology*. Albany, 2011.

The Enoch–Metatron Tradition. TSAJ 107. Tübingen, 2005.

Owens, J. E. "Asmodeus: A Less Than Minor Character in the Book of Tobit." In *Angels*, ed. Reiterer, Niklas, and Schöpflin, 277–292.

Pagels, E. *Origins of Satan*. New York, 1995.

Penney, D. L. and M. O. Wise. "By the Power of Beelzebub: An Aramaic Incantation Formula from Qumran (4Q560)." *JBL* 113 (1994): 627–650.

Perrin, A. B. "The Aramaic Imagination: Incubating Apocalyptic Thought and Genre in Dream-Visions among the Qumran Aramaic Texts." In *Apocalyptic Thinking in Early Judaism*, ed. Crawford and Wassen, 110–140.

The Dynamics of Dream-Vision Revelation in the Aramaic Dead Sea Scrolls. Göttingen, 2105.

"Tobit's Context and Contacts in the Qumran Aramaic Anthology." *JSP* 25 (2015): 23–51.

Peters, D. M. *Noah Traditions in the Dead Sea Scrolls*. Leiden, 2009.

Petersen, A. K. "The Notion of Demon: Open Questions to a Diffuse Concept." In *Die Dämonen*, ed. Lange and Lichtenberger, 23–41.

Pioske, D. *Memory in a Time of Prose: Studies in Epistemology, Hebrew Scribalism, and the Biblical Past*. Oxford, 2018.

Poirier, J. C. *The Tongues of Angels: The Concept of Angelic Languages in Classical Jewish and Christian Texts*. WUNT 287. Tübingen, 2010.

Pomykala, K. "A Scripture Profile of the Book of the Watchers." In *The Quest for Context and Meaning: Studies in Biblical Intertextuality in Honor of James A. Sanders*, ed. C. Evans and S. Talmon, 263–286. Leiden, 1997.

Popović, M. "The Emergence of Aramaic and Hebrew Scholarly Texts: Transmission and Translation of Alien Wisdom." In *The Dead Sea Scrolls: Transmission of Traditions and Production of Texts*, ed. S. Metso, H. Najman, and E. Schuller, 81–114. STDJ 92. Leiden, 2010.

"Networks of Scholars: The Transmission of Astronomical and Astrological Learning between Babylonians, Greeks, and Jews." In *Ancient Jewish Sciences*, ed. Ben-Dov and Sanders, 153–193.

"Physiognomic Knowledge in Qumran and Babylonia: Form, Interdisciplinarity, and Secrecy." *DSD* 13 (2006): 150–176.

Reading the Human Body: Physiognomics and Astrology in the Dead Sea Scrolls and Hellenistic-Early Roman Period Judaism. STDJ 67. Leiden, 2007.

Portier-Young, A. E. *Apocalypse against Empire: Theologies of Resistance in Early Judaism.* Grand Rapids, MI, 2011.

Poulakos, T. *Speaking for the Polis: Isocrates' Rhetorical Education.* Columbia, SC, 1997.

Principe, L. M. "Alchemy Restored." *Isis* 102 (2011): 305–312.

Puech, É. "Du bilinguisme a Qumran." In *Mosaique de langues, mosaique culturelle: Le Bilinguisme dans le Proche-Orient ancien,* ed. F Briquel-Chatonnet, 171–179. Paris, 1996.

Rainbow, J. "Textual Loss and Recovery in the Hebrew Bible." PhD dissertation, Harvard University, 2013.

Reed, A. Y. "Abraham as Chaldean Scientist and Father of the Jews: Josephus, *Ant.* 1.154–168, and the Greco-Roman Discourse about Astronomy/Astrology." *JSJ* 35 (2004): 119–158.

"Ancient Jewish Sciences and the Historiography of Judaism." In *Ancient Jewish Sciences,* ed. Ben-Dov and Sanders, 197–256.

"The Construction and Subversion of Patriarchal Perfection: Abraham and Exemplarity in Philo, Josephus, and the Testament of Abraham." *JSJ* 40 (2009): 185–212.

"Enochic and Mosaic Traditions in Jubilees: The Evidence of Angelology and Demonology." In *Enoch and the Mosaic Torah,* ed. Boccaccini and Ibba, 353–368.

"Enoch, Eden, and the Beginnings of Jewish Cosmography." In *The Cosmography of Paradise,* ed. A. Scafi, 67–94. London, 2016.

Fallen Angels and the History of Judaism and Christianity: The Reception of Enochic Literature. Cambridge, 2005.

Forgetting. Forthcoming.

"Gendering Heavenly Secrets? Women, Angels, and the Problem of Misogyny and Magic." In *Daughters of Hecate: Women and Magic in Antiquity,* ed. K. Stratton, 108–151. Oxford, 2014.

"Heavenly Ascent, Angelic Descent, and the Transmission of Knowledge in 1 Enoch 6–16." In *Heavenly Realms and Earthly Realities in Late Antique Religions,* ed. R. S. Boustan and A. Y. Reed, 47–66. Cambridge, 2004.

"Interrogating 'Enochic Judaism': 1 Enoch as Evidence for Intellectual History, Social Reality, and Literary Tradition." In *Enoch and Qumran Origins: New Light on a Forgotten Connection,* ed. G. Boccaccini, 336–344. Grand Rapids, MI, 2004.

"Job as Jobab: The Interpretation of Job in LXX Job 42:17b-e." *JBL* 120 (2001): 31–55.

"Knowing our Demons." In *The Immanent Frame.* Available at: https://tif.ssrc.org/2018/01/25/knowing-our-demons/

"The Modern Invention of 'Old Testament Pseudepigrapha.'" *JTS* 60 (2009): 403–436.

"The Origins of the Book of the Watchers as 'Apocalypse' and Its Reception as 'Apocryphon'." *Henoch* 30 (2008): 55–60.

"Pseudepigraphy and/as Prophecy: Continuity and Transformation in the Formation and Reception of Early Enochic Writings." In *Revelation, Literature,
and Community in Late Antiquity*, ed. P. Townsend and M. Vidas, 25–42.
TSAJ 146. Tübingen, 2011.

"Textuality between Death and Memory: The Prehistory and Formation of the
Parabiblical Testament." *JQR* 104 (2014): 381–412.

"The Textual Identity, Literary History, and Social Setting of *1 Enoch*: Reflections on George Nickelsburg's Commentary on *1 Enoch* 1–36; 81–108."
ARG 5 (2003): 279–296.

"Was There Science in Ancient Judaism? Historical and Cross-Cultural Reflections on 'Religion' and 'Science.'" *SR* 36 (2007): 461–495.

"Writing Jewish Astronomy in the Early Hellenistic Age: The Enochic *Astronomical Book* as Aramaic Wisdom and Archival Impulse." *DSD* 24 (2017):
1–37.

Reed, A. Y., and N. B. Dohrmann, "Rethinking Romanness, Provincializing
Christendom." In *Jews, Christians, and the Roman Empire: The Poetics of
Power in Late Antiquity*, ed. N. B. Dohrmann and A. Y. Reed, 1–21.
Philadelphia, 2013.

Reeves, J. C. and A. Y. Reed. *Enoch from Antiquity to the Middle
Ages: Sources from Judaism, Christianity, and Islam*, volume 1. Oxford,
2018.

Reimer, A. M. "Rescuing the Fallen Angels: The Case of the Disappearing Angels
at Qumran." *DSD* 7 (2000): 334–353.

Reiterer, F. V., T. Nicklas, and K. Schöpflin, eds. *Angels: The Concept of Celestial
Beings: Origins, Development, and Reception.* Berlin, 2007.

Reiterer, F. V., "An Archangel's Theology." In *Angels*, ed. Reiterer, Nicklas, and
Schöpflin, 255–275.

Reynolds, B. H. "A Dwelling Place of Demons: Demonology and Apocalypticism
in the Dead Sea Scrolls." In *Apocalyptic Thinking in Early Judaism*, ed.
Crawford and Wassen, 23–54.

"Understanding the Demonologies of the Dead Sea Scrolls: Accomplishments
and Directions for the Future." *Religion Compass* 7 (2013): 103–114.

Roberts, L. "Situating Science in Global History: Local Exchanges and Networks
of Circulation." *Itinerario* 33 (2009): 9–30.

Rochberg, F. "A Consideration of Babylonian Astronomy within the Historiography of Science." *Studies in the History and Philosophy of Science Part A.*
33 (2002): 661–684.

Rofé, A. *The Belief in Angels in the Bible and in Early Israel.* 2d ed. Jerusalem,
1979.

Roitman, A. D., L. H. Schiffman, and S. Tzoref, eds. *The Dead Sea Scrolls and
Contemporary Culture: Proceedings of the International Conference Held at
the Israel Museum, Jerusalem (July 6–8, 2008).* STJD 93. Leiden, 2011.

Rollston, C. A. "Scribal Education in Ancient Israel: The Old Hebrew Epigraphic
Evidence." *BASOR* 344 (2006): 47–74.

Writing and Literacy in the World of Ancient Israel. Atlanta, 2010.

Ronis, S. "Do Not Go Out Alone At Night: Law and Demonic Discourse in the
Babylonian Talmud." PhD diss., Yale University, 2015.

"Intermediary Beings in Late Antique Judaism: A History of Scholarship." *CBR* 14 (2015): 94–120.

Rosen-Zvi, I. *Demonic Desires: Yetzer Hara and the Problem of Evil in Late Antiquity.* Philadelphia, 2011.

Rothstein, D. "Text and Context: Domestic Harmony and the Depiction of Hagar in *Jubilees.*" *JSP* 17 (2008): 243–264.

Sacchi, P. "History of the Earliest Enochic Texts." In *Enoch and Qumran Origins: New Light on a Forgotten Connection*, ed. G. Boccaccini, 401–407. Grand Rapids, MI, 2005.

Said, E. W. *Beginnings: Intention and Method.* New York, 1975.

Sanders, E. P. *Paul and Palestinian Judaism: A Comparison of Patterns of Religion.* London, 1977.

Sanders, S. L. *From Adapa to Enoch: Cultures of Scribal Vision in Mesopotamia and Ancient Israel.* TSAJ 167. Tübingen, 2017.

"Enoch's Imaginary Ancestor: From Ancient Babylonian Scholarship to Modern Academic Folklore." *JAJ* 9 (2017): 155–177.

"Daniel and the Origins of Jewish Biblical Interpretation." *Prooftexts.* Forthcoming.

The Invention of Hebrew. Urbana, 2009.

"'I Was Shown Another Calculation': The Language of Knowledge in Aramaic Enoch and Priestly Hebrew." In *Ancient Jewish Sciences*, ed. Ben-Dov and Sanders, 69–101.

Schäfer, P. "Aufbau und redaktionelle Identität der Hekhalot Zutarti." *JJS* 33 (1982): 569–582.

"From Cosmology to Theology: The Rabbinic Appropriation of Apocalyptic Cosmology." In *Creation and Re-Creation in Jewish Thought: Festschrift in Honor of Joseph Dan on the Occasion of His Seventieth Birthday*, ed. R. Elior and P. Schäfer, 39–58. Tübingen, 2005.

"Magic and Religion in Ancient Judaism." In *Envisioning Magic*, ed. P. Schäfer and H. G. Kippenberg, 19–44. Leiden, 1997.

Mirror of His Beauty: Feminine Images of God from the Bible to the Early Kabbalah. Princeton, 2002.

The Origins of Jewish Mysticism. Tübingen, 2009.

"Research into Rabbinic Literature: An Attempt to Define the Status Questionis." *JJS* 37 (1986): 139–152.

Rivalität zwischen Engeln und Menschen in der rabbinischen Literatur: Untersuchungen zur rabbinischen Engelvorstellung. SJ 8. Berlin, 1975.

"Tradition and Redaction in Hekhalot Literature." Repr. in Schäfer, *Hekhalot-Studien*, 8–16. TSAJ 19. Tübingen, 1988.

Schaper, J. "The Death of the Prophet: The Transition from the Spoken to the Written Word of God in the Book of Ezekiel." In *Prophets, Prophecy, and Prophetic Texts in Second Temple Judaism*, ed. M. H. Floyd and R. D. Haak, 63–79. New York, 2006.

"Exilic and Post-Exilic Prophecy and The Orality/Literality Problem." *VT* 55 (2006): 324–342.

"A Theology of Writing: The Oral and the Written, God as Scribe, and the Book of Deuteronomy." In *Anthropology and Biblical Studies: Avenues of Research*, ed. L. J. Lawrence and M. I. Aguilar, 97–119. Leiden, 2004.

"On Writing and Reciting in Jeremiah 36." In *Prophecy in the Book of Jeremiah*, ed. H. M. Barstad and R. G. Kratz, 137–147. Berlin, 2009.

Schipper, B. U. "Angels or Demons?: Divine Messengers in Ancient Egypt." In *Angels,* ed. Reiterer, Nicklas, and Schöpflin, 1–19.

Schmidt, B. B. *Israel's Beneficent Dead: Ancestor Cult and Necromancy in Ancient Israelite Religion and Tradition.* Tübingen, 1994.

Schmitt, R. "Problem of Magic and Monotheism in the Book of Leviticus." *JHS* 8 (2008): 1–12.

Schniedewind, W. M. *How the Bible Became a Book.* Cambridge, 2004.

Social History of Hebrew: Its Origins through the Rabbinic Period. New Haven, 2013.

The Word of God in Transition: From Prophet to Exegete in the Second Temple Period. JSOTSup 197. Sheffield, 1995.

Schöpflin, K. "God's Interpreter: The Interpreting Angel in Post-Exilic Prophetic Visions of the Old Testament." In *Angels,* ed. Reiterer, Nicklas, and Schöpflin 137–147.

"On Writing and Reciting in Jeremiah 36." In *Prophecy in the Book of Jeremiah*, ed. H. M. Barstad and R. G. Kratz, 137–147. Berlin, 2009.

"YHWH's Agents of Doom." In *Angels,* ed. Reiterer, Nicklas, and Schöpflin, 125–137.

Schwartz, S. *Imperialism and Jewish Society: 200 BCE to 640 CE.* Princeton, 2001.

"Language, Power, and Identity in Ancient Palestine." *Past and Present* 148 (1995): 3–47.

The Ancient Jews from Alexander to Muhammad. Cambridge, 2014.

Scurlock, J. "Physician, Exorcist, Conjurer, Magician: A Tale of Two Healing Professionals." In *Mesopotamian Magic: Textual, Historical, and Interpretative Perspectives*, ed. T. Abusch and K. van der Toorn, 69–79. Ancient Magic and Divination 1. Gröningen, 1999.

Séd, N. *La mystique cosmologique Juive.* Paris, 1981.

Segal, A. *Life After Death: A History of the Afterlife in the Religions of the West.* New York, 2004.

Shaw, G. *Theurgy and the Soul: The Neoplatonism of Iamblichus.* University Park, PA, 2010.

Skehan, P. W. "*Jubilees* and the Qumran Psalter." *CBQ* 37 (1975): 343–347.

Smith, G. A. "How Thin Is a Demon?" *JECS* 16 (2008): 479–512.

Smith, J. Z. "Sacred Persistance: Toward a Redescription of Canon." In *Imagining Religion: From Babylon to Jonestown*, 36–52. Chicago, 1982.

"Wisdom and Apocalyptic." In *Religious Syncretism in Antiquity*, ed. B. Pearson, 131–156. Missoula, MT, 1975.

Smith, M. S. *The Early History of God: Yahweh and the Other Deities in Ancient Israel.* Grand Rapids, MI, 1990.

God in Translation: Deities in Cross-Cultural Discourse in the Biblical World. FAT 57. Tübingen, 2008.

The Origins of Biblical Monotheism: Israel's Polytheistic Background and the Ugaritic Texts. Oxford, 2001.

The Memoirs of God: History, Memory, and the Experience of the Divine in Ancient Israel. Minneapolis, 2004.

Sollamo, R. "The Creation of Angels and Natural Phenomena Intertwined in the Book of Jubilees (4QJub^a)." In *Biblical Traditions in Transmission: Essays in Honour of Michael A. Knibb,* ed. C. Hempel and J. M. Lieu, 273–290. Leiden, 2006.

Sommer, B. D. *The Bodies of God and the World of Ancient Israel.* Cambridge, 2009.

Sorensen, E. *Possession and Exorcism in the New Testament and Early Christianity.* WUNT 157. Tübingen, 2002.

Speyer, W. "The Divine Messenger in Ancient Greece, Etruria, and Rome." In *Angels,* ed. Reiterer, Nicklas, and Schöpflin, 35–47.

Steele, J. M. "The 'Astronomical Fragments' of Berossos in Context." In *The World of Berossus,* ed. Haubold, Lanfranchi, Rollinger, and Steele, 107–122 Wiesbaden, 2013.

Steiner, R. C. "The Heading of the Book of the Words of Noah on a Fragment of the Genesis Apocryphon: New Light on a 'Lost' Work." *DSD* 2 (1995): 66–71.

Sterling, G. E. *Historiography and Self-Definition: Josephos, Luke-Acts, and Apologetic Historiography.* NTSup 64. Leiden, 1992.

Stern, D. "The First Jewish Books and the Early History of Jewish Writing." *JQR* 98 (2008): 163–202.

The Jewish Bible: A Material History. Seattle, 2017.

Stern, S. "Rachel Elior on Ancient Jewish Calendars: A Critique." *Aleph: Historical Studies in Science and Judaism* 5 (2005): 287–292.

Stock, B. *Augustine the Reader: Meditation, Self-Knowledge, and the Ethics of Interpretation.* Cambridge, MA, 1996.

Stock-Hesketh, J. "Circles and Mirrors: Understanding I Enoch 21–32." *JSP* 11 (2016): 27–58.

Stokes, R. E. "Devil Made Me Do It… Or Did He? The Nature, Identity, and Literary Origins of the Satan in 1 Chronicles 21:1" *JBL* 128 (2009): 91–106.

"Satan, YHWH's Executioner." *JBL* 133 (2014): 251–270.

Stone, M. E. *Ancient Judaism: New Visions and Views.* Grand Rapids, MI, 20.

"The Book of Enoch and Judaism in the Third Century BCE." *CBQ* 40 (1978): 479–492.

"Enoch, Aramaic Levi, and Sectarian Origins." *JSJ* 19 (1988): 159–170.

"The Parabolic Use of Natural Order in Judaism of the Second Temple Age." In *Essays on Transformation, Revolution and Permanence in the History of Religions, Dedicted to R. J. Zwi Werblowsky,* ed. Gilgul, 293–308. Leiden, 1987.

Stratton, K. B. *Naming the Witch: Magic, Ideology, and Stereotype in the Ancient World.* New York, 2007.

Strootman, R. "Babylonian, Macedonian, King of the World: The Antiochos Cylinder from Borsippa and Seleukid Imperial Integration." In *Shifting Social Imaginaries in the Hellenistic Period: Narrations, Practices, and Images*, ed. E Stavrionopolou, 67–97. Leiden, 2013.

Courts and Elites in the Hellenistic Empires: The Near East After the Achaemenids, c. 330 to 30 BCE. Edinburgh, 2014.

"The Dawning of a Golden Age: Images of Peace and Abundance in Alexandrian Court Poetry in the Context of Ptolemaic Imperial Ideology." In *Hellenistic Poetry in Context*, ed. M. A. Harder, R. F. Regtuit, and G. C. Wakker, 325–341. Leuven, 2013.

"Hellenistic Imperialism and the Ideal of World Unity." In *The City in the Classical and Post-Classical World: Changing Contexts of Power and Identity*, ed. C. Rapp and H. A. Rapp, 38–61. Cambridge, 2014.

Stuckenbruck, L. T. "'Angels and God': Exploring the Limits of Early Jewish Monotheism." In *Early Jewish and Christian Monotheism*, ed. L. T. Struckenbruck and W. North. JSNTSup 263. London, 2004.

Angel Veneration and Christology. WUNT 70. Tübingen, 1995.

"Giant Mythology and Demonology: From the Ancient Near East to the Dead Sea Scrolls." In *Die Dämonen*, ed. Lange and Lichtenberger, 318–338.

"The 'Angels' and 'Giants' of Genesis 6:1–4 in Second and Third Century BCE Jewish Interpretation: Reflections on the Posture of Early Apocalyptic Traditions." *DSD* 7 (2000): 354–377.

"The Book of Jubilees and the Origin of Evil." In *Enoch and the Mosaic Torah*, ed. Boccaccini and Ibba, 294–308.

The Book of the Giants: Texts, Translation, and Commentary. TSAJ 63. Tübingen, 1997.

"The Origins of Evil in Jewish Apocalyptic Tradition: The Interpretation of Genesis 6:1–4 in the Second and Third Centuries B.C.E." In *The Fall of the Angels*, ed. C. Auffarth and L. T. Stuckenbruck, 87–118. Leiden. 2004.

1 Enoch 91–108. Berlin, 2007.

"Interiorization of Dualism within the Human Being." In *Light against Darkness: Dualism in Ancient Mediterranean Religion and the Contemporary World*, ed. E. Meyers, A. Lange, and R. Styers, 159–184. JAJSup 2. Göttingen. 2010.

"Pleas for Deliverance from the Demonic in Early Jewish Texts." In *Studies in Jewish Prayer*, ed. C. T. R. Hayward and B. Embry, 55–73. JSSSup 17. Oxford, 2005.

"Pseudepigraphy and First Person Discourse in the Dead Sea Documents: From the Aramaic Texts to Writings of the 'Yaḥad.'" In *The Dead Sea Scrolls and Contemporary Culture*, ed. Roitman, Schiffman, and Tzoref, 295–326.

"'Qumran Aramaic' Today: Reflections on the Contributions in this Issue of Dead Sea Discoveries." *DSD* 21 (2014): 277–288.

Stuckenbruck, L. and W. North. *Early Jewish and Christian Monotheism.* London, 2004.

Suter, D. "Fallen Angel, Fallen Priest: The Problem of Family Purity in *1 Enoch* 6–16." *HUCA* 50 (1979): 137–142.

Swartz, M. D. "The Dead Sea Scrolls and Later Jewish Magic and Mysticism." *DSD* 8 (2001): 182–193.

"Three-Dimensional Philology: Some Implications of the Synopse zur Hekhalot-Literatur." In *Envisioning Judaism: Studies in Honor of Peter Schäfer on the Occasion of his Seventieth Birthday*, ed. R. S. Boustan, K. Herrmann, R. Leicht, A. Y. Reed, and G. Veltri, 1:529–550. 2 vols. Tübingen, 2013.

Tambiah, S. J. *Magic, Science, Religion, and the Scope of Rationality*. Cambridge, 1990.

Thomas, S. "Eternal Writing and Immortal Writers: On the Non-Death of the Scribe in Early Judaism." In *The Authoritativeness of Scripture in Ancient Judaism*, ed. E. Mason, 2.573–588. Leiden, 2012.

Thrade, K. "Erfinder II." In *Reallexikon für Antike und Christentum*, ed. T. Klausner, 5.1191–1278. Stuttgart, 1962.

Tigchelaar, E. "Aramaic Texts from Qumran and the Authoritativeness of Hebrew Scriptures." In *The Authoritativeness of Scripture in Ancient Judaism*, ed. M. Popovic, 155–172. Leiden, 2010.

"Eden and Paradise: The Garden Motif in Some Early Jewish Texts (I Enoch and Other Texts Found at Qumran." In *Paradise Interpreted: Representations of Biblical Paradise in Judaism and Christianity*, ed. G. Luttikhuizen, 37–62. Leiden, 1999.

Prophets of Old and the Day of the End: Zechariah, the Book of Watchers and Apocalyptic. Leiden, 1996.

"Some Remarks on the *Book of Watchers*, the Priests, Enoch and Genesis, and 4Q208." *Henoch* 24 (2002): 143–145.

Tiller, P. *A Commentary on the Animal Apocalypse of I Enoch*. Atlanta, GA, 1993

Timotin, A. *La démonologie platonicienne: Histoire de la notion de daimôn de Platon aux derniers néoplatoniciens*. Leiden, 2012.

Tov, E. "Some Thoughts at the Close of the Discoveries in the Judaean Desert Publication Project." In *The Dead Sea Scrolls and Contemporary Culture*, ed. Roitman, L. Schiffman, and Tzoref, 1–13.

Textual Criticism of the Hebrew Bible. 2d ed. Minneapolis, 2001.

Tuschling, R. M. M. *Angels and Orthodoxy: A Study in Their Development in Syria and Palestine from the Qumran Texts to Ephrem the Syrian*. STAC 40. Tübingen, 2007.

Ulrich, E. "The Bible in the Making: The Scriptures Found at Qumran." In *The Bible at Qumran: Text, Shape, and Interpretation*, ed. P. Flint, 51–66. Grand Rapids, MI, 2001.

van den Hoek, A. "Aristobulos, Acts, Theophilus, Clement – Making Use of Aratus' *Phainomena*: A Peregrination." *Bijdragen* 41 (1980): 290–299.

van der Toorn, K. *Family Religion in Babylonia, Syria, and Israel: Continuity and Changes in the Forms of Religious Life*. Leiden, 1996.

Scribal Culture and the Making of the Hebrew Bible. Cambridge, MA, 2007.

"The Theology of Demons in Mesopotamia and Israel: Popular Belief and Scholarly Speculation." In *Die Dämonen*, ed. Lange and Lichtenberger, 61–83.

van der Toorn, K., B. Becking, and P. W. van der Horst. *Dictionary of Deities and Demons in the Bible (DDD)*. 2d ed. Leiden, 1999.

van Ruiten, J. "The Covenant of Noah in Jubilees 6.1–38." In *The Concept of Covenant in the Second Temple Period*, ed. S. E. Porter and J. C. R. de Roo, 167–190. JSJSup 71. Leiden, 2003.

"A Literary Dependency of *Jubilees* on *1 Enoch*? A Reassessment of a Thesis of J. C. VanderKam." *Henoch* 26 (2004): 205–209.

Primeval History Interpreted: The Rewriting of Genesis 1:1–11:26 in the Book of Jubilees. Leiden, 2000.

VanderKam, J. C. "*1 Enoch* 77, 3 and a Babylonian Map of the World." *RevQ* 42 (1983): 271–278.

"The Angel of the Presence in the *Book of Jubilees*." *DSD* 7 (2000): 378–393.

"The Angel Story in the Book of Jubilees." In *Pseudepigraphic Perspectives: The Apocrypha and Pseudepigrapha in Light of the Dead Sea Scrolls*, ed. E. G. Chazon and M. E. Stone, 151–170. STDJ 31. Leiden, 1999.

"Biblical Interpretation in 1 Enoch and Jubilees." In *The Pseudepigrapha and Early Biblical Interpretation*, ed. J. H. Charlesworth and C. A. Evans, 96–125. JSPSup 14. Sheffield, 1993.

"The Book of the Luminaries (1 Enoch 72–82)." In *1 Enoch 2: A Commentary on the Book of 1 Enoch, Chapters 37–82*, ed. G. W. E. Nickelsburg and J. C. VanderKam, 96–115. Hermeneia. Minneapolis, 2012.

The Book of Jubilees. 2 vols. CSCO 510–511. Louvain, 1989.

Calendars in the Dead Sea Scrolls: Measuring Time. London, 1998.

"The Demons in the Book of Jubilees." In *Die Dämonen*, ed. Lange and Lichtenberger, 341–530.

Enoch and the Growth of an Apocalyptic Tradition. Washington, DC, 1984.

"Enoch Traditions in *Jubilees* and Other Second-Century Sources." *SBLASP* 1 (1978): 229–251.

"Enoch's Science." In *Ancient Jewish Sciences*, ed. Ben-Dov and Sanders.

"Genesis 1 in *Jubilees* 2." *DSD* 1 (1994): 300–321.

Jubilees: A Commentary in Two Volumes. 2 vols. Hermeneia. Minneapolis, 2018.

"The Manuscript Tradition of Jubilees." In *Enoch and the Mosaic Torah*, ed. Boccaccini and Ibba, 294–308.

"The Putative Author of *Jubilees*." *JSS* 26 (1981): 209–217.

"Recent Scholarship on the *Book of Jubilees*." *CBR* 6 (2008): 405–431.

From Revelation to Canon: Studies in Hebrew Bible and Second Temple Literature. JSJSup 62. Leiden, 2000.

"The Scriptural Setting of the *Book of Jubilees*." *DSD* 13 (2006): 61–72.

"Some Thoughts on the Relationship between the Book of Jubilees and the Genesis Apocryphon." In *Is There a Text in This Cave? Studies in the Textuality of the Dead Sea Scrolls in Honour of George J. Brooke*, ed. A. Feldman, M. Cioata, and C. Hempel, 317–384. Leiden, 2017.

"Studies on the Prologue and Jubilees 1." In *For a Later Generation: The Transformation of Tradition in Israel, Early Judaism, and Early Christianity*, ed. R. A. Argall, B. Bow, and R. A. Werline, 266–279. Harrisburg, PA, 2000.

Textual and Historical Studies in the Book of Jubilees. Missoula, MT, 1977.

Vayntrub, J. *Beyond Orality: Biblical Poetry on Its Own Terms*. London, 2019.

Volk, K. *Manilius and His Intellectual Background*. Oxford, 2009.

von Heijne, C. H. *The Messenger of the Lord in Early Jewish Interpretation of Genesis*. Berlin, 2010.

Wagner, A. *Gottes Körper: zur alttestamentlichen Vorstellung der Menschengestaltigkeit Gottes*. Gütersloh, 2010.

Weitzman, S. "Lessons from the Dying: The Role of Deuteronomy 32 in Its Narrative Setting." *HTR* 87 (1994): 75–103.

Werman, C. "*Jubilees* 30: Building a Paradigm for the Ban on Intermarriage." *HTR* 90 (1997): 1–22.

———. "Qumran and the Book of Noah." In *Pseudepigraphic Perspectives: The Apocrypha and Pseudepigrapha in Light of the Dead Sea Scrolls*, ed. E. G. Chazon and M. E. Stone, 171–181. STDJ 31. Leiden, 1999.

———. "The TWRH and the T'WDH Engraved on the Tablets." *DSD* 9 (2002): 75–103.

West, M. L. "Towards Monotheism." In *Pagan Monotheism in Late Antiquity*, ed. Athanassiadi and Frede, 21–41.

Wevers, J. W. *Notes on the Greek Text of Deuteronomy*. Atlanta, 1995.

Wey, H. *Die Funktionen der bösen Geister bei den griechischen Apologeten des zweiten Jahrhunderts nach Christus*. Winterthur, 1957.

Whitmarsh, T. *Ancient Greek Literature*. Cambridge, 2004.

———. "Thinking Local." In *Local Knowledge and Microidentities in the Imperial Greek World*, ed. T. Whitmarsh, 1–16. Cambridge, 2010.

Williams, T. F. "Towards a Date for the Old Greek Psalter." In *The Old Greek Psalter: Studies in Honour of Albert Pietersma*, ed. R. J. V. Hiebert, C. E. Cox, and P. J. Gentry, 248–276. Sheffield, 2001.

Wills, L. M. *The Jewish Novel in the Ancient World*. Ithaca NY, 1995.

Wood, A. *Of Wings and Wheels: A Synthetic Study of the Biblical Cherubim*. Berlin, 2008.

Woolf, G. "Afterword: The Local and the Global in the Graeco-Roman East." In *Local Knowledge and Microidentities in the Imperial Greek World*, ed. T. Whitmarsh, 189–200. Cambridge, 2010.

———. *Tales of the Barbarians: Ethnography and Empire in the Roman West*. Malden, 2010.

Wright, A. T. *The Origin of Evil Spirits: The Reception of Genesis 6:1–4 in Early Jewish Literature*. WUNT 198. Tübingen, 2013.

Wright, B. G. "From Generation to Generation: The Sage as Father in Early Jewish Literature." Repr. in Wright, *Praise Israel for Wisdom and Instruction*, 25–47. JSJSup 131. Leiden, 2008.

———. "The Letter of Aristeas and the Question of Septuagint Origins Redux." *Journal of Ancient Judaism* 2 (2011): 304–326.

Wright, B. G., III and L. M. Wills, eds. *Conflicted Boundaries in Wisdom and Apocalypticism*. Atlanta, 2005.

Wyrick, J. *The Ascension of Authorship: Attribution and Canon Formation in Jewish, Hellenistic, and Christian Traditions*. Cambridge, MA, 2004.

Yerushalmi, Y. H. *Zakhor: Jewish History and Jewish Memory*. Seattle, 1982.

Zerubavel, E. *Ancestors and Relatives: Genealogy, Identity, and Community*. Oxford, 2012.

"Social Memories: Steps to a Sociology of the Past." *Qualitative Sociology* 19 (1996): 283–299.

Social Mindscapes: An Invitation to Cognitive Sociology. Cambridge, MA, 1997.

Time Maps: Collective Memory and the Social Shape of the Past. Chicago, 2003.

Zhmud, L. *The Origin of the History of Science in Classical Antiquity.* Trans. A. Chernoglazov. Berlin, 2006.

Index

Printed in the USA
CPSIA information can be obtained
at www.ICGtesting.com
LVHW050216160224
772017LV00033B/546

9 781108 746090